# The State and Capital in Chile

# The State and Capital in Chile

## Business Elites, Technocrats, and Market Economics

### Eduardo Silva

Westview Press
A Member of Perseus Books, L.L.C.

*For Erika and Ismael*
*Gerald and Irene*

Copyright © 1996 by Westview Press, Inc., A Member of Perseus Books, L.L.C.

Published in 1996 in the United States of America by Westview Press, Inc., 5500 Central Avenue, Boulder, Colorado 80301-2877, and in the United Kingdom by Westview Press, 12 Hid's Copse Road, Cumnor Hill, Oxford OX2 9JJ

A CIP catalog record for this book is available from the Library of Congress.
ISBN 0-8133-2751-2 (hc)

The paper used in this publication meets the requirements of the American National Standard for Permanence of Paper for Printed Library Materials Z39.48-1984.

10    9    8    7    6    5    4    3    2    1

# Contents

*List of Tables*                                                                vii
*Acknowledgments*                                                               ix


**1    Introduction**                                                             1

Capitalists and Neoliberal Economic Restructuring, 4
Upper-Class Elites and Democratization, 9
Conclusion, 10
Notes, 12


**2    Capitalists, Neoliberal Economic Reform,
       and Democracy**                                                           17

Capitalist Coalitions, the State, and External Shocks, 17
Capitalists, Landowners, and Democratization, 23
Conclusion, 25
Notes, 25


**3    Import-Substitution Industrialization
       and the Breakdown of Democracy**                                          29

Rise of the Import Substitution Coalition, 30
Unravelling of the Import Substitution Coalition, 36
Socialists and the Regime Loyalties of Chilean Capitalists, 40
Collapse of Political and Class Compromise, 48
Capitalists, Landowners,
   and the Post-Coup Political Project, 53
Conclusion, 56
Notes, 57


**4    Gradual Adjustment Under Military Rule**                                   65

The Gradualist Coalition, 68
The Sociedad de Fomento Fabril and Its Policy Reversal, 78
Regime Structure, Gradualists, and Policymaking, 83
Conclusion: Capitalists, the State, and Gradual Reform, 88
Notes, 90

**5 Radical Neoliberalism Ascendant** 97

Rise of the Radical Internationalist Coalition, 99
Consolidation of the Radical Neoliberal Coalition, 111
Conclusion: The Imposition of Radical Neoliberalism, 128
Notes, 131

**6 Triumph and Collapse of Radical Neoliberalism** 137

Triumph of the Radical Neoliberal Coalition, 139
Tensions in the Radical Neoliberal Coalition, 149
Shaping an Alternative: The Pragmatic
    Neoliberal Coalition, 155
Conclusion: Regime Structure and Policy Inflexibility, 166
Notes, 168

**7 Pragmatic Neoliberalism** 173

Rise of the Pragmatic Neoliberal Coalition, 175
Consolidation of Pragmatic Neoliberalism, 192
Conclusion: Capitalist Coalitions and Economic
    Policymaking in Authoritarian Chile, 206
Notes, 209

**8 Pragmatic Neoliberalism and the Politics of Chile's
Transition From Authoritarianism** 215

Capitalists, Pragmatic Neoliberalism,
    and Mass Mobilization, 217
Triumph of Pragmatic Neoliberalism
    and Opposition Response, 224
Capitalist Regime Allegiances and
    Chile's Transition to Democracy, 226
Notes, 236


*List of Acronyms* 243
*Selected References* 245
*Index* 263
*About the Book and Author* 273

# Tables

3.1   Voting Representation on Major Economic
        Policymaking Boards                                          37
3.2   SFF Leadership: Conglomerate Affiliation and
        Effects of Nationalization to September 1971                 46
3.3   Impact of the 91 List on Conglomerates                        50
3.4   SFF Leadership Affected by Nationalization Policy              51

4.1   The Monday Club and Conglomerates                             71
4.2   Major Traditional and International Conglomerates
        in 1970: Concentration of Companies
        by Economic Activity (Percent)                              72
4.3   El Ladrillo: Member Curriculum                                75

5.1   Bank Nationalization and Privatization                       104
5.2   Major Traditional and International
        Conglomerates, 1970 and 1977: Concentration of
        Companies by Economic Activity (Percent)                   114
5.3   Conglomerate Control of Banking Assets by end-1977           116
5.4   Conglomerate Control of Financiera Credit, 1978              117
5.5   Concentration of Wealth of the Largest 250
        Chilean Firms, 1978                                         118
5.6   Economic Interests of SFF Council Members, 1975-1977         120
5.7   Economic Interests of SNA Council Members, 1973-1977         122

6.1   Conglomerates and Key Government Economic
        Institutions, 1978-1982                                     142
6.2   Economic Interests of SNA Council Members, 1978-1980         145
6.3   Economic Interests of SFF Council Members, 1978-1980         146
6.4   Growth of Exports, 1977-1982 (Millions of US$)               149

7.1   Composition of Industrial Exports, 1973 (Millions of US$)    178
7.2   Key Domestic and International Economic Indicators,
        1970-1988                                                   180
7.3   Conglomerates and Key Government Economic
        Institutions, 1983-1987                                     188
7.4   Industrial Production Index, 1976-1980  (1979 = 100)          196
7.5   Industrial Production Index, 1980-1987 (1968 = 100)           198
7.6   SFF Council: Industrial Economic Interests, 1982-1985        200

# Acknowledgments

I started working on this book because the argument that technocrats and a strong state were sufficient to explain economic policymaking in authoritarian Chile seemed too pat, especially after the intense class conflict of the early 1970s. During the course of my research, Chile redemocratized and emerged as a paradigm of development for Latin America. Again, the arguments for elevating Chile to such stature struck me as too glib; greater caution regarding the lessons of Chile seemed more appropriate. I have accumulated many debts in the course of fleshing out those thoughts and in the writing of this book. To all those who made my sojourn possible, thank you. Because it is hard to do justice to all who helped me so generously and unselfishly, my apologies to anyone not properly recognized.

Many people read various drafts of either the whole manuscript or various chapters. Their commentary kept me from my worst excesses and enriched the content of the work immeasurably. My friends among them kept me going when my energy waned. Remaining problems, errors, and omissions are my fault alone. Special recognition must go to Paul Drake for his unflagging support over the years and his periodic descents into purgatory each time I passed him a new version of the manuscript. A very special thanks also to Bill Smith and Dennis Judd for their encouragement and help. My gratitude, moreover, extends to those who read and commented on the entire manuscript at various times including Peter Smith, Tim McDaniel, Arend Lijphart, Carlos Waisman, Bob Bauman, and Jillian Richman. Other friends and colleagues enriched separate chapters, especially Ben Schneider, Brian Loveman, Thomas Koelble, Robert Kaufman, Sylvia Maxfield, and David Bartlett.

A number of people responded to my requests for help with a generosity of spirit that warmed the heart. Among them are, Laurence Whitehead, Christopher Mitchell, Augusto Varas, Alvaro Plaza, Robert Spitch, Carlos Bascuñán, Juan Ignacio Varas, Jorge Desormeaux, Sergio de la Cuadra, Barbara Stallings, Carlos Cruz, Alberto Armstrong, and Rodrigo Montero. Alejandro Goya remained a friend through the decades. Luiz Carlos Bresser Pereira, Giorgio Alberti, Gary Gereffi, Stephan Haggard, and Eric Herschberg made me feel I was doing something worthwhile. Special thanks must go Vanessa Gray who, as copy-editor, labored over my prose and to Les Altstatt who typeset the book.

The following institutions provided crucial support: Fulbright-Hays, the Social Science Research Council, the University of California at San Diego, the University of Missouri-St. Louis, and the Department of Political

Science and the Center for International Studies of the University of Missouri-
St. Louis. The Escuela Superior de Administración de Empresa and the
Instituto de Administración de Empresas of the Pontificia Universidad
Católica de Chile gave me an institutional home in Chile. Members of the
Sociedad de Fomento Fabril, Sociedad Nacional de Agricultura, the Cámara
Nacional de Comercio, and the Confederación de la Producción y Comercio
patiently answered my questions and made contacts and data available to
me.

   For their endurance and support, I am fortunate to owe an unrepayable
debt of gratitude to my family, both nuclear and extended.

*Eduardo Silva*

# The State and Capital in Chile

# 1

# Introduction

Chile emerged from seventeen years of military rule in the 1990s as a paradigm for free market economic reform and a model of democratic stability with greater social equity.[1] These achievements did not come easily. Under military rule, boom and bust cycles and mounting social costs characterized Chile's lurching efforts to reorganize the economy radically. A short, gradual program of economic stabilization and restructuring after the overthrow of Salvador Allende was followed by draconian, ideologically rigid neoliberal policies, uneven economic recovery, and a brief spurt of rapid economic growth fueled by financial speculation that ended in Chile's worst economic decline since the Great Depression. Out of the ashes came more pragmatic free market policies with a greater focus on production that generated high economic growth rates in the late 1980s. Scarcely missing a beat, the economy roared ahead upon the restoration of democracy. Old ideological banners were furled, permitting center-left democratic governments to retain key elements of the dictatorship's economic model and to raise expenditures for poverty alleviation.[2] The cumulative effect of these policies was Chile's metamorphosis from a highly protected, regulated industrializing economy to an open, free-market economy governed by prudent fiscal and stable monetary policies.

Observers look to Chile in search of lessons for other countries. They tend to stress the competence of economic policymaking teams insulated from social forces and the capacity of policymakers to learn from past mistakes in policy design, sequencing, and timing. To a large extent, this focus on the lessons of Chile rests on a particular interpretation of the relationship between capitalists and the state. Most of the literature on Chile's economic transformation argues that two factors suffice to explain the change: strong authoritarianism under General Augusto Pinochet and cohesive teams of free market-oriented technocrats with a capacity for learning. From this perspective, technocrats backed by a labor-repressing state carried out economic reforms over the objections of capitalists. The lesson: Strong states must insulate economic policymakers from social groups, especially businessmen and landowners. If they are not insulated, business groups defending narrow, sectoral, and parochial interests will derail or distort reform efforts.[3] The lesson is considered valid for democratic governments as well. They too are advised to create highly cohesive technocratic policymaking teams with relatively high degrees of insulation from social forces. Policymakers are expected to remain in control of shaping agendas and formulating policy. Business, labor, and middle-class groups may be consulted afterwards, especially during the implementation stage of the policymaking process.

Competent policymakers, sound policy designs, social learning, and relative autonomy are undoubtedly important factors for economic reform. Yet the role of capitalists and landowners in Chile's neoliberal transformation has been consistently underplayed. This book argues that economic elites were more active in the policy process than previously thought; hence, they too are a necessary factor in the explanation of Chile's free-market economic restructuring. A comparison across three policy periods in authoritarian Chile—gradual, radical, and pragmatic neoliberalism—shows that distinctive, shifting (sometimes narrow) coalitions of businessmen and landowners, with varying power resources, played a significant part in the agenda-setting, formulation, and implementation stages of the policy process in each period. If the interaction between capitalists and the state existed in an extreme case such as the Chilean one, where the nature of the dictatorship and the cohesiveness of ideological technocrats made it difficult to discern, then it must be present in other cases as well. Furthermore, the evidence suggests that close interaction between capitalists and the state has been a central feature of economic and social policymaking in Chile's new democracy as well.

Ignoring this relationship can lead to misinterpretations of why market-oriented economic reforms succeed or fail. In authoritarian and democratic Chile, changing systems of interaction between shifting capitalist coalitions and policymakers had differential effects for policymaking styles and investment patterns. Some forms were more functional for balanced economic policy and investment in production than others. The failure to take the relationship between capital and the state into account also has other consequences. It generates a certain measure of hubris about the relationship between market economics and social equity; it blinds observers to the limitations that Chile's system of interaction between capital and state places on social reform policy; and, hence, it conceals the true nature of the state and society under construction in Chile.

To argue that capitalist and landowning groups played a greater role in economic policymaking than formerly believed is not to say that the structure of state institutions and economic ideas are unimportant to explanations of economic reform in Chile. The focus here is not so much on which factor is more important but on when and how they matter, for alone each is insufficient for an explanation of policy outcomes.[4] Consequently, this book concentrates on the role of capitalist and landowning elites in Chile's neoliberal economic restructuring, but it by no means ignores the contribution of other factors.

The emphasis on social actors stems from an interest in uncovering factors that define the content of policy and that show how agents shape policy agendas and then formulate and implement policy. State structures cannot define the content of policies because they have no agency—they cannot construct meanings or act. The ideology of policymakers can provide meaning and content, but the question then becomes, what conditions influence the triumph of one set of ideas over another? After all, at any given moment there are competing ideologically anchored policy alternatives. An examination of coalitional politics helps explain why certain outcomes "win." By the same token, social actors do not operate in institutional vacuums. State structure matters. At the simplest level, a political system's degree of openness determines which social actors have access to the policymaking process, under what conditions, with whom it may be profitable—or possible—to ally, and how to divide and conquer. Of course, the economic and political changes examined here do not depend solely on domestic variables. International factors play an important role by closing some policy options and opening others. Without this variable, it is often difficult to understand the systemic conditions that elicit reactions from domestic social actors and impel coalitional change.

Given this approach, the book analyzes when and how social groups (principally capitalists and landowners), state structure, economic ideas, and international factors affected economic policy agenda setting, formulation, and implementation in contemporary Chile. The evidence in this case study, however, does not reveal a constant relationship between those factors and policy outcomes. International factors sometimes played a stronger role; at other times domestic factors prevailed. Within this limitation, the study shows how state structure and international factors influenced intracapitalist and landowner conflict and, hence, coalition formation over different policy periods. It then shows how state structure and international factors shaped the relative power of the different coalitions and their relationship to technocrats, which, in turn, influenced the victory of one over another. This approach is key to demonstrating that capitalist coalitions—the only social class that mattered for policymaking under the military government—did in fact participate in the policy process.

In addition, a focus on capitalist coalitions in economic policymaking sheds new light on the democratization process in Chile. Why was Chile, once one of Latin America's more established democracies, among the last dictatorships to democratize? Why did Chilean capitalists and landowners—

battered by the neoliberal restructuring project—unite behind Pinochet and the preservation of military rule? What explains the democratic opposition's retention of the neoliberal model?

This book argues that part of the answer lies in the linkages between capitalist coalitions and their access to policymaking. The general literature has attributed the Chilean bourgeoisie's support of Pinochet during the redemocratization period only to its fear of resurgent socialism. Yet capitalists also formed a broad intersectoral economic policy coalition and the military government negotiated with them: These facts are crucial to understanding why businessmen and landowners did not turn against the regime. These factors, among others, also influenced the opposition's decision to placate capitalist opposition to democracy by pledging to retain the socio-political model. Adhering to this pledge, once in power, center-left politicians preserved the system of close interaction with business groups on policy formulation that had emerged toward the end of military rule. The maintenance of that system has narrowed the options of democratic administrations for addressing social equity questions, limiting them to the deepening of liberal, not social-democratic, state formation. This urges caution with respect to optimistic assumptions of the Chilean model's capability to deliver on its promise of growth with equity.

## Capitalists and Neoliberal Economic Restructuring

In the mid-1970s, several of the most developed Latin American countries—Argentina, Chile, and Uruguay—experienced deep economic, social, and political crises.[5] During those upheavals, the military overthrew democratic governments and established authoritarian regimes that replaced import-substitution industrialization (ISI) and the welfare state with neoliberal economic and social policies. The new regimes repressed organized labor. During their reign domestic markets were opened to free trade, financial and foreign exchange markets were deregulated, state enterprises were privatized, and welfare states were dismantled. Neoliberal technocrats believed that by reducing the role of the state in the economy and society—except in labor markets—adhering to monetarism, and freeing markets they would be able to lick inflation, "get the prices right," reassign resources to export activities, and spur sustained economic growth.[6]

### Strong States

The prevailing explanation for neoliberal restructuring in the Southern Cone has led to neglect of the role of capitalists and landowners in economic change. Most interpretations emphasize the importance of highly autonomous military regimes and their civilian technocratic allies.[7] The focus on the role of the state and technocratic elites in restructuring originated in the fact that military governments not only had to repress labor and leftist political parties but significant sectors of the upper classes as well.[8] Thirty years or more of import-substitution industrialization had created an entrenched industrial bourgeoisie dependent on high levels of protection from trade and on sectoral policies that shifted resources from agriculture, trade, and the financial sector to industry. Because the industrial bourgeoisie was often considered the dominant fraction of the upper classes, when it could not stave off drastic neoliberal economic reforms, statist explanations for economic policy shifts were strengthened.

The supporting evidence for state and ideologically centered explanations for neoliberal restructuring in the Southern Cone was greater in Chile than in Argentina and Uruguay. For example, Chile's military government was more centralized. It was a system of one-man rule dominated by Pinochet, which made it easier to insulate technocrats from pressure groups. At one point Chilean business associations found they had no access to the policymaking process at all. By contrast, Argentina and Uruguay had real, not decorative, military juntas and presidential successions that gave business elites alternative channels of access to rival power centers within the regime.[9] Pinochet also sponsored a more cohesive and homogeneous cadre of economic experts that controlled all major ministries of state: the so-called Chicago boys. The label was applied because most of the core group had been trained in neoclassical economics under Milton Friedman and Arnold Harberger at the University of Chicago.[10] Whereas capitalists were seen as relatively unimportant to explaining neoliberal restructuring in Argentina and Uruguay, they were considered almost irrelevant in the Chilean case. Because the explanatory factors of the statist approach appeared strongest in the Chilean case, evidence that social forces indeed mattered in Chile suggests that their role elsewhere should be examined more carefully. As the following chapters will demonstrate, the form of the interaction between capitalists and the state in Chile significantly influenced policy formulation and affected investment patterns. Such findings indicate that perhaps the designers of reform processes should pay closer attention to the relationship between capitalists and the state, instead of assuming that the chimera of insulation ensures the correct path.

## Weak Capitalists

The neglect of capitalists and landowners in most studies of neoliberal restructuring has two related causes: the characterization of the upper classes and the structural role of the state in economic development. It is generally accepted that the bourgeoisie in Latin America is weak because of the way dependent capitalist development shaped class formation, particularly that of the industrial bourgeoisie.[11] Because Latin American countries are late developers, they occupy a subordinate and exploited position in the world economy. As a result, the industrial bourgeoisie (the harbinger of modernization) remains, as does the economy, underdeveloped. The main consequence of an underdeveloped industrial bourgeoisie is that it cannot play the modernizing role—either economically or politically— that it is believed to have played in the advanced industrial countries of the West. Latin American capitalists are too weak to sweep aside anachronistic upper classes—latifundistas and the comprador bourgeoisie—so they cannot be the engine of industrialization or democratization. In other words, because the industrial bourgeoisie is not the hegemonic fraction of capital, it cannot be a progressive force for economic and political change.[12]

In the absence of an innovative capitalist class the state must take the lead in economic development, particularly when socio-economic transformation and international economic crises force economic change.[13] From this perspective, Latin America's industrial bourgeoisie was born in the crucible of the Great Depression and World War II. It was dependent on state support throughout its infancy and adolescence; the state nurtured, protected, and guided national capitalists. Then, in their stunted maturity, Latin American capitalists appear incapable of proactive economic initiatives at a time in which economic change is unavoidable. Once again the state must step in; where it leads capitalists must follow.

In sum, the interpretation outlined above emphasized state-led development as the norm in Latin America since the 1930s. The region's economic and political problems were seen to stem from the survival into the modern era of traditional classes that have all but disappeared in developed nations. A pusillanimous industrial bourgeoisie has been the legacy of dependent capitalism in the (semi) periphery of the world economic system.[14]

Kinship ties between capitalists and landowners are often seen as yet another source of the bourgeoisie's weakness.[15] In this view, extensive networks of kin relations across economic sectors dampen intra-elite conflict. Blood ties often find material reinforcement in diversified holding companies. It is believed that these kinship and business relationships strengthen intraclass accommodation and inhibit confrontation, thereby stifling dramatic departures in economic policy proposals and, of course, incapacitating the industrial bourgeoisie from playing its historical modernizing role.

In addition to these historically oriented and economic interpretations of bourgeois feebleness, other explanations stress the shortcomings of the sectoral peak associations of business and landowning groups in the policymaking process.[16] These associations represent the interests of specific economic sectors such as industry, agriculture, mining, commerce, construction, and banking. In each sector, their membership aggregates large individual firms and smaller, industry-specific associations. In this view, then, sectoral peak associations suffer from several deficiencies. First, they are not truly representative of the group they claim to serve. Usually the interests of large-scale entrepreneurs find much more consistent and forceful expression than those of smaller operators. Moreover, because of the historical consequences of class formation in Latin America, when it comes to policy initiatives peak associations tend to be primarily reactive and defensive. Lastly, even when they have ample access to the policymaking process, they are frequently unsuccessful in staving off unwanted government policies.

## The Dominant Classes and Economic Policymaking Reconsidered

The case for thinking of business and landowning elites as mainly obstacles to economic change in Latin America appears strong. Could their weakness and relative irrelevance for understanding economic policy change have been overstated? State-centric characterizations of neoliberal economic restructuring—which emphasize centralization of authority, insulation of technocrats from pressure groups, and ideological homogeneity among top policymakers—certainly address some of the key conditions that made such dramatic reforms possible. Yet state structure cannot explain the *content* of policy. Why did the Southern Cone countries turn to neoliberalism in the mid-1970s rather than "deepen" industrialization as the bureaucratic-authoritarian regimes did in the 1960s?[17] The problem with the state structure approach is that it undervalues the fact that policy requires carriers. To be sure, technocrats and their ideology may give content to policies, but to focus exclusively on those two factors leaves a deeper issue unaddressed. What factors allow one set of ideologies to triumph over another? There are always competing ideologically anchored policy alternatives, and development paths are not predetermined.[18] During crises, competing alliances of intellectual, political, and material interests that favor different policy solutions vie for supremacy. The task is how to deconstruct those alliances and their power resources to find out how one side won and how losers might later change their postures.

Another obstacle to understanding the role of upper classes in neoliberal restructuring arose from the way dependency approaches sought to elucidate the historical significance of class formation for the economic structure of developing nations and theorized about the likelihood of progressive (or socialist) political change. The focus was not on policy process and economic policy outcomes, which is what this book stresses. Shifting the object of study in this way emphasizes the politics of economic policymaking, which allows analysis to focus on the impact of a wider range of class-based actors on a more tightly bounded, less macro-historical, outcome. In short, a focus on policy outcomes rather than structural outcomes allows one to consider factors that get washed out in broad-brush interpretations.

A focus on policy process and outcomes, however, is not sufficient to understand the role of capitalists and landowners in economic policy shifts for three reasons that are related to the earlier discussion of the arguments for the bourgeoisie's weakness. First, the level of aggregation of the relevant classes in those studies is often too high. In other words, analysts tend to assume that industrialists are the only relevant class actor in labor-repressing military regimes. Second, those studies have a linear concept of power between social groups and the state. As a result, they are inclined to focus mainly on conflicts between the state and the specific group affected adversely by a policy initiative (for example, industrialists or landowners). Third, many interpretations consider only the formal links between organized business and the state to determine the degree of insulation of state actors from societal pressure.

Given these observations, discerning the role of business and landowning groups in the politics of neoliberal restructuring requires three related tasks. First, all capitalist and landowning fractions must be taken into account and further disaggregated, enabling the construction of more fluid and varied policy coalitions. Second, a relational, not linear, concept of power is needed to observe both the interaction of class-based groups with varying policy preferences among themselves and the relationships of those groups to the state. This concept of power allows one to take into account tensions among competing social groups and the coalitions they may form in support of, or in opposition to, major economic policy models. Furthermore, tracking coalitions through policy debates can reveal when dominant capitalist coalitions have a proactive policy agenda and how they negotiate their policy preferences with state actors. Third, the informal channels of access of business associations and unorganized businessmen and landowners (the top management of conglomerates, for example) to government decision makers should not be neglected.

Executing these three tasks may reveal that states that appeared to be closed to societal groups may in fact be more "porous" than previously thought. Porosity has important functions. It contributes to the exchange of information between businessmen and policymakers, providing capitalists—the implementers of policy through investment in market reforms—with confidence to commit their resources. During difficult moments in a country's history, business participation in the policy process—especially policy formulation—enhances the belief that policies will actually work; for policies may be perfectly designed, but if the relationship between state officials and business is bitterly antagonistic, it is unlikely that policies will elicit the desired response from investors. Moreover, the form of the interaction between policymakers and capitalist coalitions also affects policy outcomes. The Chilean case suggests that a well-ordered hierarchy of ministries staffed with competent personnel is key. Such a hierarchy limits and orders points of access, thus favoring policy coherence. However, extremely insulated, rigidly ideological policymakers in contact with a narrow coalition of conglomerates may contribute to skewed reform measures and inflexible policymaking styles. State interaction with a broader coalition anchored by an encompassing peak association (one composed of the sectoral peak associations) seems to foster a climate more conducive to productive investment rather than financial speculation and to encourage a more pragmatic policy style.

## Upper-Class Elites and Democratization

Is there also a relationship between capitalist policy coalitions, their shifting fortunes, and the regime loyalties of businessmen and landowners?[19] One approach argues that in general there is a positive relationship between those factors.[20] Barring a severe threat from below, the dominant fractions of the upper class tend to support democratization when they expect to have access to government decision making, perceive that they may influence policy outcomes, and can exclude subordinate groups from the process. This support for democratization is also conditioned by whether the authoritarian regime excluded the dominant classes from policymaking and whether policies were to their liking.

Because of the predominance of the state-centric view of policymaking in authoritarian Chile, most interpretations focus on the severity of the threat from below to explain the persistence of upper class loyalty to Pinochet.[21] The argument is that neoliberal economic restructuring harmed the interests of both traditional landowners and industrialists—the presumed dominant fractions of the upper class—and shut them out of the policymaking process. Therefore, the only explanation for the Chilean upper classes' continued loyalty to the authoritarian regime after the economic collapse of 1983 must have been their fear of resurgent Marxism. This fear was said to be acute when the political parties responsible for the "chaos" of the Unidad Popular administration organized mass mobilizations. In the face of these events the bourgeoisie sided with Pinochet in spite of their unhappiness over economic policy.

An analysis that focuses on upper-class disaggregation, policy coalitions, and formal and informal mechanisms of representation and access to policymaking shows that the dominant capitalist coalition did have significant access to and influence over policymaking during the transition to democracy. Furthermore, it reveals that the "threat from below," although a consideration, was less significant than some accounts suggest. Under these conditions, the regime loyalties of the Chilean bourgeoisie can be explained by variations on the same factors that were relevant for much of the rest of South America, where the threat from below was not a major variable. In the absence of this, capitalists and landowners in a number of South American countries turned against authoritarian regimes because they had been shut out of the policymaking process or because they had to compete with state enterprises. In addition, the economic restructuring projects of those states partially failed because they could not entice investment and thus induce economic growth, as in Argentina. Had they been able to, they might have diminished opposition movements or changed their thrust. In Chile, by contrast, Pinochet reequilibrated his regime in part because he negotiated changes to radical neoliberalism with a new capitalist policy coalition. Their inclusion in the policymaking process defused the threat of a multiclass coalition between industrialists and the dominant *moderate* opposition, which might have toppled him. The resulting policies contributed to investment in fixed capital and economic recovery, which further shored up the military government.

## Conclusion

This book engages three major themes with regard to the relationship between coalitions, policy, and regime change. First, the central argument stresses that shifting coalitions of capitalist and landowning groups with varying power resources were a necessary condition for neoliberal restructuring in Chile. This perspective does not imply that state structure and the ideology of technocrats were unimportant but rather that the problem is to establish how and when coalitions, state structure, and ideology matter in the analysis of economic policy outcomes. The focus is on the role played by upper-class elites because their part is not as well understood as that of the state and technocrats. Second, the book examines the contributions of state structure and international factors to coalition building and capability, providing evidence for a reappraisal of the sources of the regime loyalties of large-scale businessmen and landowners in Chile. Third, that capitalist coalitions had access and influence over economic policymaking was a major reason for their support for authoritarianism in the wake of the economic crisis of 1982-1984. This thesis gains strength when one considers that the threat from below was more attenuated than previously thought. By the same token, the reequilibration of the military government had important consequences for the process of democratization and economic policy in Chile's new democracy: It limited the capacity of democratic governments to deliver on the promise of growth with equity.[22]

Having outlined the scope of the book in this chapter, Chapter 2 provides a framework for the analysis of the role of class-based groups in economic policymaking, with a focus on the upper classes under authoritarianism. The chapter emphasizes a method for disaggregating dominant class fractions and for identifying their policy preferences and coalitions. Definitions of the institutional and economic sources of relative power among the coalitions are also examined. This, in turn, provides the basis from which to characterize systems of interaction between business and bureaucrats and from which to assess their contribution to policy formulation and investment.

The remaining chapters apply the framework to the Chilean case. Chapter 3 focuses on the position of capitalists and landowners within the larger import-substitution industrialization coalition and the reasons for the demise of that coalition. It then briefly outlines how, when, and why capitalists turned against Salvador Allende. Their struggles against his government established the initial relationships between the various capitalist and landowning groups in the authoritarian period.

Chapters 4 through 7 cover the authoritarian period proper. They show how shifting capitalist coalitions with varying power resources participated in the policy process during the three distinct policy periods of the military government: the gradualist, radical, and pragmatic neoliberal phases of economic restructuring. Several questions guide the organization of these chapters. Which was the dominant policy coalition? How did economic and international factors and state structure affect the power resources of competing coalitions? What was the relationship of the dominant coalition to state actors, in particular to the technocrats? How did collaboration between bureaucrats and capitalist coalitions shape economic policy, especially in the policy formulation stage of the process?

The concluding chapter returns to the issue of the regime loyalties of Chilean capitalists during the transition to democracy in Chile. It argues that while the threat from below was a consideration, the fact that the dominant capitalist coalition had access to and influence over economic policymaking played a larger role in their continued support for the dictatorship. During the economic and political crisis of 1983-1985 capitalists and landowners established a system of close collaboration with bureaucrats for economic policymaking, a system that has largely persisted into the newly inaugurated democratic period.

The significance of these findings is that they call into question arguments of Chilean exceptionality, even by comparativists who *do* consider the role of capitalists in economic and political change.[23] These authors show the relevance of businessmen and landowners for these processes in Mexico, Argentina, Uruguay, Brazil and other countries, but maintain that the criteria used for those cases do not apply to Chile—in their eyes, a case of almost pure Bonapartism. This study shows that the same criteria, though less obvious, do apply. Thus, the reequilibration of the military dictatorship had important consequences for Chile's transition to democracy. Redemocratization followed the conditions and timetable of the authoritarian constitution of 1980. The renewed stability of the military government reinforced the political opposition's embrace of neoliberalism because opposition forces had to placate capitalists to induce them to accept political change and to keep them from disinvesting after the transition. The opposition's need to prove their sincerity contributed to the retention of the system of collaboration between policymakers and business. This in turn has led to the deepening of a neoliberal approach to social equity and welfare statism—an outcome that indicates that the Chilean model may not be the best for resolving the problem of economic growth with social equity. This suggests that more analyses of the conditions under which upper classes can be reconciled to policies that generate greater social equality are needed.

## Notes

1. For a recent example, see Barry P. Bosworth, Rudiger Dornbusch, and Raúl Labán, eds., *The Chilean Economy: Policy Lessons and Challenges* (Washington, D.C.: Brookings Institution, 1994).

2. Timothy Scully, *Rethinking the Center: Party Politics in Nineteenth- and Twentieth-Century Chile* (Stanford: Stanford University Press, 1992); for moderation in the left, see Jeffrey M. Puryear, *Thinking Politics: Intellectuals and Democracy in Chile, 1973-1988* (Baltimore: Johns Hopkins University Press, 1994).

3. For a recent review of these arguments, see Barbara Geddes, "The Politics of Economic Liberalization," *Latin American Research Review* 30, 2, 1995.

4. For a similar view, see Thomas Risse-Kappen, "Public Opinion, Domestic Structure, and Foreign Policy in Liberal Democracies," *World Politics* 43, 4, 1991.

5. For a classic in the analysis of the crisis of populism, see Guillermo O'Donnell, *Modernization and Bureaucratic-Authoritarianism: Studies in South American Politics* (Berkeley: Institute of International Studies, University of California, 1973).

6. The literature on the economics of neoliberal restructuring in the region is extensive. For representative works, see Joseph Ramos, *Neoconservative Economics in the Southern Cone of Latin America* (Baltimore: Johns Hopkins University Press, 1986); Sebastian Edwards and Alejandra Cox-Edwards, *Monetarism and Liberalization: The Chilean Experiment* (Cambridge: Ballinger, 1987).

7. For the theoretical elaboration of the statist approach, see Theda Skocpol, *States and Revolutions: A Comparative Analysis of France, Russia, and China* (Cambridge: Cambridge University Press, 1979); Peter Evans, Dietrich Rueschmeyer, and Theda Skocpol, *Bringing the State Back In* (New York: Cambridge University Press, 1985); Stephen Krasner, *Defending the National Interest: Raw Materials Investments and Foreign Policy* (Princeton: Princeton University Press, 1978); Judith Goldstein, "The

Political Economy of Trade: Institutions of Protection," *American Political Science Review* 80, 1, 1986.

8. For applications of the statist approach to the Latin American region, see Alejandro Foxley, *Latin American Experiments in Neoconservative Economics* (Berkeley: University of California Press, 1983); Philip O'Brien and Paul Cammack, eds., *Generals in Retreat: The Crisis of Military Rule in Latin America* (Manchester: Manchester University Press, 1985); Guillermo Campero, *Los Gremios empresariales en el período 1970-1983: Comportamiento sociopolítico y orientaciones ideológicas* (Santiago: ILET, 1984). More recent studies echo these positions; see Lois Hecht Oppenheim, *Politics in Chile: Democracy, Authoritarianism, and the Search for Development* (Boulder: Westview, 1993); David E. Hojman, *Chile: The Political Economy of Development and Democracy in 1990s* (Pittsburgh: University of Pittsburgh Press, 1993). Even studies that consider the role of social forces in policy outcomes fall back on statist explanations in the Chilean case; see Jeffry Frieden, "Winners and Losers in the Latin American Debt Crisis: The Political Implications," in Barbara Stallings and Robert Kaufman, eds., *Debt and Democracy in Latin America* (Boulder: Westview, 1989).

9. For the system of one-man rule in Chile, see Arturo Valenzuela, "The Military in Power: The Consolidation of One Man Rule," in Paul W. Drake and Iván Jaksic, eds., *The Struggle for Democracy in Chile, 1982-1990* (Lincoln: University of Nebraska Press, 1991) and Genaro Arriagada, *Pinochet: The Politics of Power* (Boston: Unwin Hyman, 1988). For the Uruguayan military government, see Howard Handelman, "Economic Policies and Elite Pressures," in Howard Handelman and Thomas G. Sanders, eds., *Military Government and the Movement Toward Democracy in Latin America* (Bloomington: University of Indiana Press, 1981). For Argentina, see William C. Smith, *Authoritarianism and the Crisis of the Argentine Political Economy* (Stanford: Stanford University Press, 1989).

10. For a history of the Chicago boys, see Juan Gabriel Valdés, *La escuela de los Chicago: Operación Chile* (Buenos Aires: Grupo Editorial Zeta, 1989); Arturo Fontaine Aldunate, *Los economistas y el Presidente Pinochet* (Santiago: Editora Zig-Zag, 1988, second edition); Patricio Silva, "Technocrats and Politics in Chile: From the Chicago Boys to the Cieplan Monks," *Journal of Latin American Studies* 23, 2, 1991; and Jeffrey M. Puryear, *Thinking Politics*.

11. For the classic studies of this interpretation, see Fernando Henrique Cardoso and Enzo Faletto, *Dependency and Development in Latin America* (Berkeley: University of California Press, 1978); Fernando Henrique Cardoso, *Las ideologías de la burguesía industrial en sociedades dependientes: Argentina y Brasil* (México: Siglo XXI, 1971); and Claudio Véliz, "La mesa de tres patas," *Desarrollo Económico* 3, 1-2, 1963. For a nondependency analysis that comes to the same conclusion about upper class behavior, see Charles W. Anderson's pioneering study, *Politics and Economic Change in Latin America: The Governing of Restless Nations* (New York: D. Van Nostrand, 1967).

12. From another perspective, it can be argued that these interpretations give too much credit to the bourgeoisie of developed nations. In other words, the Latin American bourgeoisie appears so weak only because the capabilities and inclinations of European and American capitalists have been overdrawn and, to an extent, romanticized. The historical record shows that the upper classes of many developed and democratic nations could be quite reactionary. For a development of this point,

see Catherine Conaghan, *Restructuring Domination: Industrialists and the State in Ecuador* (Pittsburgh: University of Pittsburgh Press, 1988).

13. For a classic study on Brazil in the 1970s, see Peter Evans, *Dependent Development: The Alliance of Multinational, State, and Local Capital in Brazil* (Princeton: Princeton University Press, 1979); also see Phillip O'Brien and Paul Cammack, *Generals in Retreat*; and William Smith, *The Crisis of the Argentine Political Economy*.

14. For a good review of these arguments, see Arnold J. Bauer, "Industry and the Missing Bourgeoisie: Consumption and Development in Chile, 1850-1950," *Hispanic American Historical Review* 70, 2, 1990.

15. For an analysis of bourgeois weakness based on kinship ties, see Maurice Zeitlin and Richard E. Ratcliff, *Landlords and Capitalists: The Dominant Class of Chile* (Princeton: Princeton University Press, 1988).

16. For representative works, see Philippe C. Schmitter, *Interest Conflict and Political Change in Brazil* (Stanford: Stanford University Press, 1971); and Guillermo Campero, *Los Gremios empresariales en el período 1970-1983*.

17. The neoliberal cases of the 1970s were different from the bureaucratic-authoritarian (BA) experiences of Brazil and Argentina in the mid-1960s. Although economic and political crisis also contributed to their rise, and they too emphasized labor repression and economic stabilization, they did not seek to reduce the role of the state in the economy; nor did BA regimes encourage a rapid shift of resources from ISI to agricultural commodity export or pursue extreme market liberalization. To the contrary, they sought to "deepen" industrialization, which required state-directed industrial policy. For a discussion of these differences, see Hector E. Schamis, "Reconceptualizing Latin American Authoritarianism in the 1970s: From Bureaucratic-Authoritarianism to Neoconservatism," *Comparative Politics* 23, 2, 1991.

18. For an elaboration of this view in a study largely devoted to an exploration of the role of ideas in economic policymaking, see Peter A. Gourevitch, "Keynesian Politics: The Political Sources of Economic Policy Choices," in Peter A. Hall, ed., *The Political Power of Economic Ideas: Keynesianism Across Nations* (Princeton: Princeton University Press, 1989).

19. In one of the first attempts to come to grips with this problem David Collier called for a disaggregation of coalitions, policy, and regime change; see the concluding chapter to David Collier, ed., *The New Authoritarianism in Latin America* (Princeton: Princeton University Press, 1979).

20. Catherine Conaghan, James Malloy, and Luis Abugattas, "Business and the Boys: The Politics of Neoliberalism in the Central Andes," *Latin American Research Review* 25, 2, 1990; Catherine Conaghan and Rosario Espinal, "Unlikely Transitions to Uncertain Regimes? Democracy Without Compromise in the Dominican Republic and Ecuador," *Journal of Latin American Studies* 33, 3, 1990; Leigh A. Payne, *Brazilian Industrialists and Democratic Change* (Baltimore: Johns Hopkins University Press, 1994).

21. For an example of the "threat from below" interpretation, see Jeffry Frieden, "Winners and Losers in the Latin American Debt Crisis."

22. For a characterization of Chile within a typology of emerging democracies in Latin America, see Carlos H. Acuña and William C. Smith, "The Political Economy of Structural Adjustment: The Logic of Support and Opposition to Neoliberal Reform," in William C. Smith, Carlos H. Acuña, and Eduardo Gamarra, eds., *Latin*

*American Political Economy in the Age of Neoliberal Reform* (New Brunswick: Transaction, 1994).

23. Jeffry Frieden, *Debt, Development, and Democracy: Modern Political Economy and Latin America, 1965-1985* (Princeton: Princeton University Press, 1991); Sylvia Maxfield, *Governing Capital: International Finance and Mexican Politics* (Ithaca: Cornell University Press, 1990).

# 2

# Capitalists, Neoliberal Economic Reform, and Democracy

A disaggregation of social coalitions, policy outcomes, and regime change simplifies the analysis of complex and interrelated processes of economic and political change.[1] It shifts the focus from strict policy analysis and the process of democratization to the way in which coalitions influence economic policymaking and how different forms of social participation in the policymaking process shape the regime loyalties of class-based groups. This chapter develops a framework for uncovering the role of capitalist coalitions in authoritarian economic policymaking and for examining how the fortunes of those coalitions condition their support for dictatorship or democracy. The framework, however, is not intended to be a general analytic model. It aims to reintroduce social forces as a necessary component in the explanation of changes in economic policy outcomes. It does not, nor can it, establish whether social forces are more or less important than other factors. Its other purpose is to elucidate why capitalists support dictatorship or democracy and to draw some conclusions about the consequences of that support for the process of regime transition. It falls short of claiming that capitalist regime loyalties determine the outcome of transitions from authoritarianism.

## Capitalist Coalitions, the State, and External Shocks

In addition to the role of state structure, ideas, and external shocks, a full explanation of the policy shift from import-substitution industrialization to neoliberalism and export-led growth in Chile and elsewhere also requires an examination of the social bases of support—however narrow—that state elites turned to for the success of their projects. For in capitalist economies, where much of the productive apparatus is in private hands, state actors must find upper-class allies willing and able to respond to policy initiatives.[2] Again, although shifting coalitions of capitalists and landowners are a necessary factor in the explanation of policy change, other factors also played important roles in shaping the coalitions and policy. The central question is when and how external factors, domestic institutions, and social groups matter in such processes.[3] This book examines the first two factors to illuminate the role that social groups play in economic policy outcomes at different historical junctures. The case, unfortunately, does not provide sufficient material for determining a fixed set of relationships between those factors and outcomes.

With respect to external factors, many studies in the field of international political economy have argued that external conditions play a permissive role by opening some options and closing others. A world economy in expansion, contraction, or sudden crisis forces change upon countries. But external factors do not determine outcomes, except in the case of conquest. Variables related to domestic structure—state institutions and social forces— play a key role in determining variation in economic policy outcomes.[4] The state, as used here, consists of a set of civilian and military institutions—the state apparatus. The people who control those institutions are the government.[5] Regime, by contrast, refers to the system of intermediation between state and society. Classifications of regimes usually distinguish between democratic, authoritarian, and monist variants.[6]

Many analysts have explored how state structure shapes policy outcomes; and, although this study makes a distinction between state and regime, most of the effects emphasized by those scholars apply to political regimes as well. One widely recognized impact of regime type is its role in determining which social groups participate in economic policymaking. Regimes also influence the conditions of that participation and the institutional power resources at their command.[7] Highly centralized authoritarian regimes have a much freer hand in selecting social support bases than do pluralist, democratic regimes with multiple channels of access to decision making centers. The former insulate policymakers much more than the latter. When political regimes change abruptly during economic crises—say from democracy to dictatorship—the range of policy experimentation following the coup d'etat may be much greater because state elites are less constrained in their selection of social support bases. This implies that labor-repressing authoritarian regimes such as Chile's under General Augusto Pinochet tend to bar all but large-scale capitalists and landowners from the politics of economic policymaking. Under these conditions, the kinds of coalitions and policies that arise will be markedly different from those in which labor and middle classes are significant actors.[8]

In sum, external factors and domestic institutions influence the range of policy options available to state elites. They also affect which social groups are likely to be relevant for economic policymaking and under what conditions. This, however, still leaves the following question unanswered. What theories elucidate the role that large-scale businessmen and landowners play in policymaking? Each must overcome the problems discussed in the previous chapter: the tendency to focus on one or two highly aggregated capitalist fractions; a linear conception of power between class-based groups; and the inclination to consider only the links between organized business and the regime.

Peter Gourevitch and Jeffry Frieden have provided a good starting point from which to surmount these problems. [9] Both stress the importance of disaggregating class-based groups as a first step toward examining intraclass conflict and its impact on the formation of more fluid policy coalitions than those found in classic interpretations of the bourgeoisie in Latin America.[10] Frieden stresses how the economic characteristics of firms induce their directors to back either market-oriented policies or sectoral policies. He argues that liquid-asset holders (in banking, real estate, and trade) prefer the former and that fixed-asset holders (industrialists and landowners) favor the latter. The reason for the difference is that liquid-asset holders can adjust more quickly to market signals than fixed-asset holders.

It is certainly important to know when firms are likely to back government policies by investing, and Frieden's disaggregation captures the two polar types of economic interests: industrial conglomerates that rely on high levels of protection versus economic groups with a heavy concentration in highly mobile financial, commercial, and speculative assets. This approach, however, underestimates the significance of alliances that cut across liquid and fixed-asset holders and influence the policy demands of competing business coalitions.[11] One way to fill the gap is to combine Frieden's disaggregation with Gourevitch's approach to coalition-building. Then it is possible to recognize more nuanced economic interests and, thus, identify more fluid and varied economic policy coalitions.

One of Gourevitch's criteria for disaggregating social groups is to classify them according to whether they produce for international or domestic markets. For Latin America, the method seems warranted given the nature of the two major developmental strategies in contestation since the 1930s: import-substitution industrialization behind high protective barriers (ISI) and open economies seeking to exploit their comparative advantages in agriculture and extractive industries. One of the central conflicts in shifts from ISI to open economies is between producers for domestic markets who are not competitive in world markets, and who therefore tend to favor protection, and capitalists tied to internationally competitive sectors, who are inclined to support trade opening.

Although Gourevitch's approach is broader and more flexible than Frieden's, the two are not incompatible. In fact, they complement each other well. By combining them we can examine the policy stances of capitalists with fixed assets in internationally-oriented industrial and agricultural sectors (mining, fishing, logging, and fruits) as well as those of capitalists with fixed assets in industries that produce for domestic markets but that are internationally competitive (mainly the food processing industry). The policy preferences of these groups tend to be different from those of liquid-asset holders with strong connections to the international financial community, and they are also distinct from those of producers with fixed assets in internationally noncompetitive sectors in industry and agriculture (consumer durables, grains, and livestock). Fixed-asset groups oriented towards international markets should support open economies but not oppose all sectoral policy. Fixed-asset producers oriented toward domestic markets but who are internationally competitive should favor sectoral policies and not adamantly oppose gradual reductions in protection.

Having identified the relevant groups, their economic interests, and their likely policy stances, what constitutes a coalition and how does it affect policy outcomes? At the most basic level, coalitions form around common economic interests. Drawing from Poulantzas, at the center of the alliance is the core group or class fraction that dominates the coalition and sets overall policy demands. The hegemonic class fraction may draw other capitalist and landowning groups to it and form a broader coalition under its leadership: the power bloc. The core group may negotiate some policy positions with these new partners in order to form an effective alliance. Additional class fractions—allied capitalist and landowning groups—may support the overall policy positions of the dominant coalition but lack the ability to influence the alliance's policy demands.[12]

Discovering these coalitions requires a close examination of policy debates. However, in addition to the policy statements of business peak associations, one must also take into account the preferences of the directors of large-scale private enterprises for these may be at odds with those of business associations. They may, in fact, constitute the core group of a capitalist policy coalition and enter into a collaborative relationship with the regime quite independently of what other groups wish. Business associations may join them later in a subordinate position within a power bloc or simply as allied groups.

Having set the criteria for the disaggregation of capitalist and landowning groups and defined the structure of policy coalitions, the next problem is to establish a link between the policy coalitions and policy outcomes. First, to make plausible the claim that the coalition had an impact on the policy agenda, one must show that the dominant policy coalition formed before the government announced the policy and that the coalition's policy preferences were reflected in the policy outcome. The fit between demand and outcome need not be perfect because a policy coalition's starting demands only represent an initial negotiating position *vis-à-vis* bureaucrats and, perhaps, other social groups. The outcome, however, must include some of the coalition's substantive policy demands, not merely side issues.

The second step borrows from instrumentalist conceptions of the relationship between state and society. Class background and economic interest may bring key policymakers together with the principal representatives of shifting capitalist coalitions. This approach offers a window into the role that capitalist coalitions may play in policy formulation; and, by tracing the connections between policymakers and policy coalitions one also discovers the system of interaction between them in the policymaking process. Again, business peak associations are not necessarily the sole means of class representation. Careful attention must be paid to the ways in which upper-class elites also articulate their economic interests through personalistic, ad hoc channels.[13] The early literature on authoritarianism noted that the military selected influential persons to direct government economic agencies because they presumably spoke for important business and landowning constituencies, but subsequent works have rarely explored the class backgrounds of highly ideological ministers of economic affairs. The few authors that did failed to tie them to larger coalitions of capitalists and landowners both inside and outside of organized business.[14]

A few additional questions remain to be settled before tackling the issue of the regime loyalties of the bourgeoisie. Why does one policy coalition dominate over another, and why does the government take its policy demands into account? Charles Lindblom and others answer the second question by arguing that governments depend, in part, on a healthy growing economy for their stability.[15] Conversely, in hard economic times, economic recovery programs must succeed in restoring growth if governments wish to survive. In a capitalist economy many of the investment resources upon which economic performance depends are in the hands of the private sector; therefore, governments rarely oppose the interests of all of the fractions of capital. Naturally, some fractions of capital may be left out of the dominant coalition, especially those that are a drag on investment, which varies according to historical context. The structural power of capital becomes even more significant during processes of neoliberal transformation where the private sector is expected to be responsible for the bulk of investment.

A number of economic and institutional factors give some capitalist and landowning groups the ability to dominate others. The power of economic resources is related to their capacity to contribute to a country's economic growth and stability. In dependent developing economies, external factors play an especially large role. For example, an expansion of international trade and finance can strengthen exporters, import-export merchants, and the bankers they do business with. By contrast, world economic contractions tend to favor producers for domestic markets.[16] Sources of foreign investment are important economic power resources in developing nations. Capitalist groups that can tap into them are at an advantage over those that cannot, especially when international liquidity is expanding rapidly. An instrumental approach to the relationship between state and society reveals how government may turn important decision-making centers over to the representatives or agents of a coalition that is gaining economic strength.

Regime type also may bias institutional sources of power in favor of the dominant coalition. In any regime, when a social group gains control over key state institutions it has an advantage over other groups. Authoritarian regimes magnify this advantage because they often have few, if any, formal channels of representation for social groups. In a regime as exclusionary as Pinochet's Chile, a very narrow coalition may impose its policy agenda on a wide spectrum of capitalist and landowning groups opposed to it, not to mention urban and rural labor. Nevertheless, the dominant coalition, however narrow, must control the economic resources necessary to nourish the development model that it champions. Democratic regimes, to some extent, provide multiple power centers. This usually means that those who control state institutions must take into account the interests of a wider range of social actors or risk jeopardizing regime stability. However, the existence of multiple power centers does not necessarily mean uncontrolled "porosity" of the state to societal interests and, therefore, chaotic, ineffectual policymaking.[17] Democratic governments can control access to the policymaking process by establishing a clear hierarchy of authority among financial and line ministries.

These institutional considerations clearly affected the structure of the system of interaction between capitalists and state policymakers in Chile. That structure was defined by whether the military government set up a tight hierarchy of authority among financial and line ministries or not, the characteristics of the policymakers (meritocratic bureaucrats and ideological or flexible technocratic political appointees), and whether the interaction was with individual peak associations, narrow conglomerates, or with the encompassing peak association. These conditions affected the politics of policy formulation and policy outcomes; among other factors, they also influenced the type of investment that predominated in each of the policy periods in authoritarian Chile. The same logic held true for the new democratic regime as well.

A final question remains. How did international stimuli and state structure affect the role of class-based social groups in economic policymaking? Chile under Pinochet suggests that authoritarianism determined the exclusion of all but the top economic elite from the policymaking process. External factors, international capital flows in particular, influenced which fraction of capital dominated at various times. Pinochet and his policymakers listened to a certain group of capitalists that seemed to hold the key to economic growth because the regime was keen to expand private investment. After the transition to democracy, the political institutions of the Constitution of 1980, coupled with the durability of the pragmatic capitalist coalition and the expansion of the international economy, forced center-left administrations to permit ample participation by business elites in policy formulation and implementation. This situation casts a shadow on the ability of center-left governments to design and implement policies that address social equity and challenges uncritical acceptance of the Chilean model of growth with equity.

### Capitalists, Landowners, and Democratization

Upper-class elites may at times give up the right to rule for the right to make money, but if they cannot make money they may attempt to participate in the policymaking process in areas of direct concern to them. Whether capitalists play a significant role in the policymaking process, especially during crisis periods, influences their continued support for authoritarianism or their turn to democracy; and, even if their preference does not determine outcomes in transitions from authoritarianism, it has definite consequences for the process of political change. Capitalists played precisely this role in Chile.

Many studies have shown that political change—especially political liberalization and democratization—often begins with splits at the top.[18] The crucial question is: Under what circumstances do cleavages among the elites turn into conflict? Because the "top" in an authoritarian regime such as Chile's consists of the military and the upper classes, the discussion that follows examines the conditions that influence a split between military rulers and significant business and landowning groups.

The literature on authoritarianism argues that the inclusion or exclusion of significant large-scale capitalist and landowning groups in dominant economic policy coalitions colors their support for such regimes.[19] Where they are included in the policy coalition, have access to the policymaking process, and can defend themselves against measures that threaten their fundamental interests—property and profits—upper-class elites remain loyal to a regime because it is perceived to be reliable.[20] Where the opposite holds true a regime is viewed as unreliable, and excluded capitalist and landowning groups may turn against it. Disgruntled members of the upper class may prefer a more democratic form of government because such regimes offer more points of access and influence in policymaking.[21]

Democratic regimes also encourage more open and diverse sources of information, and information is crucial to decision making in business.

Nevertheless, the regime loyalties of capitalists and landowners also depend on economic performance.[22] Upper-class groups shut out of policymaking may not oppose an authoritarian regime during good economic times, but during prolonged, deep economic downturns they may cast about for alternatives. Whether they do so or not may hinge on the character of emerging political party systems.[23] Capitalists are more likely to support political liberalization and democratization when leftist, socialist, and populist political parties are weak.

Numerous empirical findings support these views. Research on Brazil, Ecuador, Peru, Bolivia, and the Dominican Republic showed that business elites supported a shift from authoritarianism to more democratic rule because they believed they would have greater access to the economic policymaking process under conditions in which the perceived threat from below was low.[24] Similar evidence exists for the cases of Argentina, Brazil, Mexico, and Venezuela.[25] Capitalists turned to democracy due to varying combinations of the following factors: their exclusion from economic policymaking, the economy's poor performance under authoritarianism, and the low salience of the threat from below.

Because Chilean capitalists apparently chafed under many of the same adverse conditions, studies that accepted an overly state-centered approach to neoliberal restructuring argued that a much higher degree of threat from below explained their continued support for military rule. In contrast to those conclusions, this book's focus on the relationship between shifting capitalist coalitions and the state revealed that during the crucial period of political and economic instability, Chilean capitalists supported Pinochet because they were *included* rather than excluded from economic policymaking under conditions in which the threat from below was minimal after 1983. This occurred during the third policy period, which began in 1983 and ended in 1989. Moreover, Chilean capitalists accepted Pinochet's defeat in the October 1988 plebiscite because the opposition committed itself to the retention of their economic model, because they enjoyed constitutional protection of their privileges, and because of sustained economic growth from 1985 on. These facts strongly caution against overestimating the commitment to democracy of the Chilean right. They suggest that Chilean capitalists only tolerate democracy because the economic model is not threatened by social-democratic policies, even in a mild form, and because their constitutional privileges remain intact. This situation reinforces the need for prudence in the face of uncritical acceptance of the Chilean model, which is being so heavily promoted.

## Conclusion

This chapter outlined a framework for uncovering the role of large-scale businessmen and landowners in economic policymaking under authoritarian rule and how their exclusion or inclusion in policymaking influenced their support for dictatorship or democracy. The analysis in the chapters that follow is based on a comparison between three distinct policy periods: gradual, radical, and pragmatic neoliberal restructuring.[26] An application of the interpretive framework shows that—in addition to such factors as international conditions, state structure, and ideology—capitalist coalitions also played a significant part in each of those economic policy shifts.[27] In each period, policymakers relied on a distinct capitalist coalition to set the policy agenda, and each coalition enjoyed privileged networks with state institutions and actors before the policies were adopted.[28] In other words, the capitalist coalitions collaborated with policymakers, principally in policy formulation, in ways that were crucial to policy outcomes. The style, content, and extent of that collaboration varied with each policy coalition in each policy period.[29] The book then draws out some of the positive and negative policy consequences of the carry-over into democracy of the system of collaboration that emerged during the pragmatic period.

Turning to the question of political change, the argument expounded here is based on a comparison of Chile to factors that applied in other countries. It concludes that Chilean capitalists supported Pinochet during the transition from military rule largely due to variations in factors that applied to other Latin American cases as well (their inclusion or exclusion from the policymaking process), not because of some exceptional condition to Chile (greater threat from below). Their loyalty to the dictatorship helped shape the process and outcome of Chile's political transition. It allowed the military government to overcome the political crisis of 1983-1986 and to follow the timetable and conditions set by the authoritarian regime's Constitution of 1980. This, along with other factors, contributed to the retention by Chile's new democracy of the system of interaction between capital and the state developed during the final years of the dictatorship.

## Notes

1. David Collier argued this point in the concluding chapter of his edited volume, *The New Authoritarianism* (Princeton: Princeton University Press, 1979).

2. For this view, see Charles E. Lindblom, *Politics and Markets* (New York: Basic Books, 1977).

3. Recent scholarship in the field of Latin American politics has called for the development of approaches that tackle these theoretical problems; see Peter H. Smith, "Crisis and Democracy in Latin America," *World Politics* 43, 4, 1991; Hector E. Schamis,

"Reconceptualizing Latin American Authoritarianism in the 1970s: From Bureaucratic-Authoritarianism to Neoconservatism," *Comparative Politics* 23, 2, 1991.

4. For the relationship between these variables, see Peter Gourevitch, *Politics in Hard Times: Comparative Responses to International Economic Crisis* (Ithaca: Cornell University Press, 1986); Steven Haggard, *Pathways from the Periphery: The Politics of Growth in Newly Industrializing Countries* (Ithaca: Cornell University Press, 1990); and Kenneth Waltz, *Man, the State, and War: A Theoretical Analysis* (New York: Columbia University Press, 1954).

5. For an elaboration of these definitions, see Nora Hamilton, *The Limits of State Autonomy: Post-Revolutionary Mexico* (Princeton: Princeton University Press, 1982).

6. For this definition of regime, see Fernando H. Cardoso, "On the Characterization of Authoritarian Regimes in Latin America," in David Collier, ed., *The New Authoritarianism in Latin America*.

7. For a similar view, see John Zysman, *Governments, Markets, and Growth: Financial Systems and the Politics of Industrial Change* (Ithaca: Cornell University Press, 1983).

8. For inclusionary and exclusionary regimes, see Alfred Stepan, *The State and Society: Peru in Comparative Perspective* (Princeton: Princeton University Press, 1978).

9. Peter A. Gourevitch, *Politics in Hard Times*; Jeffry Frieden, "Classes, Sectors, and Foreign Debt in Latin America," *Comparative Politics* 21, 1, 1988.

10. Some Marxist and dependency school analysts have made distinctions between the national and internationalized bourgeoisie. These analyses move the discussion in the right direction, but they are limited in two respects. First, the difference between the two is essentially based on the degree to which national capitalists are associated with transnational corporations (via licensing, credit arrangements, and joint ventures, etc.) instead of the markets for which they produce, the distribution of assets (liquid and fixed), or the economic sectors of which they are a part. Thus, secondly, the level of aggregation is still too high to uncover more fluid coalitions of capitalist groups.

11. The evidence presented in this book calls into question Frieden's argument that extreme class conflict produced a "Bonapartist" situation in which capitalists gave state elites a free hand in economic policymaking in return for order.

12. Nicos Poulantzas, *Political Power and Social Classes* (London: New Left Books, 1973).

13. This point is highlighted in Peter Gourevitch's treatment of Germany under Bismarck and the shift from free trade to protectionism in the 1890s.

14. For the classic statement, see Juan J. Linz, "An Authoritarian Regime: Spain," in Erik Allardt and Stein Rokkan, eds., *Mass Politics: Studies in Political Sociology* (New York: Free Press, 1970). For work that connects ministers to class backgrounds, see Guillermo O'Donnell, *Bureaucratic-Authoritarianism: Argentina, 1966-1973, in Comparative Perspective* (Berkeley: University of California Press, 1988), p. 72. For a study that does link capitalist coalitions to the state, see Sylvia Maxfield, *Governing Capital: International Finance and Mexican Politics* (Ithaca: Cornell University Press, 1990). For an instrumentalist view of the state, see Ralph Miliband, *The State in Capitalist Society: An Analysis of the Western System of Power* (New York: Basic Books, 1969).

15. Charles Lindblom, *Politics and Markets*; Adam Przeworski and Michael

Wallerstein, "Structural Dependence of the State on Capital," *American Political Science Review* 82, 1, 1988.

16. Peter Gourevitch, *Politics in Hard Times*; and Ronald Rogowski, *Commerce and Coalitions: How Trade Affects Domestic Political Alignments* (Princeton: Princeton University Press, 1989).

17. Barbara Geddes, "The Politics of Economic Liberalization," *Latin American Research Review* 30, 2, 1995.

18. Theda Skocpol, *States and Revolution: A Comparative Analysis of France, Russia, and China* (Cambridge: Cambridge University Press, 1979); Guillermo O'Donnell and Philippe C. Schmitter, *Transitions from Authoritarian Rule: Conclusions* (Baltimore: Johns Hopkins University Press, 1986); Gaetano Mosca, *The Ruling Class* (New York: McGraw Hill, 1939).

19. Douglas Chalmers and Craig Robinson, "Why Power Contenders Choose Liberalization," *International Studies Quarterly* 26, 1, 1982; Guillermo O'Donnell, "Tensions in the Bureaucratic-Authoritarian State and the Question of Democracy," in David Collier, ed., *The New Authoritarianism*.

20. Robert Kaufman, "Liberalization and Democratization in South America: Perspectives from the 1970s," in Guillermo O'Donnell, Philippe Schmitter, and Laurence Whitehead, eds., *Transitions from Authoritarian Rule: Comparative Perspectives* (Baltimore: Johns Hopkins University Press, 1986); Jeffry Frieden, "Winners and Losers in the Latin American Debt Crisis: The Political Implications," in Barbara Stallings and Robert Kaufman, eds., *Debt and Democracy in Latin America* (Boulder: Westview, 1989).

21. Douglas Chalmers and Craig Robinson, "Why Power Contenders Choose Liberalization."

22. Jeffry Frieden, "Winners and Losers in the Latin American Debt Crisis"; Douglas Chalmers and Craig Robinson, "Why Power Contenders Choose Liberalization."

23. In addition to the work of Robert Kaufman and Jeffry Frieden cited above, see Edward Epstein, "Legitimacy, Institutionalization, and Opposition in Exclusionary Bureaucratic-Authoritarian Regimes: The Situation of the 1980s," *Comparative Politics* 17, 1, 1984.

24. Catherine M. Conaghan, James Malloy, and Luis Abugattas, "Business and the Boys: The Politics of Neoliberalism in the Central Andes," *Latin American Research Review* 25, 2, 1990; Catherine Conaghan and Rosario Espinal, "Unlikely Transitions to Uncertain Regimes? Democracy without Compromise in the Dominican Republic and Ecuador," *Journal of Latin American Studies* 22, 3, 1990; Leigh A. Payne, *Brazilian Industrialists and Democratic Change* (Baltimore: Johns Hopkins University Press, 1994).

25. William C. Smith, *Authoritarianism and the Crisis of the Argentine Political Economy* (Stanford: Stanford University Press, 1989); Fernando Henrique Cardoso, "Entrepreneurs and the Transition to Democracy in Brazil," in O'Donnell, Schmitter, and Whitehead, *Transitions from Authoritarian Rule: Comparative Perspectives*; Sylvia Maxfield, "National Business, Debt-Led Growth, and Political Transition," in Stallings and Kaufman, eds.,*Debt and Democracy*; René Millán, *Los empresarios ante el estado y la sociedad* (Mexico: Siglo Veintiuno Editores, 1988); Jeffry Frieden, *Debt, Development,*

*and Democracy: Modern Political Economy and Latin America, 1965-1985* (Princeton: Princeton University Press, 1991).

26. The periods are not always given the same names used here, but the descriptions of the main policies advanced in each period are remarkably similar.

27. For a useful overview of these periods, see Carlos Hurtado, *De Balmaceda a Pinochet* (Santiago: Ediciones Logo, 1988).

28. For policy networks, see Peter Katzenstein, ed., *Between Power and Plenty: Foreign Economic Policies of Advanced Industrial States* (Madison: University of Wisconsin Press, 1978); G. William Domhoff, *The Power Elite and the State: How Policy is Made in America* (New York: Aldine de Gruyter, 1990); and Michael Mann, *The Sources of Social Power, Volume 1* (Cambridge: Cambridge University Press, 1986).

29. For studies that link the style of collaboration to rapid development, see Peter Evans, "The State as Problem and Solution: Predation, Embedded Autonomy, and Structural Change," in Stephan Haggard and Robert Kaufman, eds., *The Politics of Economic Adjustment: International Constraints, Distributive Conflicts, and the State* (Princeton: Princeton University Press, 1992); Rosemary Thorp, *Economic Management and Economic Development in Peru and Colombia* (Pittsburgh: University of Pittsburgh Press, 1991); Robert Wade, *Governing the Market: Economic Theory and the Role of Government in East Asian Industrialization* (Princeton: Princeton University Press, 1990); Alice Amsden, *Asia's Next Giant: South Korea and Late Industrialization* (New York: Oxford University Press, 1989); and Fredric C. Deyo, *The Political Economy of the New Asian Industrialism* (Ithaca: Cornell University Press, 1987).

# 3

# Import-Substitution Industrialization and the Breakdown of Democracy

Throughout Latin America, neoliberal economic restructuring emerged in reaction to tensions in the economic, political, and social structures that had sustained import-substitution industrialization (ISI) and the welfare state. Chile was no exception to these historical trends. What follows is a characterization of the conditions that held Chile's ISI coalition together and the reasons for its breakdown, crucial for understanding the politics of economic restructuring and democratization between 1973 and 1994.

This chapter divides the period between the 1930s and the breakdown of democracy in September 1973 in two parts. The first section establishes the bases for intersectoral conflict and cooperation among Chilean capitalists between the 1930s and the late 1960s. It focuses on the genesis of the ISI coalition, the domestic political institutions that mediated it, and the growing tensions within it. The argument sets the stage for the analysis of shifting capitalist coalitions after the overthrow of Salvador Allende and sheds light on why protectionists among the upper classes were not able to assert their interests vigorously after the coup.

A second section examines the sources of the regime loyalties of Chilean capitalists and landowners during this period. It argues that they supported democracy as long as they were included in multiclass coalitions and could defend their fundamental interests (property and profits) within the policymaking process. The exposition then centers on showing that Chilean capitalists turned against political democracy between 1970 and 1973 in two stages. First, the nationalization and social mobilization policies of Unidad Popular (UP) excluded them from the policy coalition and threatened to destroy their dominant position in Chilean society. Although these changes made capitalists and landowners uneasy, the political system still offered some lines of defense: the Congress and particularistic relations with the executive branch. Upper-class elites tried to negotiate concessions from the Allende government during its first year. Second, only after those attempts failed did they mobilize to destroy the regime.

The process of forging capitalist unity and mobilization against Unidad Popular brought together the actors that formed the basis of shifting capitalist policy coalitions after the coup and defined some of their starting relationships. Nevertheless, an examination of nationalization policy reveals that some business sectors were seriously weakened at this time. This period is critical for understanding which fractions of capital emerged dominant after the coup and why.

### Rise of the Import Substitution Coalition, 1931-1952

Import-substitution industrialization policies in the wake of the Great Depression cemented the implicit settlement among class-based social groups that underpinned democracy in many Latin American countries. In Chile, ISI policies promoted a mixed economy, protection for domestic industry, and social welfare. They held together an urban coalition of primarily manufacturers for domestic markets, medium and small businessmen, middle-class professionals, and organized labor groups. Industrialists and organized labor were the coalition's polar ends. High tariffs benefitted industry, social welfare aided labor, and cheap food prices served the interests of both groups. Economic growth based on industrialization and a mixed economy assisted the middle sectors. Landowners, although not directly included in the coalition, had a commitment from labor and the political left not to upset social relations on the latifundia. Political party systems, often dominated by populist (or center-left) parties, usually mediated the interests of these social groups. Class-based social groups also pursued their interests directly, most often through lobbying, but other tactics included investment strikes by upper classes and labor strikes by organized workers.

The following two sections expand on the terms of the social bargain described above. The first section, covering the period of the administration of Arturo Alessandri (1932-1938), analyzes the impact of external economic shocks on socio-economic elites. It shows that cooperation between manufacturers and landowners had its origins more in the specific economic interests expressed in their policy demands than in family ties and interlocking directorships as some have argued.[1] The second section examines the role of the party system in cementing the interclass bargain between the bourgeoisie and organized labor and in ensuring upper class support for Chilean democracy as it emerged in the 1930s. It also demonstrates that sectoral tensions between industry and agriculture only emerged *after* specific industrial policies began to discriminate against the agricultural interests. The importance of these tensions becomes evident later when, after the fall of democracy and in a new institutional context, manufacturers for domestic markets were without allies or power to effectively resist the changes to Chile's development model.

### External Shocks and Upper Class Cooperation and Tension, 1932-1938

*Alessandri*

Most of Chile's main economic sectors already existed before the Great Depression, providing the foundation for a capitalist coalition that supported a liberal economic model based on free trade and the "night watchman state," one whose basic function was the provision of law and order. This coalition—forged in the 19th century—included landowners, financiers, large scale import-export merchants, and mine owners.[2] Import-export merchants had every incentive to prefer low customs tariffs. And, although the nitrate and copper mines were largely foreign-owned by the early 1900s, their proprietors and the smaller-scale Chilean producers had every reason to support free trade because their products were internationally competitive.[3]

The preferences of landowners require more elaboration. By and large, they also supported free trade despite the fact that they now cultivated grain and vegetables largely for the domestic market rather than for export as they had done in the 19th century. For the most part, their products were competitive with imports and did not need heavy protection.[4] Landowners also had strong business and family links to the finance sector and a growing industrial sector dominated by import-competitive food and beverage firms.[5] These two factors, import competitiveness and blood ties, probably explain the lack of intersectoral conflict during this period. It was only later that perceived policy discrimination in favor of industry sharpened intersectoral tensions, with fateful consequences after the coup.[6]

By the 1920s, Chilean capitalists and landowners had developed powerful sectoral peak associations through which to advance their interests. The oldest were the landowners' Sociedad Nacional de Agricultura (SNA), founded in 1838; the large-scale merchants' Cámara Central de Comercio (CCC), founded in 1858; the mine owners' Sociedad Nacional de Minería (SONAMI), founded in 1888; and the industrialists' Sociedad de Fomento Fabril (SFF), founded in 1883.[7] The Chilean upper classes lost direct control of the state as the nation developed politically, and the peak associations became vehicles for the defense of the economic and social interests of Chilean capital.[8] For example, the SNA, SONAMI, and the SFF each lobbied for and obtained the creation of line ministries related to their economic sectors. The directors of these business and landowning associations then gained ample representation in, and access to, the new ministries charged with regulating economic activity in their respective sectors. These linkages became stronger over time.[9]

The Great Depression shattered the conditions that held together the capitalist coalition that supported the liberal economic model.[10] Most importantly, the international financial crash interrupted the flow of private capital to Chile, which had provided much of the foreign exchange needed for business, agriculture, and the trading sector.[11] Moreover, because taxes on British nitrate and U.S. copper exports had supplied the remaining portion of hard currency, low commodity prices further aggravated the foreign exchange problem.

The ISI developmental strategy and social coalition that replaced the liberal model emerged in two stages that roughly correspond to the administrations of Arturo Alessandri (1932-1938) and Pedro Aguirre Cerda (1938-1944). During Alessandri's government, external economic shock led to capitalist and landowner support for greater government intervention in the economy, including reflationary measures and state support for industrialization. During this period capitalist and landowning groups avoided intersectoral tension by proposing general policies that did not discriminate harshly against certain sectors.

The Great Depression altered the perspective on laissez-faire policies of some sectors of the Chilean bourgeoisie. The collapse of international trade and loans caused financiers and budding industrialists alike to advocate internal economic expansion to revive the economy.[12] Equally important, between 1931 and 1933 both landowners *and* manufacturers demanded policies to stimulate industrial production for domestic markets. Their demands included deficit spending, public works projects, and special loans to industry and landowners. Alessandri's administration responded by implementing such policies.

Many analysts have seized on the presence of intraclass agreement over industrialization and interlocking directorates of firms across economic sectors as early evidence of an enduring collaboration between dominant groups that should have been enemies: land and capital. In this collaboration they saw the roots of the nation's economic backwardness: Capital failed to eliminate traditional landowners, hence the absence of modernization.[13] Such interpretations, however, suffer from a rather superficial view of the nature of intersectoral conflict in Latin America and its role in explaining shifts in economic development models.

The available evidence suggests three interrelated reasons why landowner resistance to a *general* policy of industrialization was muted, but none of them would have precluded the eruption of sharp intersectoral conflict under different conditions. First, and most importantly, as long as proposed policies did not discriminate against agriculture (as was largely the case under Alessandri) there was little need for landowners to oppose industrialization. This included the retention of price supports and special credits for agriculture between 1931 and 1938.[14] Second, the early 1930s were a period of great unemployment and social unrest. Agriculture could not absorb idle labor quickly enough. Third, the interconnection between land, finance, and industry helps to explain why agriculturalists initially supported industrialization. They too could invest in it.[15] Nevertheless, the kind of industrialization landowners supported was telling of the nature of intraclass cooperation *and* conflict. They were only enthusiastic about proposals that developed existing manufacturing sectors, largely tied to food processing. These firms did not compete with the agricultural sector; they complemented it.[16] Thus, although tariff protection in general rose significantly during this period, it largely benefitted industrial sectors tied to the land: food and leather.[17]

The intersectoral battles that came later were over policies that discriminated against agriculture in favor of nontraditional industries such as metals, petrochemicals, and textiles. The SNA consistently opposed measures to lower food prices for urban consumers, to extend government credit to industry, and to differentiate tariff schedules in a way that made food imports cheaper and agricultural machinery more expensive. By contrast, the SFF supported such measures.[18] Over the decades, intersectoral conflict over these issues deepened, with important consequences for economic policy after the overthrow of Allende.[19] As will be seen in the next section, the consequences of this friction in the late 1930s largely depended on domestic institutional factors.

### Domestic Politics
### and the Consolidation of the ISI Coalition, 1938-1952          CORFO

Chile's Popular Front government (1938-1944) went beyond the general industrial policies of Alessandri's administration, which were mainly attempts to accommodate the bourgeoisie's policy demands. Instead, the Popular Front brokered a partly explicit and partly tacit multiclass alliance between industrialists, the middle class, and organized urban labor. That alliance supported an ISI model that discriminated against agriculture (as well as other business sectors like finance) by insuring cheap food, differentiated customs tariffs, and specially priced credit. The development model established by the Popular Front also promoted social security, pension plans, workers' compensation, less restrictive labor laws, minimum wage laws, and subsidized credit for housing.

The structure of the political party system was the key domestic political factor that enabled the Popular Front to forge this reformist multiclass political coalition. The Popular Front government was rooted in Chile's enduring tripolar multiparty system that included a Socialist and Communist left, a reformist center that dominated the system but could not win a majority in a presidential election by a majority on its own, and a conservative right.[20]  Thus, in the Popular Front, the Radical party (a flexible, centrist, reformist party capable of forming either center-left or center-right political coalitions) dominated an electoral coalition that included the Socialist and Communist parties as well as other minor centrist parties.[21]

The Popular Front largely worked because the centrist Radical party represented middle-class sectors and mediated the interests of both capitalists and labor. The Popular Front's economic program sought to bring together the interests of industrialists, middle classes, and labor. Manufacturers basically supported its industrial policy as well as other policies that discriminated against agriculture. There are ample signs that these policies generated lingering intersectoral tensions that played an important role in setting a new economic direction for Chile after 1973.

In the election, industrialists had backed Gustavo Ross, the candidate of the Conservative and Liberal parties who lost by a narrow margin.[22] After Ross's defeat, they mostly supported the Popular Front's industrialization program, but they disapproved of its welfare policies. Labor backed both initiatives. Meanwhile, landowners, mine owners, and large-scale merchants opposed the new industrial policy because it favored nascent firms in metal-working, petrochemicals, and textiles.[23] The multiclass nature of the Popular Front gave it the edge it needed in the legislature to press its policy agenda on both industrialization and welfare. By themselves, upper-class groups opposed to the Popular Front's policies could not stop the new laws. But when a business sector made common cause with labor against other business sectors it could turn its policy preference into law. For example, in addition to the issue of industrialization, there was a much more explicit alliance between industrialists and labor in favor of cheap food prices. Thus, they supported the Popular Front's successful efforts to establish low price ceilings and paltry tariff protection for wheat and other basic foodstuffs against the SNA's strenuous objections.[24]

 A more nuanced set of relationships between manufacturers and the Popular Front arose during the crucial policy fight over the establishment of Chile's Development Corporation (the Corporación de Fomento, CORFO) in 1939. The Popular Front government wanted CORFO to be an institution capable of planning and carrying out industrial policy; one that could target industries for growth, provide them with credit and infrastructure, build state-owned industry, and initiate joint ventures with the private sector. CORFO's planned thrust—metalworking and petrochemicals—clearly shifted the allocation of state resources away from agriculture and other business sectors.

Manufacturers, represented by the SFF, supported the Popular Front's project, although they would have preferred that CORFO's powers be limited to the provision of capital rather than direct state participation in production. Nevertheless, guarantees of participation for the SFF in the design of industrial policy allayed the fears of industrialists.[25] The SFF, as well as the other sectoral peak associations, had representation on CORFO's board of directors. More importantly for industrialists, however, they took part in CORFO's planning commissions to a much greater extent than the representatives of other economic sectors. Not once did the SFF raise a serious complaint against CORFO policy. In short, industrialists had ample input in policy formulation and in the design of policy implementation.

A number of upper-class groups, especially landowners and the Conservative and Liberal parties (in which land was heavily represented) bitterly opposed CORFO. The development corporation symbolized an unwanted expansion of the public sector's entrepreneurial activity. More concretely, for landowners CORFO threatened to expand heavy industry at the expense of the food and beverage sector. Although they did not succeed, *latifundistas* and traditional right-wing parties worked tirelessly in the legislature to block CORFO.[26]

CORFO promoted nontraditional manufactures by establishing differentiated tariffs that discriminated against both agriculture and large-scale merchants. Landowners suffered because protection for metalworking and petrochemicals made agricultural inputs, especially machinery, more expensive and of poorer quality. Large-scale merchants resented higher protection for imported textiles. They had supported tariffs on finished clothing because they operated the nation's largest clothing factories in which they used low-cost imported textiles. Now they would have to rely more on domestic textiles whose manufacture they did not control.

In conclusion, the evidence shows that, following the Great Depression, the Popular Front government and the Radical party, which dominated Chilean politics for fifteen years, gave birth to Chile's ISI model and a welfare state by mediating a tacit alliance between industry and organized labor. A number of upper-class social groups were left out of the bargain, fueling lasting discontent. Industrialization came at the expense of the development of the agricultural sector, the small Chilean-owned mining sector, and the trading houses. While the price of imports and nationally manufactured goods rose due to protectionism, food imports were subsidized and tariffs on food products were very low. Emphasis on incentives to investment in manufactures siphoned off investment from the countryside.[27]

Nevertheless, the Radical party struck a separate deal with landowners, the most significant of the social groups not directly involved in the bargain. The most important provision of the agreement stipulated that peasant organization would not be tolerated, assuring the continuation of existing social relations on the land. Landowners could thus continue to exploit peasants as a voting block, ensuring them ample representation in the legislature that would defend their interests. Successive Radical administrations managed to enforce the terms of the bargain against occasional backsliding by leftist political parties and organized labor.[28] This arrangement no doubt also helped to assuage the concerns of industrialists over the divisive issue of labor peace and the pace of social change.

### Regime Loyalties of Capitalists and Landowners

Why did capitalists and landowners tolerate the Popular Front government, a coalition of centrist and Socialist and Communist parties roughly patterned on the Western European model? A decade before they probably would not have stood for such a political alliance. What had changed? To begin with, the economic and social dislocations triggered by the Great Depression made novel economic and political combinations much less unthinkable. The pressing need to renew economic growth made an implicit compact between industrialists and organized labor more feasible. Moreover, recent social and political turmoil had briefly given rise to a "Socialist Republic" sanctioned by the military. Under these conditions, compromise with centrist and reformist political parties that included the interests of manufacturers in the dominant economic policy coalition, and that safeguarded the essential concerns of landowners, seemed prudent.

Another motivation for the regime loyalties of capitalists and landowners was that they were included in the policymaking process. Prominent industrialists, bankers, merchants, landowners, and mine owners frequently became ministers and undersecretaries of finance, economy, agriculture, and mining.[29] Moreover, as shown in Table 3.1, the SFF, SNA, CCC, and SONAMI were well represented in key state agencies (such as the Central Bank, the State Bank, and CORFO), state planning commissions, and economic development projects.[30] In short, formal and informal channels of contact with the policymaking process gave the Chilean upper classes a variety of fora within which to advance, delay, or water down economic and social reforms.

### Unravelling of the Import Substitution Coalition, 1952-1970

By the early 1950s, the economic policies of the two previous decades had created a highly protected and regulated economy. Protection ranged from differentiated tariff barriers, import prohibitions, and high import deposit rates to subsidized credit via controlled bank interest rates. Multiple foreign exchange rates also aided manufacturers. For example, in 1950 there were six foreign exchange rates. The lowest applied to export

TABLE 3.1 Voting Representation on Major Economic Policymaking Boards, 1958-64

| Government Representatives[a] | | Business Association Representatives | | Semiautonomous Agency Representatives | |
|---|---|---|---|---|---|
| Position | Number | Position | Number | Position | Number |
| Central Bank | | | | | |
| President | 2 | SFF-SNA | 1 | | |
| Senate | 2 | CCC | 1 | | |
| Chamber of | | Private Banks | 3 | | |
| Deputies | 2 | Labor | 1 | | |
| | | Private | | | |
| | | Shareholders | 1 | | |
| Total | 6 | | 7 | | 0 |
| State Bank | | | | | |
| President | 5 | SFF | 1 | Central Bank | 1 |
| | | SNA | 1 | State Bank | 1 |
| | | CCC | 1 | CORFO | 1 |
| | | SONAMI | 1 | | |
| | | Retail | | | |
| | | Merchants | 1 | | |
| | | Salaried | | | |
| | | Employees | 1 | | |
| | | Labor | 1 | | |
| Total | 5 | | 7 | | 3 |
| CORFO | | | | | |
| President | 3 | SFF | 1 | Central Bank | 1 |
| Senate | 2 | SNA | 1 | Agrarian | |
| Chamber of | | SONAMI | 1 | Colonization | |
| Deputies | 2 | CCC | 1 | Bank | 1 |
| | | Institute of | | Others | 8 |
| | | Engineers | 1 | | |
| | | Labor | 1 | | |
| Total: | 7 | | 6 | | 10 |

[a]During the 1958-64 period, the congressional representatives were eliminated. In the Central Bank, the change gave the president four representatives out of 11.

*Source*: Constantine Menges, "Public Policy and Organized Business in Chile: A Preliminary Analysis," *Journal of International Affairs* 20, 2, 1966, p. 351. Reprinted by permission.

products. By contrast, the price of dollars for imports (the "special commercial rate") was more than twice as high as the export rate and 70 percent more expensive than the official rate.[31]

In addition to these measures CORFO also subsidized industrial growth. Through CORFO, the state was also an entrepreneur in undeveloped industries such as steel, petrochemicals, and consumer durables. The private sector often participated in these ventures and obtained representation on their boards of directors. As a result of these diverse policies, the industrial sector's share of GDP rose from 13 percent in 1940 to 21 percent in 1950. Wage earners benefitted from minimum wage laws, relatively favorable labor laws, price controls on essential consumer goods, and a social security system.

Beginning in the 1930s and through the 1960s, the sources of foreign savings for development purposes favored industrialists over other business and landowning sectors. Most of the funds came from bilateral and multilateral lending institutions such as the United States Export-Import Bank, the Inter-American Development Bank, the World Bank, and the Alliance for Progress. Much of this went to CORFO. By the early 1950s, however, Chile began to suffer from the exhaustion of the "easy phase" of ISI.[32] Industrialization based on the assembly of finished products and the production of intermediate goods led to ever increasing foreign exchange requirements for imported capital goods, intermediate goods, and basic foods, all of which put pressure on Chile's balance of payments and inflation. Throughout most of this period, sluggish terms of trade for copper—Chile's major export—compounded the problem.

Chronic difficulties in the balance of payments characteristic of the limits of the easy phase of ISI forced a need to stabilize and restructure the Chilean economy. Tension arose in the coalition between industrialists and labor over who would pay the costs of adjustment. Capital succeeded most of the time in imposing these costs—especially those of economic stabilization—on labor.[33]

Economic restructuring also drove a wedge between industrialists and their political party allies and provoked intrasectoral conflict. The need to lower protection for domestic industry in order to promote industrial efficiency and exports set the majoritarian sector of the SFF—organized around conglomerates and firms that produced almost wholly for domestic markets—against the government and other sectors within the SFF organized around conglomerates and firms that also had an export component. The SFF prevailed in preventing major change because foreign exchange shortages made sustaining import liberalization difficult. In addition, the SFF used the political system to protect itself from the worst effects of tariff reform.

Two other changes threatened the terms of the bargain that held the ISI coalition (industrialists and labor) and subordinate fractions of the upper classes together. First, agrarian reform, begun under Jorge Alessandri's administration (1958-1964), endangered the settlement between landowners and the ISI coalition. The impact of the agrarian reform was increasingly felt by landowners during the administrations of Eduardo Frei (1964-1970) and Salvador Allende (1970-1973).[34] Second, shifts in the political party system disrupted the terms of the ISI bargain, which had included the presence of a flexible centrist political party ready to enter into pragmatic coalitions with both conservative and leftist political parties. Between 1958 and 1973, governing parties did not enter into coalitions or compromises with other political parties. The period of exclusionary politics had begun, radicalizing the left and labor, which heightened class and ideological conflict.[35]

In 1958, Alessandri ran as an independent with the backing of the right-wing Conservative and Liberal parties. His government was the closest the bourgeoisie had come to direct rule since the 1920s. Even though he had won with only a plurality of votes and the political parties that backed him did not control Congress, Alessandri did not invite representatives of other political currents into his cabinet as past administrations had done. Moreover, his platform pointedly favored the interests of capital over labor; and although some businessmen might not have seen it that way, labor certainly did. His economic stabilization plan, for example, was an onslaught against hard-earned gains by organized labor and its centrist and leftist political party allies. The Alessandri government's attempt to implement its project of capitalist modernization affected both centrist and leftist political parties. The unabashedly right-wing character of his program led to sharper confrontations with the left, which stepped up its revolutionary rhetoric and socialist policy preferences (such as widespread nationalization), especially in the wake of the Cuban revolution.

Meanwhile, the Christian Democratic party (PDC)—by now the major centrist political force—developed an ideological and programmatic rigidity of its own to differentiate itself from both the right and the left.[36] Although Eduardo Frei won the 1964 presidential election with right-wing support, he did not include members of the right in his cabinet. The right's uneasiness worsened when Frei began a government program that emphasized nationalization and increased regulation of business. The Frei government further contributed to the polarization of Chilean politics by angering the left when it attempted to create rival unions in the industrial sector and when it began to organize unorganized lower-class groups—peasants and shantytown dwellers—as part of a strategy to become Chile's majority party, thereby undercutting the left's historical reformist role. The left became more radicalized and stepped up its mobilizations.

The cumulative effect of the PDC's exclusionary practices polarized the parties and the electorate and escalated class conflict. The delicate system of alliances in which political parties had muted strife between the right and left broke down. By 1970, both the right and the center had had their opportunity to attempt to transform Chile. The stage was set for the left's turn under Allende.

## Socialists and the Regime Loyalties of Chilean Capitalists, 1970-1973

Between November 1970 and September 1973, conflict over socialist economic policies destroyed the political and class compromise that had sustained Chile's democratic regime since the 1930s.[37] Why did Chilean capitalists turn against political democracy? Notably, although Unidad Popular's focus on nationalization and social mobilization excluded them from the policy coalition and threatened their dominant position in Chilean society, capitalists did not abandon democracy as long as the Chilean political system still offered some lines of defense, such as Congress and direct access to the executive branch. As a result, upper-class elites tried to negotiate concessions from the government. The failure of these attempts led Chilean capitalists to mobilize to destroy the regime.

Capitalist regime loyalties changed in three stages between 1970 and 1973. Nationalization policy was the fulcrum of debate. In the first stage, from the election in September 1970 through most of 1971, the upper classes accepted the PDC's efforts to negotiate nationalization policy with Unidad Popular. In the second stage—mainly the first half of 1972—capitalists acquired the capacity to mobilize but exercised forbearance, awaiting the outcome of congressional battles to halt nationalization. Having failed to influence Unidad Popular on the nationalization issue, the third stage began when capitalists and middle-class groups mobilized and, with congressional maneuvering, sought to destabilize the regime in order to emasculate the Unidad Popular program, to force Salvador Allende's resignation, or to provoke a coup. As they forged class unity, businessmen, landowners, and the PDC also built the basis for the first post-coup capitalist coalition and lay some of the groundwork that allowed the Chicago boys to dominate economic policy after 1975.

### *The Attempt to Negotiate, September 1970 to December 1971*

The Unidad Popular program stressed nationalization, income redistribution, and a reform of labor relations in favor of workers. From the outset, Unidad Popular recognized that its program would put pressure on the fragile social and political accommodations that sustained Chilean democracy. Unidad Popular leaders were fully aware that Chile's political system provided both constraints and opportunities on its capacity to implement policy.

Unidad Popular initially pursued two coalitional strategies in order to mitigate the possibility of a coup *and* proceed with socialist transformation. The first consisted of building a multiclass alliance between labor and the middle classes, especially owners of medium and small businesses. Unidad Popular strategists used wage hikes and price controls to promote this alliance; they estimated that these measures would increase demand for basic consumer goods, promote growth in labor-intensive industries, and create jobs.[38] The second Unidad Popular strategy was to try to garner support among the rest of the lower classes—peasants and urban migrants—for the next elections.[39] Thus, it began to compete with the Christian Democrats over the organization of these groups. While working to expand its voting base for the municipal elections in April 1971 and congressional elections in March 1973, Unidad Popular also hoped to hold and win a constitutional referendum that would allow it to push through key aspects of its program, particularly nationalization policy.[40] Moreover, increasing union membership—a traditional stronghold of leftist parties in Chile—and improving labor relations policy were also aimed at strengthening Unidad Popular electorally.[41]

In addition to its coalitional strategy, Unidad Popular sought to combine structural changes with economic development.[42] The goal was a structural shift from capitalism to socialism in both industry and agriculture. Unidad Popular aspired to establish a dominant state—or "social"—area of production in the industrial sector. Besides the firms that the state already owned, Unidad Popular planned to nationalize large mines (mostly foreign-owned), the financial system, wholesale distribution, strategic industrial companies, and foreign commerce as well as some infrastructural sectors such as communications, transportation, and energy production. In agriculture, Unidad Popular wanted to break up the remaining large estates and install collective farms.[43]

To complement the social area of production, Unidad Popular planned to create a mixed area of social property, leaving a third area of the economy to the private sector. The government mainly intended to form joint ventures with foreign capital in the social property area. State participation in strategic domestic firms was not ruled out, but Unidad Popular did not intend to nationalize medium and small sized firms. The architects of the Unidad Popular program were under no illusion that they could run a command economy or win an assault on medium and small property owners—the very segment of middle-class voters that it hoped to win over.[44]

However, Unidad Popular did intend to nationalize most of the major firms in key financial and productive areas in order to make state planning a viable tool for attaining its economic development objectives. Its objectives included switching production from luxury goods to basic consumer goods, providing full employment at good wages, reducing dependency on foreign capital, encouraging nontraditional exports, controlling inflation, and overhauling commerce and distribution. Unidad Popular believed that state planning, control of credit, taxation, productive enterprises, and international trade were the appropriate means to attain these ends.[45]

Throughout 1971, the upper classes defended themselves from the government with a two-track policy. On the one hand, business peak associations pledged their willingness to negotiate with the government. Although they did so with increasing uneasiness, producer groups hoped to use the established policy process to force Unidad Popular to moderate its most radical proposals, especially its nationalization policy.[46] On the other hand, the conservative National party (PN) confronted Unidad Popular openly.[47] This dual-track tactic may not have been the explicit strategy of a unified bourgeoisie, but it delivered a clear message. If Unidad Popular did not negotiate, business peak associations would eventually join the PN in active opposition to the government. In other words, capitalists were buying time to mount an effective campaign of economic destabilization and social mobilization, if necessary, while hoping that sufficient concessions from the UP within the confines of congressional politics might make such mobilization unnecessary.

Business and landowning elites were shut out of the policymaking coalition. Unidad Popular's rhetoric and practice identified them as a class enemy and strove to break their power through nationalization. But, throughout the first year, upper-class elites believed they might defend themselves from the onslaught through direct negotiation and the PDC's efforts to extract concessions in Congress. As will be seen, the failure of businessmen and landowners to thwart nationalization through the two tactics caused Chile's socio-economic elite to unite in open rebellion, actively calling for a coup d'etat.

*Negotiation Strategies.* Despite mounting problems, throughout 1971 Chilean capitalists used two forms of direct negotiation with Unidad Popular to defend themselves from nationalization. One negotiation strategy focused on responding to the four different means that Unidad Popular used to gain control of firms. One technique involved the government purchase of controlling shares of stock in private companies in the financial, manufacturing, and commercial distribution sectors.[48] Unidad Popular also sought to incorporate firms into the social area of property via requisitions, interventions, and expropriation (without compensation). The legal mechanisms for these actions were laws dating from the shortlived Socialist Republic of 1932.[49] Powerful businessmen, or delegations from the peak associations, responded to these tactics by lobbying for better operating conditions (higher prices and more credit) to keep owners from having to sell, to obtain better prices for their shares when they had to sell, or to have their businesses returned if they had been requisitioned. They were not always unsuccessful in their endeavors.[50]

A second form of direct negotiation between capitalists and Unidad Popular followed traditional patterns of interest group participation in the policymaking process. As in the past, producer peak associations offered to help draft legislation in order to smooth out policy implementation. Landowners (the SNA) explicitly requested this privilege in November 1970. Industrialists (the SFF) were more indirect, exhorting Unidad Popular to define the "rules of the game" by introducing a formal nationalization bill in the legislature and by demanding that the UP give up the use of interventions and requisitions.[51]

In addition to direct negotiation, capitalists relied on opposition political parties to mediate for them. Upper-class elites supported the opposition's efforts to force Unidad Popular to introduce legislation on nationalization and to give up nationalization by administrative fiat. To achieve these ends, however, business elites and the National party had to rely on the Christian Democrats. But the PDC was not an unconditional ally of the upper classes: Its reformist (or left-wing) *tercerista* faction dominated the party. Because this faction supported structural reforms for the construction of progressive capitalism and favored developmentalist and redistributive programs, it often sought accommodation with Unidad Popular.[52] Capitalists' support for the PDC entailed their implicit agreement to acquiesce to some nationalization in return for a more moderate and controlled pace of ownership transfers.[53]

The Christian Democrats had attempted to bring Unidad Popular around to such negotiations from the beginning, starting with banking nationalization. Unidad Popular consistently manifested a willingness to deal but somehow always delayed action. When discussions with the PDC finally began in September 1971, Christian Democrats were unconvinced that Unidad Popular was bargaining in good faith. When the PDC introduced its own nationalization bill in mid-October 1971—the Hamilton-Fuentealba bill—they introduced it in the form of a constitutional amendment in order to be able to override an all-but-certain presidential veto.[54] Ordinary bills required a two thirds majority, which the budding PN-PDC alliance did not have.[55]

Like the Unidad Popular nationalization scheme, the Hamilton-Fuentealba bill proposed the establishment of three areas of social property. Unlike the Unidad Popular program, however, it called for a communitarian sector (cooperatives owned and managed by employees), mandated case-by-case legislative review of the firms the government proposed to nationalize, and stipulated that companies taken over after October 14, 1971, should be returned to their owners.[56] The bill's approval would have allowed the Christian Democrats to design a selective strategy of capitalist transformation of the Chilean economy, one of the party's enduring objectives. All nationalizations would have required PDC approval.

Meanwhile, Unidad Popular's radical interpretation of existing land reform legislation promised the expropriation of all significant land holdings. To contain the extent of land seizure, the Christian Democrats introduced legislation that precisely defined the size of land holdings subject to government takeover. The bill also substituted state-run collectives for land-to-the-tiller forms of land tenure for expropriated farms and latifundia.[57] The PDC's position on redistributive policy and support for selective nationalization demonstrated its resolve to move Unidad Popular away from class confrontation. The PDC wanted to bring Unidad Popular back into a more accommodative style of politics that would put less strain on the political system. Capitalists did not oppose compromise. The National party supported the Hamilton-Fuentealba bill.[58]

***Nationalization and Business Mobilization.*** Although capitalists attempted to negotiate nationalization policy with Unidad Popular, the government's recourse to administrative fiat stymied their efforts and hardened their stance. The discussion that follows highlights the junctures that galvanized businessmen and landowners into organizing a broad opposition to Allende, one capable of mobilizing a united bourgeoisie into open conflict with the government. Each of those moments in time underscored the inability of socio-economic elites, and of the PDC, to control the government's efforts to nationalize a significant portion of the Chilean economy.

A series of confrontations over nationalization in April, May, and June of 1971 brought landowners, manufacturers, and the construction sector together. In April, the landowners' peak association (the SNA) used the death of two landowners during an expropriation action to stress its opposition to land seizures and the destruction of tenurial relationships in the countryside.[59] Business peak associations affiliated with the Confederation for Production and Commerce—the Construction Chamber, the Mining Association, and the Chamber of Commerce—and the Confederation itself, issued sympathetic statements, but without abandoning a commitment to negotiation.[60] The National party, in support of landowners, initiated impeachment procedures against the governor of the province.

Scarcely a month later, the detention by company workers of a top executive of a major consumer durables firm,[61] and the requisition and intervention of over a dozen textile firms, alarmed Chilean industrialists, a group which had thus far not been aroused to opposition.[62] Before May, Unidad Popular had mostly bought out Chilean firms in the banking sector willing to sell, and  many of the firms that had been intervened or requisitioned were MNCs.[63] There had been no direct attack on the core of the economic base of Chilean capitalists.  They were uneasy over their general situation and unhappy over the loss of their share in the banking sector, but their survival was not at stake.  The industrial sector had always been heavily regulated and dominated by state banks; and, hoping to hold onto the rest of their companies, Chilean businessmen no doubt believed that they could arrive at a satisfactory arrangement with a state-controlled banking industry.

The massive nationalization of the textile industry in May 1971 broke up a number of smaller conglomerates that had not significantly diversified their portfolios.   However, the owners and top executives of these conglomerates were represented in the SFF's council—particularly the Yarur and Said economic groups (see Table 3.2).   More ominously, the textile takeovers signaled Unidad Popular's willingness to attack important Chilean businessmen who had resisted nationalization.   The textile nationalization and executives' fear of violence provoked business peak associations to condemn nationalization policy.[64] The expropriations also led to a change in leadership within the SFF.  The SFF's new president, Orlando Sáenz (a young industrialist who took a hard line against the government) subsequently said, "Our sector finally reacted, it realized that it had to try something radically different."[65]

Government takeovers in June 1971, this time of forestry industries, drew sharp criticism from various sectors.  Capitalists expressed growing frustration at the impotence of the established policy process to defend their interests.  Representing the construction sector, the Cámara Chilena de la Construcción (CChC) declared, "The government, contrary to what it professes, refuses to punish those who create a climate of subversion; instead, it encourages them." The Asociación de Industriales de Valparaíso complained, "Allende promised us that his administration would implement its revolutionary programs within the bounds of the established legal order, but his deeds belie his promise."[66] They called on him to stop the interventions saying the resulting labor-management strife would destroy Chile.

The latest nationalizations gave birth to a group of powerful businessmen who began to organize business opposition to Unidad Popular.  Because their meetings were held over lunch on Mondays, they called themselves the Monday Club.  The significance of this cabal was to reach far into the future: Its membership contained the core of both the gradualist and the radical neoliberal economic restructuring coalitions that emerged after the coup.  The Monday Club was in contact with military conspirators and first

TABLE 3.2 SFF Leadership: Conglomerate Affiliation and Effects of Nationalization to September 1971

| Member Name | Conglomerate Affiliation | Direct Experience of Nat'lization: Exec. of Firm[a] | Indirect Experience of Nationalization: Firm Part of Conglomerate in which SFF Member Participates as an Exec. | Direct and Indirect Experience of Nationalization |
|---|---|---|---|---|
| SFF Exec. Director | | | | |
| Sáenz, O. | Edwards | x | | x |
| Sahli, R. | Kunstmann | | | |
| Ipinza, I. | Ibáñez/Edwards | | x | x |
| López, S. | BHC | | | |
| (N=4) Total: | | 1 | 1 | 2 |
| | | | | |
| SFF Elected Council | | | | |
| Angelini, A. | Angelini | x | | x |
| Arata, R. | | | | |
| Arteaga, D. | | | | |
| Ayala, E. | Matte | | x | x |
| Cristofanini, J. | | | | |
| Echeverría, V. | | | | |
| Elton, C. | | | | |
| Falcón, F. | MNC | | | |
| Feliú, G. | BHC | | | |
| Fontaine, J. | | | | |
| Garib, F. | | | | |
| Ipinza, E. | Ibáñez/Edwards | | x | x |
| Izquierdo, J. | BHC | | x | x |
| Kunstmann, G. | Kunstmann | | | |
| Larraín, C. | | | | |
| Lira, P. | Angelini | | x | x |
| López, S. | BHC | | | |
| McKay, J. | | | | |
| Markman, S. | Lepe/Piquer/Lehman | | | |
| Marty, L. | Briones | | x | x |
| Menéndez, P. | Menéndez | | | |
| Nieto, A. | | | | |
| Pinto, E. | Matte | x | | x |
| Ross, G. | Edwards | x | | x |
| Sahli, R. | Kunstmann | | | |
| Sáenz, O. | Edwards | x | | x |
| Said, J. | Said | x | | x |
| Silva. A. | | | | |
| Smits, F | BHC/Briones/Lepe/Piquer/Lehman | | x | x |
| Tietzen, F. | Matte | | x | x |
| Yarur, F. | Yarur, L. | x | | x |
| Zañartu, E. | Angelini | | x | x |
| (N=32) Total: | | 6 | 8 | 14 |

[a]The firm is part of the conglomerate as well.

Source: Colegio de Periodistas, Diccionario biográfico de Chile (Santigo: Editorial Universitaria, selected years); company annual reports.

brought the Chicago boys together to prepare a post-coup economic recovery program. Monday Club regulars included seven top executives of two' of Chile's largest conglomerates, five from the Edwards group (one of the oldest), and two from the relatively new Banco Hipotecario de Chile group (BHC). Of the five Edwards group members, two were involved in the news media. One was the editor of *El Mercurio*, the establishment daily, the other owned and published the independent news weekly *Qué Pasa*, dedicated to popularizing neoclassical economic theory. The Monday Club used *El Mercurio* to whip up middle-class sentiment against Unidad Popular. It also funneled money from outside sources into the opposition movement.[67]

A major turning point for Chilean capitalists came in October 1971, the same month that the government and the PDC introduced their rival nationalization bills to the Chilean congress. Unidad Popular attempted to take over the Compañía Manufacturera de Papeles y Cartones (CMPC), also known as the "Papelera." The Papelera was the flagship company of the powerful Matte conglomerate. Jorge Alessandri, former president of Chile, and recent presidential candidate, was its chairman of the board. The Papelera was a symbol of capitalist economic and political power. It also had a virtual monopoly on newsprint in Chile.[68]

The attempted takeover failed because the owners established a fund to bid up shares. In the fight to save the Papelera manufacturers pulled together.[69] The industrialist's peak association, the SFF, emerged as the leader of concerted capitalist resistance to Unidad Popular. From then on, the SFF dedicated its resources to organizing a broad front against Unidad Popular. The SFF achieved this goal by early December 1971.[70] Meanwhile, the Edwards group used *El Mercurio* and other lesser papers to lambast the government for trying to gain a monopoly on newsprint, accusing the government of infringing on the freedom of the press. It railed against the nationalizations, characterizing them as an attempt to gain totalitarian control over Chilean society.[71]

The leaders of the SFF and the encompassing peak association of business organizations, the Confederación de la Producción y Comercio (CPC), knew that in order to form a broad, mobilizable resistance front they had to enlist medium and small businessmen to their cause.[72] Unidad Popular attempted to woo these groups too, but they nevertheless perceived themselves at risk for two reasons.[73] Rising labor-management conflicts weakened the government's stated commitment to nationalize only large-scale firms. What really drove medium and small-scale businesspeople, especially retail merchants, into the opposition, however, was the government's establishment of Juntas de Abstecimiento Popular (JAPs). The JAPs were an alternative distribution system for basic consumer goods run by Unidad Popular loyalists. Unidad Popular introduced the project in July 1971 in response to growing shortages, hoarding, black marketeering and other distribution problems.[74] In a letter to the minister of economy the retail merchants' association bluntly stated, "[JAPs] are unnecessary and unacceptable."[75] Middle-class consumers were also deeply offended by the JAPs; they believed the JAPs discriminated against them in favor of customers from the lower class. Other small businessmen and middle-class professionals began flocking to the opposition when inflation and shortages of consumer goods and inputs made their lives increasingly difficult.[76]

On December 2, 1971, the SFF and the CPC inaugurated a broad opposition front that included large-scale, medium, and small businessmen—the Frente Nacional del Area Privado (FRENAP)—at a convention called the Encuentro del Area Privado. The peak associations appealed to the interest that large and small businessmen most had in common: private property. The CPC and the SFF infused that call to arms with a strong mystique. The success of that ideological invocation was rooted in the reality that making one's living in business with a modicum of tranquility had become difficult in Chile. The JAPs, labor-management disputes, and a deteriorating economy fed the perception of medium and small businessmen that their livelihood was in jeopardy.

Orlando Sáenz, president of the SFF and a Monday Club regular, was FRENAP's principal organizer. Speaking at the opening event, Sáenz said,

> In spite of our firm goal of national conciliation, a civic panorama has developed that is so full of tensions and abnormalities that even the once most indifferent now realize that the country is in danger of social crises with unpredictable and certainly ominous results...The hour has arrived to say *no* to abuse, injustice and plunder; and because of this we have met here today.[77]

In summary, after Allende's election, capitalists accepted the PDC's attempts to blunt Unidad Popular's nationalization policy. Initially, they also tried more direct lines of defense, offering to "assist" in the design of legislation that affected them, ostensibly under the guise of ironing out policy implementation problems. But Unidad Popular repeatedly rebuffed business and landowning elites, as well as the Christian Democrats. That prompted capitalists to organize a broad-based resistance movement more or less openly dedicated to the overthrow of Allende's government.

## Collapse of Political and Class Compromise, 1972

FRENAP enabled the private sector to mobilize against the government, but capitalists did not act immediately on that capability. As long as there was hope that the Hamilton-Fuentealba bill might succeed, private sector peak associations held back. As long as there was a chance that they might be able to defend their fundamental interests within established political institutions, they showed forbearance. For example, when the Hamilton-Fuentealba bill was virtually approved in Congress in January 1972, FRENAP, the CPC, and the SFF held a series of meetings from which they issued dire warnings about the consequences of a presidential veto.[78] At this stage, major Unidad Popular concessions might have stopped a full-scale capitalist mobilization. But by June large-scale capitalists had irreversibly committed themselves to destabilizing the regime.

Several events between January and June 1972 convinced capitalists that they could no longer rely on the political system to defend their property from nationalization. In January, Unidad Popular unveiled a new nationalization policy that contained some concessions to the opposition: The three areas of property were defined more clearly, and the number of firms to be nationalized was reduced from over 250 to 91.[79] The concessions, however, gave little comfort to Chile's capitalists because those 91 firms were the core of the nation's most powerful conglomerates. The targets included the Edwards, Matte, BHC, and Lúksic groups, which were Chile's four largest conglomerates and controlled many of the nation's most important banks, consumer durables, food processing, pulp and paper (newsprint), beverages, construction materials, and fishing companies. Many of the top executives or members of the board of targeted firms were members of the SFF and the Chamber of Commerce. In addition to the conglomerates mentioned above, SFF leaders also had close ties to the Menéndez (shipping), Briones (consumer durables), Lepe-Piquer-Lehman (consumer durables), Angelini (fishing and wood processing), and Said (banking and textiles) groups (see Table 3.3).[80]

In February and March the conflict over nationalization policy came to a head. Congress approved the Hamilton-Fuentealba bill in late February, Allende vetoed several of its clauses, and a conflict over constitutional interpretation erupted between the opposition-dominated congress and the executive. The opposition insisted that the constitutional amendment of 1970 specified that future amendments only required a majority to override a veto. Allende insisted that such legislation required the same number of votes as ordinary legislation: two thirds of both chambers. Negotiations to resolve this conflict began in March, but the PDC was unable to extract concessions from the government and Unidad Popular soon walked out of the deliberations.[81] To capitalists it was a clear signal that the main centrist political party could not effectively defend their most fundamental interests within established institutions.[82]

Confirming capitalists' worst fears, shortly after the failure of the PDC's negotiations with the government, Unidad Popular took over (intervened) two of Chile's most important consumer durables firms—Fensa and Mademsa. These were the flagship firms of the powerful and relatively new (1960s) BHC conglomerate, a key participant in the Monday Club. Other

TABLE 3.3 Impact of the 91 List on Conglomerates

| Conglomerate | Sector | Before the List of 91 | | | Number of Companies on the 91 List |
| | | Number of Firms Per Sector Eligible for Nationalization | Nat'ized with Compensation | Nat. w/o Comp.[a] | |
| --- | --- | --- | --- | --- | --- |
| Edwards | Industry | 10 | 3 | | 6 |
| | Banking | 1 | 1 | | |
| Matte | Industry | 7 | | | 7 |
| | Banking | 1 | 1 | | |
| BHC | Industry | 5 | | 2 | 2 |
| | Banking | 2 | 1 | 1 | |
| | Distribution | 1 | | | 1 |
| | Shipping | 1 | | | 1 |
| Lúksic | Mines | 2 | 2 | | |
| | Industry | 7 | 6 | | |
| Menéndez | Shipping | 5 | | | 3 |
| Angelini | Fishing | 2 | | | 2 |
| | Commercial | 1 | | | 1 |
| | Industrial | 1 | | | 1 |
| Said | Banking | 2 | 2 | | |
| | Industrial | 3 | | | 1 |
| Yarur L. | Industrial | 1 | | | 1 |
| | Banking | 1 | | | 1 |
| Yarur B. | Industrial | 3 | | | 1 |
| Yarur A. | Industrial | 3 | | 2 | |
| Hirmas | Industrial | 1 | | | 1 |
| | Commercial | 1 | | | 1 |
| Sumar | Industrial | 3 | | 1 | 2 |
| Furman | Industrial | 2 | | | 2 |
| Briones | Industrial | 3 | | | 3 |
| Pollak | Industrial | 2 | | | 2 |
| Total: | | 71 | 16 | 6 | 39 |

[a]Requisitioned, intervened, or expropriated.

Source: Fernando Dahse, El mapa de la extrema riqueza (Santiago: Editorial Aconcagua, 1979) and MAPU, El libro de las 91 (Santiago: Ediciones Barco de Papel, 1972).

TABLE 3.4 SFF Leadership Affected by Nationalization Policy

| Name | To May 1972 | | 1973 |
|---|---|---|---|
| | Executive of Firm Nat'lized By Unidad Popular | Linked To Firms on 91 List[a] | Exec. of a Firm Nat'lized After May 1972 |
| Executive Director | | | |
| Sáenz, O. | x | x | x |
| Sahli, R. | | x | |
| Ipinza, I. | | x | x |
| López, S. | x | x | x |
| (N=4) Total: | 2 | 4 | 3 |
| Elected Council | | | |
| Angelini, A. | x | x | x |
| Arata, R. | | | |
| Arteaga, D. | | | |
| Ayala, E. | | x | |
| Cristofanini, J. | x | x | x |
| Echeverría, V. | | | |
| Elton, C. | | | |
| Falcón, F. | | x | |
| Feliú, G. | x | x | x |
| Fontaine, J. | | | |
| Garib, F. | | | |
| Ipinza, E. | x | x | x |
| Izquierdo, J. | | x | x |
| Kunstmann, G. | | x | x |
| Larraín, C. | | | |
| Lira, P. | | x | x |
| López, S. | x | x | x |
| McKay, J. | | | |
| Markman, S. | x | x | x |
| Marty, L. | | x | x |
| Menéndez, P. | x | x | x |
| Nieto, A. | | x | x |
| Pinto, E. | x | x | x |
| Ross, G. | x | x | x |
| Sahli, R. | | x | |
| Sáenz, O. | x | x | x |
| Said, J. | x | x | x |
| Silva. A. | | | |
| Smits, F | x | x | x |
| Tietzen, F. | | x | x |
| Yarur, F. | x | x | x |
| Zañartu, E. | | x | x |
| (N=32) Total: | 13 | 23 | 20 |

[a]The SFF member was either an executive of a firm nationalized or a nationalized company was part of a conglomerate in which the SFF member participated.

*Source:* Colegio de Periodistas, *Diccionario biográfico de Chile* (Santiago: Editorial Universitaria, selected years); company annual reports.

prominent conglomerates also owned stock in those firms. The SFF harshly denounced the government for those actions.[83] Table 3.4 gives a graphic portrait of the extent of the Unidad Popular attack through May 1972.

Capitalists and conservative political parties began to plot the government's downfall in earnest. Before the end of March, 33 right-wing leaders met to begin the destablization campaign. They declared, "Our liberty, our democracy, and our human rights are seriously threatened...faced with this situation we cannot afford cowardice or hesitancy. The time has come to act."[84]

In May and June, Unidad Popular took over eight more textile firms and a number of companies in other manufacturing sectors. Executives who were on the SFF's council were directly affected. Two of the firms (in the ocean freight business) belonged to the Menéndez group; Pedro Menéndez was a prominent member of the SFF who had served as its president several times. Another member of the SFF's elected council had his forestry firm requisitioned, and a distribution firm controlled by yet another prominent conglomerate (the Hirmas group) also passed into the state sector with a final transfer of stocks.[85]

Later in June, when the PDC and Unidad Popular resumed talks to overcome the constitutional crisis over the Hamilton-Fuentealba bill, the CPC declared that business no longer supported the negotiations. The SFF condemned the talks and reaffirmed its commitment to fight against "economic totalitarianism."[86] Landowners, engulfed by widespread expropriation and rising violence in the countryside, also rejected those talks. The SNA strengthened its links to opposition political parties. Retail merchants staged a one day "strike" by not opening their shops. The rhetoric of combative opposition escalated, and business peak associations began to dedicate their energies to the destabilization of the government with an eye towards provoking a coup.[87]

After capitalists and landowners repudiated the negotiations over nationalization, the PDC walked out on the June discussions just as Unidad Popular was preparing to make substantive concessions.[88] It is probable that the PDC abandoned the discussions because capitalists condemned them—the party leadership feared that in a climate of increasing polarization right-wing political parties were drawing away PDC voters for the March 1973 congressional elections.[89]

After business elites concluded that negotiation was fruitless they stepped up efforts to mobilize. Beginning in August 1972, upper and middle-class groups staged "bosses strikes" in response to the activities of the JAPs, which, in turn, had been prompted by rapidly deteriorating economic conditions. Requisitions and interventions of firms followed. In October, a month-long truckers strike broke out; massive lock-outs accompanied their action.

The mobilization of Chilean business culminated in the creation of a more militant organization and a list of demands, the Pliego de Chile. Opposition political parties supported the demands, most of which turned on the issue of property rights and property owners' recourses for defending their interests. Specifically, the Pliego de Chile demanded that Unidad Popular return firms taken over after August 21, 1972, refrain from nationalizing the Papelera, sign the Hamilton-Fuentealba bill into law, privatize the banking industry, limit agrarian reform, enact legislation guaranteeing medium and small business exemption from nationalization, dismantle the JAPs, and give business peak associations a greater role in economic policymaking by including them on planning commissions and on the boards of utility companies. Unidad Popular refused to negotiate over the Pliego de Chile.[90]

The movement that climaxed in the October bosses strike and the Pliego de Chile gave property owners a heightened sense of power. They openly advocated "entrepreneurs' power" *(poder gremial)*, a concept introduced by the president of the SNA during an annual international trade fair in November 1972. This was a setting traditionally used by business leaders to either praise or upbraid governments for their economic policies with high administration officials in attendance.[91] *Poder gremial* became business' rallying cry for the overthrow of the government.

Meanwhile, conservative political parties and the Christian Democrats united in an electoral alliance—the Confederación Democrática (CODE)—for the congressional election in March 1973. The results disappointed the opposition. Although it claimed victory, CODE failed to get the two thirds majority needed to impeach Allende.[92] Moreover, Unidad Popular did better than expected given the chaotic state of Chile's economy and high levels of social unrest. Historically, support for government political parties during mid-term elections generally declined from the level of the preceding presidential race. Unidad Popular's votes, however, increased from 36 percent to 44 percent. Electoral support for opposition political parties dropped from 64 percent during the presidential election to 54 percent during the congressional election.[93] These results, and the social conflict that exploded after the elections, isolated those the factions within the PDC and Unidad Popular that still wished to negotiate a solution to Chile's political crisis. The stage was set for the *golpe de estado*.

### Capitalists, Landowners, and the Post-Coup Political Project

Unidad Popular's nationalization policy, and the creation of alternative forms of commercial distribution (the JAPs), drove business to orchestrate the economic and political destabilization of Allende's government. As Chilean capitalists gave up hope that they could defend themselves within the system, their peak associations—the *gremios empresariales*—organized the *gremios* of medium and small businesses in opposition to Unidad Popular. The CPC and the SFF, the main organizers, wooed small and medium business with an ideological discourse that stressed a common interest in private property. The effort succeeded because Unidad Popular's policies made the perception of a threat to the economic survival of all businesspersons credible. As 1972 wore on, the collapse of the Hamilton-Fuentealba bill, the widespread use of JAPs, and the deteriorating economy, led to mobilizations of businesspeople and middle-class professionals in the streets.

By mid-1972, the political and class compromise that sustained Chilean democracy had been replaced by class conflict. The upper and middle classes and their political party allies no longer desired a negotiated settlement with the UP. They had ceased to believe they could defend their fundamental interests within the context of existing political institutions. They would settle only for the capitulation of Unidad Popular. The opposition staged mass mobilizations and general strikes that even included some working-class groups, creating confidence that the government could be brought down.

The combative period that began in the middle of 1972 led to competing views of what type of government should follow and the role of organized business in it. Business groups aligned around two projects. Neither project envisioned a strictly military—much less personalist—government. Both wanted a government in which the military ruled along with organized business. The two projects proposed differing systems of interest intermediation and different degrees of power for political parties. The projected plans of the opposition may have influenced some of Pinochet's decisions. In his quest for absolute power, Pinochet had a motive for shutting organized business out of the economic policymaking process and for adopting policies that would weaken them: These were social groups that might seek to circumscribe his authority.

Between November 1972 and March 1973, capitalists and landowners not only developed a mobilization strategy but two visions of Chile's future political system. Large-scale capitalists had long understood that a successful mobilization and destabilization strategy required the participation of medium and small scale business as well as middle classes. But large-scale business groups disagreed over the place of medium and small-scale business in Chile's post-Allende policymaking process. The SNA supported the development of *gremialismo*, a political current based upon the more numerous but economically less powerful business groups. The term *gremios* applied to the representative associations of society's functional groups, often based on employment categories. Thus, *gremialismo* essentially referred to a political movement made up of the representative associations of "freedom loving" entrepreneurial groups and professionals.[94] In mid-

December 1972, *gremialista* leaders established the Movimiento de Acción Gremial. They defined themselves as a movement that was independent of political parties, born out of a pressing need to fight Marxism. The movement's leaders insisted that is should take an active role in Chile's reconstruction.[95]

Benjamín Matte, president of the SNA and a leader of Fatherland and Freedom, a new extremist right-wing party, defined some of the movement's goals at the international trade fair in November 1972. He urged entrepreneurs to overthrow the government and outlined the role that entrepreneurial organizations should play in the authoritarian regime he hoped would follow. Echoing these ideas, Pablo Rodríguez, the head of Fatherland and Freedom, argued for the establishment of an authoritarian corporatist regime after the overthrow of Allende. In their view, Chile had progressed the most during the historical periods when authoritarian governments ruled. In the new government, the *gremios* should have voice and vote in Congress and in a national development council. *Gremios* would also participate directly in policymaking through regional planning and development councils in a regionally defined decentralized administrative system.[96] The *gremialista* movement took great pains to establish its independence from traditional opposition political parties, although it allied with them in pursuit of a common cause.[97] In their view, most policymaking should take place in development councils and not in a legislative arena where political parties play a larger role. Landowners, medium and small-scale producers, and professionals wanted an active role in a corporatist government that gave elite deal-makers and political parties less room to maneuver.

By contrast, big business (the CPC, the SFF, and the CCC) only participated in the *gremialista* movement as part of a mobilization strategy to overthrow Allende. They did not, however, support the corporatist project.[98] Chile's most important businessmen defined *gremialismo* as a current of opinion, a movement that could help guarantee liberty. But, according to Orlando Sáenz, president of SFF, it should neither have a direct role in policymaking nor should there be corporatist political institutions.[99] In both November 1972 and March 1973, Jorge Fontaine (president of the CPC) called for a political order based on a tripartite relationship between *gremialistas*, political parties, and the military. He also supported administrative decentralization through regionalization.[100] Fontaine's declarations suggest that most of the leadership of big capital preferred a system of interest intermediation in which they, together with "acceptable" political parties (reluctantly including the Christian Democrats), would play a dominant role in policymaking. In any case, the traditionally most powerful economic and political elites were not in favor of a corporatist regime. As will be seen, big business also had the best connections to military conspirators and, initially, the military government. As a result, corporatism did not flourish in Chile to any significant degree despite widespread rhetoric acclaiming it.

## Conclusion

This chapter examined the roots of intersectoral cooperation and tension in Chile, the sources of capitalist regime loyalties from the 1930s to the early 1970s, and the incentives for greater cooperation among business peak associations fostered under the reformist governments preceding the military coup. These relationships offer a reference point from which to assess the opportunities and obstacles offered by the military government to competing capitalist groups.

Intersectoral conflict began in earnest with the creation of CORFO and acute discrimination against landowners, mine owners, and merchants in favor of manufacturers. During the democratic period, industrialists prevailed over other sectors because of their critical role in a multiclass alliance mediated by centrist or center-left political parties that included middle-class groups and labor. After the fall of democracy the opponents of the manufacturing sector were able to strike back at the sector that had grown at their expense. Military rule robbed industrialists of the tacit "partners" and institutional structures they had relied on to stave off previous efforts to restructure the economy.

The evidence suggested that capitalists and landowners tolerated democracy as long as they could defend their property and profits. That condition held more or less through Frei's Christian Democratic administration and ended with Unidad Popular's nationalization, land reform, labor, and commercial distribution policies. Unidad Popular's attempts to organize peasant and urban migrant groups, often in response to capital's resistance to nationalization, exacerbated the conflict. When capitalists and landowners became convinced they could not defend their fundamental interests within the political institutions of Chilean democracy, they turned against democracy itself.

The process of mobilizing a cohesive intraclass force aligned capitalists in a series of complex relationships that shaped the immediate post-coup period. During the process, groups that would be relevant for economic policymaking in the dictatorship rose to the fore although other social actors were excluded. Large-scale capital was in. Medium-sized businesses, and the middle classes barely had a toehold (through both their participation in the *gremialista* movement and through the Christian Democratic party's position within the larger coup coalition). Although some labor and shantytown groups were also part of the coup coalition, their interests were only weakly represented by the PDC. From the outset, the military government repressed labor.

The Allende period also established the power relationships among large-scale capitalists in the coup coalition for the beginning of the military government. The more influential ones formulated policy within the state itself from the very beginning. Others only had access to the policymaking process at later points. Specifically, the conglomerate executives that had participated in the Monday Club obtained choice economic policymaking positions in the new government. Business peak associations had no direct mechanisms of interest representation, such as boards or commissions, but they had access to hearings.

The large-scale capitalists in the coup coalition rejected corporatism, but they expected a share of power in the military government and called for the establishment of a protected democracy as soon as possible. Their preferences suggest why the corporatist project did not flourish in Chile and why Pinochet (intent on setting up one-man rule) embraced the free-market economic ideologues. Both Pinochet and the ideologues opposed traditional business groups because they could benefit from a more exclusionary form of dictatorship.

Finally, the increasingly reformist governments of Frei and Allende forged greater internal cohesiveness among the business associations and politicized them to a greater extent than ever before. This stage in the development of business peak associations enabled them to take the lead in formulating an alternative economic program to radical neoliberalism during the economic crisis of 1982-1983. Chapter 8 will show how capital's capacity to engage in collective action also played an important role in shaping the process of Chile's transition to democracy.

## Notes

1. Maurice Zeitlin and Richard Earl Ratcliff, *Landlords and Capitalists: The Dominant Class of Chile* (Princeton: Princeton University Press, 1988).

2. Claudio Véliz, "La mesa de tres patas," *Desarrollo Económico* 3, 1-2, 1963.

3. Michael Monteón, *Chile in the Nitrate Era: The Evolution of Economic Dependence, 1880-1930* (Madison: University of Wisconsin Press, 1982); Thomas F. O'Brien, *The Nitrate Industry and Chile's Crucial Transition: 1870-1891* (New York: New York University Press, 1982); Frederick B. Pike, *Chile and the United States, 1880-1962* (Notre Dame: University of Notre Dame Press, 1965). The best single volume on the Chilean copper industry is Theodore Moran, *Multinational Corporations and the Politics of Dependence: Copper in Chile* (Princeton: Princeton University Press, 1974); also see Paul E. Sigmund, *Multinationals in Latin America: The Politics of Nationalization* (Madison: University of Wisconsin Press, 1980).

4. For cattlemen's advocacy of protection, see Thomas C. Wright, "Agriculture

and Protectionism in Chile, 1880-1930," *Journal of Latin American Studies* 7, 1, 1975. For analyses of Chilean landowners into the early 20th century, see Arnold J. Bauer, *Chilean Rural Society from the Spanish Conquest to 1930* (New York: Cambridge University Press, 1975); also see part one of Cristóbal Kay and Patricio Silva, eds., *Development and Social Change in the Chilean Countryside: From the Pre-Land Reform Period to the Democratic Transition* (Amsterdam: CEDLA, 1992).

5. For the development of the Chilean economy before the Great Depression, see Henry W. Kirsch, *Industrial Development in a Traditional Society: The Conflict of Entrepreneurship and Modernization in Chile* (Gainesville: University of Florida Press, 1977); Oscar Muñoz, ed., *Crecimiento industrial de Chile, 1914-1965* (Santiago: Universidad de Chile, Instituto de Economía y Planificación, second edition, 1971); Markos Mamalakis, *Growth and Structure of the Chilean Economy: From Independence to Allende* (New Haven: Yale University Press, 1976). For the best single collection of historical statistics and summaries of Chilean economic policies, see Markos J. Mamalakis, *Historical Statistics of Chile* (Westport: Greenwood, 1978-1989).

6. Maurice Zeitlin and Richard Earl Ratcliff, *Landlords and Capitalists: The Dominant Class of Chile*; Henry Kirsch, *Industrial Development in a Traditional Society*.

7. Both the SFF and SONAMI were founded under the auspices of the SNA in the 19th century. For an account of Chilean peak associations before 1970, see Genaro Arriagada, *La oligarquía patronal chilena* (Santiago: Ediciones Nueva Universidad, 1970).

8. Marcelo Cavarozzi, "The Government and the Industrial Bourgeoisie in Chile, 1938-1964," Ph.D. Dissertation, University of California, Berkeley, 1975; James Petras, *Politics and Social Forces in Chilean Development* (Berkeley: University of California Press, 1970). For an analysis of how the SNA operated in the first half of this century, see Thomas C. Wright, *Landowners and Reform in Chile: The SNA, 1919-1940* (Urbana: University of Illinois Press, 1982).

9. David F. Cusack, "The Politics of Chilean Private Enterprise under Christian Democracy," Ph.D. Dissertation, University of Denver, 1972; Constantine Menges, "Public Policy and Organized Business in Chile: A Preliminary Analysis," *Journal of International Affairs* 20, 2, 1966.

10. For the effects of the Great Depression, see P.T. Ellsworth, *Chile: An Economy in Transition* (New York: Macmillan, 1945).

11. For U.S. capital flows to Latin America and the Great Depression, see Paul W. Drake, *The Money Doctor in the Andes: The Kemmerer Missions, 1923-1933* (Durham: Duke University Press, 1989); Barbara Stallings, *Banker to the Third World: U.S. Portfolio Investment in Latin America, 1900-1986* (Berkeley: University of California Press, 1987).

12. For the economic policy demands of upper classes during the 1931-38 period, as well as general economic policy, see Paul Drake, *Socialism and Populism in Chile, 1932-52* (Urbana: University of Illinois Press, 1978); Paul Drake, "The Political Responses of the Chilean Upper Class to the Great Depression and the Threat of Socialism, 1931-33," in Frederic Cople Jaher, ed., *The Rich, the Well Born, and the Powerful* (Urbana: University of Illinois Press, 1973); P.T. Ellsworth, *Chile: An Economy in Transition*; Oscar Muñoz and Ana María Arriagada, "Orígenes políticos y económicos del estado empresarial en Chile," *Estudios Cieplan* no. 16, September 1977, pp. 12-20.

13. Maurice Zeitlin and Richard Earl Ratcliff, *Landlords and Capitalists: The Dominant Class of Chile*; Arnold J. Bauer, "Industry and the Missing Bourgeoisie: Consumption and Development in Chile, 1850-1950," *Hispanic American Historical Review* 70, 2, 1990.

14. Jean Carriere, *Landowners and Politics in Chile: A Study of the Sociedad Nacional de Agricultura, 1932-1970* (Amsterdam: CEDLA, 1981), pp. 175-180.

15. The fact that landowners primarily produced for domestic markets, instead of export, might have facilitated their support for inward-looking solutions to the economic crisis as well.

16. Brian, Loveman, *Chile: The Legacy of Hispanic Capitalism* (New York: Oxford University Press, 1979), pp. 258-59; Oscar Muñoz, *Crecimiento industrial de Chile*, especially Chapter 3.

17. The government also protected the textile industry, which made large-scale merchants unhappy because they had invested heavily in clothing assemblies based on textiles imported by them. Henry W. Kirsch, *Industrial Development in a Traditional Society*, pp. 77-81.

18. Paul Drake, *Socialism and Populism in Chile*, pp. 114-118 and pp. 190-192; Paul Drake, "The Political Responses of the Chilean Upper Class," pp. 316-30; Brian Loveman, Chile, pp. 258-259.

19. For intersectoral conflict between agriculture and industry, see Markos Mamalakis, "La teoría de los choques entre sectores," Universidad de Chile, Instituto de Economía, publication no. 83, 1966; Markos Mamalakis, *Growth and Structure of the Chilean Economy*; Brian Loveman, *Struggle in the Countryside: Politics and Rural Labor in Chile, 1919-1973* (Bloomington: University of Indiana Press, 1976); Jean Carriere, *Landowners and Politics in Chile*.

20. For the Chilean party and electoral system, see Federico Gil, *The Political System of Chile* (Boston: Houghton Mifflin, 1966); Manuel Antonio Garretón, *The Chilean Political Process* (Boston: Unwin Hyman, 1989); Arturo Valenzuela, *The Breakdown of Democratic Regimes: Chile* (Baltimore: Johns Hopkins University Press, 1978).

21. For the composition of the Radical party, see Federico Gil, *The Political System of Chile*; Paul W. Drake, *Socialism and Populism in Chile*; Julio César Jobet, *Ensayo crítico del desarrollo económico-social de Chile* (Santiago: Editorial Universitaria, 1955); John Reese Stevenson, *The Chilean Popular Front* (Westport: Greenwood, 1945); James Petras, *Politics and Social Forces in Chilean Development*. For additional sources on the history of the Popular Front, see Mariana Aylwin, Carlos Bascuñán, Sofía Correa, Cristián Gazmuri, Sol Serrano, and Matías Tagle, *Chile en el Siglo XX* (Santiago: Emisión, n.d.); Brian Loveman, *Chile* and *Struggle in the Countryside*; Marcelo Cavarozzi, "The Government and the Industrial Bourgeoisie." For a different interpretation of centrist political parties, see Timothy R. Scully, *Rethinking the Center: Party Politics in Nineteenth- and Twentieth-Century Chile* (Stanford: Stanford University Press, 1992).

22. For Gustavo Ross' candidacy, in addition to sources already cited, see Tomás Moulián and Isabel Torres Dujisin, *Discusiones entre honorables: Las candidaturas presidenciales de la derecha, 1938-1946* (Santiago: FLACSO, n.d.).

23. For the opposition of these groups to sectorally discriminatory ISI policies, see Jean Carriere, *Landowners and Politics in Chile*; Marcelo Cavarozzi, "The Government and the Industrial Bourgeoisie"; Markos Mamalakis, "La teoría de los

choques entre sectores"; David Cusack, "The Politics of Chilean Private Enterprise," pp. 98-100.

24. Jean Carriere, *Landowners and Politics in Chile*.

25. Marcelo Cavarozzi, "The Government and the Industrial Bourgeoisie in Chile, 1938-1964," pp. 120-148.

26. Brian Loveman, *Chile*, pp. 258-259.

27. Markos Mamalakis, *The Growth and Structure of the Chilean Economy*; and "La teoría de los choques entre sectores."

28. For the political arrangement between landowners and the Radical party, see Brian Loveman, *Chile: The Legacy of Hispanic Capitalism* and *Struggle in the Countryside*.

29. Marcelo Cavarozzi, "The Government and the Industrial Bourgeoisie in Chile."

30. Constantine Menges, "Public Policy and Organized Business in Chile."

31. For the multiple exchange rate, see Teresa Jeannerette, "El sistema de protección a la industria chilena," in Oscar Muñoz, ed., *Proceso a la industrialización chilena* (Santiago: Ediciones Nueva Universidad, 1972), pp. 74-75. For an analysis of the role of multiple exchange rates between 1934 and the 1940s, see P.T. Ellsworth, *Chile: An Economy in Transition*.

32. For general works on the development of ISI, see Celso Furtado, *Economic Development of Latin America: Historical Background of Contemporary Problems* (New York: Cambridge University Press, 1976, second edition); Joseph Grunwald, ed., *Latin America and the World Economy: A Changing International Order* (Beverley Hills: Sage Publications, Inc., 1978); Guillermo O'Donnell, *Modernization and Bureaucratic-Authoritarianism: Studies in South American Politics* (Berkeley: Institute of International Studies, University of California, 1973); Albert Hirschman, *Journeys Toward Progress* (Garden City: Doubleday and Company, 1966); Fernando Henrique Cardoso and Enzo Faletto, *Dependency and Development in Latin America* (Berkeley: University of California Press, 1979).

33. Marcelo Cavarozzi, "The Government and the Industrial Bourgeoisie in Chile"; Barbara Stallings, *Class Conflict and Economic Development in Chile, 1958-1973* (Stanford: Stanford University Press, 1976).

34. For English language sources on agrarian reform in Chile, see Brian Loveman, *Struggle in the Countryside*; and Robert Kaufman, *The Politics of Land Reform in Chile, 1950-1970* (Cambridge: Harvard University Press, 1972).

35. For English language overviews of this process of political and ideological radicalization between 1958-1970, see Arturo Valenzuela, *The Breakdown of Democratic Regimes: Chile*; Manuel Antonio Garretón, *The Chilean Political Process*; Barbara Stallings, *Class Conflict*; Paul Sigmund, *The Overthrow of Allende and the Politics of Chile, 1964-1976* (Pittsburgh: University of Pittsburgh Press, 1977).

36. For the ideological roots of Chilean Christian Democracy, see Jaime Castillo Velasco, *Las fuentes de la Democracia Cristiana* (Santiago: Editorial del Pacífico, 1963); Jaques Maritain, *Christianity and Democracy* (Santiago: Charles Scribner's Sons, 1947).

37. For this interpretation of Chilean democracy, see Manuel A. Garretón and Tomás Moulián, "Procesos y bloques políticos en la crisis chilena," *Revista Mexicana de Sociología* 41, 1, 1979; Brian Loveman, *Chile*, pp. 256-302. For a rational choice analysis, see Youssef Cohen *Radicals, Reformers, and Reactionaries: The Prisoner's*

*Dilemma and the Collapse of Democracy in Latin America* (Chicago: University of Chicago Press, 1994).

38. Ian Roxborough et al., *The State and Revolution*, pp. 74-77; Sergio Bitar, "The Interrelationship between Economics and Politics," in Federico Gil, Ricardo Lagos, and Henry A. Landsberger, eds., *Chile at the Turning Point: Lessons of the Socialist Years* (Philadelphia: ISHI, 1979), pp. 106-116; Tomás Moulián, "Las fases del desarrollo político chileno entre 1973 y 1978," FLACSO Chile, Documento de Trabajo no. 155, p. 26, 1982; Brian Loveman, *Chile*, p. 335; Paul Drake, *Socialism and Populism in Chile*, p. 324.

39. For urban migrants, see Mónica Threlfall, "Shantytown Dwellers and People's Power," in Philip O'Brien, ed., *Allende's Chile*. For peasant organization, see Peter Winn and Cristóbal Kay, "Agrarian Reform and Rural Revolution in Allende's Chile," *Journal of Latin American Studies* 6, 1, 1974.

40. For a detailed discussion of this policy, see Joan Garcés, *Allende y la experiencia chilena* (Barcelona: Editorial Ariel, 1976), especially pp. 215-52.

41. Patricia Santa Lucía, "The Industrial Working Class and the Struggle for Power in Chile," in Philip O'Brien, ed., *Allende's Chile*; Barbara Stallings, *Class Conflict*, p. 129 and note number 6, p.279; Oscar Guillermo Garretón, "Concentración monopólica en Chile: Participación del estado y de los trabajadores en la gestión económica," in *Economía política en la Unidad Popular* (Santiago: Editorial Fontanella, 1975).

42. Barbara Stallings, *Class Conflict*; "Basic Program of the Popular Unity Government, in *New Chile* (Berkeley, 1972); Stefan de Vylder, *Allende's Chile* (Cambridge: Cambridge University Press, 1976); Gonzalo Martner, *El gobierno del Presidente Salvador Allende, 1970-1973* (Concepción: Ediciones LAR, 1988), pp. 67-176; Mark Falcoff, *Modern Chile* (New Brunswick: Transaction, 1989), pp. 53-159; Edy Kaufman, *Crisis in Allende's Chile: New Perspectives* (New York: Praeger, 1988), pp. 191-204.

43. For agrarian policy, see Cristóbal Kay, "Agrarian Reform and the Transition to Socialism," in Philip O'Brien, *Allende's Chile*; David Baytelman, "Problems of Collective Land Exploitation in Chilean Agriculture," in Federico Gil et al., eds., *Chile at the Turning Point*.

44. Ian Roxborough et al., *Chile: The State and Revolution*, pp. 78-81.

45. Barbara Stallings, *Class Conflict*, p. 126.

46. Guillermo Campero, *Los gremios empresariales en el período 1970-1983: Comportamiento sociopolítico y orientaciones ideológicas* (Santiago: ILET, 1984), pp. 42-49.

47. For the National party's stance, see Luis Maira, "The Strategy and Tactics of the Chilean Counterrevolution in the Area of Political Institutions," in Federico Gil et al., eds., *Chile at the Turning Point*, pp. 250-251; Edy Kaufman, *Crisis in Allende's Chile*, p. 152; Hugo Zemelman and Patricio León, "Political Opposition to the Government of Allende," in Federico Gil et al., eds., *Chile at the Turning Point*, p. 73.

48. Gonzalo Martner, *El gobierno del Presidente Allende*, pp. 137-139. For a more critical view of bank nationalization, see Mark Falcoff, *Modern Chile*, pp. 125-126. However, top executives and major shareholders of non-financial firms who resisted government buy-outs often complained of the government's unfair practices to force them to sell. The usual mechanism involved manipulation of price controls.

Businessmen bitterly recriminated UP officials for keeping the prices of their products too low to compensate for rising labor costs and inflation. Consequently, the financial and operating conditions of their industries deteriorated to the point were shareholders were glad to sell. These data were obtained from annual reports of FENSA and Compañía Manufacturera de Papeles y Cartones for 1971 and interviews in 1989 with Jorge Fontaine (then president of the Confederation of Production and Commerce) and Manuel Valdés (a member of the National Agricultural Association).

49. Eduardo Novoa, "Vías legales para avanzar hacia el socialismo," *Revista Mensaje*, 1971. The government could requisition firms when owners curtailed production to create artificial shortages and intervene in firms paralyzed by labor-management conflicts. During an "intervention" a government-appointed board of directors replaced the original one, although the shareholders did not lose their stock. In principle, although not always in practice, the government was supposed to negotiate the sale of the firm at some later date. For a detailed study of nationalization policy, see Lois E. Athey, "Government and Opposition during the Allende Years," Ph.D. Dissertation, Columbia University, 1978, especially pp. 264-344.

50. Lois Athey, "Government and Opposition," pp. 304-5; and company annual reports.

51. Guillermo Campero, *Los gremios empresariales*, pp. 44-45.

52. Joan E. Garcés, *Allende y la experiencia chilena*, p. 208; Michael Fleet, *The Rise and Fall*, p. 137; Ian Roxborough et al., *The State and Revolution*, pp. 62-63; Ian Roxborough, "Reversing the Revolution," pp. 198-199; also see, Radomiro Tómic, "Christian Democracy and the Unidad Popular," pp. 213-214; Edy Kaufman, *Crisis in Allende's Chile*, p. 145; Paul Sigmund, *The Overthrow of Allende*, pp. 72-73, 77-79, 111-112; Michael Fleet, *The Rise and Fall*, pp. 128-139.

53. Michael Fleet, *The Rise and Fall*, pp. 141-145; Lois Athey, "Government and Opposition," p. 168; Pío García, "The Social Property Sector: Its Political Impact," in Federico Gil et al., eds., *Chile at the Turning Point*, p. 175.

54. Paul Sigmund, *The Overthrow of Allende*, pp. 158-160; Mark Falcoff, *Modern Chile*, p. 145; Lois Athey, "Government and Opposition," pp. 168-169.

55. For details of the constitutional conflict, see Arturo Valenzuela, *Breakdown*, pp. 73-74 and p. 124, note 52.

56. For details of the Hamilton-Fuentealba bill, see Barbara Stallings, *Class Conflict*, pp. 130-131; Mark Falcoff, *Modern Chile*, p. 145; Ian Roxborough, "The Chilean Opposition to Allende," p. 204.

57. Luís Maira, "Political Strategy of the Counterrevolution," p. 236; Michael Fleet, *Rise and Fall*, p. 146; Paul Sigmund, *The Overthrow of Allende*, pp. 181-182.

58. Zemelman and León, "Political Opposition to the Government of Allende," pp. 91-94.

59. *El Campesino* 4, April 1971. *El Campesino* is the SNA's monthly publication.

60. They declared, "These alarming events should give pause to all and clearly suggest that we should denounce the strategies and tactics of those who wish to promote violence. Ideological differences should be resolved within the bounds of fair play guaranteed by true democratic principles." Guillermo Campero, *Los gremios empresariales*, p. 52.

61. FENSA annual report, 1970-1971.

62. Lois Athey, "Political Opposition," p. 293; Ian Roxborough et al., *The State and Revolution*, pp. 91-92.

63. Ibid.

64. The Textile Institute suggested that the expropriations constituted a violation of legal procedures, and by extension a violation of the constitutional guarantees Unidad Popular had pledged to uphold. *El Mercurio*, May 28, 1971.

65. Guillermo Campero, Los gremios empresariales, p. 54.

66. El Mercurio, "His Deeds Belie his Statements," July 7, 1971.

67. Philip O'Brien, *The Pinochet Decade* (London: Latin American Bureau, 1983), pp. 34-35. Prosopographical data were drawn from the annual reports of Edwards group companies.

68. Paul Sigmund *The Overthrow of Allende*, pp. 157-158; Mark Falcoff, *Modern Chile*, pp. 126 and 231; for the impact of the Papelera conflict on the PDC and its negotiations with the UP, see Michael Fleet, *The Rise and Fall*, p. 148.

69. CMPC executives, for example, chided other companies for not having fought harder to defend their property. They then expressed satisfaction that their example had finally shaken businessmen out of their lethargy and the mistaken idea that they could negotiate separate deals with the UP. See CMPC annual report, 1972.

70. Guillermo Campero, *Los gremios empresariales*, pp. 58-61; Barbara Stallings, Class Conflict, p. 139.

71. *El Mercurio*, months of October and November, passim.

72. Author interview with Manlio Fantini, council member of the Mining Association (SONAMI), April 1989.

73. Joan Garcés, *Allende y la experiencia chilena*, pp. 232-233.

74. This may help to explain the apparent paradox cited by Chilean analysts who prefer ideological explanations. They point out that retail merchants were making more money than ever as a result of the government's wage policy, yet they joined the opposition.

75. Guillermo Campero, *Los gremios empresariales*, p. 56.

76. Paul Sigmund, *The Overthrow of Allende*, p. 172; Alec Nove, "The Political Economy of the Allende Regime," in Philip O'Brien, ed., *Allende's Chile*, pp. 61-64; Guillermo Campero, *Los gremios empresariales*, p. 57.

77. Barbara Stallings, *Class Conflict*, p. 139.

78. For details on those threats, see Guillermo Campero, *Los Gremios Empresariales*, pp. 62-63. For the course of the Hamilton-Fuentealba bill in the Chilean legislature, see Alejandro Rojas, *La transformación del estado: La experiencia de la Unidad Popular* (Santiago: Ediciones Documentas, 1987), pp. 103-112; Mark Falcoff, *Modern Chile*, pp. 145-150; Pío García, "The Social Property Sector," pp. 174-176.

79. Lois Athey, "Government and Opposition," pp. 269-270. For additional information on the list of 91 and the debate over the Hamilton-Fuentealba bill, see Movimiento de Acción Popular Unitaria, *El libro de las 91: Las empresas monopólicas y el área social de la economía chilena* (Santiago: Ediciones Barco de Papel, 1972).

80. Prosopographical data from Colegio de Periodistas, *Diccionario biográfico* (Santiago: Editorial Universitaria, selected volumes); and from company annual reports.

81. For details about the constitutional conflict, see Michael Fleet, *The Rise and*

*Fall*, pp. 150-154; Arturo Valenzuela, *Breakdown*, p. 73 and pp. 124-125, note 52; Lois Athey, "Government and Opposition," pp. 169-179.

82. Many interviewees still expressed great bitterness at this fact, which to this day fuels their mistrust of the PDC.

83. For details, see Guillermo Campero, *Los gremios empresariales*, pp. 67-68.

84. Barbara Stallings, *Class Conflict*, p. 140.

85. For the list of firms, see Lois Athey, "Government and Opposition," pp. 316-326; prosopographical data from Colegio de Periodistas, *Diccionario biográfico de Chile* (various years); and from company annual reports.

86. Guillermo Campero, *Los gremios empresariales*, p. 68; Arturo Valenzuela, *Breakdown*, p.75.

87. Guillermo Campero, *Los gremios empresariales*, p. 69.

88. Most observers believe that Unidad Popular scuttled the first negotiations in March 1972 because a by-election was coming up and it wanted to make a show of strength against the opposition to boost votes. Had the government caved in to PDC-PN attempts to force Unidad Popular to its knees, a radicalized labor sector would have been less likely to continue supporting the government coalition. Unidad Popular lost the election anyway and, after a cabinet shakeup, prepared to make some real concessions; see Michael Fleet, *The Rise and Fall*, pp. 152-3.

89. Michael Fleet, *The Rise and Fall*, p. 154 and pp. 162-66; Arturo Valenzuela, *Breakdown*, pp. 83-86.

90. Guillermo Campero, *Los gremios empresariales*, pp. 71-72.

91. The SNA's monthly *El Campesino* gave excellent coverage of the trade fair.

92. Paul Sigmund, *The Overthrow of Allende*, pp. 198-201.

93. Arturo Valenzuela, *Breakdown*, pp. 40 and 85.

94. For the *gremialismo* movement, see Alec Nove, "The Political Economy of the Allende Regime," pp. 69-70; Paul Sigmund, *The Overthrow of Allende*, pp. 221-222; and Edy Kaufman, *Crisis in Allende's Chile*, pp. 74-81.

95. *El Mercurio*, December 23, 1972.

96. *El Mercurio*, November 11, 1972.

97. Philip O'Brien, *The Pinochet Decade*, pp. 35-36.

98. Ibid., pp. 72-78.

99. Ibid., p. 78.

100. *El Mercurio*, November 11, 1972, and March 14, 1973.

# 4

## Gradual Adjustment Under Military Rule

The violence and brutality of the coup against Allende astonished Chileans and the rest of the world. The repression under the military governments of Brazil and Argentina in the 1960s, and Uruguay earlier in 1973, paled in comparison. Then, as if in a perverse rivalry, in 1976 a new Argentine military government unleashed even greater state terror in its "dirty" war. After absorbing these rather disturbing events, observers noticed that the new labor-repressing military governments were not following the Brazilian development model. Instead, Argentina, Chile, and Uruguay strove to restructure their economies along neoliberal lines, which meant dismantling the institutions of import-substitution industrialization (ISI). As the dictatorships began to entrench themselves, the scope of analysis broadened from a preoccupation with human rights violations to an examination of the economic experiments being conducted.

As noted in Chapter 1, most analyses of neoliberal economic restructuring in these countries emphasized the importance of state autonomy in the policymaking process. In the case of policymaking in Chile, the personalist, one-man rule of General Augusto Pinochet (as opposed to rule by military junta elsewhere) was seen to almost completely insulate fiercely ideological technocrats from other social groups. These interpretations accorded no role to the interaction between policymakers and business and landowning groups. Moreover, the perceived lack of input by these groups was seen as beneficial to the advance of neoliberal reform.

The following chapters on authoritarian Chile, however, argue that this characterization has been overdrawn. A comparison across three policy periods—of gradual, radical, and pragmatic reform—shows that shifting capitalist coalitions with varying power resources played a vital part in the policymaking process. The role of state structure and international factors in the shaping of those coalitions and their power resources are also examined. In each of these policy periods, the representatives of distinct coalitions of capitalists and landowners helped to shape policy agendas, participated in policy formulation, and fleshed out plans for policy implementation. In part, they were able to do so because market-based economic development strategies made state elites more attentive to the demands of the dominant fractions of capital; inasmuch as neoliberalism gives capitalists significant control over investment.

This chapter examines the formation of the first capitalist coalition in authoritarian Chile and its relationship to the state in the short-lived gradualist policy period, which lasted roughly from October 1973 to April 1975. It also focuses on the ways in which state institutions, domestic political forces, and international economic crises affected the relative power capabilities of capitalist and landowning groups. These findings undermine the argument that radical neoliberalism was inevitable because the economic team that designed extreme free market reforms had dominated economic policymaking since the formulation of a policy agenda some months before the coup.

Development paths and their champions are rarely without alternatives at decisive historical turning points. The gradual approach to free market-oriented economic restructuring was an alternative to either radical neoliberalism or maintaining ISI after the overthrow of Allende. In a climate of intense violence and massive repression, on January 10, 1974, the newly installed military government decreed a gradual approach to both economic stabilization and trade opening. Gradual stabilization policies liberated prices in careful phases, froze wages, and reduced the public sector by privatizing industrial and financial enterprises. In the trade sphere, gradualism meant reducing tariffs from an average rate of 94 percent to 60 percent over three years; this schedule only threatened highly inefficient firms. Devaluations of a unified exchange rate offered additional protection. The idea was to allow manufacturers to gradually adjust to stiffer competition from regional markets (principally the Andean Common Market).

The gradualist coalition that developed this agenda and formulated the policies to carry it out was the result of a compromise between two major capitalist and landowning groups. At its core stood internationally competitive industrial producers for domestic markets. They could adjust easily to a gradual and shallow economic opening that would not radically alter the economic structure they once flourished in. The focus on regional rather than world trade further cushioned the effect of the reforms and provided continuity with past efforts, particularly those advocated during the administration of Eduardo Frei. Other business and landowning sectors, which had historically opposed high tariff barriers and occasionally backed more rapid openings, supported gradualism as well, although from a subordinate position in the gradualist coalition. They were producers for international markets in both fixed and liquid-asset sectors (fishing, mining, fruits, banking) and included large scale import-export merchants as well. Landowners who produced grains, meat, and dairy products for domestic markets joined the subordinate faction of the coalition. They too had traditionally resisted high tariff barriers because it siphoned off investment from agriculture into industry. Although they were not competitive internationally, they supported gradual trade liberalization because they obtained nontariff protection for their products, such as price floors. The main losers under the gradualist coalition were internationally uncompetitive industrialists, the capitalist fraction that had dominated the old import-substitution industrialization coalition.

Although international factors played an attenuated role in shaping the coalition, regime structure and control of state institutions strongly influenced its emergence and capabilities. Groups that had direct access to power holders in the new regime (the military and well-placed civilian authorities) were privileged over those that did not enjoy such connections. The interests of civilians appointed to the top economic ministries corresponded closely with those of the proponents of gradual economic restructuring. The men who headed key ministries and economic advisory committees were either drawn from the dominant capitalist policy coalition or they had analogous economic interests and, thus, would not oppose its agenda. In other words, top government policymakers and key business leaders essentially agreed on a strategy of gradual trade liberalization and economic stabilization. In essence, they all belonged to the same broad, loosely constituted coalition.

This arrangement created a distinctive system of interaction between capital and the state. From within the state, important individual businessmen—and technocrats closely linked to them—personally represented the interests of the gradualist coalition, set the policy agenda, and were mostly responsible for policy formulation. Although these policymakers did not generally belong to organized business, the peak associations of large-scale businessmen and landowners generally agreed both with their policy agenda and the pace of implementation. The relationship between capitalists and policymakers differed from that of the pragmatic policy period (1983-1989) in that business organizations did not play a large role in policy formulation. However, the encompassing peak organization, the Confederación de la Producción y Comercio (CPC), played a key supportive role within the gradualist coalition by ratifying the agenda, formulating early versions of the gradual approach to economic restructuring, and forming a strong lobby for it. Individual sectoral peak associations, however, did participate in the policy process. Although never in the lead, they did take part in policy formulation and were especially active in the implementation stage of the policy process. Moreover, from time to time, the interests of the conglomerates affected the policy stances of those organizations because they had heavy representation in them.[1]

In this constellation of forces, capitalists and landowners with dissenting policy preferences found themselves out in the cold. The proponents of continued high protectionism were without defenses. Under authoritarianism, lone or isolated dissenters within the large-scale business community, not to mention from middle-class and labor groups, were simply ignored. By the same token, although radical free marketeers fared much better (many held economic advisory posts in the government) they chafed because they occupied positions subordinate to gradualists. Their incessant, aggressive maneuvering to dominate policymaking imparted a measure of fragility to the gradualist coalition.

10/73 - 4/75

## The Gradualist Coalition

The economic and political crisis unleashed by Unidad Popular's socialist experiment united capitalists, landowners, middle classes and their political party allies against labor, peasants, and leftist parties. The coup coalition, especially its upper-class component, agreed on much. Chilean capitalists, relieved that they no longer had to contend with organized labor, made two goals their highest priority.[2] They wanted nationalized properties returned and an economic program capable of spurring economic growth. There was a consensus that the Chilean economy needed agile capital markets to generate investment funds and a hefty reduction of government regulations on business. Most entrepreneurs also backed a gradual approach to deflation to tame hyperinflation.

One policy issue on which Chilean capitalists and landowners openly disagreed was international trade policy. Business and landowning groups wrangled over the extent to which Chilean markets should be opened to external competition, the speed of the implementation of such a shift, and the economic sectors destined to reap the benefits of investment in export diversification. Intraclass competition was fed by the knowledge that diminished protection would set in motion a major overhaul of the national economy in which there would be winners and losers. Trade liberalization invoked open intraclass conflict that spilled over to other areas such as financial sector reform and deflation. The struggle over tariff policy offers a window through which to observe the forging of the gradualist policy coalition and the differences of that alliance from other groups.

The fragile, short-lived gradualist coalition formed just prior to and immediately following the coup. Two business actors—each defined internally according to market orientation and asset specificity—participated in the coalition. First, before the coup, business conglomerate heads (and an economic team closely allied to them) played a preponderant role in setting the policy agenda and in early policy formulation. These were powerful conglomerates that, given the nature of Chile's highly oligopolistic economy, controlled many of the nation's most important firms.[3] These early participants included both proponents of gradualism and of more drastic measures; the former, however, dominated. They produced a policy document dubbed *El Ladrillo* (the Brick), which proposed sweeping reforms but did not specify the timing, sequencing, or the speed with which they should take place. Second, after the coup, the gradualist coalition expanded dramatically from this small nucleus when Chile's encompassing business organization—the CPC—embraced a gradual approach to economic restructuring in December of 1973. CPC endorsement meant that the five peak associations of large-scale businessmen and landowners backed the gradualist plan. In addition to organized business, the heads of conglomerates whose firms had similar structures to those already in the coalition joined after the coup. In one capacity or another, the coalition came to include most of Chile's large-scale businessmen and landowners by the time the military government decreed gradual economic restructuring in January 1974.

The gradualist policy coalition was forged in a period of chaotic economic and political crisis. Over the course of a year, between 1973 and 1974, a diverse set of actors with varying motives was brought together by the belief that economic restructuring was necessary in Chile. It was a fragile, tension-laden, jerry-built coalition. At different points in time each of the groups belonging to it struggled to ensure that gradual reform prevailed over drastic, swift change or a return to the status quo ante.

## Policy Agenda Setting Before the Coup

The gradualist agenda had its origins in the Monday Club, where members plotted the mobilization of business against Allende. Before the coup, military conspirators had turned to the Monday Club for a post-coup economic program.[4] The businessmen of the Monday Club selected and controlled the young technocrats and businessmen who designed the Brick. Among the Brick's creators were, as will be seen in later chapters, the radical neoliberal ideologues whom Pinochet later appointed to top economic posts in the military government, although for the moment they only formed part of a team that also included gradualists. Monday Club leaders probably chose these economists to develop the post-coup economic program because they were young men with a fresh vision, not because the leadership supported shock treatment methods. Within the Monday Club, and in the period right after the coup, the radical neoliberals remained firmly subordinate to businessmen who believed in the necessity of significant change but whose conglomerates and firms could not flourish under drastic applications of free market policies. Businessmen linked to multisectoral conglomerates that could handle gradual but not radical change acted to moderate the stances of the more radical neoliberals.

*The Monday Club.* As seen in the previous chapter, the Monday Club was the core of the business conspiracy to overthrow Allende. Its regular members consisted of the top executives of two of the conglomerates most beleaguered by nationalization in Allende's Chile: the well-established and powerful Edwards group and the newer, take-over hungry Banco Hipotecario de Chile, or BHC conglomerate (popularly known as the "piranha" on account of its propensity to gobble up companies ruthlessly). Key leaders of the Sociedad de Fomento Fabril (SFF) also participated in the Monday Club.

The roster of its regular members reveals that economic interests inclined toward significant but gradual economic reform dominated the Monday Club; those with a preference for rapid, radical change occupied a subordinate position. The Monday Club was controlled by five businessmen linked to the Edwards conglomerate and two executives from the BHC economic group (see Table 4.1).[5] All agreed that the economic distortions introduced into the Chilean economy since the 1930s required broad, free-market reforms to eliminate them. They did not, however, agree on the pace as was later revealed. The Edwards group, which dominated the Monday Club, preferred gradual change, especially on trade issues but also in economic stabilization. This position was articulated publicly when the Edward group's flagship daily, and Chile's leading conservative newspaper, *El Mercurio*, backed the gradualist approach in early policy debates before the military government decreed gradual economic reform.[6] As will be seen in following chapters, the BHC conglomerate was led by men who would forcefully advocate radical restructuring.

A closer examination of the Edwards conglomerate-linked members of the Monday Club illustrates the dominance of gradualist predilections. Orlando Sáenz, who was on the board of directors of a leading Edwards group company, was also the president of the SFF. As mentioned in the previous chapter, he was the architect of business mobilization against Allende. Given that the industrial sector was accustomed to protection and a regulated economy, the SFF could support gradual reforms but not drastic restructuring in which many member firms would perish. Since two of the other members of the Monday Club linked to the Edwards conglomerate controlled important news media—one edited *El Mercurio* and the other owned the conservative news weekly *Qué Pasa*—the Monday Club possessed a powerful tool for shaping public opinion.[7]

TABLE 4.1 The Monday Club and Conglomerates

| Name | Conglomerate Affiliation | Media Executive | Economics Degree from U. of Chicago |
|------|--------------------------|-----------------|-------------------------------------|
| H. Cubillos | Edwards | | |
| Jorge Ross | Edwards | | |
| R. Silva E. | Edwards | x | |
| O. Sáenz[a] | Edwards | | |
| E. Sanfuentes | Edwards | x | x |
| Javier Vial | BHC | | |
| M. Cruzat | BHC | | x |

[a]Also President of the SFF.

*Sources:* Philip O'Brien, *The Pinochet Decade* (London: Latin American Bureau, 1983); Fernando Dahse, *El mapa de la extrema riqueza* (Editorial Aconcagua, 1979); annual company reports of conglomerate firms.

Viewed this way, the Monday Club was a complex microcosm of forces. As will be seen in the next chapters, it harbored economic interests that vied for dominance later. Immediately after the coup, however, there was an uneasy alliance in the gradualist coalition's power bloc that was dominated by internationally competitive producers for domestic markets and supported by internationally oriented sectors.

The economic composition of the conglomerates represented by Monday Club members helps to explain why some supported gradualism and others harbored more radical tendencies. If a conglomerate was linked to industrial sectors producing for domestic markets to what degree could it be internationally competitive? Or, in contrast, did the conglomerate's activities focus on production for international markets (mining, fishing, logging) or liquid-asset sectors such as banking, insurance, real estate, and commerce (see Table 4.2)? These factors reveal the link between economic interest and policy stance. Differences among the conglomerates were a matter of degree. Many of them controlled firms that produced both for the domestic and international markets in fixed and liquid-asset sectors, but the bulk of a conglomerate's activities was weighted in one direction or another.[8] As it turned out, the top well-established, traditional conglomerates that could compete with imports dominated the gradualist coalition. Newer, internationally oriented economic groups—internationalist conglomerates— occupied a subordinate position.

In 1970, the Edwards group and a few others like it (Matte and Lúksic) could be classified as industrial conglomerates oriented toward domestic

TABLE 4.2 Major Traditional and Internationalist Conglomerates in 1970: Concentration of Companies by Economic Activity (Percent)

| Conglomerate | Total Companies | Fixed-Asset Domestic Market Oriented Internat'lly Noncompetive Sectors[a] | Fixed-Asset Domestic Market Oriented Internat'lly Competitive Sectors | Fixed-Asset Primary Product Export Sector | International Commerce Sector | Liquid-Asset Sectors | Total in Fixed-Asset Domestic Market Oriented Sectors | Total in Liquid-Asset, Internat'lly Oriented & Speculative Sectors |
|---|---|---|---|---|---|---|---|---|
| Traditional | | | | | | | | |
| Edwards | 30 | 6.6 | 33.3 | 6.6 | 6.6 | 33.3 | 43.2[b] | 56.5[c] |
| Matte | 26 | 34.5 | 19.2 | 7.6 | 15.3 | 19.2 | 53.7[b] | 45.9[c] |
| Lüksic | 16 | 25.0 | 43.7 | 24.6 | 6.2 | – | 68.7 | 31.1 |
| Yarur-Bana | 7 | 43.0 | – | – | – | 57.0 | 43.0 | 57.0 |
| Briones | 5 | 80.0 | 20.0 | – | – | – | 100.0 | – |
| Lepe | 4 | 50.0 | 50.0 | – | – | – | 100.0 | – |
| International | | | | | | | | |
| BHC (1970) | 27 | 14.8 | 14.8 | 11.1 | 3.7 | 51.8 | 29.6 | 70.3[c] |
| BHC (1974) | 18 | 16.7 | 5.5 | 11.0 | – | 66.7 | 22.2 | 77.7 |
| Cruzat-Larraín (1974) | 11 | 9.0 | 27.2 | 36.4 | – | 27.2 | 36.2 | 63.6 |
| Menéndez | 8 | – | – | 25.0 | 62.5 | 12.5 | – | 100.0 |
| Angelini | 4 | – | – | 75.0 | 25.0 | – | – | 100.0 |

[a]Competitiveness was established by industrial sector, not by individual firm; the criteria were taken from Guillermo Campero and José Valenzuela, El movimiento sindical an el régimen militar chileno (Santiago: ILET, 1984).

[b]The difference is made up by investment in agricultural production for domestic markets.

[c]The difference is made up by investments in financial-sector related real estate, a highly speculative activity.

Source: Fernando Dahse, El mapa de la extrema riqueza (Santiago: Editorial Aconcagua, 1979).

markets but competitive internationally. These traditional, well-established conglomerates could adjust to a gradual opening to external competition with relative ease. Although roughly half of the companies controlled by the Edwards group were in the industrial or fixed-asset sectors, they were mostly in the food processing, beverage, and printing industries—all capable of competing with imports. The other half of its companies were in liquid-asset sectors (banking, insurance, and real estate), further easing the conglomerate's ability to adjust to gradual change.[9]

Internationalist conglomerates such as BHC were qualitatively different. They tended to concentrate in liquid-asset sectors such as finance and trade and in primary product export industries, with a third or less of their firms in manufacturing for domestic markets. In 1974, fully two-thirds of BHC's 18 companies were in banking, investment, and insurance and another tenth were in trading firms. Only about a fifth were in sectors that produced for domestic markets (mostly in internationally uncompetitive industries). In accordance with Jeffry Frieden's observations, the BHC group's liquid-assets made it relatively easy to adjust to rapid trade liberalization compared to most traditional conglomerates. A more rapid opening to external trade provided a vehicle for conglomerate expansion at the expense of other economic groups.[10] Key backers of radical neoliberalism, both in the Monday Club and later, were linked to the BHC conglomerate and its 1974 spin-off, the Cruzat-Larraín group.[11] The fact that its leaders were subordinate to Edwards group members in the Monday Club helps to explain why the gradual approach prevailed.[12]

*The Brick.* What were the links between the Monday Club, the military, and the establishment of a post-coup policy agenda? While preparing the coup d'etat, the military conspirators, especially the navy, developed close ties with Monday Club members. Navy officials tapped Roberto Kelly, a retired navy captain with intimate connections to the Edwards group (and hence to the Monday Club) to inform the private sector of the military's need for an economic program in the event of a coup d'etat. The business conspirators put together a team to design an economic plan that went to work in March 1973.[13] The SFF's economic department coordinated the effort and code named it the Brick (*El Ladrillo*).[14]

The Brick set an agenda for economic restructuring upon which the forces within the Monday Club and the larger coup coalition could agree. These included conglomerate heads, the leadership of the SFF, and probably the CPC (through Jorge Fontaine who was very close to Orlando Sáenz). The Monday Club also invited Christian Democratic economists to participate in order to make the effort more representative of the larger coup coalition. All participants supported the opening of Chilean markets to international competition as a first step toward export-led economic growth.

They welcomed the privatization of firms taken over by Unidad Popular as well as other parts of the public sector. They wanted to reduce inflation largely by liberating prices and freezing wages and salaries. They sought to build more extensive private capital markets.[15] The PDC economists tried to mediate labor and middle-class interests on three fronts. They exacted a commitment to a basic level of social welfare expenditures, they sought to preserve key aspects of agrarian reform, and they promoted their favorite form of ownership: cooperatives.[16]

The Brick advanced a policy agenda that reflected the interests of the major actors of the coup coalition because its authors represented the various components of the broad-based alliance against Allende. Table 4.3 shows that of the ten men who met regularly to create the Brick six were businessmen; three from the Edwards group and three from the BHC group. Two of these six were also members of the National party (PN). Of the two PN members, the one from the BHC group was a member of the SNA's council; while the one linked to the Edwards group was the director of the SFF's economic department. The remaining four individuals were economists who belonged to the Christian Democratic party and had held important positions in the Central Bank during the Frei administration.[17] Within the Brick they were subordinate, reflecting the secondary role to which the PDC had been relegated in the larger coup coalition. The businessmen who controlled the Monday Club and the Brick did not trust the Christian Democrats who they blamed for Allende's victory.[18]

Table 4.3 highlights the remarkable connecting factor shared by eight out of ten of the Brick's authors: master's degrees in economics from the University of Chicago. Most analyses focus on this factor, which cut across conglomerate, political party, and business association membership lines, to conclude that radical neoliberal reform in Chile originated with the Brick. But this was not the case. The Brick's overall policy prescriptions were broader than what the ideological zealotry of the radical monetarists among its authors allowed for. Why was this?

In general, the Chicago boys (radical or not) who participated in formulating the Brick shared an interest in unfettered internal markets and the free flow of international commerce. But they were divided over the desired degree and speed of deregulation. To some extent, individuals were probably influenced by which conglomerate employed them: the internationalist (radical) BHC or the internationally competitive (gradualist) Edwards. Yet at least one of the Chicago boys employed by the Edwards group was quite radical. This meant that the economic ideology of approximately half of the ten led them to prefer radical to gradual restructuring.[19] Thus, the question remains, why did the central recommendations of the Brick not more closely reflect their ideological predilections?

TABLE 4.3 El Ladrillo: Member Curriculum

| Name | Conglomerate Affiliation | Political Party Affiliation | Prior Gov't Service | Economics Degree from U. of Chicago |
|---|---|---|---|---|
| E. Undurraga[a] | Edwards | PN | | |
| E. Sanfuentes | Edwards | | | x |
| S. de Castro | Edwards | | | x |
| M. Cruzat | BHC | | | x |
| J. Braun | BHC | | | |
| P. Baraona[b] | BHC | PN | | x |
| A. Bardón | | PDC | C. Bank | x |
| A. Sanfuentes | | PDC | C. Bank | x |
| J.L. Zabala | | PDC | C. Bank | x |
| J. Villarzú | | PDC | C. Bank | x |

[a] Also in SFF; [b] also in SNA.

*Sources:* Arturo Fontaine, *Los economistas y el Presidente Pinochet* (Santiago: Editora Zig-Zag, 1988); Philip O'Brien, *The Pinochet Decade* (London: Latin American Bureau, 1983); Fernando Dahse, *El mapa de la extrema riqueza* (Santiago: Editorial Aconcagua, 1979); annual company reports of conglomerate firms.

Although radical elements figured prominently in the economic team that designed the Brick, and the ideology imparted by their training colored their recommendations, the plan itself reflected the broader interests of the anti-Allende coalition. The leaders of the coalition were the ones who controlled the process; the Chicago boys were their subordinates. Moreover, most of the Christian Democrat economists, in spite of their academic training, did not adhere to the radical version of neoclassical economics. They decidedly favored the gradual model that their party had proposed in the late 1960s. The Brick was a blueprint for restructuring the Chilean economy upon which the members of the Monday Club, the leadership of the SFF and the CPC, and the Christian Democrats could agree. It set an agenda without specifying degree of implementation or timetables.[20] As a result, the questions of how much restructuring and how fast dominated the policy debates in the first months after the coup.[21] Therefore, economic restructuring was not set on an irrevocably draconian course from the beginning. On the contrary, radical internationalists were held in check within the Monday Club, within the larger coup coalition, and even within the economic team that fashioned the Brick itself. That the radical option prevailed later depended on factors other than the ideology of a faction of the Brick's designers and the authoritarian nature of the new regime.

### Post-Coup Expansion of the Gradualist Coalition

The Monday Club and the Brick team were the forerunners of a coalition in favor of significant, but gradually applied, economic reform. Nevertheless, forces within those two nuclei chafed to apply more radical measures; although important business groups outside of them probably preferred a return to the status quo ante. The core economic interests that favored gradualism in the pre-coup period managed to expand their base of support after the coup but before the government's announcement of gradual restructuring in January 1974. The policy debates immediately after the coup—especially those related to protection—revealed that business and landowning peak associations, in addition to several other powerful conglomerates, favored the gradual option. As a result, the groups that backed other solutions found few politically significant social allies for their projects in the early post-coup period.

The CPC's support for the gradual approach helped legitimize it because the CPC was the encompassing organization of large-scale business and landowning interests; this provided the broadest possible upper-class seal of approval. A month after the coup, CPC president Jorge Fontaine said, "We are in the process of preparing studies and plans that we will soon make public; we are quite clear about what needs to be done to initiate national recovery."[22] Those "plans" were a gradual application of the policy prescriptions outlined in the Brick. The significance of the CPC position was that since the Confederación was an encompassing organization, it advocated policies reflecting a consensus arrived at by its member organizations, the sectoral peak associations. The CPC's board of directors consisted of the presidents and vice presidents of the sectoral organizations.

The CPC did not throw its official weight behind the gradualist approach until after the sectoral peak associations had ironed out their differences on broad policy issues at CPC summit meetings.[23] In those discussions most of the producer peak associations supported gradual adjustment, including tariff reductions. Backing for continued high protection was scant and largely confined to the subsector associations of manufacturers for domestic markets that could not compete with imports—metals, electronics, and textiles. The fact that the SFF joined the landowner's peak association (the SNA) in support of a gradual reduction of tariffs underscored the isolation of those who wished for a return to the status quo ante. Mine owners (SONAMI), the large-scale commercial sector (the CCC), and the Construction Chamber (the CChC) also supported gradual tariff reductions. With the exception of the SFF, all of these organizations welcomed the change in tariff policy because they eagerly awaited an increased share of national wealth once Chile restructured its economy along its international comparative advantages.[24]

Landowners were the most explicitly in favor of tariff reductions of all of the peak organizations. The SNA considered that protectionism had discriminated against agriculture for 30 years by decapitalizing the sector and by making it pay dearly for imported capital inputs, although prices for their products had been kept artificially low to satisfy industry's need for cheap food for its labor force.[25] Nevertheless, a sizeable proportion of the SNA's leadership produced traditional crops such as grains, cereals, and dairy products that required a certain amount of protection from international competition. The support of these producers for gradual tariff reduction was not inconsistent with their economic interest. The SNA wanted protection; it simply favored a different policy instrument. In November 1973, the SNA made it clear that it wanted price floors and ceilings for traditional products, reiterating its position at a CPC summit meeting in May 1974.[26]

The internationally oriented mining and large-scale commerce sectors (SONAMI and the CCC) also advocated gradual tariff reduction. After the military coup, the CCC reported that it had collaborated extensively with the CPC and government authorities in the search for tariff structure reform, which the CCC wholeheartedly supported. The Cámara Central de Comercio also went on record advocating a gradual approach to controlling inflation.[27] Meanwhile, SONAMI, greatly weakened as an organization due to the nationalization of the foreign-owned copper mines, also favored gradual tariff reductions. SONAMI believed tariff reductions would lead to increased investment in mining and hoped they would reorient industrial production more efficiently. From the mining industry's perspective, it was more efficient for industry to link production to the mining sectors' needs than to manufacture automobiles and electronics.[28]

The peak association of the industrial sector—the SFF—joined the others in support of gradual tariff reduction, although not enthusiastically. The SFF noted that even before 1970 Chile's development model had run into serious difficulty. Thus, Chile needed a new socio-economic model— a social market economy—to overcome the system-wide crisis that had engulfed it. The SFF accepted that the success of the new model required the elimination of economic activities rendered unprofitable by free markets. But it advocated a gradual phasing out that would give those affected time to adjust.[29]

In addition to business peak associations, many internationally competitive conglomerates with heavy investments in fixed assets also backed a gradual policy of economic restructuring. The Edwards economic group—dominant in the Monday Club and involved in the Brick—was the most visible because it owned *El Mercurio*. Between October 1973 and January 1974, *El Mercurio* called for gradual tariff reductions.[30] Similar conglomerates, such as the Matte and Lúksic groups, supported gradualism, albeit less publicly.[31] Together, these three conglomerates accounted for some of the most powerful and prestigious economic groups in Chile. They had the economic resources to adjust and modernize. Their flagship firms were solid institutions with long-standing relationships to foreign suppliers who were willing to extend the necessary credit once they regained control over their nationalized banks.

Given their silence in policy debates, internationally oriented fixed and liquid-asset conglomerates at least tacitly supported gradualism at this stage. Although some of their directors may have preferred more far-reaching changes, gradual economic restructuring was an advance over the previous policies. In the meantime, they could fortify themselves in order to advance more radical policy proposals in the future. They set up the first private-sector financial firms and consolidated their holdings in sectors of the economy that were either competitive with imports or that had an international comparative advantage.[32]

Overall, then, the immediate post-coup period witnessed a dramatic expansion of business and landowner support for a gradual approach to free market restructuring. The coalition now included all of the large-scale sectors of organized business and, with the inclusion of additional conglomerates, a substantial proportion of Chile's largest firms. As a result, business groups that preferred other options initially found themselves with few partners with which to pursue them. The gradualist coalition was a loose amalgam of different actors without a centralized locus or hierarchical organization and, often, with quite distinctive agendas. The size of the coalition, however, was a factor that hindered the advance of challengers immediately after the coup.

## The SFF and Its Policy Reversal

Although most of the producer peak associations, and the SNA in particular, had long wanted tariff reductions in order to end discrimination against their sectors, the position of the SFF was a major change. As seen in Chapter 3, during the Alessandri and Frei administrations the SFF had resisted all attempts at gradual opening. Why, then, did it offer only weak resistance in 1974 and 1975? Put differently, how did the internationally competitive wing of the SFF wrestle control away from the internationally noncompetitive faction? This issue is one of the main unexplained puzzles of business' political behavior during this period. After responding to these questions, the discussion shifts to how regime structure accorded disproportionate power to the gradualist coalition over the supporters of continued high protection and those who favored more radical economic change.

## International Economic Change

External factors partially explain the sudden weakening of internationally noncompetitive fixed-asset producers in the SFF. ISI policies typically caused foreign exchange bottlenecks. Chile, like other Latin American countries, was essentially a monocrop exporter with copper accounting for over 75 percent of foreign exchange earnings. Import-substitution policies required very high hard currency outlays for intermediate and capital inputs. Moreover, food imports for urban workers further strained foreign accounts. In the latter part of the 1960s, this situation had prompted the Frei administration to promote export diversification and gradual tariff reform within the framework of the Andean Common Market.[33]

In 1973, rising oil prices and a drastic decline in bilateral and multilateral aid to Chile drove the government to seek additional sources of foreign exchange by diversifying its exports.[34] Between 1973 and 1974 oil prices quadrupled, and Chile depended on imported oil for over 50 percent of its petroleum requirements. Multilateral lending banks, especially the International Monetary Fund (IMF), did not respond to the dramatic increase in the need for foreign capital. According to one estimate, the IMF provided financing for barely three percent of developing nations' current account deficits after the oil crisis began.[35]

Internationally noncompetitive industrialists were weakened because the state could no longer afford to provide high protective barriers for manufactures. In countries with small internal markets import substitution seemed to have reached its limits. By itself it could no longer fuel economic growth. On the contrary, it reinforced stagnation, drained hard currency, and fueled balance of payments deficits.[36] Consequently, if the exhaustion of the ISI development model had contributed to Chile's social and political crisis, then the nation could hardly expect to continue with it.[37] Orlando Sáenz, president of the SFF, said as much in a speech in early 1974.[38]

Chile's balance of payments crisis, inherited from the Allende government, further debilitated protectionist interests and compounded the effects of structural changes in international trade and finance. In September of 1973, foreign exchange reserves had fallen from a surplus of 350 million dollars in 1970 to a deficit of 600 million dollars. The foreign debt also surged by 800 million dollars.[39] Exclusive reliance on import substitution to save foreign exchange was no longer a viable option.

In addition, the consolidation and growth of international trade and finance strengthened internationalists in finance, trade, and agro-export products. Just as the collapse of international trade and finance had brought the ISI coalition of industry and labor together in the 1930s, the rebirth of international trade in the 1960s and 1970s placed internationalists in a much better position to advance their interests. They gained greater freedom and more resources with which to do business.[40] The expansion of the international financial interests that lubricated international trade placed Chilean financiers, especially those with international connections, in a highly privileged position *vis-à-vis* other economic sectors.[41]

Between 1965 and 1975, then, a number of international factors forced Chilean manufacturers for domestic markets—the dominant business group in the old ISI coalition—to consider the need for economic adjustment seriously. Those factors included the decline in multilateral and U.S. government loans, the corresponding increase in international bank lending, the explosive growth of international finance, and the oil crisis. A large portion of internationally uncompetitive industries—especially in metalworking, electronics, and textiles—became a net drain on dwindling hard currency reserves. By the same token, given the boom in international trade, a gradual reduction of tariff barriers and regional competition allowed internationally competitive industries to adjust. But, because manufacturers were still dominant among the bourgeoisie, industrial development remained Chile's primary goal.[42] This reinforced the preference for gradual over radical adjustment, which would have favored liquid assets and agro-extractive exports. Nevertheless, it was hoped that the promotion of nontraditional exports, and the liberalization of capital markets would provide a net receipt of dollars for Chile.

### Domestic Factors

The aggravation of international trends that began in the mid-1960s no doubt contributed to the SFF's support for gradual adjustment. Those trends, however, were already evident in the late 1960s, a time when the SFF was successfully blocking attempts at gradual tariff reductions. The shift in the SFF's position between 1969 and 1973, then, is only partially explained by gradual international changes. Domestic factors were also at work. One such factor was the reaction of Chilean property owners to Unidad Popular's socialist policies. Many industrialists and other business groups were induced to accept more liberal positions than they had in the past in order to reverse Unidad Popular policies, especially the extensive nationalizations.[43]

Although this change in outlook colored the perceptions of the Chilean bourgeoisie, three other factors carried much more weight. First, Allende's nationalization policy had weakened industrialists economically and diverted attention from tariff policy. Nationalization had hit the manufacturing sector the hardest, and after the coup many businessmen spent most of their time negotiating their recovery. Physical control of firms, however, was not their only concern. Once they regained ownership, they had to get their companies back into shape. They needed to replace machinery, hire new personnel, and obtain operating capital in a country with no private capital markets and few government funds. Given these preoccupations, many industrialists simply assumed that tariff reform was not a serious threat to them. They believed that with a little effort they would be able to muster enough support among the authorities and the military to stop any serious lowering of protection. They miscalculated.[44]

Second, the change from a democratic to an authoritarian regime had an even greater impact on the internal balance of power in the SFF. Regime change unleashed sectoral conflicts between the SFF and all the other business and landowning sectors that had long sought to reduce tariffs to increase investment in their sectors. In the democratic period, manufacturers for domestic markets had tacitly relied on a non-business coalitional partner—organized labor—that had benefitted from increased employment. According to a former finance minister from the Frei administration, the SFF also staved off government-sponsored tariff reform by threatening to incite labor unrest.[45] But the Allende experience, and the labor repression that followed, destroyed those relationships. Thus, in the new context of more or less unmediated relations with the state, the SFF found itself both bereft of allies against other capitalist and landowning sectors and with reduced economic power due to the nationalizations. Under these circumstances, the SFF had to compromise with other sectors that wanted to reduce protection.

Moreover, the policy process that emerged after the coup shifted influence from the individual sectoral peak associations to the CPC, reinforcing the SFF's need to negotiate and compromise. In the new regime, business and agricultural leaders dealt directly with the corresponding economic authorities in government. If these did not respond, they went to the junta in the hopes that the military leaders—the real power holders— would instruct their ministers to change a given policy. In the absence of formal, regular, and institutionalized channels of communication between peak associations and government, businessmen had to make appointments every time they wished to discuss a topic. They frequently resorted to the use of memoranda in an effort to communicate with government officials.[46]

The preferences of individual peak associations carried less weight than the combined position of business and agriculture expressed through the CPC. Both the junta and government policymakers, convinced of the need for thoroughgoing economic and political change, could more or less isolate themselves from the particularistic demands of individual business associations, such as the SFF.[47] As it turned out, only industry subsectors that represented noncompetitive manufacturers resisted gradual tariff reductions. They were even easier to ignore because they got little publicity as isolated subsectors within the SFF, which—along with other sectoral peak associations—supported gradual decreases in protectionism.

An exchange of memoranda between the SFF and the ministries of finance and economy between July and November of 1974 illustrates the point. In June of 1974, the Ministry of Finance created the Comité Asesor de Política Arancelaria (CAPA). As a dependency of the Central Bank, it was charged with working out a tariff reduction schedule in accord with the goals set in January, an average tariff of about 60 percent. The CAPA gave industry subsectors a channel through which to suggest a program suitable to their needs; that is, a means to influence policy implementation.

In July 1974, the Electronics Industry Association, an SFF affiliate, sent a memorandum to Minister of Finance Jorge Cauas. In the memo, the association affirmed its support for the government's economic program, including tariff reductions. However, faced with what it called a sudden, violent reduction in protection for televisions from about an average of 130 percent to 90 percent in the recent past, the Electronics Association suggested that 110 percent was much more compatible with an orderly restructuring of operations. The memo added, that if the government did not accede to this petition it might be held responsible for creating unemployment in the northern city of Arica where most of the industry was located. Enzo Bolocco, the Electronics Association president, signed the cover letter.[48]

They either got no reply or an unsatisfactory one. In November, the SFF fired off two memoranda in quick succession to Undersecretary of the Ministry of Economy Sergio de Castro. It reiterated most of the points made in July. These SFF memos, however, did not carry the full weight of the SFF because they were only signed by the chairman of the Tariff Policy Committee, Enzo Bolocco.[49]

Later that month, the issue erupted within the CAPA. Most of the government delegates to the CAPA argued that the electronics industry was crying wolf; in their view, proposed tariff reductions would not destroy the industry. Less protection, however, would force some firms to forego profits and to restructure more quickly. The Confederación de la Producción y Comercio's private sector representative to the CAPA suggested a compromise: that the average tariff for televisions be set at 100 percent rather than 90 percent.[50] If the electronics industry received any satisfaction at this time it was short-lived. Seven months later a more drastic and swifter tariff schedule went into effect. Most of the electronics industry went under.[51]

Third, the varied economic interests of the SFF's leadership, combined with its isolation in the CPC, constituted another reason why the SFF accepted a gradual reduction in protectionism. The majority of the elected members of the SFF either worked in internationally competitive firms or had multiple economic interests. The burden of adjustment was more manageable for them. Between 1973 and 1974, of a total of 31 elected members, 16 were linked to internationally noncompetitive activities (metals, textiles, electronics, and chemicals). However, 12 of those 16 also had interests in competitive sectors (mostly food processing) that mitigated their need to give vigorous support to existing levels of protection. Furthermore, six had interests in commerce, finance, and agriculture; four were executives of firms controlled by the BHC internationalist conglomerate, which had a high concentration of firms in liquid assets; and two worked for MNCs. Manufacturers for domestic markets with economic interests firmly planted in internationally uncompetitive sectors were a minority within the SFF. Their complaints and demands lacked clout. Even when the issue of retaining high levels of protection got on the agenda of the SFF's general council, it was voted down.[52] Faced with a social and institutional conflict where the SFF had little support or capacity for defense, the majority of its members fell back on their second best option: Their capacity to adjust.

### Regime Structure, Gradualists, and Policymaking

So far, this chapter has concentrated on establishing the existence of a broad coalition of capitalist and landowning interests in favor of gradual adjustment. The gradualist coalition favored an economic development strategy that remained strongly focused on industrialization because internationally competitive industrialists producing for domestic markets dominated it. It included industrialists in fixed-asset sectors (fishing, mining, and processed agro-exports). Internationalists with a heavy concentration in liquid assets occupied a subordinate position within the coalition; their preference for deeper, more rapid reform was a source of tension within the coalition. In the period immediately before and after the coup, the supporters of gradual change—which included the top executives of some of Chile's most powerful conglomerates and the leadership of business peak associations—shaped the agenda-setting, formulation, and implementation stages of the policy process.

A crucial question, however, remains. Why did gradualists and not radical neoliberals or supporters of the status quo ante dominate policymaking, and how did different components of the coalition influence policy outcomes? The answer is that a bias in the structure of the authoritarian regime favored gradualists and permitted them to use government appointments and access to "friendly" policymakers to influence policy formulation.

Studies on the effect of regime structure on the power of social groups have shown that authoritarian regimes often exclude or control the organizations of the masses but give preferential treatment to capitalists and landowners. In authoritarian regimes, the upper classes naturally seek to penetrate decision-making circles and authoritarian rulers often provide them with formal channels of access to the policymaking process on boards, commissions, and planning committees and also via informal channels. Prominent capitalists and landowners are frequently appointed to ministerial positions. Thus, some private interests outside of the government find that they have the ear of sympathetic policymakers in the government.[53]

Although the bargaining that ensues may resemble the lobbying that takes place in polyarchies, there are crucial differences. A two-way relationship between peak associations and the regime is pivotal. The peak associations seek to influence public policy; once the business leadership and government officials agree on a policy, the associations are used to control the membership and keep the "rank and file" in line.[54]

Another contrast with lobbying in pluralist systems is that the authoritarian rulers, rather than the organizations, may decide who participates. As a result, the quality of representation is affected, but representation occurs nonetheless. When authoritarian regimes appoint members of the bourgeoisie to important positions in government they are not selected at random.[55] They can be chosen for their loyalty, for their success in particular economic activities, or both. When appointees are picked for their economic significance, they represent the business community at large that shares similar interests. The regime may target a given sector through such appointments to garner crucial support for a particular policy. Such a system of interest representation can degenerate into patrimonialism and corruption, as was the case in some Central American countries.[56] But although a system of representation based on peers selected and appointed by authoritarian rulers is not as genuine as it may be in democracy, it may be considered a midpoint between full representation and patrimonialism, at least for the upper classes.

"Representation" is used here to describe a function of particular capitalists and landowners who are highly representative of the economic sectors and subsectors they belong to. Representatives are understood to represent the interests of their social group and not necessarily act purely on a personal and corrupt basis even though their peers have not selected them. This particular style of representation is at its strongest when newly appointed businessmen-cum-policymakers belong to private sector forces that defined the basic policy agenda before the new economic authorities took office. In short, government appointments elevate elements of the capitalist policy coalition to positions of power and authority within the state apparatus. The members of the coalition left in civil society establish specific modes of interaction with them in the policy process. They may participate in policy formulation or implementation, or they may act as significant support groups for the general policy agenda.

## *Appointments, "Representation," Power, and Policymaking*

One of the principal features of the post-coup policy process in Chile was the unmediated relationship between social groups and the state. It favored the supporters of gradual adjustment because the military appointed persons who represented their policy stances to key economic ministries and advisory positions. As a result of those appointments, the supporters of gradual adjustment among the bourgeoisie found sympathetic counterparts at the highest level of government. Consequently, in the new authoritarian regime direct access to military and civilian power holders privileged gradualists over other groups that did not enjoy similar connections.

The distribution of civilians in top economic policymaking positions corresponded closely to the composition of the civilian anti-Allende coalition, in which gradualists were dominant. Representatives of the interests of internationally competitive but domestic market-oriented conglomerates occupied the most important ministerial positions. Subordinate to them, the radical Chicago boys—close allies of the internationalist conglomerates— became important advisors in the Ministry of Economics and ODEPLAN, the planning ministry. The ministers who supported gradual adjustment checked the ambitions of the more radical Chicago boys during this period. Meanwhile, the relatively less important offices and ranks to which Christian Democrats were appointed reflected the PDC's precarious position in the coalition and the anti-political party stance of the military and business.

Prosopographical data on the junta's first high-level appointments strongly support the conclusion that the military initially favored business groups that backed gradual economic restructuring. In October 1973, the junta made Fernando Léniz minister of economy and named Raúl Sáez to head the military government's civilian economic advisory team. Léniz was a prominent businessman with close ties to the Edwards and Matte conglomerates; both of which were internationally competitive conglomerates that ranked among the oldest and most powerful in the country. Sáez, well known within ISI business circles, had been one of the first directors of CORFO, the holding company for state enterprise, which also financed joint ventures and purely private enterprises. Other appointments indicated a similar trend. Orlando Sáenz, president of the SFF, became coordinator for the team that handled the renegotiation of Chile's foreign debt. Roberto Kelly, who had close ties to the Edwards conglomerate, became head of ODEPLAN, the government planning agency.

A number of other ministries, such as finance and agriculture, remained under military control.

In addition to these appointments, the military also approached former members of the Monday Club (again through Roberto Kelly) seeking recommendations for civilian economic advisors. Kelly drew up a list of names with the help of Orlando Sáenz and Sergio Undurraga. At the time, Orlando Sáenz was on the board of directors of Edwards group companies, was a Monday Club regular, and was president of the SFF. Sergio Undurraga, also on the board of Edwards group firms, was the director of the SFF's economics department and was one of the framers of the Brick. Not surprisingly, Sáenz and Undurraga recommended the architects of the Brick who then were made key advisors to civilian and military ministers of state. Of these men, the more radical economists went to the Ministry of Economy. Christian Democrats advised the president of the Central Bank and directed the budgetary agency. Sergio Undurraga himself became advisor to the navy official heading the Ministry of Finance.[57]

The appointment of gradualists—who tended to be businessmen without significant links to business organizations—gave the leaders of the business and landowner peak associations, who also favored the gradual approach, congenial counterparts in government with whom to interact in the policy process. Whenever they chose, the leadership of the business peak associations could hold meetings with ministers, undersecretaries, and top military personnel.[58] Their access enabled them to participate in both policy formulation and implementation. These privileges notwithstanding, their role in policy formulation tended to be ancillary to that of the government policymakers. Their role in the design of policy implementation, however, was stronger. According to prominent participants of the period, such as Orlando Sáenz (SFF) and Manuel Valdés (CPC), this interaction greatly minimized disagreements between the business associations and the policymakers.[59]

The interaction usually consisted of sectoral peak associations approaching policymakers to give their input on the formulation or implementation of policies that most affected their individual sectors. For example, in November 1973, the SNA reported to its members, "Our leadership has met many times with the minister of agriculture and the director of its planning agency. During those meetings we have detailed our positions on a number of issues."[60] The SNA's requests included free markets in land sales, price freedom for agricultural products, pre-announced price supports for crops, and liberalized agricultural exports and imports. Similarly, the SFF held repeated meetings with Minister of Economy Fernando Léniz on the privatization of firms taken over by Unidad Popular.[61] The CCC (large-scale commerce) convened with government authorities over tax structure.[62] Thus, to the extent that they could, producer peak associations continued to perform their traditional tasks. They resolved intrasectoral conflicts, which allowed them to approach government officials with unified policy positions. They also advanced special sectoral interests. Moreover, their members had long-standing connections to government and were well acquainted with their operating procedures.

For their part, the ministries were very receptive to businessmen. Business leaders persuaded the junta to appoint an economic coordinator to iron out difficulties in policy implementation. The junta asked Colonel Gastón Frez, who had close business ties to the Edwards group, to meet with the CPC leadership on a weekly basis.[63] Moreover, during the first months after the coup, the Ministry of Economy had an open-door policy for top business leaders concerned about privatization policy. Business leaders frequently sent delegations to the ministry with some petition or another. Although these petitions were not always granted, businessmen usually did not leave empty-handed either. In the main, business leaders wanted an orderly return of their property in order to avoid a reconcentration of wealth in the hands of competitors. They found the minister most receptive to this approach.[64]

Although not significantly involved in the policy process itself, the Confederación de la Producción y Comercio nevertheless played a vital role within the gradualist coalition and assured that gradual economic reform prevailed over other options. It convened the Second Convention of the CPC in December 1973, where it provided crucial support to gradualists in and out of government. The leadership of the individual peak associations used the CPC to publicize what they had already agreed on in private, that organized business supported a gradual approach to the economic reform measures set forth in the Brick. The convention, however, was also for the "rank and file" of the business organizations. It offered symposia on the Brick's proposals, suggesting that the business leadership also used the convention to build greater support for gradualism in the larger business community.[65] Finally, the CPC held the convention in the Diego Portales—which housed most government ministries at the time—symbolizing the unity of purpose between the policymakers of the military government and organized business.

The timing of the convention was also part of the business leadership's strategy to lobby for a gradual approach to economic restructuring. The convention closed on the eve of an important high-level government meeting to plan economic strategy. As if to dramatize the close connection between government and the private sector, on the last day of the convention the CPC leadership held a closed-door, all-day conference with top government authorities. Before the meeting, business leaders and government officials had already agreed on the main policy objectives: privatization, price deregulation, agile capital markets, devaluation, deflation, and tariff reform. It was during the meeting that business leaders pressed for gradual implementation of policies, especially the deregulation of financial markets and tariffs and anti-inflation measures.[66]

Although the CPC and the sectoral peak associations were not directly involved in policy formulation, they generated significant support for gradualism from outside of the state. Foreshadowing deeper labor repression (which came after the PDC's ouster from the gradual coalition) and revealing capital's lack of commitment to social equity questions, business leaders sharply criticized a key component of the government's "social development" policy: a labor co-management plan sponsored by Christian Democrats and their sympathizers in the armed forces, especially the air force. Businessmen adopted a tactic of noncompliance to defeat the plan. To justify their foot dragging, they loudly complained about impractical implementation guidelines. Their strategy worked.[67]

In conclusion, regime structure favored groups that supported gradual adjustment. Men with close ties to internationally competitive conglomerates—those with the most interest in gradual adjustment—headed key economic ministries. The peak associations of business and landowners had privileged access to key policymaking institutions. Other societal actors occupied subordinate positions within the new post-coup policy coalition. The Chicago boys—allies of the internationalist conglomerates based on an affinity of ideology and economic interest—held second-rank positions within the top economic ministries. These groups acknowledged their subordinate position, the outspokenness of their more flamboyant members notwithstanding.[68]

### Conclusion: Capitalists, the State, and Gradual Reform

The disaggregation of capitalists and landowners, and the examination of the policy preferences of business actors outside of business associations as well as within them, revealed that most of the Chilean bourgeoisie initially supported a gradual policy of economic restructuring. Executives of internationally competitive but domestic market-oriented conglomerates and the leadership of Chile's peak associations agreed on the need for both broad economic reform and gradual implementation. Christian Democratic technocrats also favored gradualism. The pattern of appointments of civilians to ministries and advisory positions then biased institutional power in favor of the gradualists.

The coalition and its institutional sources of power either checked or isolated business groups that preferred other options, such as more drastic economic reforms or a return to the status quo ante. The directors of internationally oriented firms—and the Chicago boy technocrats linked to them—wanted a more radical approach to economic restructuring, but their subordination to gradualists at the time postponed realization of their aims. Businessmen who wanted policies from the 1950s and 1960s resurrected—principally internationally uncompetitive industrialists who produced for domestic markets—found themselves completely isolated. They had no allies in government and precious few outside of it.

The various elements of this loosely knit, tension-filled policy coalition played different roles in the policymaking process over time depending on the system of interaction between capitalists and the state. During the last year of Allende's government, when there was no real system of interaction, conglomerate heads and technocrats linked to the largest firms, or to political parties, shaped the agenda for reform and formulated early versions of policies to carry out that agenda after the overthrow of Allende. Organized business did not play a significant role here because it was done in secret.

After the coup but before the government announced a gradual approach to economic reform in January 1974, a particular system of interaction between policymakers and businessmen and landowners facilitated the fragile triumph of the gradual option. Prominent businessmen-thinkers with economic interests compatible with gradual economic reform, some related to the core conglomerates of the pre-coup period and some not, continued to formulate policy on the basis of the Brick's recommendations, emphasizing gradual implementation. In addition to representing their own economic interests, these individuals were also representative of broader economic interests. The military chose its appointees because they represented currents of opinion and economic power within business that seemed likely to provide a good base for future economic and political stability. Meanwhile, individual sectoral peak associations performed traditional policymaking roles. In general agreement with the agenda advanced by policymakers, they involved themselves in policy formulation, and especially in the design of policy implementation, to influence the process according to their sector-specific preferences.[69]

Despite its relatively weak role in agenda setting and policy formulation, organized business provided crucial support for the forces within the state that advocated gradualism. The CPC in particular worked to build consensus across business sectors in favor of gradual economic restructuring. It smoothed out policy differences between the different sectors so that a concerted effort by organized business could tip the balance of forces within the government in favor of officials that eschewed the more drastic application of reforms. Within the CPC, the sectoral peak associations formed a policy coalition on the basis of a shared interest in gradual reform, allowing the CPC to perform more effectively as a pressure group on behalf of the conglomerate heads in and out of government who preferred gradualism. Although the CPC was not heavily involved in policy formulation, its support for gradualism diminished the strategic choices of business groups that preferred other options.

In conclusion, effective access and influence in economic policymaking in Chile's new regime was limited to the large-scale producers that participated in the dominant policy coalition. Business subsectors and conglomerates outside of that circle lacked avenues for the redress of their grievances. The effectiveness of the business peak associations in the policy process depended on the capacity of their leadership to find common policy positions and to articulate them to government policymakers who also represented distinctive fractions of capital. Moreover, this policy period revealed that the business peak associations' capacity for concerted action had advanced since the 1950s. The Allende experience had sharpened the class consciousness of capitalists and fortified their capacity for collective action. In the interim, the SFF had greatly strengthened its planning department, developing the capacity to produce well-documented, technically-based policy positions (the Brick was forged in the offices of the SFF's research department). But, as the next chapter reveals, these changes in business association development were insufficient for them to maintain their influence relative to non-association business and landowning actors.

## Notes

1. For this view of peak associations, see Genaro Arriagada, *La oligarquía patronal chilena* (Santiago: Ediciones Nueva Universidad, 1970).

2. For an account of labor's fortunes under the military government, see Guillermo Campero and José A. Valenzuela, *El movimiento sindical en el régimen militar chileno, 1973-1981* (Santiago: ILET, 1984); and Jaime Ruiz-Tagle, *El sindicalismo chileno después del plan laboral* (Santiago: Programa de Economía del Trabajo, 1985).

3. For data on Chilean conglomerates of the period, see Fernando Dahse, "El poder de los grandes grupos empesariales nacionales," *Contribuciones FLACSO*, Santiago, June 1983; Fernando Dahse, *El mapa de la extrema riqueza* (Santiago: Editorial Aconcagua, 1979); Philip O'Brien, *The Pinochet Decade* (London: Latin America Bureau, 1983); Guillermo Sunkel, *El Mercurio: Diez años de educación político-ideológica, 1969-1979* (Santiago: ILET, 1983); and Andrés Sanfuentes, "Los grupos económicos: Control y políticas," *Colección Estudios Cieplan* no. 15, December, 1984.

4. For the Monday Club and the Brick (*El Ladrillo*), see Philip O'Brien, *The Pinochet Decade*; Arturo Fontaine Aldunate, *Los economistas y el Presidente Pinochet* (Santiago: Editorial Zig-Zag 1988); Ascanio Cavallo, Manuel Salazar, and Oscar Sepúlveda, *La historia oculta del régimen militar* (Santiago: Editorial La Epoca, 1988). A version of the document itself was published after the inauguration of the new democratic regime in Chile, see Centro de Estudios Públicos, *"El Ladrillo": Bases de la política económica del gobierno militar chileno* (Santiago: CEP, 1992).

5. Edwards conglomerate company annual reports and Fernando Dahse, *El mapa de la extrema riqueza*.

6. *El Mercurio*, October 26, 1973; December 15, 1973; and January 9, 1974.

7. Edwards group company annual reports for Compañía Cervecerías Unidas (Emiliio Sanfuentes was on the board of directors); Colegio de Periodistas, *Diccionario biográfico de Chile* (Santiago: Editorial Universitaria, selected years); *Qué Pasa* mastheads; Arturo Fontaine, *Los economistas*; Philip O'Brien, *The Pinochet Decade*.

8. Conglomerates were categorized according to the concentration of companies in various economic sectors. Fixed-asset conglomerates producing for domestic markets had about half of their companies in such sectors. Whether they were competitive or not internationally was established by the industrial sector the company was in, not by individual firm performance. The criteria for the international competitiveness of sectors were taken from Guillermo Campero and José Valenzuela, *El movimiento sindical en el régimen militar chileno* (Santiago: ILET, 1984). By contrast, internationalist conglomerates had about two thirds or more of their companies distributed between sectors that produced for export and in liquid assets such as finance and insurance, in addition to trading firms and investments in real estate speculation.

The lack of systematic data precluded the categorization of conglomerates on the basis of assets rather than firms. However, the system employed here highlights the influence of financial institutions in conglomerate strategy, which is not proportional to a financial firm's assets. Moreover, although some may feel that the criteria for distinguishing between fixed-asset domestic market-oriented and internationalist conglomerates are too loose, empirically, conglomerates' initial policy positions largely corresponded to the expectations raised by the criteria used here. According to the available data, unequivocally internationalist conglomerates (particularly those most intimately linked to the policy process) favored a radical policy. The two conglomerates closer to a 50-50 split between the two major orientations could, in principle, go either way: support radical change or the status quo. In fact, they initially backed a middle path—gradual adjustment to export led growth. Both later shifted their holdings to conform to an unequivocally internationalist profile. Conglomerates that were 100 percent fixed-asset and domestic market-oriented (with 50 percent or more of firms in internationally uncompetitive sectors—particularly metalworking and electronics) supported continued high protection. They had too much at stake in their uncompetitive sectors and lacked financial institutions to make production shifts easier.

9. The Matte group was another prominent competitive domestic market oriented conglomerate, and its directors favored gradual adjustment as well. Jorge Alessandri, the chairman of the board, had sponsored a gradual trade liberalization project during his tenure as president of the republic between 1958 and 1964.

10. Not all internationalist conglomerates were so heavily weighted towards liquid assets, although those most connected to the government until 1982 were. Others had a higher proportion in primary product export and trade. This was particularly true of the Angelini, Hochschild, and Menéndez groups.

11. This was particularly the case of Manuel Cruzat who, along with his lieutenants, later had privileged access to policymakers. Cruzat split off from the

BHC group (which was left under the control of Javier Vial) and quickly built an economic empire that rivaled it.

12. A third type of conglomerate, whose leaders did not participate in pre-coup policy proposals, were economic groups with close to half or more of their companies in internationally uncompetitive industrial sectors. The more extreme cases, such as the well-known Lepe and Briones groups, had no investments in liquid-asset sectors. As predicted by both Gourevitch and Frieden's system of disaggregation, these groups supported continued high protection. Their position found little favor in policymaking circles. Their directors were not included in the Monday Club or The Brick; they were not favored with high office; and they found little support in the SFF.

13. Philip O'Brien, *The Pinochet Decade*; Arturo Fontaine, *Los economistas*; Ascanio Cavallo et al., *La historia oculta*.

14. For an edited version of the document released by a conservative think tank, see Centro de Estudios Públicos, *"El Ladrillo"*.

15. Philip O'Brien, *The Pinochet Decade*, p. 40; author interviews with Raúl Sáez (economic coordinator in 1974), December 1988 and Juan Villarzú (budget director in 1974), December 1988; Ascanio Cavallo et al., *La historia oculta*; Arturo Fontaine, *Los economistas*.

16. Philip O'Brien, *The Pinochet Decade*, p. 40 and p. 51; author interview with Juan Villarzú, December 1988.

17. Prosopographical data from Philip O'Brien, *The Pinochet Decade*; Edwards and BHC conglomerate company annual reports; and Colegio de Periodistas, *Diccionario biográfico*.

18. For the role of the PDC in the breakdown of democracy, see Arturo Valenzuela, *The Breakdown of Democratic Regimes: Chile* (Baltimore: Johns Hopkins University Press, 1978).

19. After the coup, the strong policy affinity between the non-Christian Democratic Chicago boys and the internationalist conglomerates with a heavy concentration in liquid assets led to their employment by those conglomerates upon completion of their government service. See Centro de Estudios Públicos, *"El Ladrillo"*.

20. See Centro de Estudios Publicos, *"El Ladrillo"*.

21. Author interview with Orlando Sáenz (president SFF, Monday Club participant, and chief foreign debt negotiator in 1974), August 1988.

22. *El Campesino* 10, October 1973.

23. For the CPC's policy position I relied on author interviews with Manuel Valdés, March 1989 (in 1973 he was vice president of the CPC, and organizer of the second CPC convention in December 1973), and media accounts of the convention in *El Mercurio, Ercilla,* and *El Campesino* as publicized in November and December 1973.

24. For the minority position in the SFF I relied on author interviews with Gustavo Ramdohr (former director of the metal sector association), August 1988 and Orlando Sáenz (president of the SFF at the time), August 1988. For the majority position of the SFF, see Orlando Sáenz's speech in *Informativo SFF* no. 71, February-March 1974. For SNA policy stances, see *El Campesino* 11, November 1973 and *El Campesino* 1-2, January-February 1974; for the CCC, see *Memorias Anuales*, 1973 and 1974. I derived SONAMI's position from author interviews with Manlio Fantini (a

long-time member of SONAMI's elected board), April 1988 and Carlos Rodríguez, SONAMI's director of planning January 1989. Data for the CChC were from an author interview with Pablo Araya (director of studies), May 1989.

25. *El Campesino* 1-2, January-February 1974. The same report says that the SNA issued press releases to *El Mercurio* and other news media on these subjects.

26. *El Campesino* 11, November 1973, editorial; and *El Campesino* 5, May 1974.

27. Cámara Central de Comercio, *Memoria Anual*, 1973 to 1974.

28. Author interviews with Manlio Fantini (SONAMI), April 1988; Carlos Rodríguez, SONAMI director of planning, January 1989; Hernán Danús, president of the Mining Engineer's Association, January 1989.

29. *El Mercurio*, December 15, 1973 and January 9, 1974; also see Orlando Sáenz' speech in *Informativo* SFF, February-March 1974.

30. For *El Mercurio*'s position within the Edwards group, see Fernando Dahse, *El mapa de la extrema riqueza*; for the paper's position on gradual tariff reduction, see *El Mercurio*, October 26, 1973, December 15, 1973 and January 9, 1974. For *El Mercurio*'s role in organizing the opposition to Allende, see Osvaldo Sunkel, *El Mercurio*; Patricio Dooner, *Periodismo y política: La prensa de derecha e izquierda* (Santiago: Editorial Andante, 1989); and Philip O'Brien, *The Pinochet Decade*.

31. See the annual reports for 1973 and 1974 of CMPC (Matte), Luchetti (Lúksic), and CCU (Edwards). All of these companies were among the flagship companies of these conglomerates, and were either internationally competitive or internationally oriented fixed-asset concerns.

32. Author interviews with Rolf Lüders, economist and former director of the internationalist Vial conglomerate, December 1988; Juan Andrés Fontaine and Efraín Friedman, former executives of the internationalist Cruzat-Larraín conglomerate, both in November 1988; Alvaro Plaza, director of the Catholic University's Escuela Superior de Administración de Empresa, August 1988.

33. Ricardo Ffrench-Davies, *Políticas económicas de Chile, 1952-1970* (Santiago: Ediciones Nueva Universidad, 1973); and Oscar Muñoz, ed., *Proceso a la industrialización chilena* (Santiago: Ediciones Nueva Universidad, 1972).

34. For the relationship of Latin America to the world economy, see Jonathan Hartlyn and Samuel A. Moreley, eds., *Latin American Political Economy: Financial Crisis and Political Change* (Boulder: Westview, 1986); Celso Furtado, *Economic Development of Latin America: Historical Background and Contemporary Problems* (Cambridge: Cambridge University Press, 1976, second edition); Joseph Grunwald, *Latin America and the World Economy: A Changing International Order* (Beverly Hills: Sage Publications, 1978). For figures on the decline of bilateral and multilateral aid to Latin America, see Stephany Griffith-Jones and Osvaldo Sunkel, *La crisis de la deuda y del desarrollo en América Latina: El fin de una ilusión* (Buenos Aires: Grupo Editor Latinoamericano, 1987), p. 83.

35. Stephany Griffith-Jones and Osvaldo Sunkel, *La crisis de la deuda y del desarrollo en América Latina*, p. 92.

36. See Chapter 3 for details of this process.

37. Guillermo O'Donnell, *Modernization and Bureaucratic-Authoritarianism: Studies in South American Politics* (Berkeley: Institute of International Studies, 1979).

38. *Informativo* SFF no. 71, February-March 1974.

39. Howard Handelman and Thomas G. Sanders, *Military Government and the*

*Movement Towards Democracy in South America* (Bloomington: University of Indiana Press, 1981), p. 294.

40. For a theoretical treatment of these movements, see Ronald Rogowski, "Political Cleavages and Changing Exposure to Trade," *American Political Science Review* 81, 4, 1987.

41. Stephany Griffith-Jones and Osvaldo Sunkel, *La crisis de la deuda*, pp. 95-96.

42. *Informativo SFF* no. 71, February-March 1974.

43. For a good overview of these policy debates, see Philip O'Brien, *The Pinochet Decade*; Tomás Moulián and Pilar Vergara, "Ideología y política económica," *Colección Estudios Cieplan* no. 3, June 1980; and Guillermo Campero, *Los gremios empresariales en el período 1970-1983: Comportamiento socio-político y orientaciones ideológicas* (Santiago: ILET, 1984).

44. Author interviews with, Orlando Sáenz, August 1988; Sergio Albornoz (Business School of the Catholic University), September 1988; Rolf Lüders, December 1988; and Jaime Alé, director of the SFF's planning department, September 1988.

45. Author interview with Sergio Molina, minister of finance in the mid-1960s, May 1989.

46. This description of the policy process follows from numerous accounts in *Informativo SFF*, *El Campesino*, and Cámara Central de Comercio *Memorias Anuales*. Also see Arturo Fontaine, *Los economistas y el Presidente Pinochet*.

47. This was true for other sectors as well. Almost from the very beginning the SNA insisted on the need for more formal and institutionalized channels of communication between peak associations and government. See issues of *El Campesino* for the end of 1973 and 1974.

48. Asociación de Industrias Electrónicas, Memorandum dated July 11, 1974 to the ministers of finance (Jorge Cauas), economy (Fernando Léniz), and economic coordination (Raúl Sáez).

49. SFF memorandum to Undersecretary of the Ministry of Economy Sergio de Castro, November 6 and 7, 1974.

50. Banco Central de Chile, Comité Asesor de Política Arancelaria, minutes of the meeting of November 22, 1974.

51. See *Informativo SFF*, July 1976, where O. Sáenz mourned the bankruptcy of Bolocco Industries.

52. Author interview with Gustavo Ramdohr, former official of the metal sector association, Asociación de Industriales Metalúrgicos, August 1988.

53. For these views, see Juan Linz, "An Authoritarian Regime: Spain," in Erik Allardt and Yrjo Littunen, eds., *Cleavages, Ideologies, and Party Systems* (Helsinki: Academic Bookstore, 1964); Guillermo O'Donnell, "Corporatism and the Question of the State," in James M. Malloy, ed., *Authoritarianism and Corporatism in Latin America* (Pittsburgh: University of Pittsburgh Press, 1977); and Fernando Henrique Cardoso, "On the Characterization of Authoritarian Regimes in Latin America," in David Collier, ed., *The New Authoritarianism in Latin America* (Princeton: Princeton University Press, 1979).

54. For further details, see Guillermo O'Donnell, "Corporatism and the Question of the State."

55. Fernando Henrique Cardoso, "On the Characterization of Authoritarian Regimes," pp. 43-44.

56. For a Central American example, see Rose J. Spalding, *Capitalists and Revolution in Nicaragua: Opposition and Accommodation, 1979-1993* (Chapel Hill: University of North Carolina Press, 1994).

57. Data on appointments from Arturo Fontaine, *Los economistas*; and newspaper accounts of the period, principally *El Mercurio* and *Ercilla*.

58. These data were culled from business peak association monthly publications. Only the SNA, which had advocated corporatism for the post-coup political order, consistently demanded more formal, institutionalized access to government authorities.

59. Author interviews with Orlando Sáenz and Manuel Valdés, September 1988 and March 1989 respectively.

60. *El Campesino* 11, November 1973, editorial.

61. Author interview with then SFF president Orlando Sáenz, August 1988.

62. Cámara Central de Comercio, *Memoria Anual*, November 1974 to October 1975.

63. Compañía Cervecerías Unidas annual report, 1974; SFF, *Memoria*, 1974; *El Campesino*, various issues in 1974; Arturo Fontaine, *Los economistas*.

64. Author interview with Orlando Sáenz, August 1988.

65. Author interview with Manuel Valdés, organizer of the CPC convention, March 1989. Also see accounts of the convention in *El Mercurio*, *Ercilla*, and *El Campesino*.

66. Author interview with Manuel Valdés, March 1989.

67. Author interviews with Orlando Sáenz, August 1988; and Juan Villarzú, December 1988.

68. Jorge Cauas and Sergio de la Cuadra, "La política económica de la apertura al exterior en Chile," *Cuadernos de Economía de la Universidad Católica de Chile*, August-December 1981, especially p. 2308.

69. Nevertheless, CPC president Jorge Fontaine must have known about The Brick. He had a close working relationship with SFF president and Monday Club regular Orlando Sáenz during the period of business mobilization against Allende.

# 5

# Radical Neoliberalism Ascendant

Chile began to implement a draconian policy of economic restructuring in mid-1975, which set it apart from its authoritarian counterparts. Brazil attempted to sustain high levels of industrial substitution and agricultural expansion in the wake of quadrupled energy prices; Uruguay continued with its own version of gradual neoliberal restructuring; and Argentina faced a paralyzing economic and political crisis following the death of President Juan Domingo Perón. Chile had its economic problems during this period: hyperinflation, lack of investment, low foreign exchange reserves, declining export earnings, and general economic disorder in the wake of Unidad Popular's failed attempt at socialist transformation.

Until April 1975, Chile had relied on a gradual approach to economic adjustment to address those problems. Over the next two and a half years, however, policy shifted dramatically as Chile inaugurated the first phase of a radical neoliberal economic restructuring program. The new policy measures included drastic deflation, swift privatization of state owned companies, rapid deregulation of markets (especially in the financial sector), and deep and fast reductions in protectionism.[1]

The policies were radical for several reasons. First, the draconian nature of the stabilization measures and the speed and thoroughness of market liberalization were without parallel in the recent history of Chile or Latin America. Second, the policies were intended to set in motion a sweeping transformation of the Chilean economy. Neoliberalism in Chile was also radical in its insensitivity to adversely affected economic sectors, including many capitalists and landowners. The indifference of reformers differed in comparison to both the post-Depression era in Chile and to contemporary policies in the Southern Cone and Brazil.

Changes in the dominant capitalist coalition—a reversal of the balance of forces within the fragile gradualist coalition—played a crucial role in the shift from gradual to radical economic restructuring. Between the middle of 1974 and the middle of 1975, internationally oriented conglomerates with a heavy concentration in liquid assets became the dominant capitalist fraction displacing internationally competitive industrialists that produced for domestic markets. Internationalist capitalists preferred radical neoliberal restructuring long before the military government adopted such policies. They supported extensive financial sector deregulation, sharp tariff reductions, major deflation, and rapid privatization. They stood to benefit from those policies because a depressed economy and preferential access to finance gave internationalist conglomerates the pick of privatized companies. Those policies would also weaken groups more heavily involved in the production of products for domestic markets. And, since the internationalist groups were more competitive in world markets, lower tariffs promised to increase their share of national income. Investment in internationally oriented production, and especially finance, promised to outstrip growth in traditional economic activities such as manufactures for domestic markets or grain and dairy production.

Before policy changes were announced, the radical internationalist conglomerates were allied with radical Chicago boy policymakers in the government, many of whom had employment histories linking them to the internationalist conglomerates. This connection gave the heads of the core radical conglomerates liberal access to policy formulation. The alliance between these forces inside and outside of the government grew out of a common social history and a web of shared ideological and economic interests. The radical Chicago boys, and some of the coalition's important entrepreneurs, had all studied economics during the same time period either at the University of Chicago or the Universidad Católica in Santiago, Chile. In addition to being ideological technocrats, the most important radical Chicago boys were often executives of the flagship companies of the radical internationalist conglomerates as well. Given the connections between technocrats and conglomerates, investment was sure to follow on the heels of policy change.

For the sake of exposition, this chapter is divided into two policy subperiods. Each traces coalition formation, examines coalitional power resources, and explains the consequences of the system of interaction between capitalist coalitions and the state for policymaking. The first subperiod, from the middle of 1974 to the middle of 1975, examines how radical internationalists gained sufficient economic and political strength to challenge the gradualist coalition. A complicated conjuncture of international and domestic factors emboldened these challengers. The deepening international economic crisis produced by the first oil shock, and the continuing shift in the sources of foreign savings, were the most important external factors. Domestic factors that strengthened the radical coalition included the expansion of their economic power as a result of privatization and financial deregulation, the displacement of gradualists in the government economic advisory team, and changes in regime structure. These last two elements involved crucial modifications of the system of interaction between capitalists and policymakers that favored radical internationalists.

During the second subperiod, from the middle of 1975 to the end of 1977, two interrelated processes favored radical internationalists. First, the constellation of business and landowning forces that supported radical neoliberalism expanded. The core radical internationalist conglomerates that had participated in the Monday Club increased their holdings, augmenting their significance to the Chilean economy. Meanwhile, other business and landowning groups also began to support radical neoliberalism. These groups remained allied fractions of the radical coalition. They did not join the coalition explicitly through formal proclamations, agreements, or participation in the policy process. Instead, their investment decisions indicated that they had given up on gradualism and cast their weight behind the movement for more radical reform. The investment decisions of several internationally competitive conglomerates that produced for domestic markets were key to this process of coalition expansion. These conglomerates began to restructure their holdings along the lines of the radical international conglomerates. They demonstrated to policymakers that firms could restructure and they made a positive impact on national accounts.

While support for the radical internationalists expanded in this manner, General Augusto Pinochet consolidated one-man rule. The change in regime structure biased the power of state institutions in favor of the radical neoliberals because Pinochet appointed them to the highest economic policymaking positions, replacing gradualists who had previously held them. The personalization of Chilean authoritarianism consolidated tendencies in the system of interaction between policymakers and capitalists that had emerged by 1975. A narrow alliance of the core radical internationalist conglomerates and the radical Chicago boys was able to expand and perpetuate its role in the policymaking process—from the shaping of policy agendas, to control over policy formulation, and to the virtual exclusion of organized business and other economic groups. The consequences of these changes were a rigid policymaking style that emphasized unswerving commitment to radical neoliberalism, a through dismantling of tariff barriers, and more daring financial sector reform.

## Rise of the Radical Internationalist Coalition, 1974-1975

The tone of policy debates between the middle of 1974 and the middle of 1975 began to change as radical international capitalists mounted a campaign for drastic neoliberal economic reforms. During the formulation of the Brick and in the first months of the military government, when gradualists had kept their ambitions in check, radical internationalists had confined their advocacy for deeper reforms to closed-door policymaking sessions. Beginning in November 1974, however, they publicly and forcefully advocated drastic change. By April 1975, they had won.

The three conglomerates that had dominated the Monday Club (and therefore had participated in the policy process from the beginning) stood at the core of the radical neoliberal coalition long before the military government decreed deeper reforms. The Banco Hipotecario de Chile (BHC) and its spin-off Cruzat-Larraín, both relatively new conglomerates, led the radical coalition. As discussed previously, the BHC group concentrated most of its holdings in liquid-asset sectors. Cruzat and Larraín left BHC and formed their own conglomerate in 1974. Of the eleven firms that Cruzat and Larraín began with, roughly two-thirds exported primary products or were in liquid-asset sectors, while a quarter were in internationally competitive domestic market manufactures. The rest were in sectors that were not internationally competitive. Toward the end of 1973, the two conglomerates began an aggressive strategy of acquisitions and mergers, building economic empires at the expense of other business groups and living up to their reputation as "the piranhas."

The public policy stance of the Edwards conglomerate made it the third member of the core radical neoliberal coalition. Why did the Edwards group, which had supported gradual economic change in the immediate post-coup period, shift its policy stance? In 1974, the Edwards group began shifting the composition of its holdings towards an internationalist profile. That decision affirmed a long-standing collaboration between the Edwards group and the newer, more radical conglomerates. Before the coup, the Edwards and BHC conglomerates had worked together closely in the Monday Club and the Brick. After the coup, many of the economic advisors to the military government were drawn from these conglomerates, which meant that they had an inside track in the new regime. In 1974, however, the economic power of the BHC and the Cruzat-Larraín conglomerates, and their network of connections to policymakers, began to overtake the Edwards group. In order to protect itself the Edwards group took action. It pursued a tactical alliance with the radical internationalist conglomerates by developing close ties between its financial institutions and those of the Cruzat-Larraín group. The Edwards group then began a rapid internal conversion to an internationalist profile.

The economic composition of the Edwards group facilitated its transition. Of all of the internationally competitive domestic market-oriented conglomerates, its economic structure most resembled that of the radical internationalists. Put differently, among internationally competitive conglomerates it had the weakest profile. Only 43 percent of its companies produced for domestic markets versus 54 and 69 percent for comparable conglomerates (Matte and Lúksic). The restructured Edwards conglomerate also expanded its holdings in the print media, which complemented Cruzat-Larraín's and Vial's (BHC) lack of holdings in that area.[2] As a result, the core radical neoliberal coalition and its allies acquired *El Mercurio*.

The alliance between the BHC, Cruzat-Larraín, and the Edwards groups in favor of radical neoliberal economic restructuring proved formidable. It fired its opening salvos during the policy debates of November 1974 by running editorials in *El Mercurio* that advocated drastic deflation, rapid privatization, and draconian tariff reductions.[3] *El Mercurio* argued that oil price shocks contributed to the Chilean government's fiscal imbalance, which fueled inflation. Privatization and deflationary policies would relieve those inflationary pressures. *El Mercurio* exhorted the nation to lower tariff barriers quickly so that international competition could reassign resources to more internationally competitive sectors, increase foreign exchange reserves, and alleviate balance of payments pressure. *El Mercurio* did not emphasize that the policies it was advocating would "reassign" national resources to the internationalist conglomerates with which the Edwards group was forging close ties.

Gradualists were not persuaded by *El Mercurio* and recognized that more drastic reforms would undermine their interests. In January 1975, Orlando Sáenz denounced radial proposals to change the Chilean economy. He exposed the economic motives behind "shock treatment," the demand for rapid privatization, and libertine banking deregulation. He warned that such policies would lead to a rapid and dramatic concentration of wealth in certain sectors of the Chilean economy and to financial speculation at the expense of investment in production. Without demand, he argued, industrial growth would wither.[4]

In early March 1975, the radical internationalist conglomerates made their final and most direct attack against gradualist policies. The BHC group organized a widely publicized conference on economic policy and invited noted neoconservative economists from the University of Chicago to legitimize the claims of the radical coalition. Arnold Harberger and Milton Friedman obliged them by strenuously arguing against the gradualist approach.[5] A month later, the government applied shock treatment to the Chilean economy; shortly thereafter, it began the rapid privatization of the many financial and nonfinancial firms controlled by the public sector.[6]

An economically powerful but narrow capitalist coalition openly supported radical neoliberal economic restructuring before such policies were adopted. But what was the connection between this coalition and the policy shift? What factors allowed the radical internationalists, who had been a subordinate group in the gradualist coalition, to prevail? The next sections of this chapter examine the sources of the radical coalition's economic and political power to shed some light on this question.

The arguments that follow suggest that three factors—external shocks, privatization, and superior financial capability—gave the radical international conglomerates the economic power to wrestle control of the economy away from the traditional, long-established, internationally competitive conglomerates that supported gradual adjustment. Trade account deficits and rising inflation compelled the government to consider more severe stabilization measures. In the context of Chile's chaotic and disarticulated economy, a draconian stabilization program was in the international conglomerates' economic interest, provided that rapid privatization of financial and nonfinancial assets accompanied it. Drastic deflation was bound to trigger a severe recession. In an economy starved for capital, the comparatively capital-rich conglomerates would be able to purchase key industries from the government and from bankrupt owners at bargain prices. Moreover, they could concentrate on buying firms in what would become the most dynamic sectors of the economy: import competitive industries.

The sources of the radical coalition's political power were two elements of regime structure that began to bias capabilities in favor of the radical internationalists. First, shifts within the Central Bank and among other economic advisors bolstered the radical internationalists. Second, the increasingly exclusionary nature of Chilean authoritarianism—the establishment of one-man rule—barred a growing number of capitalist groups (especially from organized business) from the economic policymaking process.

### External Factors and the Rise of Radical Internationalists

External shocks strengthened international conglomerates over other capitalist groups. In the third quarter of 1974, copper prices—which accounted for approximately 80 percent of Chile's export earnings—plunged from a high of $1.26 to $.78 and kept sinking.[7] Chile's hard currency earnings plummeted just as import bills were soaring. The global recession and skyrocketing energy prices were not brief blips in the world economy, and it seemed that Chile would face chronic and steadily worsening foreign exchange shortages. These conditions favored internationalist groups over those who produced for domestic markets because the latter were a drain on hard currency reserves. They always had been, but with the increased cost of oil imports and lower copper receipts foreign exchange for importing raw and intermediate goods would be more scarce.

An added problem was that bi and multilateral financial institutions were lending less. Foreign exchange increasingly would have to come from exports. If traditional exports proved too unreliable to fill the gap, new sources had to be developed. This view favored internationalist groups, especially those who produced semi-elaborated industrial goods (fish meal, wood pulp, processed fruits and vegetables) and landowners in the central valley who could grow export crops (mainly fresh fruit). Landowners, as represented by the Sociedad Nacional de Agricultura (SNA), recognized the possibilities. In January 1975, the leadership of the SNA predicted, "Chile can be certain that the international economic crisis will hit it hard. In the last six months copper prices have fallen precipitously." On the heels of this assessment, the SNA proposed that Chile massively develop its agribusiness capacity.[8]

While the SNA explored the possibilities of long-term investment, in the short term, both the increased lending by private commercial banks and rising quantities of recycled petrodollars gave the radical internationalist conglomerates an enormous advantage.[9] They had privileged access to international banking at a time when Chile was in a severe credit crunch.[10] Moreover, import-substitution industrialists, the ones most interested in gradual adjustment, by and large did not have similar access. Since the radical internationalists were in a better position to contribute foreign exchange reserves, they were more attractive to the military. Over time, the availability of foreign capital, and the mediation of those funds by the radical internationalist conglomerates, helped to fuel a speculative boom in Chile.

### *Privatization, Financial Reforms, and Radical Internationalists*

International economic conditions, although important, were too diffuse to fully explain the triumph of radical internationalists. Unidad Popular's nationalization of large-scale business and banking had weakened import-substitution industrialists greatly, setting the stage for a reorganization of capital that was quite different from the experiences of Argentina and Uruguay. After the overthrow of Allende, privatization, recession, and deregulation of the financial system allowed internationally connected financiers—radical internationalists—to acquire leading Chilean firms at bargain prices.[11]

Unidad Popular's nationalization of the financial sector had great significance for intracapitalist conflict in the post-coup period. In its struggle against the Chilean bourgeoisie, Unidad Popular had seized control of a crucial component of many Chilean conglomerates: their banks (see Table 5.1).[12] These and other policies had weakened and disorganized segments of the private sector targeted for extinction. After the coup, the distributional consequences of the reprivatization of capital markets played a crucial role in determining the relative economic power of business groups. Radical internationalists saw draconian market liberalization as an opportunity to increase their economic empires at the expense of other conglomerates.

TABLE 5.1 Bank Nationalization and Privatization

| Bank | % Owned by CORFO | Date Sold | %Sold | Conglo-merate | Conglomerate Type |
|------|------------------|-----------|-------|---------------|-------------------|
| Español | 94 | 9-75 | 94 | Puig | Internationalist |
| Osorno | 89 | 9-75 | 89 | | |
| Chile | 48 | 9-75 | 30 | Vial | Internationalist |
| Israelita | 96 | 10-75 | 96 | | |
| Sudamericano | 85 | 11-75 | 73 | Lúksic | Traditional |
| Talca | 90 | 11-75 | 90 | Calaf | Traditional |
| Concepción | 92 | 11-75 | 92 | Ascuí | Traditional |
| Trabajo | 84 | 12-75 | 84 | Said/ Edwards | Traditional |
| Yugoslavo | 78 | 1-76 | 78 | | |

*Sources:* CORFO, *Privatización de empresas y activos* (Santiago: Gerencia de Normalización de Empresas, n.d.); Fernando Dahse, *El mapa de la extrema riqueza* (Santiago: Editorial Aconcagua, 1979).

Nationalization under Allende had been *the* issue that galvanized business and landowning groups against the government. The restoration of nationalized companies to private ownership was business' first priority after the coup, and most of the meetings between the Sociedad de Fomento Fabril (SFF) and the Ministry of Economy were related to that issue.[13] In those meetings, business leaders demanded more than a simple return to the status quo ante. They also wanted the privatization of companies that had always had majority public ownership. In early 1974, Orlando Sáenz, president of the SFF declared, "The establishment of a social market economy requires the elimination of public ownership, with the exception of areas crucial to economic development or social benefit. Privatization is especially necessary in activities where the state directly competes with the private sector."[14]

The radical internationalists understood that their future economic strength depended on their ability to gain control over key firms destined for privatization. They also knew that in a country starved for capital gaining an edge over future competitors required a head start in the new private financial markets. Most large-scale businessmen were relying on the reputation of their flagship firms to get supplier credits from foreign banks and manufacturing companies.[15] Domination of the new financial system would provide the resources with which to acquire newly privatized firms or buy out companies strapped for operating funds.

On the issue of privatization, Chilean businessmen distinguished between firms in which the state had bought assets and firms that Unidad Popular had requisitioned or intervened in against the owners' will. The sentiment among capitalists was that intervened and requisitioned firms should be returned to their former owners as soon as possible. The fragility of the banking system and the lack of liquidity in Chile's capital markets, however, meant that most conglomerates had a stake in a gradual sale of state-owned assets. In the gradualist policy period, the post-coup government returned most of the requisitioned or intervened firms to their former owners but did not do so with firms in which the state had bought assets.

Unintentionally, this policy favored the Vial (BHC) and the Cruzat-Larraín internationalist conglomerates. Unlike many other Chilean businessmen, Vial, Cruzat, and Larraín had refused to sell assets to the Unidad Popular government, which proceeded to intervene in and requisition many of their firms. Since firms nationalized this way were the first to be privatized, the BHC group regained most of its assets, including the Banco Hipotecario, soon after the overthrow of Allende. After Cruzat-Larraín split off from BHC in 1974, the holdings of both of these radical internationalist conglomerates were concentrated heavily in the banking and financial services sectors, although Cruzat-Larraín also controlled some mining and fishing companies.[16] With so many of their assets in financial services, the BHC and Cruzat-Larraín groups dominated the Chilean financial sector. Many of the directors of the Banco Hipotecario were former executives of the nationalized First City National Bank (now Citibank).[17] Their contacts and experience made it easier for them to seek out foreign commercial bank loans at a time when few Chilean economic groups were thinking along those lines.[18]

The radical international conglomerates also took advantage of financial sector deregulation to capture the lion's share of Chile's emerging capital markets, quickly dominating the Chilean economy. In May 1974, the Central Bank created a new type of non-bank financial institution with unregulated interest rates—the *financieras*. They offered interest rates on deposits that were much higher than the heavily regulated state controlled banking sector. They were also the only financial institutions authorized to offer very short-term loans (about seven days), which carried very high interest rates.[19]

The Cruzat-Larraín and BHC groups established *financieras* at a much earlier date than the more traditional economic groups. Their contacts with New York banks provided them with cheap hard currency that the *financieras* turned into local currency at favorable exchange rates. Then they loaned those funds at very high interest rates to firms strapped for operating capital, turning a handsome profit for the conglomerates that controlled the *financieras*. Moreover, with the *financieras* in place, the radical internationalist conglomerates managed to capture a large percentage of national savings. By contrast, the conglomerates that backed gradualism were not as quick to set up *financieras*. To cover operating expenses they borrowed from abroad using their nonfinancial assets as collateral.[20]

In sum, in an economy starved for hard currency, early control of financial institutions through which to channel the first inflows of foreign loans gave the radical international conglomerates an edge over more traditional conglomerates. Two additional factors strengthened the international conglomerates' position. The traditional conglomerates were still struggling to regain control of assets they had sold to the government, and the traditional conglomerates did not have financial service companies and banks of their own.

### Regime Structure: Institutions, Power, and Policy Change

Economic strength alone, of course, does not explain how the radical internationalists turned the tables on gradualists between April and July of 1975. So far, we have seen that the internationalist conglomerates had become strong enough to elicit the policies that would elevate them into a position of dominance. But how did they translate that moment of opportunity into political victory in an authoritarian system?

An examination of how state institutions and a change in regime structure biased the distribution of power among competing capitalist coalitions completes that connection. The evidence suggests that radical internationalists used the lack of a clear hierarchy of authority among state economic institutions to carve out a power base. The subsequent replacement of key ministers together with an alteration of regime structure permanently tipped the scales in their favor. These events created a system of interaction between policymakers and capitalists in which a now tight hierarchy of authority among ministries gave control over policy formulation to a narrow group of conglomerate heads and the technocrats who were closely linked to their concerns.

*Policy Networks, Radical Internationalists, and Financial Reform.* The previous section argued that the radical international conglomerates' early control over the financial sector was one of the keys to their success. These entrepreneurs, however, did more than capitalize on policy-generated economic opportunities; nor did they limit their involvement in the policy process to simple demand raising. The radical internationalist conglomerates secured a head start in the financial sector because their increasingly privileged access to the policy process gave them two key resources: information and an expanding role in policy formulation. The lack of clear-cut lines of command and authority between ministries and agencies was largely responsible for providing this early advantage.

The deregulation of the financial sector was largely designed in the Central Bank and by the economic advisory team of the junta. Although the Central Bank was nominally under the control of the Ministry of Finance, general administrative disorganization meant that the institution enjoyed great independence.[21] This was also true for the economic team; their members were officially attached to different government agencies, but they operated more as an autonomous unit. The radical Chicago boys—allies of the radical internationalist conglomerates by ideology and employment—were ascendant in both the Central Bank and the junta's advisory team. In the Central Bank they had been quietly displacing the more moderate voices of Christian Democratic Chicagoans for some time. Their efforts were facilitated when a key PDC Chicago boy defected from the party, turned radical, and became president of the Central Bank. Radical neoliberal Chicagoans also gained control of the civilian advisory team.[22]

The radical Chicago boys in the government then invited a few radical internationalist businessmen from the core conglomerates to participate in the deliberations that shaped financial sector reform. These policymakers and businessmen shared a long-standing association dating back to the Monday Club, the Brick, and even before in some cases. The deliberations evaluated the investment and operational consequences of the policy proposals being considered. More moderate PDC-affiliated advisors objected to the presence of the businessmen in the planning meetings to no avail.[23] As a result of their privileged participation in policy formulation, businessmen of the internationalist conglomerates possessed significant insider information that they used to expand their business empires.

In addition to these meetings, capital market reform was being discussed in a broader forum also. In mid-March 1974, the Central Bank held a seminar on the issue sponsored by the Organization of American States. Many of those who attended were members of the technical staffs of government agencies and also had ties to business.[24] Seminar participants agreed on many general points. Chile needed extensive and agile private capital markets. Foreign savings should come more from international commercial banks than from traditional governmental and international financial institution sources.[25] Interest rates should not be controlled, least of all at levels below the rate of inflation. Differential interest rates between the various types of financial institutions should be eliminated. The development of efficient capital markets required inflation control.[26] Beyond these areas of agreement, participants disagreed on many specifics of design, emphasis, priority, and pace for the reform of capital markets.

At this juncture the insider connections of the internationalist businessmen who shared the radical Chicago boys' economic ideology proved most valuable. The resolution of the disagreements took place in the inner sanctums of the Central Bank and among the junta's economic advisory team. These venues were precisely the ones in which radical internationalist businessmen had privileged direct access to policymakers and participation in policy formulation. Other business groups, not to mention organized business, were less fortunate.

Advance knowledge that interest rates would be liberalized in non-banking financial institutions before banks gave radical internationalists a competitive edge over other economic groups. Businessmen of the gradualist movement had their sights trained on the banking sector proper; they did not pay much attention to the establishment of non-bank institutions that would disporportionately capture pools of savings and investment. Gradualists such as Orlando Sáenz, president of the SFF, and José Zabala, a PDC economist and government economic advisor, favored a different instrument to rebuild capital markets and to gain access to foreign savings. They advocated the establishment of development banks at the service of industry, commerce, and agriculture.[27]

*Institutional Power and the Rise of Radical Neoliberals.* For the radical international conglomerates and their Chicago boy allies, however, shifting from gradual to more radical neoliberal economic policies required more than growing economic strength and the advancement of their cohorts in middle levels of the government bureaucracy. The key to their victory lay in their ability to capture the "commanding heights" of the economic policymaking bureaucracy. The takeover proceeded in several steps. First, Minister of Economy Fernando Léniz had to be replaced by someone who shared their economic vision. This goal was accomplished in April 1975, just before the "shock treatment" policy went into effect. The junta dismissed Léniz and replaced him with Sergio de Castro, a radical Chicago boy of long standing who had been employed by the Edwards conglomerate, and who later became an executive of the Cruzat-Larraín group.

Meanwhile, the Ministry of Finance supplanted the Ministry of Economy in the hierarchy of power of Chile's economic policymaking institutions. The finance minister, Chicago boy sympathizer Jorge Cauas, had insisted on this reorganization as a condition for going ahead with "shock treatment." The switch gave the Ministry of Finance control over the ministries of economy, agriculture, mining, public works, housing, health, transportation, labor, as well as cabinet rank agencies such as ODEPLAN and CORFO.[28] These changes reflected the growing importance of the finance sector in the economy and the monetarist emphasis of the Chicago boys themselves.

The differences between these men on the issue of gradualism versus "shock treatment" were well known among Chile's socio-economic elites. Gradualists Fernando Léniz and Raúl Sáez (economic coordinator) strongly disagreed with radical neoliberals Sergio de Castro and Jorge Cauas on these issues. Their disputes often reached the highest levels within the military government. Personnel changes, however, extended beyond top-level appointments. Officials who opposed "shock treatment" from subordinate posts also left. Among these was the budget director, PDC loyalist Juan Villarzú. CORFO, the agency in charge of privatization came under the direction of Francisco Soza, a business associate of the internationalist Cruzat-Larraín conglomerate.[29] And, by the end of 1974, radical Chicago boys were displacing gradualists on the government economic teams, and monetarist views had gained more influence with the armed forces, especially the army.[30]

Why was Léniz replaced with de Castro, a necessary act for power consolidation by the Chicago boys? Part of the answer to this question lies in the power struggle within the junta itself. The navy, not the army, organized the coup d'etat that overthrew Allende. The navy contacted the Monday Club and asked it to draft an economic plan for post-Allende Chile. After the coup, the navy took charge of economic affairs and most civilians believed that courting patrons in the navy high command offered the key to policymaking.[31] But the civilians who had gambled on the navy—mainly traditional economic elites that backed gradualism—lost when Pinochet began to consolidate his personal power.

Immediately after the coup, a four-man junta (the commanders of the army, navy, air force, and militarized police, *Carabineros*) governed Chile. As commander-in-chief of the army and also commander of the armed forces, Pinochet became the head of the junta. Initially the junta considered their titular leader to be a *primus inter pares*.[32] Pinochet, however, was not content with that. Unlike the view of the air force, he was not interested in restoring democracy. His goal was absolute personal political power. To that end, he consolidated the intelligence forces under army control in June of 1974 and formally took over the role of president of the junta. In December, he became president of Chile.[33]

As Pinochet's political star rose, the Chicago boys in the government economic advisory teams and ministries began to court him.[34] Pinochet responded to their overtures and promoted them while he demoted or fired the supporters of gradualism. The gradualists represented traditional business groups that had grown powerful under a democratic form of government and wanted Chile to return to representative government as soon as the Marxists had been purged. The radical Chicago boys, by contrast, had few loyalties to social actors who favored a return to democracy.

Meanwhile, PDC loyalists who held important positions in the government suffered the same fate as gradualist businessmen for similar reasons. PDC demands at the end of 1974 that the military government set a timetable for the return to democracy angered military men, especially

Pinochet, who brooked no critiques of their intentions. It also placed officers sympathetic to the PDC, or its goals, in a difficult position. Their views on democratization ostracized them, or so they claimed.[35]

In addition to the political advantages of promoting radical Chicagoans, both the policy debates of the day and his own relationship to the Chicago boys must have revealed to Pinochet that they were connected to powerful business actors that seemed at odds with the traditional business community he sought to circumvent.[36] Therefore, radical neoconservative economic policies that nurtured a new concentration of wealth could shore up an alternative base of support, albeit a narrow one, for Pinochet's government. That social base would expand once the economy had adjusted, or so believed the capitalists who had either been top executives of the radical internationalist conglomerates or who had been involved in the design of tariff policy. The perception was that the radical internationalist conglomerates had to expand for radical neoliberal economic restructuring to be implemented and sustained. It was said that a new generation of entrepreneurs directed the internationalist conglomerates. This new breed of Chilean capitalists supported the new policy direction and prospered while those who opposed it did not. Their prosperity gave government officials a model of dynamic and successful entrepreneurs that regime propaganda then built up to legendary proportions. The authorities pointed to the internationalist conglomerates with pride and could, in essence, say: "See, our economic model works."[37]

***Policy Consequences of the Gradualist Coalition's Defeat.*** The displacement of the gradualist coalition by the radical internationalist coalition ended gradual economic restructuring with an emphasis on industrial development. The ascendant radical internationalist coalition stressed draconian stabilization, financial intermediation, and primary product exports. It also favored semi-elaborated industrial exports, such as fruit paste and fish meal. The new policy coalition assumed an uncompromising stance toward traditional business sectors from the very beginning. Immediately after the internationalist coalition took over the ministries of economy and finance in April 1975, it imposed a program of drastic deflation. The government slashed total expenditures by 27 percent in real terms in 1975 and reduced public investment by half. It sharply increased public enterprise rates and reduced real wages.[38] In July 1975, the military government accelerated the schedule for tariff reductions and, with a median tariff of 33 percent, quickly implemented the 60 percent ad valorem ceiling originally programmed for the end of 1976. The revised schedule fixed the new ceiling at 35 percent, to be reached by mid-1977.[39]

In addition to these policies, rapid privatization, especially of banks, also began in July 1975. The process was virtually complete by March 1976, less than a year later.[40] At the same time, the military government liberated interest rates, which shot up from negative 23 percent in the second quarter of 1975 to 178 percent in the following quarter.[41] Capitalists, mostly those in radical internationalist conglomerates that had gained early possession of financial institutions, made enormous profits.

### Consolidation of the Radical Neoliberal Coalition, 1976-1978

So far this chapter has examined how a narrow group of capitalists and landowners—both from within the state and from outside of it—participated in the formulation of radical neoliberal policies in Chile. The policies were not just the result of authoritarianism and the ideological fervor of a cohesive team of technocratic economists. The radical neoliberal technocrats were allied both intellectually and materially to the core radical international conglomerates, with ties dating back to the Monday Club. The collaboration between technocrats and businessmen in policy formulation decisively influenced the shift from gradual to radical neoliberal economic restructuring.

The radical internationalist coalition owed its victory to three factors. First, a conjuncture of international and domestic economic conditions strengthened radical internationalist conglomerates over the traditional conglomerates. Second, as Pinochet consolidated one-man rule he relied on the internationalist conglomerates as the core of his business support, passing over traditional conglomerates that were closer to the navy. Third, Pinochet's appointment of radical Chicago boys in key economic ministries, and a tight hierarchy of authority among state economic institutions, rounded out the early success of the radical internationalist coalition.

Having consolidated the coalition and its relationship to the state, over the next three years radical internationalists accelerated Chile's opening to the international economy. Between December 1976 and January 1977, after Chile's withdrawal from the Andean Pact, the government intensified its already dramatic reduction of tariffs. The authorities lowered the average tariff to 24 percent ad valorem and then to 20 percent. In August 1977, the Pinochet administration violated previous guidelines and fixed all import duties between 35 percent and 10 percent ad valorem. Finally, in December 1977, the authorities announced that within 18 months, with few exceptions, no import would be subject to a duty exceeding 10 percent.[42] The dismantling of trade barriers was accompanied by an unswerving dedication to the deflationary and deregulatory policies initiated in April to July of 1975.

The rest of the chapter examines the factors that strengthened the position of the radical internationalists during this period, allowing the coalition to pursue its policies virtually unhindered over the next few years. The first factor was the expansion of the radical coalition as the core internationalist conglomerates grew and new capitalist and landowning groups allied themselves with the coalition through their investment decisions. The growth of this sector began to pull Chile out of its economic slump and validated the neoliberal policies. Second, continuing changes in regime structure—the consolidation of Pinochet's rule—drastically skewed institutional sources of power in favor of radical internationalists in and out of the government. Pinochet's appointments ensured that the radical Chicago boys controlled virtually all of the government's economic and social policymaking agencies, and they became the region's most (in)famously cohesive team of technocrats. Moreover, Pinochet's emphasis on a strict hierarchy of authority among ministries ensured the virtual exclusion from policymaking of other capitalist and landowning groups, rendering their opposition ineffective. These two developments consolidated a tight system of interaction between a cohesive team of ideological technocrats and a narrow group of capitalists that had emerged in 1975. The system was to persist into the early 1980s.

### Expansion of the Radical Neoliberal Coalition

Between 1975 and 1977, the three core radical internationalist conglomerates—the key organizers of the Monday Club and the most overt and ardent advocates of radical neoliberalism—expanded and consolidated their holdings. As predicted by Orlando Sáenz, deflationary policy and financial sector reform after mid-1975 gave the BHC and the Cruzat-Larraín economic groups commanding positions in the Chilean economy. Demand shock treatment triggered a tremendous contraction of the Chilean economy, and gross domestic product plunged 15 percent. In the economic reactivation that began in 1976, internationally competitive sectors of the economy began to recover but ISI-related businesses and agriculture continued to suffer, particularly in the textile, metalworking, and electrical industries.[43] With the advantage of greater access to financing, internationalist conglomerates gained increasing control over the most dynamic sectors of the Chilean economy: financial services, forestry, fishing, export agricultural crops, mining, and import-export firms. Some internationalist conglomerates also acquired internationally competitive manufacturing industries in such sectors as food and beverages, energy, and utilities.[44] Rapid privatization of state owned firms at subsidized prices helped the internationalist conglomerates in their task.[45]

The growth of the radical internationalist coalition's core influenced the application of radical neoliberal policies and aided Pinochet in his rise to power. The conglomerates' multiplying investments demonstrated that they could generate economic growth and, therefore, contribute to political stability. Having backed them against other capitalist groups, Pinochet's position as supreme dictator became even more secure once other capitalists and landowners got on the bandwagon. Had these sectors of capital and land not been successful, lack of investment and economic growth might have produced an immediate policy failure that could have disarticulated this policy coalition and its supporters. Such policy failure might have given gradualists a reprieve.

In 1975, the BHC and Cruzat-Larraín conglomerates yearned to dominate the Chilean economy and to be the material vanguards of a new order for Chile. They probably exceeded their wildest dreams. Table 5.2 shows that by 1977, BHC and Cruzat-Larraín had each amassed control of over twice as many firms as their closest competitors (62 and 85 respectively). In both conglomerates, two thirds of these companies were in financial and internationally oriented activities—one third in finance and the other third in primary product export industries and international commerce. Approximately a fifth of the remaining companies were in internationally competitive manufactures for domestic markets. As Tables 5.3 to 5.5 show, this meant that these two conglomerates alone controlled 37 percent of the assets of Chile's largest 250 companies, 40 percent of private sector banking assets, and 29 percent of *financiera* credit.

Meanwhile, the Edwards group had successfully shifted its holdings to an internationalist profile and solidified its ties to Cruzat-Larraín's financial operations. Thus, the Edwards and Matte groups came to constitute a category of formerly traditional conglomerates; conglomerates that shifted to an internationalist profile from one focused on internationally competitive production for domestic markets. By the end of 1977, almost three quarters of the 34 companies in the Edwards group were in liquid-asset sectors and the rest were in internationally competitive industries producing for domestic markets. None were in internationally uncompetitive areas.

These changes meant that even though the core capitalist coalition that supported radical neoliberalism was narrowly based in terms of membership, it commanded extraordinary economic power. The three conglomerates that formed the core policy coalition controlled 40 percent of the assets of Chile's largest 250 companies, 46 percent of private sector banking assets, and 33 percent of *financiera* credit.[46] As the power of the core coalition expanded, efforts to mold public opinion through editorials in *El Mercurio* were redoubled.[47]

Radical neoliberalism received an added boost when the policy coalition expanded through the tacit, investment-driven support of additional capitalist and landowning groups. Their addition broadened the radical coalition's appeal for the authoritarian regime. Table 5.2 shows that other internationalist conglomerates such as Angelini, a new group called

TABLE 5.2 Major Traditional and International Conglomerates, 1970 and 1977: Concentration of Companies by Economic Activity (Percent)

| Conglomerate: Year and Name | Total Firms | Fixed-Asset Domestic Market Oriented Internat'lly Noncompetitive Sectors[a] | Fixed-Asset Domestic Market Oriented Internat'lly Competitive Sectors | Fixed-Asset Primary Product Export Sector | International Commerce Sector | Liquid-Asset Sectors | Real Estate | Total in Fixed-Asset Domestic Market Oriented Sectors | Total in Liquid-Asset, Speculative, & Internat'lly Oriented Sectors |
|---|---|---|---|---|---|---|---|---|---|
| International | | | | | | | | | |
| 74/Cruzat-L. | 11 | 9.0 | 27.2 | 36.4 | – | 27.2 | – | 36.2 | 63.6 |
| 77/Cruzat-L. | 85 | 7.0 | 23.5 | 25.6 | 18.8 | 15.9 | 9.4 | 30.5 | 69.7 |
| 74/BHC | 18 | 16.7 | 5.5 | 11.0 | – | 66.7 | – | 22.2 | 77.7 |
| 77/BHC | 62 | 12.9 | 22.5 | 14.4 | 11.3 | 35.4 | 3.2 | 35.4 | 64.3 |
| 70/Angelini | 4 | – | – | 75.0 | 25.0 | – | – | 0 | 100.0 |
| 77/Angelini | 18 | 5.5 | 5.5 | 50.0 | 22.2 | 16.6 | – | 11.0 | 88.8 |
| 70/Menéndez | 8 | – | – | 25.0 | 62.5 | 12.5 | – | 0 | 100.0 |
| 77/Menéndez | 10 | 10.0 | 10.0 | 40.0 | 30.0 | 10.0 | – | 20.0 | 80.0 |
| 77/Hochschild | 12 | 8.3 | 16.6 | 41.6 | 25.0 | 8.3 | – | 24.9 | 74.9 |
| Former Traditional[c] | | | | | | | | | |
| 70/Edwards | 30 | 6.6 | 33.3 | 6.6 | 6.6 | 33.3 | 10.0 | 43.2 | 56.5 |
| 77/Edwards | 34 | – | 26.4 | 2.9 | 2.9 | 52.9 | 14.7 | 26.4 | 73.4 |

| | | | | | | | | |
|---|---|---|---|---|---|---|---|---|
| 70/Matte | 26 | 34.5 | 19.2 | 7.6 | 15.3 | 19.2 | 3.8 | 53.7 | 45.9 |
| 77/Matte | 39 | 7.6 | 7.6 | 15.1 | 23.0 | 19.9 | 28.2 | 15.2 | 84.2 |
| Traditional | | | | | | | | | |
| 70/Lúksic | 16 | 20.5 | 43.7 | 24.2 | 6.2 | – | – | 68.7 | 31.1 |
| 77/Lúksic | 29 | 3.4 | 41.3 | 20.6 | 17.2 | 6.9 | 6.9 | 48.1 | 51.6 |
| 77/Sáenz | 15 | 13.3 | 46.6 | – | – | 26.6 | 13.3 | 59.9 | 39.9 |
| 70/Lepe | 4 | 50.0 | 50.0 | – | – | – | – | 100.0 | 0 |
| 77/Lepe | 11 | 36.3 | 45.4 | – | 9.0 | 9.0 | – | 81.7 | 18.0 |
| 70/Yarur-B. | 7 | 43.0 | – | – | – | 57.0 | – | 43.0 | 57.0 |
| 77/Yarur-B. | 9 | 44.4 | 22.2 | – | 11.1 | 22.2 | – | 66.6 | 33.3 |
| 70/Briones | 5 | 80.0 | 20.0 | – | – | – | – | 100.0 | 0 |
| 77/Briones | 7 | 14.3 | 57.1 | – | 14.3 | 14.3 | – | 71.4 | 28.6 |

[a]Competitiveness was established by industrial sector, not by individual firm; the criteria were taken from Guillermo Campero and José Valenzuela, *El movimiento sindical en el régimen militar chileno* (Santiago: ILET, 1984).
[b]The difference is made up by investment in agricultural production for domestic markets.
[c]Conglomerates that shifted from a traditional to an internationalist profile.

*Source:* Fernando Dahse, *El mapa de la extrema riqueza* (Santiago: Editorial Aconcagua, 1979).

TABLE 5.3 Conglomerate Control of Banking Assets by end-1977

| Conglomerate:<br>Type and Name | US$ Millions | % of Total<br>State & Private | % of Private |
|---|---|---|---|
| Internationalist Groups | | | |
| Vial (BHC) | 114.2 | 18.9 | 37.9 |
| Cruzat-Larraín | 5.2 | 1.0 | 1.7 |
| Other[a] | 44.3 | 7.3 | 14.4 |
| Former Traditional<br>(turned Internat'l) | | | |
| Edwards | 20.4 | 3.4 | 6.7 |
| Total International | 184.1 | 30.5 | 61.1 |
| | | | |
| Traditional Groups | | | |
| Yarur-Bana | 35.9 | 6.0 | 12.0 |
| Lúksic | 22.6 | 3.7 | 7.5 |
| Other[b] | 9.1 | 1.5 | 3.0 |
| Total Traditional | 67.6 | 11.2 | 22.4 |
| Foreign Sector | 49.5 | 8.2 | 16.4 |
| State Sector | 302.3 | 50.1 | N.A. |
| Total | 603.5 | 100.0[c] | 100.0[c] |

[a]Puig and Ascuí-Cueto.
[b]Abalos y González and Picó-Cañas.
[c]Figures may not add up to 100 due to rounding.

*Source:* Fernando Dahse, *El mapa de la extrema riqueza* (Santiago: Editorial Aconcagua, 1979).

Hochschild, and the Menéndez conglomerate had common economic interests with the radical internationalist conglomerates from the outset. Any policy that favored production for export benefitted them.

Meanwhile, the Matte group began to spin off most of its firms that produced for domestic markets and significantly expanded its holdings in export agriculture, international commerce, and real estate. The Matte conglomerate's actions had deep political implications. Jorge Alessandri, former president of the republic and a once staunch supporter of gradualism, headed the Matte group. Thus, the shift in the conglomerate's holdings mirrored Alessandri's assessment of the political situation. Although he disapproved of radical economic restructuring, he saw no way to stop it:

TABLE 5.4 Conglomerate Control of Financiera Credit, 1978

| Conglomerate: Type and Name | Credit US$ Millions | % of Total |
|---|---|---|
| Internationalist | | |
| Vial (BHC) | 40.2 | 19.5 |
| Cruzat-Larraín | 20.2 | 9.8 |
| Other [a] | 55.2 | 26.7 |
| Former Traditional (Turned International) | | |
| Matte | 9.8 | 4.7 |
| Edwards | 6.8 | 3.3 |
| Total International | 132.2 | 64.0 |
| Other Conglomerates and Firms[b] | 74.2 | 36.0 |
| Total | 206.4 | 100.0[c] |

[a]Sahli-Tassara, Marín-Acuña, Andes, Ascuí-Cueto, Goycolea.
[b]May include international as well as traditional groups.
[c]Figures may not add up to 100 due to rounding.

*Source:* Fernando Dahse, *El mapa de la extrema riqueza* (Santiago: Editorial Aconcagua, 1979).

Radical neoliberals had monopolized the policy process and Pinochet had become too powerful to oppose. As a result, economic survival and future prosperity demanded rapid conglomerate restructuring. With this capitulation, gradualists lost an invaluable ally.

Landowners who produced for international markets constituted another group that at least tacitly supported radical neoliberalism during this period. Certain groups developed rapidly as the land reform sector was privatized. By the middle of 1978, nearly half of the expropriated lands had been returned to their former owners.[48] The return of these lands to the private sector did not mean their return to traditional, inefficient types of production. Overall, farms were smaller, and rapid tariff reductions and price decontrol had induced many landowners to modernize their agricultural production processes.[49] Under the new policies, producers of fruits and timber for export did quite well. Between 1976 and 1977, agricultural exports, of which fruits constituted the bulk, expanded by 68 percent.[50] Moreover, lower tariffs significantly reduced inputs such as fertilizers and machinery.

TABLE 5.5 Concentration of Wealth of the Largest 250 Chilean Firms, 1978

| Conglomerate: | Control of Firms | | Assets in 1978 | |
|---|---|---|---|---|
| Type and name | Number | % of Total | US$ Millions | % of Total |
| International | | | | |
| Cruzat-Larraín | 37 | 14.8 | 936.9 | 24.7 |
| Vial (BHC) | 25 | 10.0 | 477.3 | 12.6 |
| Angelini | 8 | 3.2 | 141.8 | 3.7 |
| Hochschild | 4 | 1.6 | 70.7 | 1.9 |
| Former Traditional | | | | |
| (Turned International) | | | | |
| Matte | 12 | 4.8 | 325.3 | 8.6 |
| Edwards | 9 | 3.6 | 96.0 | 2.5 |
| Traditional | | | | |
| Lúksic | 8 | 3.2 | 141.8 | 3.6 |
| Yarur-Bana | 4 | 1.6 | 92.0 | 2.4 |
| Lepe | 3 | 1.2 | 67.6 | 1.8 |
| Briones | 3 | 1.2 | 54.9 | 1.4 |
| 31 Lesser | | | | |
| Conglomerates | 64 | 25.6 | 531.1 | 14.0 |
| Foreign Capital | 35 | 14.0 | 493.1 | 13.0 |
| 37 Businessmen | 37 | 14.8 | 363.2 | 9.6 |
| Totals | 250 | 100.0[a] | 3,791.7[a] | 100.0[a] |

[a]Figures may not add up due to rounding.

*Source:* Fernando Dahse, *El mapa de la extrema riqueza* (Santiago: Editorial Aconcagua, 1979).

Although landowners did not participate openly in the policy debates of the period, their objective economic interests probably led most to welcome the lower tariffs championed by the radical international conglomerates. The actions of two prominent export-oriented members of the SNA who occupied high government office certainly supports this assumption. Both Alfonso Marquez de la Plata, who became minister of agriculture, and Pablo Baraona who was minister of economy, ardently advocated a radical neoliberal approach to economic restructuring. As shown in Tables 5.7 and 6.1 both of these men had business links to the Cruzat-Larraín conglomerate. In fact they were the only members of the

SNA to have strong ties to those core radical internationalist conglomerates. In addition to these bonds, both also had connections to Chilean financial circles.

## Regime Structure, State Institutions, and the Consolidation of the Radical Neoliberal Coalition

In addition to the growing economic strength of the core radical internationalist conglomerates and the expansion of the radical neoliberal coalition, a change in regime structure—the consolidation of one-man rule in Chile—added to the power of radical neoliberals by further biasing state institutions in their favor in two ways. The first one was a shift in the relationship of the army to the other branches of the armed forces. After the coup, the armed forces had divided governing responsibilities among themselves. The army took charge of internal security; the air force attended to social development; the national police watched over labor and agricultural affairs; and the navy, possessors of the economic plan, directed economic policy. They formalized and rationalized this arrangement in the middle of 1974 with the establishment of legislative commissions.

This arrangement set up a nominal policy process for routine matters until Pinochet became president of Chile in December 1974. When Pinochet acquired ultimate control over all policymaking areas, he gave himself the power to make ministerial appointments without the approval of the other junta members. With ministers of state who now served exclusively at his discretion, those positions acquired greater authority. Pinochet named radical internationalists to head key ministries and agencies; his appointees, in turn, filled important subordinate posts with their followers. A cohesive economic team in a tight hierarchy of ministerial authority virtually eliminated policy dissent among policymakers.

Pinochet's relentless efforts to institutionalize the military regime in ways that perpetuated his dominance over the political system smothered dissent from within the regime. Between December 1975 and 1976, Pinochet promulgated four constitutional acts that buried the possibility of a return to political democracy, elevated Pinochet to supreme dictator, and severed the participation of the other branches of the armed services in policymaking. These measures made the regime even more exclusionary, further reducing the institutional paths to power that gradualists and supporters of the status quo might have used to defend their interests. The detractors of radical neoliberalism were effectively deprived of venues in which to appeal their grievances. Following that, in January 1978, Pinochet held a plebiscite to ratify the junta's and, therefore, his own authority. The government claimed that 75 percent voted "yes." Finally, in mid-1978, Pinochet outlined a plan for a transition to a new "institutionality." The plan called for an anti-

TABLE 5.6 Economic Interests of SFF Council Members, 1975-1977

| Name | Economic Interest | | | | | Conglomerate Affiliation | Conglomerate Type |
|---|---|---|---|---|---|---|---|
| | MDM/NC | MDM/C | X/M | Fin. | MNC | | |
| Abumohor | x | | | x | | | Tradtional |
| Agüero | x | | | | | Lepe/Piquer/Lehman | Internationalist |
| Amunátegui | | x | | | | BHC & Cruzat/Larr. | |
| Arteaga | x | | | x | | | |
| Aspillaga | | x | | | | de Caso | Traditional |
| Ayala | | x | x | x | | Matte | Former Traditional[a] |
| Bolocco | x | | | | | | |
| Casanova | x | | | | | | |
| Daroch | x | | | | | BHC | Internationalist |
| Elton | x | | | | | | |
| Falcón | x | | | | x | | |
| Garcés | x | | | | | Said | Traditional |
| Garib | x | | | | | | |
| Ipinza | | x | | | | Ibáñez | Traditional |
| Krumm | | x | | | x | | |
| Kunstmann | | x | | | | | |
| Lira | | x | x | | | Angelini | Internationalist |
| López | x | | | | | Vial | Internationalist |

| Name | MDM/NC | MDM/C | X/M | Fin. | MNC | Conglomerate | Profile |
|---|---|---|---|---|---|---|---|
| Menéndez | x | x | | | | Menéndez | Internationalist |
| Pinto | x | x | | | x | Matte | Former Traditional[a] |
| Piquer | x | | | | | Lepe/Piquer/Lehman | Traditional |
| Riveros | x | | | | | | |
| Ross | x | | | | | Cruzat/Larr. | Internationalist |
| Sáenz | x | x | | | x | Sáenz | Traditional |
| Sahli | x | x | | x | x | Sahli/Tassara | Internationalist |
| Sarquis | x | | | | | | |
| Simonetti | x | | | | | | |
| Smits | x | | | | | Vial | Internationalist |
| Urquidi | x | | | | x | | |
| Vergara | | x | | | | Andina | Internationalist |
| Zañartu | | x | | x | | Angelini | Internationalist |

MDM/NC: Manufacturers for domestic markets in internationally noncompetitive sectors
MDM/C: Manufacturers for domestic markets in internationally competitive sectors (mostly food and beverage industries).
X/M: International commerce.
Fin.: Financial activities.
MNC: Is an executive in a Multinational Corporation.
[a] A formerly traditional conglomerate is one that shifted from a traditional to an internationalist profile.

*Sources:* SFF, *Memoria Anual*, selected years; Colegio de Priodistas, *Diccionario biográfico* (Santiago: Editorial Universitaria, selected years); SFF, *Informativo SFF*, selected years; Superintendencia de Asociaciones Bancarias y Financieras, *Nómina del directorio de instituciones financieras* (Santiago, n.p., selected years); annual reports of conglomerate firms.

TABLE 5.7 Economic Interests of SNA Council Members, 1973-1977

| Name | Markets Crops Produced for | | Non-Agricultural Interests | | |
| | Domestic [a] | Export [b] | Fin. | MDM | X/M |
|---|---|---|---|---|---|
| Ariztía R. | | x | | | |
| Arrau U. | x | | x[d] | | |
| Balmaceda V. | x | | | | |
| Baraona U.[c] | x | | x | | |
| Bascuñán A. | x | | | | |
| Bismarck E. | x | | | | |
| Correa Va. | x | | | | |
| Correa Vi. | | x | | | |
| Covarrubias L. | x | | | | |
| Godoy M. | | x | | | x |
| Infante G. | x | | | x | |
| Infante L. | x | | | | |
| Márquez d.l.P.[c] | | x | x | | |
| Matte G. | x | x | | | |
| Montt M. | x | | | | |
| Moore R. | x | | | | |
| Moreno A. | | x | | | |
| Moreno M. | x | | | | |
| Munita V. | x | | | | |
| Ochagavía V. | x | | | | |
| Ruíz-Tagle F. | x | | | | |
| Tagle V. | x | | | | |
| Ulloa M. | | x | x[d] | | |
| Valdés L. | x | | | | |
| Valdés V. | | x | | | |
| Valdés Va. | x | | | | |
| Valdés Vi. E. | x | | | | |
| Valdés Vi. M. | | x | | | |
| Valdés Z. | x | | | | |

Fin.: Financial interests.
MDM: Manufactures for domestic markets.
X/M: International commerce
[a]Traditional crops: mostly grains, cereals, cattle, and dairy products.
[b]Mostly fruits.
[c]Were connected to firms of the internationalist Cruzat-Larraín conglomerate.
[d]On the Board of Banco O'Higgins, an agricultural bank.
Sources: SNA, El Campesino, selected years; Colegio de Periodistas, Diccionario biográfico (Santiago: Editorial Universitaira, selected years); SNA central office; Superintendencia de Asociaciones Bancarias y Financieras, Nómina del directorio de instituciones financieras (Santiago, n.p., selected years); annual reports of conglomerate companies.

democratic regime that prohibited party competition as a source of opposition to the government.[51]

The consolidation of one-man rule in Chile aided the expanding core radical internationalists in another way. Pinochet increasingly relied on them to be the core of his social support. First, he could count on them to back his political ambitions because without his help they could never have triumphed so completely. Radical internationalists depended on his iron-fisted rule because it insulated economic policymakers from all other business and landowning groups in addition to other classes, such as the middle class, labor, and peasants. In a less closed authoritarian regime, these social groups, especially traditional landowners and industrialists, might have found allies in the government to protect them. During Chile's democratic era and the immediate post-coup period, the radical internationalist's ambitions were limited by different institutional arrangements. In Chile's democratic regime, where votes were a power resource, the radical internationalists would have been much too narrow a support group to sustain both an economic policy and a governing coalition. By the same token, the more permeable policy process in the wake of the coup had helped gradualists strike a bargain with more moderate internationalists and keep radical ones in check.

Second, when Pinochet placed the representatives of the core internationalist conglomerates in an unassailable position of political strength, he probably gambled that they could successfully restructure the Chilean economy and, with it, Chilean society. Policies that promoted deindustrialization had the potential to extirpate Marxism from Chilean society and break the power of organized labor, both long-term goals of Pinochet.[52]

Once again, changes in regime structure biased institutional power in favor of radical neoliberals. As the internationalist conglomerates gained strength, Pinochet relied even more heavily on them as his core support group. He promoted Sergio de Castro from minister of economy to minister of finance and elevated the director of the Central Bank, Pablo Baraona, to minister of economy. These two men had been the behind-the-scenes architects of the shock treatment, banking policy, and tariff reduction programs—all policies that the internationalist conglomerates had supported. Both men also had close business ties to the core radical internationalist conglomerates.

It was a system of interaction between state and capital in which a narrow coalition of radical internationalist capitalists enjoyed virtually exclusive rights to participation in the policymaking process with an equally narrow, cohesive band of technocrats, many of whom had business and university ties to these same radical capitalists. The system produced a rigid, inflexible policymaking style in which other fractions of capital and organized business had no access to policymaking. These subordinate fractions of capital were left with three alternatives: resist, adapt, or succumb.

## Opposition to Radical Internationalists

Although vast, the power of the Chicago boys was not absolute. Policy debates revealed that occasionally Pinochet had them bow to demands from peak associations. It was very difficult, however, for business organizations to get Pinochet's attention and still more difficult to get him to act on their behalf. The exclusion of business organizations from the policy process itself was one of the Chicago boys' greatest triumphs. Moreover, Pinochet helped them to resist pressure to institutionalize channels of access for business and landowning groups.[53] The only avenue open to business associations for redress of their grievances was to petition Pinochet directly. Since Pinochet backed the Chicago boys and their allies almost unconditionally, more often than not private sector opposition went unheeded.

The closed policymaking process stacked the cards against organized business in another way. The most effective means to get attention was to present a united and forceful front through the Confederación de la Producción y Comercio (CPC). Businessmen and landowners had to show that the general interests of the private sector were at stake, not just petty sectoral or personal ones. As a result, the demands of individual peak associations, to say nothing of subsectoral organizations, generally went unattended. A high degree of intersectoral conflict during this period made it nearly impossible for sectoral peak associations to present a united front. Individual peak associations, such as the SFF and the SNA—as well as the subsectoral organizations of wheat and dairy farmers or electronics and metalworking industrialists—insisted on approaching the authorities on their own. They persistently lobbied for their most narrow economic interests. It was a tactic that had worked in democracy and even in the first months after the coup. But it was unsuitable after Pinochet consolidated one-man rule.

Even where official institutionalized channels of access to the policy process existed, the extreme concentration of power in authoritarian Chile rendered them tenuous and ineffectual. For example, in mid-1974, the Central Bank created an agency to handle tariff structure reform, the Comité Asesor de Política Arancelaria (CAPA). The Chicago boys directed the CAPA and contracted policy design out to the Department of Economics of the Catholic University, an intellectual stronghold of the Chicago boys. The CAPA had only one private sector representative for all five branches of production affiliated with the CPC. Given strong sectoral differences over tariff policy within the CPC, this person was not even a member of any of the peak associations. He was a professor of economics at the Catholic University. His duties were limited to attending and reporting on weekly meetings, which the CPC distributed to the sectoral peak associations. This representative of the private sector was not privy to key policy deliberations because they did not take place during those weekly meetings. Consequently, business organizations had only a general idea of the direction in which policy was moving and lacked direct input into policy formulation.[54]

The tendency of the SFF and the SNA to approach policymakers individually rather than collectively undermined their efforts to influence policy implementation.[55] Nevertheless, ineffectual as it was, the internationalist coalition faced opposition from more traditional business and landowning sectors. They voiced their discontent publicly and privately, although landowners tended to be more confrontational than industrialists.[56]

***Industrialists and Quiet Diplomacy.*** A number of industrial subsectors—metalworking, textile, chemical, and leather—strongly opposed drastic deflation, radical tariff reductions, and high interest rates. Orlando Sáenz spoke for businessmen from these industries when he warned that these draconian policies were leading to predictable results: bankruptcies and a fantastic concentration of wealth.[57] In contrast to the strong, open stances those subsectors, the industrialists' peak association—the SFF— took a milder course and raised no public outcry. The SFF leadership's first response to the government's new tariff reduction program was to attempt to pacify its constituency. In an SFF meeting held in September 1975, SFF president Raúl Sahli insisted there was no need for a confrontational stance. He attempted to calm fellow industrialists by telling them that he was convinced that the government had no intention of letting entire sectors collapse. Sahli put it this way, "I have no doubt that the government will revise customs tariffs if the circumstances [mass bankruptcies] demand it, but you must understand that shrill demands and pressure on our part will yield no results."[58]

Privately, however, the SFF expressed concern, especially about tariff reductions. In meetings and communiques with government officials between August 1974 and December 1977, the leadership of the SFF stressed that drastic, across-the-board reductions hurt many industrial sectors. The leadership of the SFF, however, realized that the ideology of the Chicago boys made them deaf to demands for changes in proposed tariff schedules. The Chicago boys refused to contemplate policies that discriminated between economic sectors, so the SFF sought protection by arguing that they faced disloyal competition from abroad—dumping. SFF leaders hoped that such an approach would get a better hearing because it fit the neoclassical paradigm: It was legitimate to seek compensatory measures in blatantly distorted market situations.

Throughout 1976 and 1977, the SFF kept its members apprised of its efforts to obtain special dispensations for sectors afflicted by disloyal international competition. Early in September, the SFF informed Central Bank officials that some industrial sectors were concerned about dumping.[59] Towards the beginning of 1977, possibly out of wishful thinking, SFF leaders waxed optimistic over their prospects for success: Imports had not yet flooded Chilean markets. Yet, in the same breath, they were forced to acknowledge that some sectors had suffered heavily as a result of tariff reductions.[60]

Early 1977 was the last time the SFF leadership mustered optimism in reports to members. In mid-1977, the leadership of the SFF met with the junta and top economic authorities to express concern over tariffs and foreign exchange rates. They requested that the authorities clarify the rules of the game. Pinochet, the ministers of economy and finance, and the president of the Central Bank declined to alter policy.[61] In October 1977, the SFF appealed to Minister of Economy Pablo Baraona one more time. The leadership insisted that the authorities clarify the tariff reduction program and adopt anti-dumping legislation.[62] This attempt also failed to move the authorities. In a perverse way, however, they did clarify policy. In December, the government issued the decree that reduced most tariffs to an across-the-board 10 percent by mid-1979.

***Opposition by Landowners.*** Regardless of the size of their holdings, landowners who produced traditional agricultural products, such as corn, grains, and milk also fought for protection. Although they supported tariff reduction, they wanted price floors and ceilings to keep imports out and to make agriculture profitable. The landowners' peak association, the SNA, argued that these agricultural products had "strategic" value.[63] No doubt, they hoped that this argument would appeal to the military mindset.

Despite the fact that the SNA occasionally disparaged the government for lowering tariffs on specific agricultural products (especially milk and wheat), it concentrated on lobbying for the maintenance of price supports. In January 1976, the SNA reminded Pinochet of the commitment he had made in 1975 to maintain prices at adequate levels.[64] In June, landowners firmly asserted their right to "respectfully continue to make demands on the authorities."[65] In October, they insisted on the need for price supports for strategic products as long as imperfect market conditions made them necessary.[66] In December, they complained about inadequate price support for wheat.[67]

In the first quarter of 1977, the SNA leadership complimented the government for establishing price supports for wheat, rapeseed, and beets. It also argued that a high exchange rate was necessary for effective protection from the dumping of cheap imports.[68] In June and August, the SNA asked why the government was not expanding price supports to the rest of the strategic products.[69] The fall in production of all traditional agricultural products in 1978 ultimately demonstrated the inadequacy of price support levels.[70] These developments, and greater open turmoil among landowners, especially in southern Chile, moved the authorities to take minimal conciliatory action. However, the measures were deliberately insufficient to maintain production of the products in question. In this way policymakers forced adjustment despite the more active opposition by a lone peak association.

*Intersectoral Conflict and the Failure to Build an Opposition Industrial-Landowner Coalition.* Given that government policies hit them hard, why did uncompetitive manufacturers for domestic markets and landowners in internationally uncompetitive areas not join forces to resist the rapid opening of Chile's once highly protected economy?[71] Long standing intersectoral conflict between industrialists and landowners provides a partial explanation. Divisions within the membership of the SFF and SNA based on their relationship to traditional and internationalist conglomerates reinforced those splits.

Although difficult to measure, intersectoral conflict between town and country probably played the greater role in explaining the absence of a joint opposition.[72] For decades, high tariffs for industrial goods (including farm machines) and low tariffs for agricultural products (food for workers) had rankled landowners. Landowner resentment at the decline of their sector in favor of industry was at the root of the intersectoral divide.[73] Even though manufacturers and landowners both wanted protection, they preferred different policy instruments. Manufacturers wanted tariffs, landowners opposed them and sought price supports.

The policy debates after the coup illustrate the position of landowners. If anything, they wanted tariffs for industrial goods lowered faster. In November 1974, the SNA expressed satisfaction with tariff reductions. The leadership expected tariffs between industry and agriculture to level out, thus, ending discrimination between the two sectors.[74] After passage of the new, more radical, tariff laws in July 1975, the SNA urged the authorities not to tarry in devising a new schedule—lest industrialists have time to gain concessions under the existing one.[75]

For their part, businessmen, particularly from the internationalist conglomerates, lambasted landowners' petitions for price supports. In January 1976, the SNA monthly *El Campesino* covered an *El Mercurio* story disparaging landowners. *El Mercurio* was critical of landowners who did not diversify their production, shift to export crops, or specialize in agricultural inputs for agribusiness.[76]

Different levels of opposition to government trade policy within each peak association partly explains the lack of cooperation between the peak associations of industrialists and landowners. Although the SFF's protests were muted, the SNA dissented more aggressively. Variation in the relationship between elected council members and conglomerates or economic subsectors partially explains these stances. Table 5.6 shows that SFF members had close ties to conglomerates capable of adjustment, or they had interests in other sectors of the economy that might benefit from the new foreign economic policy. For example, of the 22 members active in manufacturing companies that were not competitive internationally (MDM/ NC), only eight had no connection to conglomerates or economic interests in other sectors of the economy. Of an additional eight persons who only had ties to the MDM/NC sector, four were executives in companies of internationalist conglomerates, one worked for an MNC, and three were active in companies that belonged to traditional conglomerates capable of adjusting, although not without some difficulty. The remaining six members either participated in other economic sectors or had close ties to conglomerates (three internationalist and one traditional). Table 5.7 shows that SNA members had fewer of these connections and most of them produced exclusively traditional agricultural products. Of the 20 members involved in such activities, only two of them had overlapping internationalist economic interests, and only one of those two had a connection to internationalist conglomerates.

### Conclusion: The Imposition of Radical Neoliberalism

The intensification of intracapitalist conflict between 1974 and 1978 led to the shift from gradual to radical market reforms in Chile. This chapter argued that a core of radical internationalist conglomerates with a heavy concentration in liquid assets, together with their Chicago boy allies, wrestled control over policymaking away from gradualists. In 1974, while gradualists were still dominant, the radicals publicly raised the demand for more drastic action. Then, after outmaneuvering gradualists, the radical internationalist coalition excluded them from the policy formulation process. Radical internationalists overcame obstacles placed by gradualists and more radical measures followed apace.

The chapter also examined the influence of external economic shocks and changes in the structure of the authoritarian regime in the victory of radical capitalists over gradualists. The manner in which these factors combined to usher in gradual or radical policy coalitions was not constant. External factors played a more significant role in the rise of the radical coalition than they had in the establishment of the gradual one. The impact of the oil price shock was not fully understood at the beginning of the gradual period. It was more of a diffuse background variable immediately after the coup. The presence of some external economic pressure, combined with the internal problems of ISI that had been worsening since the 1960s, indicated that export expansion and diversification were highly desirable. Conditions were not so dramatic, however, that they required drastic action.[77]

Beginning in late 1974, international liquidity began to rise as increasing quantities of petrodollars were recycled. This enabled radical internationalist conglomerate heads to step up intracapitalist competition aggressively. Their heavy involvement in the financial sector allowed them to gain preferential access to foreign savings. Radical internationalists then rapidly increased their holdings in the most dynamic sectors of the Chilean economy.

Domestic factors refracted the effect of external economic influences. Differences in regime structure and the system of interaction between capitalists and bureaucrats shaped intracapitalist conflict, its effect on coalition formation and strength, and policy. In the gradualist period, regime structure muted intracapitalist conflict. A junta of the armed forces governed the immediate post-coup authoritarian regime. Multiple avenues of access to decision-making were available to many fractions of large-scale capital. Moreover, both radical internationalists and supporters of pre-coup import-substitution industrialization policies were held in check within the business coup coalition that had formulated the initial economic recovery plan. Ministerial and other appointments initially biased power in favor of gradualists who dominated policy formulation. Intracapitalist conflict existed, but it was not sharp. Internationally competitive producers for domestic markets managed to keep radical internationalists in check and to defeat the erstwhile dominant fraction of capital: producers for domestic markets that were not competitive internationally.

A shift within the structure of the military regime unleashed more virulent intracapitalist conflict. A brash breed of entrepreneurs that had built up holdings in financial and internationally oriented sectors seized the opportunity to challenge established capitalist fractions. External factors may have increased the economic power of radical internationalists; but continued centralization of authoritarian rule—from the junta to Pinochet—made it possible for this narrow constellation of business interests to have a much greater impact than it would have otherwise. They offered Pinochet the dual promise of investment and economic growth along with unconditional support for his rule.

The shift in the structure of the military regime facilitated the emergence of a special system of interaction between the executives of the core internationalist conglomerates and the radical Chicago boy technocrats. This form of collaboration between capitalists, technocrats, and policy outcome differed strikingly from that of the gradual adjustment period.

The gradual policy period rested on an accommodation between the civilian coup coalition and the military junta. Here, regime structure permitted the participation of business peak associations in the policy process. Moreover, the military sought out individual capitalists who represented a general consensus among all capitalist and landowning fractions. Because of the participation of a wider spectrum of *large-scale* businessmen and landowners, policy change was not brusque.

By contrast, during the radical policy period, the change in authoritarian regime structure permitted the exclusion of business associations and individual capitalists who represented some form of intracapitalist consensus. Under Pinochet, direct collaboration in policy formulation between the executives of three conglomerates and technocrats who shared their economic and ideological interests made radical neoliberalism feasible. An intimate link existed between the men who favored radical neoliberalism in the private sector and policymakers who shared their views in the government. Pinochet elevated the radical Chicago boys from their subordinate position in the gradualist coalition by appointing them to the top economic policymaking posts. But these men, members of the economic team that produced the Brick, were not just ideologues; they had all been executives of the core radical conglomerates (BHC, Cruzat-Larraín, and Edwards) that, in turn, had dominated the Monday Club before the coup. They probably regarded themselves as both the ideological and material sources of a new order for Chile.

In this new order, the exclusion from the policy process of capitalists and landowners who preferred a more gradual course curbed the need for accommodation. The expansion of the core radical internationalist conglomerates, the growth of other internationalist conglomerates, and the decision by some leading internationally competitive conglomerates that produced for domestic markets to acquire a more internationalist profile, broadened explicit and tacit support for swift change. These developments also created investment that contributed to economic recovery, albeit of an uneven nature. Growth in the sectors targeted for expansion by radical neoliberalism helped Pinochet to stabilize his regime both economically and politically. But the narrow system of interaction between a handful of capitalists and ideological technocrats produced an inflexible policy style that did not adapt policy quickly to new, more adverse circumstances. This inflexibility was not without consequence for the stability of Pinochet's rule, as will be seen in the next two chapters.

## Notes

1. For an overview of those policies, see Sebastian Edwards and Alejandra Cox-Edwards, *Monetarism and Liberalization: The Chilean Experiment* (Cambridge: Ballinger, 1987); Alejandro Foxley, *Latin American Experiments in Neoconservative Economics* (Berkeley: University of California Press, 1983); Joseph Ramos, *Neoconservative Economics in the Southern Cone* (Baltimore: Johns Hopkins University Press, 1986).

2. Fernando Dahse, *El mapa de la extrema riqueza* (Santiago: Editorial Aconcagua, 1979).

3. *El Mercurio*, November 9, 1974.

4. *Ercilla* no. 2058, January 1975.

5. *El Mercurio*, March 8, 1975 and other dates around that time. For an argument of how local elites use foreign advisory missions, see Paul W. Drake, *The Money Doctor in the Andes: The Kemmerer Missions, 1923-1933* (Durham: Duke University Press, 1989). For an extension of the argument, see Paul W. Drake, ed., *Money Doctors, Foreign Debts, and Economic Reforms in Latin America from the 1980s to the Present* (Wilmington: Scholarly Resources, 1994).

6. By 1976, the government had spun off most nationalized banking assets. The internationalist conglomerates, which controlled the financial system, began to buy up industries in export-import and primary product industries, the dynamic industries of an open economy. For privatization policies, in addition to the texts cited in note 1, see Corporación de Fomento de la Producción, *Privatización de empresas y activos 1973-1978* (Santiago: Gerencia de Normalización de Empresas, n.d.).

7. Laurence Whitehead, "Inflation and Stabilisation in Chile, 1970-77," in Rosemary Thorp and Laurence Whitehead, eds., *Inflation and Stabilisation in Latin America* (New York: Holms and Meier, 1979); Alejandro Foxley, *Neoconservative Economics*.

8. *El Campesino* 1-2, January-February 1975, editorial.

9. Stephany Griffith-Jones and Osvaldo Sunkel, *La crisis de la deuda y del desarrollo en América Latina: El fin de una ilusión* (Buenos Aires: Grupo Editor Latinoamericano, 1987).

10. Company annual reports and annual reports of key financial institutions revealed that key officers had been employed by Citibank in Chile. The concentration of financial intermediation of foreign loans is a testimony to their privileged position. See Fernando Dahse, *El mapa de la extrema riqueza*.

11. For an account of this process, see Fernando Dahse, *El mapa de la extrema riqueza*; Andrés Sanfuentes, "Los grupos económicos: Control y políticas," *Estudios Cieplan* no. 15, December 1984. Moreover, the radical Chicago boys who controlled the Central Bank during the period of financial sector reform had close business ties to the internationalist conglomerates, and they invited executives from those conglomerates to participate in the discussions. These data from a personal interview with Juan Villarzú, who was budget director at the time, and from Banco Central de Chile, *Estudios monetarios III: Seminario de mercados de capitales* (Santiago: n.p., 1974). For a description of how the Chicago boys took over key offices from more moderate persons, see Verónica Montecinos, "Economics and Power: Chilean Economists in Government, 1958-1985," Ph.D. Dissertation, University of Pittsburgh,

1988; and Arturo Fontaine Aldunate, *Los economistas y el Presidente Pinochet* (Santiago: Editorial Zig-Zag, 1988).

12. For nationalization policy, see Corporación de Fomento de la Producción, *Privatización de empresas y activos 1973-1978;* Markos Mamalakis, *The Growth and Structure of the Chilean Economy: From Independence to Allende* (New Haven: Yale University Press, 1976), passim; Tomás Moulián, "Fases del desarrollo político chileno entre 1973 y 1978," FLACSO, *Documento de Trabajo* no. 155, September 1982; James Petras, "Nationalization, Socioeconomic Change, and Popular Participation," in Arturo Valenzuela and Samuel Valenzuela, eds., *Chile: Politics and Society* (New Brunswick: Transaction, 1976); Alec Nove, "The Political Economy of the Allende Regime," in Philip O'Brien, ed., *Allende's Chile* (New York: Praeger, 1976).

13. Author interview with Orlando Sáenz, August 1988, and *Informativo SFF* no. 71, February-March 1974.

14. *Informativo SFF* no. 71, February-March 1974.

15. Company annual reports of key firms for 1973 and 1974, for example, those of the Compañía Cevecerías Unidas, Fensa, Mademsa, Compañía Manufacturera de Papeles y Cartones.

16. Fernando Dahse, "El poder económico de los grandes grupos empresariales nacionales," *Contribuciones FLACSO,* Santiago, June 1983, pp. 13-17.

17. Annual reports of Banco Hipotecario list short biographies of their executives. Listing work experience in First City on the vita of their executives was assumed to instill confidence in BHC.

18. Philip O'Brien, *The Pinochet Decade,* p. 72.

19. For financial deregulation and *financieras,* see José Pablo Arellano, "De la liberalización a la intervención: El mercado de capitales en Chile, 1974-83,"*Colección Estudios Cieplan* no. 11, December 1983, p. 7; Ricardo Ffrench-Davis, "El problema de la deuda externa y la apertura financiera en Chile, " *Colección Estudios Cieplan* no. 11, December 1983, p. 117; Dahse, *El mapa de la extrema riqueza. Financieras* were different from banks because they were mostly savings and loan organizations, and they were restricted in terms of the types of brokerage operations they could carry out.

20. For the relationship between conglomerates and *financieras,* see Dahse, *El mapa de la extrema riqueza;* and Alejandro Foxley, *Latin American Experiments in Neoconservative Economics.*

21. Sergio de la Cuadra, economic advisor and former finance minister, elucidated the policy process for me in an author interview, September 1988; also see Central Bank-sponsored conference volumes, Banco Central de Chile, *Estudios monetarios III.*

22. For descriptions on how the Chicago boys took over key offices and displaced more moderate officials, see Verónica Montecinos, "Economics and Power: Chilean Economists in Government, 1958-1985"; Arturo Fontaine Aldunate, *Los economistas y el Presidente Pinochet* (Santiago: Zig-Zag, 1988, 2nd edition).

23. Manuel Cruzat—one of the principals of the internationalist Cruzat-Larraín conglomerate—was most frequently mentioned during interviews. Juan Villarzú was the interviewee who most explicitly described the relationship between businessmen and the Chicago boys in government in an author interview, December 1988.

24. Banco Central de Chile, *Estudios monetarios III*.

25. José Zabala, Humberto Díaz, Carlos Berner, "Bancos de Fomento en America Latina," in Banco Central de Chile, *Estudios monetarios III*, pp. 204-6.

26. Banco Central, *Estudios monetarios III*, pp. 385-388.

27. For Orlando Sáenz, see *Informativo SFF* no. 71, February-March 1974; for José Zabala, see José Zabala et al., "Bancos de Fomento en America Latina," in Banco Central de Chile, *Estudios Monetarios III*.

28. Ascanio Cavallo, Manuel Salazar, and Oscar Sepúlveda, *La historia oculta del régimen militar* (Santiago: Ediciones Epoca, 1988), pp. 63-70. The authors add that Jorge Cauas himself wrote the decree that gave him these powers, along with the independent authority to appoint all subordinates below the rank of minister. Heretofore, the junta had to approve proposed appointments.

29. Ibid.

30. For a more detailed account, see Ascanio Cavallo et al., *La historia oculta del régimen militar*, pp. 63-70; and Arturo Valenzuela, "The Military in Power: The Consolidation of One Man Rule in Chile," in Paul W. Drake and Iván Jaksic, eds., *The Struggle for Democracy in Chile, 1982-1990* (Lincoln: University of Nebraska Press, 1991).

31. Philip O'Brien, *The Pinochet Decade* (London: Latin America Bureau, 1983), pp. 46-55.

32. Ibid., p. 46.

33. Ibid.; also see Ascanio Cavallo et al., *La historia oculta del régimen militar*, pp. 47-62; and Arturo Fontaine, *Los economistas y el Presidente Pinochet*; Mary Helen Spooner, *Soldiers in a Narrow Land: The Pinochet Regime in Chile* (Berkeley: University of California Press, 1994).

34. Philip O'Brien, *The Pinochet Decade*, pp. 46-55; Ascanio Cavallo et al., *La historia oculta*, pp. 63-70.

35. Ascanio Cavallo et al., *La historia oculta*, pp. 47-54.

36. For a similar argument with respect to the labor movement, see Laurence Whitehead, "Inflation and Stabilization in Chile." Moreover, the connection between international conglomerates and government soon became a revolving door.

37. Author interviews with Sergio de la Cuadra, December 1988; Juan Ignacio Varas, November 1988; Rolf Lüders, December 1988; and Juan Andrés Fontaine, November 1988.

38. Alejandro Foxley, *Neoconservative Experiments*, pp. 55-56 and Table 8, pp. 50-52.

39. Tomás Moulián and Pilar Vergara, "Ideología y política económica," *Colección Estudios Cieplan* no. 3, June 1980, pp. 86-89.

40. CORFO, *Privatización de empresas y activos 1973-1978*, pp. 23-25, and Anexo no. 21.

41. Alejandro Foxley, *Neoconservative Experiments*, pp. 56-57.

42. Business Latin America, *Trading in Latin America: The Impact of Changing Policies* (New York: n.p., 1981), p. 76; Guillermo Campero, *Los gremios empresariales en el período 1970-1983* (Santiago: ILET, 1984), p. 153.

43. Guillermo Campero, *Los gremios empresariales*, chapter 3.

44. Fernando Dahse, *El mapa de la extrema riqueza*.

45. Ibid.; and Alejandro Foxley, *Neoconservative Economics*, pp. 106-107, and p. 170.

46. Fernando Dahse, *El mapa de la extrema riqueza*, see the section on the Edwards conglomerate, pp. 61-64.

47. *El Mercurio*, May 8, 1976.

48. Alejandro Foxley, *Neoconservative Economics*, p. 67.

49. Sergio Gómez, "Nuevos empresarios y empresas agrícolas en Chile," FLACSO, *Documento de Trabajo* no. 277, January 1986.

50. Business Latin America, *Trading in Latin America*, p. 76; Guillermo Campero, *Los gremios empresariales*, p. 153.

51. Brian Loveman, *Chile: The Legacy of Hispanic Capitalism* (New York: Oxford University Press, 1979), pp. 349-357.

52. Manufactures as share of GDP fell from 26 percent in 1972 to 21.8 percent in 1980. The average growth rate for that sector fell from 5.4 percent from 1960 to 1970 to 1 percent for the 1974-1980 period. The value added of practically all manufacturing activities declined between 1970 and 1979. Hardest hit were textiles, rubber, ceramics, glass, hardware goods, machinery, electrical equipment, transport, and professional equipment. Their share of total industrial production fell from 36 percent in 1970 to 23 percent in 1979. These data are from Guillermo Campero and José Valenzuela, *El movimiento sindical en el régimen militar chileno, 1973-1981* (Santiago: ILET, 1983), pp. 60-63, especially tables 4.10 and 4.11. For a detailed account of deindustrialization, see Jaime Gatica Barros, *Deindustrialization in Chile* (Boulder: Westview, 1989). Laurence Whitehead advances the argument about reducing the power of labor in, "Inflation and Stabilisation in Chile."

53. See *El Campesino* no. 11, November 1973 and no. 7, July 1975.

54. See Comité Asesor de Política Arancelaria files in CPC archives. Author interview with Juan Ignacio Varas, then private sector representative to the CAPA, November 1988.

55. For interesting anecdotes concerning meetings between aggrieved businessmen, Pinochet and the junta, see Arturo Fontaine, *Los economistas*. Issues of *Informativo SFF* and *El Campesino* from 1975 to 1977 constantly report on meetings with Pinochet, the junta, and ministers of state. Usually they got a sympathetic hearing and vague promises but no results.

56. For the public differences between landowners and the government on price supports, see Guillermo Campero, *Los gremios empresariales*, pp. 155-158.

57. *Ercilla* no. 2135, June-July 1976.

58. *Informativo SFF*, September 1975.

59. *Informativo SFF* no. 98, October 1976.

60. *Informativo SFF* no. 101, February-March 1977.

61. *Informativo SFF* no. 103, June-July 1977.

62. *Informativo SFF* no. 105, October 1977.

63. The SNA adopted this justification in June 1974. *El Campesino* 7, July 1974.

64. *El Campesino* 1-2, January-February 1976.

65. *El Campesino* 6, June 1976, editorial.

66. *El Campesino* 10, October 1976, editorial.

67. *El Campesino* 12, December 1976.

68. *El Campesino* 4, April 1977.

69. *El Campesino* 6, June 1977 and 8, August 1977.

70. In 1978, the production of 10 of 14 traditional agricultural products declined by the following percentages: wheat, 27 percent (wheat accounts for 40 percent of the total production in traditional agriculture); barley, 12 percent; oats, 25 percent; rye, 34 percent; rice, 13 percent; corn, 28 percent; beans, 0.3 percent; lentils, 20 percent; rapeseed, 17 percent; and beets, 62 percent. By contrast, the four traditional products that increased production (potatoes, garbanzo beans, peas and sunflowers) only accounted for approximately 18 percent of total traditional product production. Data taken from Guillermo Campero, *Los gremios empresariales*, p. 173.

71. Some Chicago boys felt that industrialists and landowners might have been more successful in opposing government policy if they had joined forces. Author interview with Juan Andrés Fontaine, director of the planning department of the Central Bank, November 1988.

72. For an early interpretation of this conflict, see Markos Mamalakis, "Teoría de choques entre sectores," *Universidad de Chile, Instituto de Economía*, Publicaciones del Instituto de Economía, no. 83, 1966.

73. *El Campesino* 1-2, January-February 1974.

74. *El Campesino* 11, November 1974.

75. *El Campesino* 10, October 1975.

76. *El Campesino* 1-2, January-February 1976.

77. Chile, for example, had managed to renegotiate its foreign debt and was receiving foreign aid from the U.S. once again.

# 6

# Triumph and Collapse of
# Radical Neoliberalism

To a much larger extent than in either Argentina or Uruguay, an economic boom between 1979 and 1981 created a sense of euphoria in Chile, a traditionally poor, austere nation. The traumas, suffering, and sacrifices of the last eight years added to historical feelings of pent up demand among the citizenry. Thus, during this short-lived period of plenty many Chileans reveled in a luxury that had long been denied to them: consumerism. Imported cheeses, consumer durables, and foreign travel, once difficult to obtain, were suddenly available. Scotch whisky, formerly almost impossible to find, became a symbol of the new consumerism. Meanwhile, the media bombarded the population with messages and images lionizing and romanticizing rugged individualism, entrepreneurship, and the benefits of the unfettered marketplace. The Chilean upper and middle classes consoled themselves over their nation's isolation from the international community for human rights abuses with the following belief: Chile had vanquished Marxism and was in the forefront of capitalist development in the developing world.

In Chile, economic success seemed to have vindicated the radical neoliberal model and the means of its implementation. The supporters of radical neoliberalism took advantage of these sentiments to deepen and extend the model. They fixed the exchange rate, let the level of international reserves control of the money supply (automatic adjustment), liberalized capital accounts, and slashed all tariffs to 10 percent, an unusually low rate for Latin America at the time. The government also extended neoliberal principles to social and educational policy.

The neoliberal model, however, began to come under stress in 1981 in Chile as well as Argentina and Uruguay. Like most other Latin American nations, Chile had contracted a large foreign debt in the 1970s and early 1980s. Debt obligations eventually strained the financial system to the breaking point. In 1982, the international debt crisis precipitated the collapse of the Chilean financial system. The economy, the most open in the region, contracted more violently than those of either Argentina or Uruguay. GDP plunged 14 percent and unemployment soared to over 25 percent. Initially, however, the regime granted few policy concessions to mounting criticism. Significant policy change did not occur until the middle of 1983.

This chapter examines how the expansion and contraction of international liquidity contributed to the extension and demise of the radical neoliberal coalition. The first section argues that between 1978 and 1981, high levels of international liquidity were responsible for the enlargement of the power bloc that backed deepening radical neoliberalism. It drew in other business and landowning groups (and even middle-class groups) to support it. The flood of foreign savings fed the economic boom and sustained social groups excluded from the policy process. Easy credit allowed producers for domestic markets to cope with the negative effects of very low tariffs. They borrowed to expand, diversify or survive in an atmosphere of prosperity. The middle class, as never before, borrowed cheap dollars and consumed goods and services, many of them imported, that had been the preserve of the upper classes.

Although the expansion of the core radical neoliberal coalition contributed to a climate of acceptance for further radicalization, explaining the adoption of those policies requires an examination of domestic structure. Regime structure—Pinochet's system of one-man rule—was key. Not only did he protect technocrats, Pinochet also sustained the system of interaction between capitalists and the state that had developed from 1975 to 1978. This assured the core radical internationalists exclusive participation in policymaking. The revolving door between the executive officers of those economic groups and the economic ministries was testimony to the power of these conglomerates.

The next two sections of this chapter examine how external factors contributed to the unravelling of the radical neoliberal coalition and the formation of an alternative, "pragmatic," neoliberal coalition. It will be argued that changes in the level of international liquidity led to shifts in the economic interest of capitalist groups, which awakened dormant intracapitalist conflict. High levels of foreign lending had sustained the radical neoliberal coalition until U.S. actions to curb inflation and strengthen the dollar in 1981 dried up international liquidity. U.S. monetary policies induced a world recession, the Latin American debt crisis followed, and the region faced its worst economic crisis since the Great Depression.

In Chile, the cut off of foreign lending and the global recession activated latent intraclass tensions. The core conglomerates had controlled the bulk of the financial intermediation of external credit and had used much of it for their own expansion. When loans became scarce they drove up internal interest rates to usurious levels to keep from going bankrupt. In 1982, business associations that had been shut out of the policy process began to demand a devaluation to spur exports. Because automatic adjustment had precipitated a sharp recession, business groups also asked for policies that would lower interest rates to stimulate the economy. Moreover, they protested the radical model's emphasis on sectorally neutral policies and demanded policies tailored to the needs of individual economic sectors, such as selective protection for producers for domestic markets.

By 1983, Chile's encompassing peak organization, the Confederación de la Producción y Comercio (CPC), had organized a pragmatic neoliberal coalition around these demands. The coalition offered its program as an alternative to that of the radical neoliberal coalition. Businessmen and landowners with international market-oriented *fixed assets* (logging, fishing, mining, agro-exports, not financial enterprises) dominated the emerging coalition. The coalition also attended to the interests of producers for domestic markets.

Until the middle of 1983, however, regime structure served to inhibit policy concessions to the new coalition. Pinochet retained as much of the radical approach as he could despite rising pressure for change and the collapse of radical neoliberalism's major supporters—the core conglomerates. It was easier to usher in radical policies during a period of regime transition between 1973 and 1975 than to change policy direction after a highly exclusionary regime was consolidated. A real shift from radical to pragmatic neoliberalism, as will be seen in the next chapters, did not occur until after mid-1983 when Pinochet was confronted with mass mobilization and a resurgence of political opposition. The potential for a multiclass opposition that included capitalists persuaded Pinochet to seek to recapture solid business support, which he accomplished by embracing the pragmatic neoliberal model.

## Triumph of the Radical Neoliberal Coalition, 1978-1981

The previous chapter reconstructed the rise of the radical neoliberal coalition. It showed that radical neoliberal restructuring followed apace with the consolidation of the core conglomerates' hold over the Chilean economy and their capacity to forge tight networks with radical Chicagoans in the government. This section examines radical neoliberalisms' heyday between 1978 and 1981; years that witnessed the deepening of market-oriented economic and social reforms. The radical neoliberal capitalist coalition owed its stunning victory to a combination of factors: the economic dominance of the core radical conglomerates, the expansion of their network of relations to the Chicago boys in the state, and the addition of allied and supporting classes and class fractions who, although they did not participate in policymaking, nevertheless reaped economic benefits from the new policies.

### Expansion and Consolidation of the Core Radical Conglomerates

Since 1975, the core radical internationalist conglomerates had gained increasing control of the capitalist power bloc by expanding more rapidly than other economic groups in key economic activities and by participating in the policy process to the exclusion of other capitalist groups. By 1979, two additional liquid-asset business consortia had joined Cruzat-Larraín, Banco Hipotecario de Chile (BHC), and Edwards in the core coalition. These were Banco Concepción and, more tenuously, Aetna, a foreign financial group.

The economic and political power that the radical neoliberal coalition had amassed by 1979 left it ready, willing, and able to deepen radical neoliberalism. Economically, the radical internationalist conglomerates had every incentive to advocate the foreign exchange and banking deregulation policies implemented in 1979 and 1980. They stood head and shoulders above their competitors in the financial intermediation of foreign loans. They managed 30 percent of external credit contracted by the private sector, 23 percent of the entire banking system's international obligations, and 16 percent of Article 14 loans.[1] Their closest competitor only handled one fourth of the Article 14 volume they did.[2] Politically, as shown in Table 6.1, the core internationalist conglomerates and their closest allies had extended and deepened their links to the Chicago boys. Meanwhile, the structure of the authoritarian regime, and the fact that other capitalist groups did not enjoy the same access to the policymaking process, ensured the dominance of the radical neoliberal coalition.

Relations between the core conglomerates and the Chicago boys were particularly close in the ministries of finance and economy. Sergio de Castro, the minister of finance for this entire period, was an intimate friend of Manuel Cruzat, one of the main directors of the core internationalist Cruzat-Larraín conglomerate. De Castro was also on the board of directors of Edwards group companies just prior to his appointment to government office and immediately after leaving government service. Three of the four ministers of economy between 1978 and 1982 were also former executives, or were on the board of directors, of either the Cruzat-Larraín or BHC groups.

Although less blatant, the record for Central Bank presidents and vice presidents and CORFO vice presidents follows the same pattern. Of the three Central Bank presidents, the one with the longest tenure—Alvaro Bardón—was a Chicago boy and fervent supporter of radical neoconservative economic policies. He also had been the president the Banco de Concepción, a powerful banking concern.[3] The directors of the Banco de Concepción channeled loans to companies that they controlled in areas that were internationally competitive or that were not sensitive to foreign competition. Of the remaining two Central Bank presidents, although no data was available for one of them, the other, Sergio de la Cuadra, had close ties to international finance and was an advisor for the Aetna consortium in Chile.[4] De la Cuadra also served as Central Bank vice president from 1976 to 1981 and became minister of finance in 1982. The other two Central Bank vice presidents had very short stays. One was a lawyer who had worked for the internationalist BHC conglomerate until 1975. No data was found for Iván de la Barra. Of the CORFO vice presidents, Luis Danús (1976-1979), an army officer, had also been a director of an important company of the Edwards conglomerate. The other two CORFO vice presidents were also army officers but with no discernable connections to business.

These data suggest a reinforcement of the trend established during the policy period examined in Chapter 5: Many of the key radical Chicago boys and other economic authorities (Minister of Agriculture Marquez de la Plata, for example) were not only academics and economic ideologues. They also were connected intimately to a handful of internationalist businessmen whose investment decisions (aided by information gained from their privileged role in policymaking) contributed to the success of the new policies. Moreover, the tight links between the Chicago boys and the core conglomerates blurred the boundary between technocrat and capitalist so much that the relevance of the distinction was eroded. As technocrats, the Chicago boys had a vision of what to do. As the former and future directors and executives of internationalist conglomerates, they possessed the investment capital to put their ideas into practice.

### Policy Consequences of Coalitional Expansion

Between 1979 and 1981, the Chicago boys, intertwined with and supported by the radical internationalist conglomerates, designed and implemented their most extreme policies, which spanned economic, social, and administrative measures. In 1979, Sergio de Castro fixed the nominal exchange rate at Ch$39 to one U.S. dollar. He developed a "neutral" money supply policy, one that automatically adjusted it to supply and demand. Under automatic adjustment, variations in international reserves determined the levels of liquidity in Chile within the framework of a balanced budget and stable bank reserve obligations. The extreme monetarist approach to the balance of payments, with its neutral monetary policy based on a dollar standard, lasted for three years (from 1979 to 1982). In 1982, the authorities used automatic adjustment to implement a recessive policy to bring internal prices back in line with international prices.[5]

TABLE 6.1 Congolmerates and Key Government Economic Institutions, 1978-1982

| Institution/ Position | Name | Tenure | Conglomerate Affiliation of Official | Conglomerate Type | Official Linked to Finance Sector[a] | Official is Chicago Boy |
|---|---|---|---|---|---|---|
| Ministers of Finance | de Castro | 12/76-04/82 | Cruzat-Larraín | Radical International | Yes | Yes |
| | de la Cuadra | 04/82-08/82 | Aetna | MNC | Yes | Yes |
| | Lüders | 08/82-02/83 | BHC | Radical International | Yes | Yes |
| Ministers of Economy | Baraona[b] | 12/76-12/78 | Cruzat-Larraín | Radical International | Yes | Yes |
| | Kelly | 12/78-12/79 | BHC | Radical International | Yes | |
| | Federici | 12/79-12-80 | Cruzat-Larraín | Radical International | | |
| | Ramos[c] | 12-80-04/82 | | | | |
| | Danús[c] | 04/82-08/82 | Edwards | Radical International | | |
| | Lüders | 08/82-02/83 | BHC | Radical International | Yes | Yes |
| Central Bank Presidents | Bardón | 1976-1981 | Banco Concepción | Undefined | Yes | Yes |
| | de la Cuadra | 1981-1982 | Aetna | MNC | Yes | Yes |
| | Kast | 1982-1982 | | | | Yes |
| Vice Pres. | Cáceres | 1982-1983 | Ibáñez-Ojeda | Neutral | Yes | Yes |
| | de la Cuadra | 1976-1981 | Aetna | MNC | Yes | Yes |
| | Errázuriz | 1981-1981 | BHC | Radical International | Yes | |
| | de la Barra | 1981-1982 | | | | |
| | Tapia | 1982-1983 | Matte | Internationalist | | |

| | | | | | | |
|---|---|---|---|---|---|---|
| CORFO Vice Presidents | Danús[c] | 10/75-07/79 | Edwards | Radical International | | |
| | Ramos[c] | 08/79-12/80 | Cruzat-Larraín | Radical International | | |
| | Varela[c] | 12/80-03/81 | | | | |
| | Ramírez[c] | 03/81-08/83 | | | | |
| Budget Office Directors | Méndez | 1975-1981 | Cruzat-Larraín Lúksic & Matte | Radical International | | Yes |
| | Costábal | 1981-1984 | | Radical Internat. & MDM/C | | Yes |
| Ministers of Agriculture | Marquez | 04/78-12/80 | Cruzat-Larraín (Agro-export) | Radical International | Yes | |
| | Toro[d] | 12/80-12/81 | | | | |
| | Prado | 12/81- | (Agro-export-import) | | | |

Neutral: Food distribution (supermarkets) gives it an interest in open trading (imports) but also in healthy domestic food processing manufactures. The Ibáñez group had no holdings in the financial sector.

MDM/C: Executive of a firm in the internationally competitive manufactures for domestic market sector (mainly food processing).

MNC: Multinational Corporation

[a]Official is on the board of directors of, an executive with, or a consultant to a private financial institution.

[b]On the elected council of the SNA and SFF.

[c]Army officer.

[d]Carabineros officer (national police).

Source: Colegio de Periodistas, Diccionario biográfico (Santiago: Editorial Universitaria, selected years); company annual reports; Superintendencia de Asociaciones Bancarias y Financieras, Nómina del directorio de instituciones financieras (Santiago: n.p., selected years); Hoy no. 346, March 7, 1984; Fernando Dahse, El mapa de la extrema riqueza (Santiago: Editorial Aconcagua, 1979).

The radical coalition introduced a series of "social modernizations" to organize social services according to market principles. They privatized retirement benefits (AFPs) and health insurance (ISAPRES), decentralized administrative functions, and enacted a new labor code. These initiatives bore the stamp of Chicagoans Miguel Kast and José Piñera, another executive of the core internationalist Cruzat-Larraín conglomerate.[6]

The radical neoliberal coalition also continued to liberalize Chile's capital accounts in 1979 and 1980. These measures phased out restrictions on bank intermediation of foreign funds. Two mechanisms had restricted banks in this area. In June 1979, the government lifted the cap on the amount of foreign liabilities that banks could contract. In April 1980, it eliminated restrictions on the level of foreign liabilities banks could incur monthly. As a result, in 1979 loans under Article 14 of the foreign exchange law increased by almost 100 percent, and foreign credits obtained by Chilean private banks more than tripled in 1980.[7]

Financial deregulation policies fed the continued expansion of the core radical internationalist conglomerates and strengthened their hegemony over other capitalist groups. The high profits they earned brokering foreign lending facilitated the take over of troubled Chilean corporations in highly leveraged operations and financed the modernization and rationalization of uncompetitive companies producing for domestic markets.[8] For example, by June 1982, BHC's Banco de Chile—Chile's largest bank with a 20 percent share of all credit in the country—had loaned 17 percent of its funds to other BHC companies. Cruzat-Larraín's Banco de Santiago—the nation's second largest bank and responsible for 12 percent of total credit in Chile—had placed 44 percent of its loans in firms controlled by Cruzat Larraín.[9]

### Allied Capitalists, Regime Structure, and Opposition Demise

High levels of international liquidity added allied capitalist fractions to the radical neoliberal coalition.[10] As discussed in Chapter 1, these groups were allied in the sense that Poulantzas uses the term. Virtually every sectoral peak association supported the new policies after 1979 because most of their members benefitted from them, although they were excluded from the policy process. New found support by the most politically significant private sector peak associations lent an aura of broader legitimacy to the economic restructuring process. By silencing the "legitimate" sources of dissent it created a receptive climate for further economic reforms.

The conversion of the Sociedad de Fomento Fabril (SFF) and the Sociedad Nacional de Agricultura (SNA) mattered to the core radical neoliberal coalition because they had been supporters of a different economic adjustment model. Several factors induced this change of heart. Massive infusions of foreign loans fueled an economic "boom" that allowed

TABLE 6.2 Economic Interests of SNA Council Members, 1978-1980

| | Crop Type and Market Orientation | | | Other Economic Interests | | |
|---|---|---|---|---|---|---|
| | Domestic Tradtional Internat'lly | Domestic Traditional Internat'lly | | | | |
| Member Name | Noncompetitive | Competitive | Export | Financial | Miscellaneous | |
| Ariztía | x | x | x | | | |
| Arrau | x | | | x | | |
| Balmaceda | | | x | | | |
| Bascuñán | x | | | | | |
| Bismarck | x | | x | | | |
| Correa Val. | x | | | | | |
| Correa Vill. | x | | | | | |
| Covarrubias | | x | | | | |
| Fuchslocher | x | | | | | |
| Godoy | | | x | | Export/Import | |
| Hevia | | | x | | | |
| Infante G. | x | | x | | | |
| Infante L. | | x | | | | |
| Moreno | | | x | | | |
| Ochagavía | x | | x | x | | |
| Riesco | | | x | | Imports | |
| Tagle | x | | | | | |
| Ulloa | | | x | x | | |
| Valdés V. | | | x | x | BHC industry | |
| Valdés Val. | x | x | x | | | |
| Valdés Vial | | | x | | | |

*Source:* SNA, *El Campesino*, selected numbers; Colegio de Periodistas, *Diccionario biográfico* (Editorial Universitaria, selected years); SNA central office; Superintendencia de Asociaciones Bancarias y Financieras, *Nómina del directorio de instituciones financieras* (Santiago, n.p., selected years); conglomerate company annual reports.

producers for domestic markets to borrow to survive, diversify, or change economic activity in an atmosphere of prosperity.[11] Many representatives of the SFF and the SNA had multiple economic interests; so rapid economic growth in the financial, import-export, real estate, and agro-extractive sectors brought them prosperity that could offset their losses in their domestic market-oriented enterprises. Table 6.3 shows that between 1978 and 1980 less than half of the SFF's representatives (16 of 34) had economic interests exclusively in manufacturing sectors that were not internationally competitive. Moreover, five of the sixteen members who did not personally have multiple economic interests worked for companies controlled by

TABLE 6.3 Economic Interests of SFF Council Members, 1978-1980

| Member Name | Economic Interest | | | | Conglomerate Affiliation | Conglomerate Type |
|---|---|---|---|---|---|---|
| | MDM/NC | MDM/C | X/M | Fin | | |
| Abumohor | x | | | x | | |
| Agüero | x | | | | Lepe/Piquer/Lehman | Traditional Noncompetitive[a] |
| Arteaga | x | | | x | | |
| Aspillaga | | x | | | de Caso | Traditional Competitive[b] |
| Ayala | | x | x | x | Matte | International |
| Baraona | | | | x | BHC | Core Radical International |
| Behrmann | | x | x | | BHC | Core Radical International |
| Bolocco | x | | | | | |
| Calderón | | | | x | | |
| Casanova | x | | | | | |
| Daroch | x | | | | BHC | Core Radical International |
| Elton | x | | | | | |
| Fell | | x | | | BHC | Core Radical International |
| Garib | x | | | | Edwards | Core Radical International |
| Ipinza | | x | | | Ibáñez | Neutral[c] |
| Krumm | | x | | x | | |
| Kunstmann | x | | | | | |
| Lira | | x | | x | Angelini | International |
| Lizana | x | | | | | |
| López | x | | | | BHC | Core Radical International |
| Mendoza | x | | x | | Cruzat-Larraín | Core Radical International |
| Ovalle | x | | | | | |
| Piquer | x | | | | Lepe/Piquer/Lehman | Traditional Noncompetitive[a] |

| | | | | | |
|---|---|---|---|---|---|
| Reisenegger | x | | | | |
| Riveros | x | | | | |
| Ross | x | | x | Cruzat-Larraín | Core Radical International |
| Sahli | x | x | | Sahli-Tassara | International |
| Sarquis | x | x | | | |
| Smits | x | | | BHC | Core Radical International |
| Tocornal | | | x | Angelini | International |
| Urquidi[d] | x | | | | |
| Vergara | x | | | Andina | International |
| Vidaurre | x | | x | BHC | Core Radical International |
| Zañartu | | | x | Angelini | International |

MDM/NC: Executive of a firm in the internationally noncompetitive manufacturers for domestic markets sector

MDM/C: Executive of a firm in the internationally competitive manufactures for domestic market sector (mainly food processing).

X/M: Executive of a firm in the international commerce sector: export/import

Fin.: Executive of a firm in the financial sector

[a] Fixed-asset firms concentrate in internationally uncompetitive industrial sectors.

[b] Fixed-asset firms concentrate in internationally competitive industries (mainly food and construction).

[c] Only active in service sector supplied by imports and domestic sources (also see note 50).

[d] Is also an executive of a multinational corporation.

*Source:* SFF, *Memoria Anual,* selected years; Colegio de Periodistas, *Diccionario biográfico* (Santiago: Editorial Universitaria, selected years); SFF, *Informativo SFF,* selected numbers; Superintendencia de Asociaciones Bancarias y Financieras, *Nómina del directorio de instituciones financieras* (Santiago, n.p., selected years); conglomerate company annual reports.

internationalist conglomerates and, thus, had every chance of surviving. By the same token, Table 6.2 demonstrates that only five of twenty-one of the SNA's elected council members dedicated themselves exclusively to the cultivation of traditional crops.

Although they, too, were excluded from the policymaking process, internationalist business peak associations such as the Cámara Nacional de Comercio (CNC) and the Asociación de Bancos e Instituciones Financieras (ABIF) had little grounds for complaints.[12] The trading and financial services sectors boomed as a result of the fixed exchange rate, low import duties, and capital account liberalization. Imports of consumer goods jumped by 150 percent from 596.9 million dollars in 1978 to almost 1.5 billion in 1980.[13] Between 1978 and 1981, in real terms, the financial sector expanded 75 percent on top of a 50 percent increase between 1975 (when financial deregulation began) and 1978. The construction sector, represented by the Cámara Chilena de Construcción (CChC) expanded by 86 percent between 1978 and 1981 thanks to the abundance of credit. This heretofore depressed sector gained back its 1974 GDP share of approximately 6 percent.[14] Exporters within the SFF and the SNA reaped substantial benefits as well. Between 1978 and 1980, industrial exports increased by 51 percent, and farm and sea exports expanded by 56 percent.

The fixed nominal exchange rate, however, eventually caused problems for net exporters, such as those represented by the Sociedad Nacional de Minería (SONAMI). When the Chilean peso became overvalued it would be expected that these exports would suffer as their relative price in world markets rose. Serious problems did not emerge until 1981 when the U.S. dollar began to appreciate rather than depreciate. (Given the fixed exchange rate, as the dollar became stronger Chilean products became more expensive and harder to sell.) Consequently, as Table 6.4 shows, mineral exports did not really suffer until 1981 when the world slid into deep recession.

Business association support for radical neoliberalism was important in that it silenced the main sources of potentially effective advocacy for an alternative economic model. The shift from either guarded or open critique to enthusiastic backing for the new policies by the SFF and the SNA had a dampening effect on political opposition to Pinochet as well. The economic boom, the lack of upper-class allies, the quiescence of the middle classes (and even some sectors of labor), and the disastrous experience with the plebiscite that ratified the new constitution, led opposition political parties, such as the Christian Democrats, to despondency and despair.[15] They all but gave up hope that the dictatorship could somehow be derailed.

Support from business associations was valuable to the reigning radical coalition, but the retention and refinement of the policymaking process described in the previous chapter was more important for the success of the radical neoliberal coalition's free market project. The process continued to

TABLE 6.4 Growth of Exports, 1977-1982 (Millions of US$)

| Export Sector | 1977 | 1978 | 1979 | 1980 | 1981 | 1982 |
|---|---|---|---|---|---|---|
| Traditional | | | | | | |
| Mining | 1,377.7 | 1,412.6 | 2,241.1 | 2,902.6 | 2,177.5 | 2,123.7 |
| Copper | 1,178.3 | 1,201.5 | 1,799.6 | 2,200.4 | 1,737.8 | 1,684.6 |
| Semi-Traditional | 215.4 | 259.9 | 382.5 | 513.1 | 443.0 | 464.3 |
| Non-Traditional | 589.2 | 735.3 | 1,139.8 | 1,402.4 | 1,215.9 | 1,117.7 |
| Farm & Sea | 155.6 | 190.4 | 264.5 | 339.9 | 365.4 | 374.9 |
| Industrial | 416.1 | 535.2 | 862.5 | 1.045.7 | 850.5 | 742.8 |
| Total Exports | 2,183.2 | 2,407.8 | 3,763.4 | 4,818.1 | 3,836.5 | 3,705.7 |

*Source:* Ricardo Ffrench-Davis, "Origen y destino de las exportaciones chilenas, 1965-80," *Notas Técnicas Cieplan* no. 31, 1981; and Banco Central de Chile, *Boletín Mensual*, selected issues.

insulate policymakers and the core capitalist coalition from organized business and landowning groups that occasionally solicited a more nuanced policy approach. Under these institutional conditions, slight adjustments to existing policy, to say nothing of changes in policy direction, required much more concerted pressure than in the previous policy period. Since the economy was growing, business and landowning groups had little incentive to use their peak associations to mount the effort required to change policy, especially after the Chicago boys and their coalition allies expanded their control over economic policymaking institutions. As will be seen in the following sections, even when hard economic times led erstwhile allied capitalist groups to form an alternative coalition, regime structure made it very difficult for them to extract policy concessions from the government.

## Tensions in the Radical Neoliberal Coalition, 1981

Ostensibly, Chile was doing well in 1980, from the point of view of those who ruled. The Constitution of 1980 offered the prospect of regime institutionalization and the opposition was in disarray. Rapid economic growth rates augured well for the future. Fiscal deficits, inflation, foreign exchange shortages, labor unrest all seemed a thing of the past. Construction was booming, credit for consumption was at an all-time high, interest rates were coming down, and middle-class groups were investing in such novelties as mutual funds. Meanwhile, the international business press hailed Chile's reforms, eclipsing the international opprobrium heaped on the regime for human rights violations. It was a rosy, self-congratulatory time for the supporters of the regime who believed that their economic model had put Chile on the launching pad for economic "takeoff."

By the middle of 1981, however, the signs of "trouble in paradise" could no longer be ignored. The Chilean economy was slowing down. The fixed exchange rate to a rapidly appreciating U.S. dollar made for an increasingly expensive peso. Chilean exports became uncompetitive and the diminishing influx of foreign savings and high world interest rates led to a net loss of international reserves. By the end of the year, Chile had lost 300 million dollars. The policy of automatic adjustment jacked up real short-term interest rates to a ruinous 39 percent. Aggregate production and sales dropped. Heavily indebted entrepreneurs worried about whether their ability to roll over loans would last.

The world recession and high international interest rates shook up the capitalist power bloc that supported radical neoliberalism. Policy debates erupted over interest rates kept high by automatic adjustment, inadequate protection of domestic markets, and the fixed exchange rate. The core internationalist conglomerates continued to back the entire policy package, but allied capitalist fractions among fixed-asset producers for both international markets and domestic markets began to balk. Capitalists and landowners who wanted more nuanced policies turned to their peak associations to raise policy demands and lobby for change. Sectoral peak associations overcame intersectoral conflict on a few issues and began to act in concert through the CPC.

The expectation that the world slump would be short and shallow and that international lending would soon resume tempered demands, however. Interest rate policy was the only radical neoliberal measure that came under strong, concerted attack from the CPC. Individual peak associations also made relatively modest sectoral policy demands. Meanwhile, the patterns of support and opposition for fixed exchange rates shifted. Fixed-asset producers for international markets opposed them because exports were down due to an overvalued peso. But the core radical internationalists found allies in an unexpected quarter. Producers for domestic markets supported the fixed exchange rate because devaluation would drive up the amount in pesos of their heavy dollar-denominated debt. These cracks and realignments strained the radical neoliberal coalition but did not break it. In the face of divided opposition the regime did not have to accommodate demands for change.

## Organized Business and Shifting Policy Preferences

Given their economic interests, the core internationalist conglomerates unconditionally supported the Chicago boys in their commitment to radical neoliberalism. Cruzat-Larraín and BHC adamantly opposed demands for devaluation, government intervention to lower interest rates, or "discriminatory" sectoral policies.[16] These groups had concentrated their holdings in liquid assets and defended the fixed exchange rate because they had accumulated very high dollar debts in their bid for rapid expansion. A devaluation would have increased their liabilities many times over. Firms of the radical coalition opposed sectoral policies that would benefit their competition within Chile's small markets.

For similar reasons, the core internationalist conglomerates opposed manipulation of interest rates. Their financial institutions had made large loans to companies that they controlled. Consequently, in order to survive in a time of tight credit, the conglomerates had to eliminate competition for credit or go under. Moreover, because their banks were overextended, they could not afford lower interest rates. They needed to capture savings, not encourage spending. Furthermore, because they were net creditors, their fear of inflation led them to oppose currency emissions to increase liquidity.

Although the core capitalist support for radical neoliberalism held firm, allied class fractions (those who had supported radical neoliberalism without the benefit of participating in the policy process) began to waver. The first tentative attempts to formulate more flexible policies emerged after the external shock that affected Chile. Nevertheless, dissident businessmen and landowners did not forge a cohesive alliance that repudiated all of the central economic policy components of radical neoliberalism, nor did they advance a cohesive alternative set of policies. The embryonic coalition was divided over key elements of the radical's program. As a result, the core conglomerates and the radical Chicago boys retained the support of important allied capitalist groups on crucial issues and only faced moderate to weak opposition on others.

Because Pinochet's personalized dictatorship protected the policy network between the Chicago boys and the core internationalist conglomerates from the demands of other groups, capitalists outside the privileged circle once again turned to their peak associations. Those organizations gave them a legitimate vehicle for the public expression of their concerns and provided businessmen and landowners with institutional mechanisms for airing differences, building consensus, and applying pressure on government. Concerted action expressed through the CPC was by far the strongest means available to persuade the government to take a different course.

Exchange rate policy was at the center of the policy debate. Most Chilean businessmen, landowners, and technocrats believed that the future of the radical neoliberal model depended on its retention or abrogation. The core conglomerates and the Chicago boys still had substantial support for their policy from allied capitalist groups, as expressed by the CPC. The CPC's position was the product of intracapitalist conflict and cooperation. On one side, the Sociedad de Fomento Fabril and the Sociedad Nacional de Agricultura—the most powerful of the sectoral peak associations— strenuously defended the fixed exchange rate.[17] On the other, disgruntled fixed-asset producers for international markets in SONAMI and the CNC only half-heartedly opposed it.[18]

These patterns of support and opposition had their roots in the economic interests of the large-scale capitalists and landowners that dominated the sectoral peak associations. Many of the members of the SFF and the SNA, especially producers for domestic markets, had large debts in dollars. They expected international lending to resume, so they sought to ward off drastic measures that would exponentially increase their financial obligations. In contrast, SONAMI and the CNC opposed the fixed exchange rate because the stronger dollar drove up the price of Chilean goods, making them uncompetitive in world markets.

On high interest rates, however, dissident internationalists in SONAMI and the CNC, together with producers for domestic markets in the SFF and the SNA, advanced a first, small step toward a cohesive opposition to radical neoliberalism. These four peak associations wanted interest rates reduced. This policy consensus led the CPC to lobby against aspects of automatic adjustment that affected interest rates.[19] This nascent alternative capitalist coalition turned against the core radical internationalist conglomerates because they had been crowded out of credit markets. In times of plenty, dominant economic groups had taken advantage of their control of the financial system to expand rapidly. Now, overexposed, the core internationalist conglomerates soaked up the lion's share of available credit to service their debts and keep from going bankrupt. Given their weak market power, erstwhile allied capitalist groups sought government action on interest rates to gain access to credit.

Protection against subsidized imports was another policy issue that contained the early seeds of a broader alternative coalition. The SFF, the SNA, and the CNC all supported antidumping policies.[20] Although they were not able to get the issue on the agenda of the CPC in the early 1980s, their positions, nevertheless, established the parameters for future cooperation on trade issues in the mid-1980s. The reappearance of the protection issue, however muted, underscored the increased strength and influence of domestic market producers within the SFF and the SNA. Global recession had weakened the relative economic strength of internationalists in those associations. Temporary, product-specific protection against unfair foreign competition—as opposed to resuscitating the debate over differential tariffs (preferred by the SFF) or price bands (preferred by the SNA)—was the softest and least conflictive line of defense against unrestricted imports.[21] The SFF could count on SNA support because the policy instrument (a surcharge on specific items) did not threaten landowners the way that differentiated tariffs had. (The belief that international liquidity would be restored accounted for the SFF's and the SNA's more restrained position in 1981.) Moreover, the commercial sector could not reject the proposal because it fell well within accepted international norms and affected a limited range of imports.

Access to credit, investment funds, and the desire for cost-cutting measures to weather the recession until international liquidity resumed were also behind a number of sector-specific demands raised by individual peak associations.[22] Those sectoral demands revealed a desire for change among groups that did not have the capacity to force change. For example, the SFF asked the government not to discriminate against national products in free zones and state purchases. The SNA sought greater public investment in agriculture, particularly in transportation infrastructure. It also wanted laws against anti-price fixing to curb the food industry's monopsonistic power. Furthermore, the SFF, the SNA, and the CNC backed petitions for reduced tax burdens. SONAMI requested that the government establish a compensatory loan fund to cover the difference between the actual price and the suggested trigger price of 95 cents, to be paid back when the price of copper rose above the trigger.[23]

In the midst of budding policy debates and shifting allegiances, financiers remained isolated and fearful. Recent decrees gave the banking superintendency wide discretionary powers to intervene in the financial sector without appeal. Financiers were particularly concerned over the broadly defined criteria permitting intervention: "financial instability, deficient management, and portfolio concentration."[24]

In 1981, then, the challenge to radical neoliberalism was weak. Key organizations still supported the fixed exchange rate. Of all of the policy demands advanced by the peak associations, only the request for reduced interest rates had the backing of the CPC. By challenging the integrity of the policy of automatic adjustment, it was also the only demand that threatened a core tenet of the radical neoliberal model. By contrast, the approach to tariffs was well within neoliberal economic theory, if not in the practice of radical Chicago boys. Nor did the cost-cutting, sector-specific policies advanced by individual business associations challenge the radical model the way a demand for industrial policy would.

For the time being, the business associations petitioned for palliative measures during a temporary economic downturn. Nevertheless, these halting steps and respectfully articulated demands were a new development. Hard economic times had prodded the business peak associations to make their first forays back to their traditional role as pressure groups for large-scale businessmen and landowners. The lack of urgency in their demands can be explained by the perceived mildness of the recession. Moreover, they had been humbled by the humiliating experience of having been so pointedly excluded from the policy process in the recent past. Nevertheless, their tentative efforts marked a first step towards the construction of a cohesive capitalist coalition that could stand up to the radical internationalists and their Chicago boy allies.

### Coalitional Tensions and Official Policy Inflexibility

Pinochet and the Chicago boys ignored all of these demands for change. In July 1981, Sergio de Castro, with Pinochet's support, bluntly stated that the Central Bank would not increase the money supply to bring down interest rates nor would he devalue.[25] In late October, Pinochet declared that it was not the government's responsibility to solve the problems of individual economic sectors. Government should limit itself to the design of general, sectorally neutral policy.[26] In December, he reiterated these sentiments and, in response to growing speculation over devaluation, he indicated that the government would not devalue the peso.[27]

Three factors contributed to government recalcitrance in the issue areas where capitalists had forged new policy alliances: interest rates and mild forms of protection. These factors dulled the effectiveness of the sectoral peak associations. First, one of the major weaknesses of dissident businessmen and landowners in 1981 lay in their divided loyalties. Their attempts to develop an alternative policy agenda were only supported by a partial, fragmented coalition that sought limited change. Although they backed some changes in automatic adjustment, key members, such as the SFF and the SNA, still sided with the radical coalition on the fixed exchange rate. Moreover, the subdued approach to protection and other sector-specific policies emphasized a willingness to work within the framework of free-market ideology. Some sectors even publicly insisted that their demands constituted adjustments to the economic model, not attempts to replace it.[28]

Second, the expectation that international lending would soon resume further diminished the partial coalition's strength. The economic power of dissenting business and landowning groups ultimately depended on their contribution to foreign exchange and economic growth. The belief in renewed flows of foreign lending tended to bolster the radical coalition because such a restoration of external financing would revitalize the conditions that had made the neoliberal coalition viable.

Finally, as described in the previous chapter, the policy process in Pinochet's personalized authoritarian regime also contributed to the lack of policy change. It insulated top policymakers from most social groups and restricted access to policymaking to a privileged, narrow range of capitalists. The limited access to institutional power resources meant that concerted pressure from a broad business coalition would be necessary to even begin to sway Pinochet toward policy change. This effort the dissidents could not yet muster.

## Shaping an Alternative:
## The Pragmatic Neoliberal Coalition, 1982-1983

In 1982, the recession capitalists had hoped would be mild and brief turned brutal and prolonged. By the end of the year, international reserves had fallen by almost 1.5 billion dollars; and, after a comfortable 1.2 billion dollar surplus in 1980, the balance of payments revealed an alarming 1.1 billion dollar deficit. Real short-term interest rates remained ruinously high at around 35 percent, and the government's pro-cyclical policies contributed to a wrenching 14 percent drop in GDP.

Growing indicators that Chile's economic downturn would be long and deep tore the radical coalition apart. The severity of the economic depression that engulfed Chile set virtually all producer groups against the core internationalist conglomerates and the Chicago boys. The core conglomerates had relied heavily on external finance. But in the absence of private international capital flows, economic recovery depended on a revival of internal production and the stimulation of exports rather than foreign savings. Thus, by the middle of 1982, the allied capitalist groups that had supported radical neoliberalism, even though they did not participate in the policy process, abandoned the core radical neoliberal coalition. By 1983, they had forged an alternative, pragmatic neoliberal coalition; one whose policy preferences corresponded closely to their economic interests as dictated by changes in the international economy. Fixed-asset producers for international markets dominated the pragmatic neoliberal coalition, but it also included internationally competitive producers for domestic markets without ignoring the interests of economic sectors that were not competitive internationally.

### Forging the Pragmatic Neoliberal Coalition

Deepening economic crisis galvanized organized business into action. Capitalists and landowners used their sectoral peak associations to stake out policy positions and relied on their technical staffs to give their demands solid economic justification. The individual peak associations of large-scale capital also used their encompassing peak association—the CPC—to hammer out common policy demands on which all sectors could agree. In short, working in concert through the CPC, the business peak associations and their upgraded technical departments forged the pragmatic neoliberal coalition.

The pragmatic neoliberal coalition emerged in several steps. By June 1982, the economic crisis had set virtually every capitalist group in Chile against the core conglomerates and the Chicago boys who sought to maintain as much of the radical neoliberal model as they could. Over the course of 1982, the CPC extended and formalized the pragmatic coalition's demands. At first it limited itself to a critique of government policy. But by the second quarter of 1982, it had fleshed those demands out; and, in January 1983, the CPC embarked on the development of a full-fledged alternative program.

The radical neoliberal coalition had supported pro-cyclical policies, such as the fixed exchange rate and automatic adjustment, and was committed to sectorally neutral policies. The pragmatic coalition was neoliberal too. It preferred open and free markets. It rejected differentiated tariffs, advocated protection only against unfair competition, and supported the price system and private enterprise. But it was "pragmatic" because it advocated greater flexibility in the management of economic problems than the Chicago boys' orthodoxy allowed. Coalition members wanted counter-cyclical policies such as high real exchange rates, low interest rates, an expansionary monetary policy, public works projects, internal debt relief, and lower wages.

The pragmatic neoliberal coalition started to coalesce in March 1982 when the CPC began to demand that the government devalue the peso in order to reactivate the economy.[29] Shortly thereafter, a powerful internationally oriented conglomerate that had begun the authoritarian period as an internationally competitive domestic market producer, the Matte economic group, publicly defected from the radical coalition. In mid-April 1982, Jorge Alessandri, chairman of the board of the Matte group's flagship company, the venerable Papelera, man of great prestige, former president of the republic, and erstwhile supporter of gradual change, attacked the policy of automatic adjustment.[30] With the CPC and powerful conglomerates against them, the ideologically rigid Chicago boys became isolated.

Asset specificity and the markets the capitalist groups of the pragmatic coalition produced for explain the shift in policy preference. Without hope of renewed external financial flows, business and landowning groups that produced for domestic markets joined fixed-asset internationalists in demanding devaluation. A softer peso would give dissident internationalists a boost. For producers for domestic markets a devaluation would discourage imports and offer the prospect that the resulting hard currency savings would be channeled into economic reactivation. The common support for devaluation built upon the convergence of other policy preferences on taxes, interest rates, and anti-dumping.

During the second half of 1982, more combative leaders were elected to the CPC and the SFF, signaling a breakthrough for the pragmatic coalition. The economic interests of the new leaders corresponded to those of the emerging pragmatic coalition: fixed-asset internationalists in alliance with producers for domestic markets. The membership had rebelled against the old leadership because economic crisis had altered their economic interests and created a profound dissatisfaction with passive acceptance of the government's policy choices. The new leadership pressed vigorously for policy change. To illustrate, during the CPC's executive committee meeting of July 1, 1982, member association presidents sharply criticized CPC president Domingo Arteaga, arguing that he had misrepresented the tenor of a June 16 meeting with Pinochet at a subsequent press conference. His declaration to the press had implied solid business support for the government's recent policies, including the need for monetary contraction to combat inflation. But during the meeting with Pinochet, the leadership of the member peak associations had made it clear that they wanted the money supply expanded to ease pressure on interest rates and to spur demand. CPC members had pointed out that immediate measures were necessary to avoid an economic collapse that could have broader political consequences. Confronted with these accusations, Arteaga offered his resignation.[31]

By mid-July, the CPC had a new president: Jorge Fontaine. His economic interests reflected the balance of power within the pragmatic coalition: Dissident internationalists dominated, but they did not exclude the concerns of producers for domestic markets. Fontaine's economic activities involved him in virtually every sector of the Chilean economy: His interests ranged from the export of fruits, wine, and minerals to production for domestic markets. His investments in firms that imported textiles, raw materials, and intermediate inputs for industry further sensitized him to the needs of producers for domestic markets.

The CPC's new leadership moved quickly to advance well-articulated alternative policy solutions and exert pressure on the government. Between July 27, 1982, and December 6, 1982, the CPC increasingly insisted on a more integrated and coherent set of policy demands. By January 1983, it had begun to develop a full-fledged alternative policy program. Policy recommendations included debt rescheduling (with generous grace periods, preferential credit, and long repayment terms), increased monetary emissions, a public works and housing plan, a preferential dollar for debtors, a high exchange rate to promote exports and protect domestic market producers, an effective law against subsidized imports, and better channels of communication between the private sector and the government.[32] On these all of the peak associations could agree. Most of them also lobbied for sector-specific policy recommendations as well.[33]

Also in mid-1982, fixed-asset producers for international and domestic markets in the SFF decided their association should do more than just make the authorities aware of how government policy affected industry. They believed that the SFF should offer policy recommendations and be aggressive when necessary.[34] Thus, in July, after a highly publicized and potentially divisive internal debate, the SFF elected a new board of directors.

As had been the case in the CPC, the economic interests of the SFF's new board typified those of the evolving pragmatic coalition: dissident internationalists in alliance with producers for domestic markets. Although producers for domestic markets regained dominance of the SFF, its president, Ernesto Ayala, also maintained a strong link to the SFF's internationalist sector. Ayala was a high-ranking executive of the Papelera, a key Matte conglomerate firm of which Jorge Alessandri was chairman of the board. The other new SFF officers were connected to industries that were not traditionally competitive internationally, such as textiles (Eugenio Ipinza), metal manufacturing (Fernando Agüero), and plastics (Pedro Lizana).[35]

The SFF's outgoing, more passive board had quite a different profile, much more internationalist in its composition. Its president, Bruno Casanova, was best known as the director of one of the few surviving and prosperous rubber products companies in Chile. Through borrowed financing he had modernized and expanded his plant and equipment. Less publicized was the fact that he was also the president of two import-export businesses. Of the remaining three former SFF officers, two (Fernando Krumm and Alberto Llona) worked for transnational corporations. The treasurer, Gonzalo Eguiguren, was general manager of a large printing company.[36]

Beginning in August of 1982, the SFF delivered a barrage of sharp critiques of government policies and pressed hard for policy change. The SFF was especially critical of the ineffectiveness of existing rules against dumping, the scarcity of soft loans and preferential dollars, the meager extent of government help in debt restructuring, and the discriminatory buying practices of government agencies against national products.[37]

The customs tariff issue remained a divisive one for the nascent coalition. Steady, world-wide economic decline had led the SFF to reopen the debate over the desirability of a differentiated tariff structure. In early 1982, it formed a commission to study the matter.[38] By October 1982, the SFF officially supported a differential tariff schedule over the objections of a minority group within the SFF.[39] Meanwhile, all the other sectoral peak associations continued to oppose differentiated tariffs.[40] Some business leaders were more circumspect while others roundly condemned the idea, attesting to the controversy over the issue. The way that the conflict was resolved—support for anti-dumping measures—left no doubt that internationalists dominated the pragmatic neoliberal coalition.

The policy debates of the period reveal that, in his capacity as president of the CPC, Jorge Fontaine—a dissident internationalist—carefully avoided the question. Nonetheless, for the record, he revealed a personal preference for low across-the-board tariffs with effective anti-dumping rules. The debate within the CPC heated up in November 1982. In a CPC executive committee meeting, the CNC delicately tried to sidestep the issue. It argued that there were more pressing problems than the tariff schedule debate. On the basis of historic intersectoral conflict, the SNA flatly declared itself against differentiated tariffs.[41] SONAMI had previously announced its opposition to them; and, as previously seen, the ABIF and the CChC were at best ambivalent.[42] Under these circumstances, the CPC did not support the SFF's position on differentiated tariffs.

On the issue of protection, then, aside from general agreement on the need for effective anti-dumping and unfair competition rules, the SFF, SONAMI and SNA had to seek private deals for government aid within their respective ministries. Thus, the SFF fought for differentiated tariffs. The SNA reopened its bid for price floors and ceilings for traditional crops.[43] SONAMI lobbied for price supports as long as the international price for copper remained below 95 cents per pound.[44] Of all of these, only the SONAMI petition was granted in late 1982. The SNA had to wait until 1983, and the SFF was consistently rebuffed.

In conclusion, the asset specificity and the position in the international and domestic economy of capitalists explained most of this period's coalitional behavior. Once Chilean business groups saw that international lending would not soon resume at pre-1981 levels, they recognized that the radical model would lead to a long, deep recession and bankruptcy for many. That realization induced an alignment of fixed-asset producers for international markets, who dominated the coalition, and producers for domestic markets. They agreed on the need for devaluation and other measures to mitigate the effects of the global recession and to reduce the cost of doing business. Over the course of 1982, business and landowning groups refined, extended, and then explicitly coalesced around those demands.

Proposals for a differentiated tariff structure did not prosper because the SFF alone wanted the policy. Within the SFF, as opportunities in the external sector declined, manufacturers for domestic markets acquired the incentive and economic strength to place the question of tariffs on the national policy agenda. But economic sectors with more involvement in the international economy (mining and commerce) or in nontradables (construction) preferred low across-the-board tariffs. Intersectoral conflict between agriculture and industry induced the SNA to support the existing tariff structure, while agreeing with the SFF on the need for rules to protect producers for domestic markets from unfair foreign competition.

## Coalitional Change and Partial Policy Correction

In 1981, Pinochet unconditionally backed radical Chicagoans and made virtually no policy concessions to demands for change from the business peak associations. In 1982, the government grudgingly ceded ground over three policy subphases. These policy changes were incremental, met the pragmatic coalition's demands only partially, and were formulated with minimal or no input from the alternative coalition's leadership. In other words, Pinochet maneuvered between the growing strength of the pragmatic coalition and his desire not to change policy. He wanted to continue to discipline traditional capitalists whom he held partially responsible for the crisis prior to military intervention in 1973. Pinochet also feared they might attempt to curtail his power.

In spite of the partial nature of policy change in each of the policy subperiods, two factors support the argument that there was a positive relationship between the rise of the pragmatic neoliberal coalition and policy change. First, policy shifts responded to demands that the pragmatic coalition—usually the CPC—had articulated well in advance of policy modifications. Second, major policy changes often occurred shortly after meetings between Pinochet and the CPC leadership. This sequencing reinforces the argument that concerted action by policy coalitions developed within the CPC had better results than individual action by sectoral peak associations in authoritarian Chile. For on matters of substantial disagreement within organized business, such as the SFF's struggle to reintroduce differentiated tariffs, the government took no action.

Why was policy change only partial? First, the pragmatic coalition's cohesiveness depended on the level of internal consensus on specific policy demands. Internal consensus also depended on the extent to which the coalition's claims revealed a broad, well-integrated agenda or, even better, a well-developed, detailed alternative policy proposal. Second, the relative economic strength of coalitions and their ability, or potential, to contribute to economic growth was shifting. The third reason was regime structure; the absence of formal mechanisms of interest intermediation between state and society meant that the pragmatic coalition lacked institutional bases of power—ministerial positions—from which to advance its interests. Thus, the coalition played no significant role in policy formulation. Nevertheless, as the pragmatic coalition gathered strength Pinochet modified the system of interaction between capitalists and the state somewhat. He appointed new ministers (equally committed to radical neoliberalism but not identified with the initial policies) and allowed the pragmatic coalition greater access to them. As that process unfolded, more concessions followed.

Of the three factors just mentioned, not all were equally significant in each of the three subperiods. In the first subperiod, the pragmatic coalition's relative lack of cohesion, in combination with the extreme exclusionary policy process, largely accounted for the minor character of policy change. During the second subperiod, all three variables became important. In the last subperiod, with coalition strength relatively constant, change in access to the policy process acquired greater significance. Over the course of 1982, then, organized business went from raising demands, to hammering out an agenda for change, to lobbying for its agenda. At the same time, although Pinochet changed some ministers, policymakers in general remained committed to radical neoliberalism and the members of the pragmatic coalition never got to participate in policy formulation. That too changed, although not until 1983-1984.

*Minimal Reforms, March 1982.* The first subperiod of incremental and partial policy change began in March 1982 when it became clear that international liquidity would not soon be restored. By March, the CPC had forged the nucleus of the pragmatic coalition around demands for devaluation and reflationary policies. But the pragmatic coalition was still relatively loose and weak. It demanded that the government do something but it had not yet developed a well-integrated policy agenda, much less a detailed policy proposal amounting to an alternative economic model. Its weakness was compounded by its lack of institutional footholds in the state. Business groups were shut out of the policymaking process and, stubborn and aloof, Minister of Finance Sergio de Castro continued in his post.

Consequently, in March 1982 the pragmatic coalition obtained only minor policy concessions on points proposed to Pinochet at a meeting in October 1981. For SONAMI, the government reinstated credit against future sales. The CNC and the SNA received tax relief. Landowners gained the right to pay taxes on either estimated or real net income; previously they had to pay estimated taxes.[45] Meanwhile, the SFF claimed credit for two changes. The first was an announcement that the Central Bank would streamline its procedures for anti-dumping claims. The second ended discrimination against national products in duty-free zones.[46]

*Devaluation, April to June 1982.* During the second subperiod of incremental policy change, between April and June 1982, the government made additional partial policy changes as the pragmatic coalition gained in cohesiveness and potential economic strength. The CPC drafted a set of well-integrated policy recommendations, although they stopped short of detailed programmatic propositions. Well in advance of any policy change, the CPC let it be known that it wanted a one-time devaluation of 30 to 35 percent, surcharges on imports that were the product of unfair competition, subsidies for exports (drawbacks), lower interest rates, debt rescheduling, and a 15 to 20 percent wage cut.[47] The pressure for devaluation, a challenge to the radical model's keystone policy, escalated in April 1982.

The pragmatic coalition's cohesiveness and combativeness manifested itself in other ways. It mounted a frontal attack against the institutional sources of the radical coalition's power. In April, the CPC concluded that since Finance Minister Sergio de Castro would not change policy he had to be replaced.[48] Pressure for his removal intensified after Jorge Alessandri, dean of traditional conservatives, made his speech condemning both de Castro and the radical model he so inflexibly supported.

The regime's need for support from capitalist groups capable of promoting economic growth strengthened the pragmatic coalition. The deepening recession and sharp decreases in the rate of foreign lending made the pragmatic coalition a strong potential contributor to future economic growth. A devaluation would aid exporters and contribute to foreign exchange earnings; it would also protect domestic market producers. Meanwhile, debtors needed relief if they were to survive, and survive they must if politically explosive high rates of unemployment were to be avoided. By contrast, the core internationalist conglomerates were becoming more of an obstacle than a valuable support group for Pinochet. They no longer contributed to economic growth. As will be discussed below, their high incidence of self-lending compelled them to drive up interest rates. The authorities responded by trying to break up the conglomerates in an orderly fashion to reduce pressure on interest rates.

Following Alessandri's speech in April 1982, Pinochet dismissed de Castro and other key economic authorities. The economic interests of the new appointees were well-suited to serve Pinochet's dual agenda: maintaining his independence and addressing the increasingly public criticism of his government by the pragmatic coalition. In the ministries of finance and economy—the top positions—he placed men with strong sympathies for the radical model but who were not directly linked to the core conglomerates, which had become a political liability. In more subordinate positions, he placed men with internationalist backgrounds who, nevertheless, also had ties to economic concerns more acceptable to the emerging pragmatic coalition. Pinochet's replacement of key cabinet members suggested that policy concessions might follow; it remained to be seen which policies would be modified and to what extent.

Prosopographical data on key minsters support the argument that cabinet changes served Pinochet's need to distance himself from the core radical internationalist conglomerates and underscored his inability to continue to ignore the pragmatic coalition. Accordingly, Pinochet appointed Sergio de la Cuadra as minister of finance and General Luis Danús as minister of economy. De la Cuadra was a staunch Chicago boy but did not have overt ties to the core radical internationalist conglomerates. His connections to international finance were with the Aetna group, a well known MNC. Luis Danús was an army general with business ties to the Edwards conglomerate and well-known for his sympathy for the radical project.[49]

Pinochet's selections for the Central Bank and the Ministry of Agriculture, on the other hand, were an attempt to mollify dissident internationalists and producers for domestic markets and to keep the former in a dominant position. Carlos Cáceres, the new president of the Central Bank, had close links to the Ibáñez conglomerate, which specialized in food distribution and higher education in business administration. He had no direct stake in either the core internationalist conglomerates or in the traditional conglomerates.[50] Agriculture Minister Jorge Prado, who had been appointed in late 1981, had a similar profile. He was vice president of the SNA prior to his appointment, and his business was the cultivation of export products (mainly fruits) and grains for domestic markets.

In the wake of the cabinet changes and the pragmatic coalition's increased cohesiveness, the authorities devalued the peso on June 14, 1982. The actual devaluation illustrated the Pinochet administration's desire to retain as much independence as possible from the groups it was ceding to. The CPC had hammered out an integrated set of policy recommendations for a meeting scheduled with Pinochet. But Pinochet canceled the meeting and went ahead with a devaluation that was little more than half of what the private sector had wanted. Nor did Pinochet address the other policy issues that were on the CPC's well-publicized agenda.

Pinochet probably snubbed the pragmatic coalition for two reasons. There was continuing tension within the CPC, especially over tariff policy.[51] More importantly, Pinochet believed that the weakness of key leaders in the CPC and the SFF kept them from pressing their demands with greater insistence. The authorities expected to gain time by exploiting differences between pro-administration leaders and the membership.

Pinochet and his advisors evidently miscalculated the cohesiveness of the emerging coalition. Government obstinacy and arrogance seemed to stiffen the resolve of coalition members. Two days after the devaluation the CPC forced a meeting with Pinochet to discuss the policies he had failed to enact when he ordered the devaluation: debt rescheduling, exchange rate loss protection, an end to automatic adjustment for inflation, flexibilization of wages, public works and housing programs, export promotion, and more external financing.[52]

The significance of such meetings cannot be understated. Given that the policy process at this time was closed to the CPC, any orders for substantive change had to come from Pinochet himself. Pinochet's direct involvement was important because the current ministers of finance and economy supported the radical model (even though they were not close to the core internationalist conglomerates).

A week after Pinochet met with the CPC, the government reacted with another partial response—it changed labor legislation to permit wage reductions. But it did not budge on the key policy demand for an expansionary monetary policy or public works to reflate the economy. The administration remained committed to a neutral monetary policy. Its fear of inflation exceeded its fear of economic depression, and Pinochet enjoyed a wide margin of discretion since the CPC had no role in policy formulation.

The government's new policymakers differed with the pragmatic coalition on various issues, but they recognized that less usurious interest rates would stimulate economic recovery. Adverse to expanding the money supply, the method that they settled on revealed a deep rift between the government and the core internationalist conglomerates, whose voracious need for credit during recessionary times kept interest rates high. They had to borrow at any cost to keep from going under because their financial institutions had loaned such a large proportion of their funds to related companies in order to finance their explosive expansion.[53]

To ease pressure on interest rates, the Central Bank offered to buy unrecoverable loans from private banks and the *financieras*, which had ten years to buy them back at low interest rates. In addition, new edicts sought to force financial institutions to spin off their interest in companies not in the financial sector. These measures failed to reduce interest rates because the core internationalist conglomerates managed to evade the rules and struck private deals with the government to avoid relinquishing control of related companies.

Moreover, Finance Minister de la Cuadra failed to dismantle the core internationalist conglomerates. His lack of knowledge of their ownership structure, especially their links to offshore financial institutions, allowed them to thwart his efforts.[54] Interest rates—one of the principal points of friction between most of the private sector and the government—remained high. As a result, criticism from dissenting capitalist groups did not abate. The stage was set for the third subphase of incremental policy change.

***Policy Concessions Proliferate, July to December 1982.*** The third subperiod of policy change spanned the months between July and December

1982. All policy modifications enacted during those months addressed demands articulated by the pragmatic coalition months before. Policy concessions, which began in August, included debt relief in the form of soft loans, protection against exchange-rate losses (the preferential dollar), and defense against unfair external competition (price floors for wheat and measures for textiles, shoes and other products). As before, the government retained a latitude of discretion. The new policies, with perhaps the exception of the preferential dollar, still fell short of the pragmatic coalition's expectations.

What accounted for the military government's sudden willingness to address so many of the pragmatic coalition's demands? Because the pragmatic coalition was well established long before the policy change, it seemed unlikely that a change in the degree of its cohesiveness could have been a determining factor. Moreover, the worsening economic situation only marginally increased the pragmatic coalition's potential contribution to economic recovery in the short run. Therefore, change in the degree of access to the policymaking process was the most important element in these new, albeit partial, policy concessions.

The new ministers modified the bias of state institutions so as to favor the pragmatic coalition. In August 1982, Pinochet replaced Finance Minister de la Cuadra, who could not control the core conglomerates and, thus, bring down interest rates, with Rolf Lüders who hopefully could. Pinochet also appointed Lüders as minister of economy, earning him the appellation "superminister." Lüders had been second in command of the BHC conglomerate until a recent falling out with its head Javier Vial. Their dispute was over Vial's unwillingness to negotiate BHC's unrecoverable loans with the Central Bank, a move that Lüders supported. This cabinet change introduced a superminister who possessed detailed knowledge of conglomerate operations.

There was another reason Lüders appealed to Pinochet. He was a Chicago boy by training but had never been embraced by their inner sanctum. He represented a further step away from the hard-line Chicago boys and the core internationalist conglomerates, and yet he was a committed internationalist. He also opposed an expansionary monetary policy to bring down interest rates.

With Lüders' appointment came greater access to the policymaking process for the pragmatic coalition.[55] CPC and other peak association leaders who had been making the rounds of ministerial offices suddenly found themselves much more welcome. The pragmatic coalition could now pursue its quest for policy change at a level of authority below Pinochet himself, which increased the possibility of more sustained contact. In Lüders, they found a minister who was willing to receive them, listen to their proposals, and partially implement them. Moreover, since other ministries depended on him for their cues, Lüders' greater flexibility gave men like Agriculture Minister Prado greater latitude for action.[56] Nevertheless, organized business did not participate in the drafting of new policy, which assured Lüders a large degree of discretion in his decisions.

Initially the core internationalist conglomerates successfully resisted Lüders' efforts to dismantle them. With a great deal of secrecy, he arranged to place their top financial institutions in receivership in order to break them up forcibly, which he did in January 1983. Given the ownership structure of the conglomerates (related companies were indebted to their banks), Lüders' action placed their major enterprises under state control and marked the demise of the once powerful core internationalist conglomerates.

In sum, throughout three subperiods of incremental and partial policy change Pinochet tried to retain as much of the radical model as possible. That model allowed him simultaneously to pursue the capitalist transformation of Chile, to discipline both business and labor groups, and to wield power with little challenge to his decisions. But, in 1982, shifting capitalist coalitions and power relations among his capitalist supporters forced Pinochet to make some changes. He then used appointments to state office to build a coalition dominated by radical internationalists that were not linked to the core conglomerates but still connected to liquid-asset holders. The increased importance of the pragmatic coalition, however, led Pinochet to place men more sympathetic to interests of fixed-asset holders in subordinate and somewhat marginal positions. The lack of formal institutions of intermediation between state and society allowed ministers to address the pragmatic coalition's policy demands selectively and to keep its representatives from directly participating in policymaking.

## Conclusion: Regime Structure and Policy Inflexibility

This chapter examined the triumph of the radical neoliberal coalition, its unravelling, and the formation of an alternative pragmatic neoliberal coalition. In 1980, because of high levels of international liquidity, skeptical business and landowning groups tolerated or supported extreme neoliberal policies and became the allied fractions of a broader neoliberal coalition. The radical internationalist conglomerates at the core of the coalition were the ones who participated in policy formulation. The allied fractions were excluded from the policy process but backed the policies that the core of the coalition promoted. The international debt crisis of the early 1980s ripped the radical neoliberal coalition asunder. The economic crisis had two immediate effects. First, the radical internationalist conglomerates fell victim to it. Second, the end of the foreign debt-financed boom demonstrated just how thin upper class ideological commitment to radical neoliberalism had been. During the boom years, business and landowning peak associations extolled the virtues of the market. Beset by economic hard times, however, the peak associations—under the umbrella of the CPC—developed an agenda for significant adjustments to radical neoliberal policies.

By the end of 1982, the economic crisis had also left the peak associations of large-scale business poised for a new phase in their development, one that crystallized and matured between 1983 and 1988. Political and economic crisis between the late sixties and early seventies had spawned new levels of collective action among business peak associations in the political arena. After the coup, business peak associations progressed to a new stage when they agreed on a common economic policy agenda. In 1982, economic crisis and Pinochet's highly exclusionary personalist dictatorship pushed the peak associations one step further to more proactive positions on economic policy. Between 1973 and 1974 they were still in a more passive, defensive role. They mostly studied the Brick and then hammered out their position on it. In 1982, they began to build a coalition with an alternative policy agenda of their own making. They were also more aggressive in their demands for changes in the policy process.

Although the business peak associations made great strides in developing an alternative to the radical neoliberal coalition, the regime did not make many policy concessions. Instead, Pinochet steered a careful course between policy continuity and change. He kept the pragmatic coalition out of the policymaking process and replaced most radical internationalist policymakers connected to the core conglomerates with men who supported the same general agenda but who were not closely associated with the core conglomerates. He probably feared that giving in to the budding pragmatic coalition would compromise his hold on power, opening the floodgates to demands for political as well as economic change. With state institutions biased against them, the fledgling alternative coalition extracted few policy changes from the regime. Radical neoliberals remained in the most sensitive ministerial positions and deflationary policies continued unabated.

Regime structure, then, sustained radical neoliberalism even though the core capitalist support coalition had crumbled. The radical economic program was installed with relative ease during the consolidation of a personalist military dictatorship with a closed policymaking process. After Pinochet established his position, reversing the process was another matter entirely. In the wake of the breakdown of democracy, but before Pinochet had consolidated one-man rule, shifting coalitions of capitalist and landowning groups with varying power resources had been sufficient to implant both the gradual approach to economic restructuring and the radical neoliberal experiment. After he had gained control of the state, however, the new pragmatic capitalist coalition alone could not induce major policy change. Subsequent events showed that only threats to Pinochet's rule could elicit substantive policy corrections. The potential threat of a multiclass coalition of capitalists, middle classes, and some labor sectors in the context of sharpening political instability would challenge not only Pinochet's economic policies but also his reign. As the next chapter argues, the need to preempt such a menace induced Pinochet to offer the pragmatic neoliberal coalition more significant policy concessions and a greater role in economic policymaking.

## Notes

1. Beginning in January of 1978, Article 14 of the capital account allowed financial firms to borrow foreign currency for any purpose. Until December 1977, they could do so only for foreign trade transactions.

2. Fernando Dahse, *El mapa de la extrema riqueza* (Santiago: Editorial Aconcagua, 1979), pp. 154-55 and p. 191.

3. The Banco de Concepción was the sixth largest bank in terms of assets, 25.5 million dollars or 3.3 percent of total banking assets in 1978. It was also the sixth largest bank in Chile in terms of its control over banking loans, 5.4 percent. It was fourth in capturing dollar-denominated foreign loans, $48.7 million or 5.2 percent of total inflows. Fernando Dahse, *El mapa de la extrema riqueza.*

4. Patricio Rozas and Gustavo Marín, *El mapa de la extrema riqueza: 10 años después* (Santiago: Ediciones Chile-América, 1989).

5. Ricardo Ffrench-Davis, "El problema de la deuda externa y la apertura financiera en Chile," *Colección Estudios Cieplan* no. 11, December 1983, p. 127. For more detailed accounts, see Sebastian Edwards and Alejandra Cox Edwards, *Monetarism and Liberalization: The Chilean Experiment* (Cambridge: Ballinger, 1987).

6. For reforms in retirement benefits, health insurance, and the restrictive labor code, see José Pablo Arellano, "Sistemas alternativos de seguridad social: Un análisis de la experiencia chilena," *Colección Estudios Cieplan* no. 4, November 1980; Dagmar Raczynski, "Reformas al sector salud: Diálogos y debates," *Colección Estudios Cieplan* no. 10, June 1983; Jaime Ruiz-Tagle, *El sindicalismo chileno después del plan laboral* (Santiago: Editorial Interamericana, 1985). For more recent texts, see David E. Hojman, *Chile: The Political Economy of Development and Democracy in the 1990s* (Pittsburgh: University of Pittsburgh Press, 1993); Tarsicio Castañeda, *Combating Poverty: Innovative Social Reforms in Chile During the 1980s* (San Francisco: International Center for Economic Growth, 1992); and Carol Graham, *From Emergency Employment to Social Investment: Alleviating Poverty in Chile* (Washington, D.C.: Brookings Institution, 1991).

7. That limit was 1.6 times a bank's equity until December 1978 and 1.8 times equity until June 1979; see Edwards and Cox-Edwards, *Monetarism and Liberalization*, p. 56.

8. See company annual reports of BHC's leading consumer durables company

Compañía Tecno Industrial and its subsidiaries and affiliates. The same holds true for Cruzat-Larraín's Compañía de Petróleos de Chile.

9. José Pablo Arellano, "De la liberalización a la intervención: El mercado de capitales en Chile, 1974-1982," *Colección Estudios Cieplan* no. 11, December 1983, p. 24.

10. For the impact of international variables, see Stephany Griffith-Jones and Osvaldo Sunkel, *La crisis de la deuda y del desarrollo en América Latina: El fin de una ilusión* (Buenos Aires: Grupo Editor Latinoamericano, 1987); also see Jonathan Hartlyn and Samuel A. Morley, eds., *Latin American Political Economy: Financial Crisis and Political Change* (Boulder: Westview, 1986).

11. All interviewees agreed on this point. For a relatively detailed study of selected cases, see Alejandra Mizala, "Liberalización financiera y quiebra de empresas industriales: Chile, 1977-82," Cieplan, *Notas Técnicas* no. 67, January 1985. For a more general overview of the process, see Alejandro Foxley, *Latin American Experiments in Neoconservative Economics* (Berkeley, University of California Press, 1983).

12. The annual reports of the SFF, SNA, and CNC as well as sectoral association publications—such as *Informativo SFF* and *El Campesino*—were notably uncritical during this period as compared to the previous years, and especially as compared to the period between 1982 and 1985.

13. Banco Central de Chile, *Memoria Anual, 1980* (Santiago: Imprenta Nacional, 1981) p. 126.

14. For the financial service and construction sectors, see Banco Central de Chile, *Boletín Mensual*, no. 650, April 1982, pp. 848-49; and no. 728, October 1988, pp. 2810-11.

15. Pinochet held a plebiscite in 1980 for a constitution to replace that of 1925, which had been in force up to the coup. In the campaign for the plebiscite the regime managed to neutralize political opposition.

16. For positions on sectoral policies, see Rolf Lüders (a top BHC conglomerate executive), *La Tercera de la Hora*, July 15, 1981. For positions on interest rates, see Rolf Lüders, *La Tercera de la Hora*, March 17 and 24, 1982, and April 24, 1982. For positions on devaluation, see top executives of Cruzat-Larraín conglomerate forestry and fishing companies in *Estrategia*, March 31-April 6, 1981. For Lüders' position on devaluation, see *Estrategia*, October 27-November 2, 1981; as well as his column in *La Tercera de la Hora* during those months.

17. For the SFF's position on devaluation, see statements by SFF presidents Hernán Daroch, *El Mercurio*, April 9, 1981; and Bruno Casanova, *Informativo SFF* no. 131, January-February 1982, p. 2. For the SNA's stance, see an interview with SNA president Germán Riesco in *El Mercurio*, September 6, 1981.

18. The diffident quality of their opposition took the following form. In early 1981, SONAMI, whose members were all net exporters, stated that an overvalued currency played a large part in their sector's depressed condition, but SONAMI fell short of advocating devaluation. The CNC declared that exporters within the association favored devaluation, but any policy recommendation on the matter would require a full assessment of its impact on the economy as a whole. For SONAMI, see "Informe: Situación de la pequeña y mediana minería nacional," annex to SONAMI letter no. 1284 to Pinochet's Chief of Staff, General Santiago Sinclair Oyander, dated November 30, 1981. For the CNC, see Cámara Nacional de

Comercio, Memorandum no. 347/81 to Domingo Arteaga, President of the CPC, "CNC Position with respect to Customs Tariffs and Exchange Rates," December 16, 1981. For the opinion of other exporters, see *Estrategia*, March 31-April 6, 1981, declaration by former president of wine exporters.

19. *El Campesino* 10, October 1981, reported on a CPC-arranged meeting with Pinochet in which the leaders of the various peak associations raised the question of interest rates. Meanwhile, the ABIF (the banking association) did not offer a public opinion on these matters. However, since it was dominated by the core internationalist conglomerates, and Javier Vial was its president, it seems doubtful that it could have supported such a policy.

20. For the SFF's positions, see *Informativo SFF* no. 124, June 1981, p. 17; no. 125, July 1981, pp. 2-3; no. 126, August 1981, p.1; no. 128, October 1981, pp. 4-6. For the SNA's positions, see *El Campesino* 8, August 1981, p. 7; and 10, October 1981, editorial; declarations to the press by Germán Riesco, SNA President, *El Mercurio*, September 6, 1981; *Ercilla* no. 2405, September 2, 1981; and *El Campesino* 11, November 1981, p. 4. For the CNC's positions, see Cámara Nacional de Comercio, *Memoria Anual, 1981-1982*; Cámara Nacional de Comercio, Circular no. 32, November 20, 1981, "El GATT, el dumping y las subvenciones"; and Cámara Nacional de Comercio, Memorandum no. 347/81 to Domingo Arteaga, President of CPC, "CNC Position with respect to Customs Tariffs and Exchange Rates," December 16, 1981. For SONAMI's position, see *El Mercurio*, March 28, 1981. For the CChC's position, see *Ercilla* no. 2400, July 1981, pp. 17-18.

21. Price bands fixed the price of a traditional agricultural product within a range of historical international prices. In other words, they established a price floor and ceiling for the product according to historical world highs and lows. Chilean landowners hoped to use price bands to counteract dumping.

22. The individual peak associations expressed those concerns at a meeting the CPC held with Pinochet in October 1981. *Informativo SFF* no. 128, October 1981, pp. 5-7; *El Campesino* 10, October 1981, pp. 4-5; *El Campesino* 11, November 1981, editorial.

23. For the SFF's positions, see *Informativo SFF* no. 124, June 1981; no. 125, July 1981; no. 126, August 1981; and no. 128, October 1981. For the SNA's position, see *El Campesino* 8, August 1981; and 10, October 1981; declarations to press by Germán Riesco, SNA President, *El Mercurio*, September 6, 1981; *Ercilla*, 2405, September 2, 1981; and *El Campesino* 11, November 1981. For the CNC's positions, see Cámara Nacional de Comercio, *Memoria Anual, 1981-1982*. For SONAMI's position, see Sociedad Nacional de Minería, Memorandum no. 1284 to President Pinochet's Chief of Staff, Brigadier General Santiago Sinclair Oyander, November 30, 1981.

24. For the ABIF, see Association of Banking and Financial Institutions, declaration, September 1, 1981.

25. *Ercilla* no. 2400, July 29, 1981, pp. 8-10.

26. *La Tercera de la Hora*, October 29, 1981.

27. *La Tercera de la Hora*, December 31, 1981.

28. The SNA, for example, stressed that it merely sought to perfect and complement the prevailing economic model, not to distort or to overturn it. *Estrategia*, week of August 25, 1981.

29. Confederación de la Producción y Comercio, memorandum that defined what the private sector understood by the term social market economy, March 22,

1982. It pointedly stated that a fixed exchange rate was a violation of economic freedom.

30. His address to the stockholders of the CMPC received wide coverage in the press.

31. CPC, minutes of the executive committee meeting no. 564, July 1, 1982.

32. *La Tercera de la Hora*, July 22, August 1, December 6, 1982; *Ercilla* no. 2453 and no. 2470, August 4 and December 1, 1982, respectively; *Estrategia*, August 2-8, 1982; *El Mercurio*, August 15, 1982.

33. For the SFF's positions, see *Informativo SFF* no. 137, August 1982; *El Mercurio* and *La Tercera de la Hora*, August 1, 1982; *Estrategia*, August 16-22, September 6-12, October 25-31, 1982; *La Tercera de la Hora*, August 27, 1982; *Ercilla* no. 2475, January 5, 1983. For the SNA's positions, see *El Campesino* 8 and 11, August and November 1982; *Estrategia*, August 16-22, 1982. For the CNC positions, see *Estrategia*, August 16-22, 1982; letter no. 248/82 to Minister of Finance and Economy Lüders dated October 12, 1982 following the CNC's general assembly of October 7-8. For SONAMI policy positions, see *El Mercurio*, June 20, 1982; letter to Pinochet dated August 3, 1982; *Estrategia*, August 16-22. For the CChC's policy positions, see *La Tercera de la Hora*, June 20 and 27, 1982; *El Mercurio*, June 20 and December 23, 1982. For the ABIF's policy position, see *Estrategia*, August 16-22, 1982.

34. *Estrategia*, July 12-18, 1982.

35. SFF, *Memoria Anual 1982-1983*. Pedro Lizana was also representative of a minority among industrialists who did not support the SFF's stance on differentiated tariffs.

36. SFF, *Memoria Anual 1981-1982*.

37. *Informativo SFF* no. 136, July 1982 and December 1982; *El Mercurio*, August 1, 1982; *La Tercera de la Hora*, August 1 and 27, 1982; *Ercilla* no. 2455, August 18, 1982; *Estrategia*, October 25-21, 1982.

38. *Informativo SFF* no. 131, January-February 1982, p. 2.

39. See SFF, "Informe final de la comisión designada por el consejo de la Sociedad de Fomento Fabril para estudiar una alternativa al sistema arancelario actualmente en vigencia," Santiago, October 20, 1982. For the dissident minority position, see Efraín Friedman, "La situación económica," August 1982.

40. Confederación de la Producción y Comercio, memorandum that defined social market economy, March 22, 1982. It explicitly supported low across-the-board tariffs.

41. Minutes of the CPC executive committee meeting, no. 577, November 25, 1982.

42. *La Tercera de la Hora*, November 9, 1982.

43. *Estrategia*, August 16-22, 1982.

44. *Estrategia*, August 16-22, 1982.

45. For SONAMI, see Memorandum to President Pinochet, August 3, 1982; for the CNC, see *Memoria Anual, 1981-1982*; for the SNA, see *El Campesino* 3, March 1982, p. 9.

46. For the first policy change favorable to the SFF, see *Informativo SFF* no. 131, January-February 1982, p. 8. Nevertheless, in April 1982, SFF President Bruno Casanova declared that industrialists still awaited the regular, timely, and effective operation of anti-dumping measures. For the second policy change, see SFF,

*Memoria Anual, 1981*, p. 3. This annual report covered the period from May 1981 to May 1982. *Informativo SFF* no. 132, March 1982, pp. 7-8.

47. For the CPC's position on these issues, see Guillermo Campero, *Los Gremios Empresariales en el período 1970-1982* (Santiago: ILET, 1984), p. 253; Minutes of CPC executive council meeting no. 557, May 27, 1982; *La Tercera de la Hora*, June 6, 1982.

48. Minutes of the CPC's executive council meeting no. 552, April 23, 1982.

49. Ascanio Cavallo, Oscar Sepúlveda, Manuel Salazar, *La historia oculta del régimen militar* (Santiago: Ediciones La Epoca, 1988), p. 290.

50. The Ibáñez conglomerate did not export or have heavy financial holdings, nor did it engage in activities for domestic markets in manufacturing industries. On the internationalist side, its agricultural import needs made its directors partial to relatively open economies. On the more traditional side, they also had an interest in healthy internal markets for food consumption.

51. The SFF wanted differentiated tariffs within GATT limits (a maximum of 35 percent). The SNA, in a meeting with Pinochet, opposed them in favor of protection against unfair competition from imports; it also sought export subsidies (drawbacks). Meanwhile, SONAMI limited itself to narrow sectoral issues, such as the ones it had raised in November 1981. For the position of the SFF, see *La Tercera de la Hora*, May 8, 1982; for the SNA, see *El Campesino* 4, April 1982 and 5, May 1982; *La Tercera de la Hora*, April 30, 1982; for SONAMI, see *La Tercera de la Hora*, April 7, 1982.

52. CPC, minutes of executive committee meeting no. 562, June 16, 1982; *El Mercurio*, June 17, 1982.

53. Sergio de la Cuadra and Salvador Valdés, "Myths and Facts about Instability in Financial Liberalization in Chile: 1974-1983," in Philip L. Brock, ed., *If Texas were Chile: A Primer on Banking Reform* (San Francisco: ICS Press, 1992).

54. De la Cuadra and Valdés, "Myths and Facts."

55. Author interviews with Rolf Lüders, December 1988; Jorge Fontaine, former president of the CPC, April 1989; Manuel Valdés, former president of the SNA, March 1989.

56. I am grateful to Sergio de la Cuadra, Rolf Lüders, Raúl Sáez, Jaime Alé (SFF), and Lee Ward (ministry of economy) for their insight into the policy process and the relationship between ministries. Author interviews in September and December 1988.

# 7

## Pragmatic Neoliberalism

The 1980s have become known as Latin America's lost decade. In compliance with International Monetary Fund (IMF) requirements to restructure loans, governments slashed fiscal deficits and curtailed imports. Economic activity contracted as investment funds dried up. Government services in health, education, and welfare declined, precipitously in some cases. Hyperinflation ravaged currencies and living standards, real wages plummeted, and unemployment soared. It seemed as if economic calamities had no end.

Chile shared many of the rest of Latin America's misfortunes with employment, wages, and investment funds especially affected. Because of the budget-balancing, monetarist policies of the Chicago boys, however, Chile's fiscal condition was sounder and inflation lower. Continuing along the trajectory established by its radical economic team, Chile initially responded to the crisis with orthodox deflationary policies to restrict the money supply and boost foreign exchange reserves. Then the trickle of reforms to the radical neoliberal model begun in 1982 became significant modifications between 1983 and 1985. Further adjustments followed between 1985 and 1988. Chile's reflationary and sectoral policies set it on a course of robust economic recovery and sustained economic growth that made it the envy of crisis-ridden neighbors and the darling of the international financial community.

The rise and consolidation of the pragmatic neoliberal coalition between 1983 and 1988 played an important part in shaping the policies and the institutional relationships between capital and labor that facilitated Chile's economic recovery. Unlike the radical neoliberal coalition, fixed-asset rather than liquid-asset internationalists dominated a broadly inclusive capitalist coalition that also embraced domestic market producers. Working through the Confederación de la Producción y Comercio (CPC), the pragmatic neoliberal coalition formulated a detailed policy agenda for Chile's economic recovery by the middle of 1983, well in advance of major policy changes. That agenda, and the initial formulation of key policies, stressed reflationary and sectoral policies that changed the emphasis of the neoliberal model but did not seek its replacement. By 1988, the pragmatic coalition had achieved virtually all its goals. Differences between policy demands and the content of the policies enacted were due to the fact that the program had been a platform for negotiation with the regime, not an ultimatum for capitulation.

What conditions facilitated the triumph of the pragmatic coalition in the face of Pinochet's initially steadfast support of radical neoliberalism? First, both external and organizational factors played necessary but not sufficient roles in strengthening the pragmatic neoliberal coalition. The lack of high liquidity caused by the Latin American debt crisis precluded a return to radical policies and endowed the pragmatic coalition with great economic strength because its policy proposals had the most to contribute to future economic growth. Meanwhile, the pragmatic coalition reached a new stage of organizational cohesiveness. By negotiating consensus on the basis of detailed sectoral policy documents, the CPC developed a sophisticated, coherent policy agenda for economic recovery.

Pinochet's initial responses to the pragmatic coalition in 1983, however, showed that those factors alone were not sufficient to explain the shift from tottering radical neoliberalism to pragmatic neoliberalism. Two additional conditions were crucial. First, and perhaps most important, the rapidly growing political opposition made overtures to the pragmatic neoliberal coalition, with some initial success. Given this context, Pinochet opted to regain the support of Chilean capitalists by giving in to their policy demands. Otherwise, continued inflexibility by Pinochet on economic policy could have helped the political opposition to forge a broad multiclass alliance that included significant capitalist fractions. Such an alliance could have negotiated an early transition to democracy.

Second, gaining control over key economic ministries and participating in policy formulation permitted the pragmatic coalition to translate its policy demands into policy outcomes. Pinochet sweetened his overtures to the upper classes by changing the system of interaction between capital and the state. In a complex and evolving process, Pinochet appointed to key policymaking positions technocrats who were less ideological and men who represented the various groups in the new pragmatic coalition. The new officials opened policy formulation to participation by organized business. This arrangement facilitated more flexible free market policies.

The rise and consolidation of the pragmatic neoliberal coalition had important consequences for future developments in Chile. First, the flexible economic program that the coalition had managed to formulate and implement set Chile on a path of sustained growth. Second, the system of interaction between state and capital that had emerged persisted relatively intact into the democratic period. Technocratic policymakers collaborated with organized business in the formulation of economic and social policy, which facilitated exchange of information regarding policy effects on investment and production. It also gave businessmen and landowners greater confidence that government policy would not run roughshod over the private sector's interests, which contributed to creating a good investment climate.

### Rise of the Pragmatic Neoliberal Coalition, 1983-1984

The shift from radical to pragmatic neoliberalism occurred over two distinct periods. In the first (1983-1984), the regime continued to give in grudgingly to some of the pragmatic coalition's demands, as it had done during the previous year. Then, in a stunning reversal, the regime adopted the core of the pragmatic coalition's program between the middle of 1983 and the end of 1984. During the second period (1985-1988), the pragmatic coalition consolidated its policy posture and expanded its material base. As the next chapter shows, the consolidation of the pragmatic neoliberal coalition, coupled with sustained economic growth, enabled the coalition to negotiate the retention of the neoliberal economic model with the democratic opposition during Chile's transition to democracy.

### *Forging a Policy Agenda*

The collapse of Chile's economy over the course of 1981 and 1982 prompted the upper-class allies of the radical neoliberals to abandon the economic team and begin trying to reach a consensus on alternative policies. Chilean capitalists and landowners turned to their business peak associations to negotiate a policy agenda for economic recovery on which they could all agree. Between December 1982 and July 1983, business peak associations forged the pragmatic neoliberal coalition within the bosom of the CPC. They took an increasingly proactive role in defining a detailed policy agenda for economic recovery and forcefully demanded participation in the policy formulation process to convert their vision into reality. The shift from simply raising demands to the independent formulation of a concerted, well-prepared policy agenda represented a new stage in the development of organized business in Chile. It provided the basis for responsible participation by business and landowning sectors in the policymaking process and reduced the tendency of those sectors to react defensively to the government's policy proposals.

During the first half of 1983, Chile's sectoral peak associations worked increasingly within the institutional framework of the CPC as they laboriously went from raising demands to the formulation of a policy package that challenged monetarist orthodoxy. Above all, they wanted the government to abandon its extreme laissez-faire stance, believing that reflationary and sectoral policies offered the best hope for economic recovery.

As long as the sectoral peak associations and the CPC merely raised scattered, isolated demands through the media or in meetings with the authorities, they got few results. Their demands included higher foreign exchange rates, debt relief for firms, lower interest rates, larger fiscal deficits, higher inflation and lower wages, and tax relief. They also sought greater access to the policymaking process and a plethora of sector-specific policies.[1] The government responded to these demands with an emergency program in March 1983. It offered to renegotiate 30 percent of eligible firms' debt, proposed real interest rates of 7 percent over the Unidad de Fomento (the UF is an inflation-adjusted measure of value), and acquiesced to a paltry fiscal deficit of 2.3 percent with an inflation rate of 20 percent. The CPC felt that the plan fell far short of the private sector's needs, especially in the areas of debt relief and fiscal stimulation.[2]

Stung by the government's tepid response to its appeals, organized business swung into action. Over the next few months, individual peak associations developed detailed sectoral programs to aid their economic recovery. They met under the institutional framework of the CPC to negotiate a consensus over crucial issues of general interest and to hammer out the parameters of acceptable sector-specific demands. The process culminated in the release in 1983 of a formal document, titled *Recuperación económica: Análisis y proposiciones*, which outlined concrete policy proposals to overcome the economic crisis. The document presented a coherent statement about what businessmen and landowners needed if they were to be the agents of economic recovery. It also defined the rising pragmatic coalition's maximum bargaining position.

*Recuperación económica* proposed that the government reschedule 100 percent of the private sector's crushing debt load with preferential credit at lower than market interest rates (5 percent over the UF); enact a spate of reflationary policy proposals, including bringing market interest rates in line with international rates to make credit more available and to stimulate economic activity; maintain a 4 percent deficit in fiscal spending; tolerate 30 percent annual inflation; and begin public works and housing programs. *Recuperación económica* also petitioned the government for measures that would benefit both exporters and producers for domestic markets, such as high real exchange rates and export incentives (drawbacks). Last, but not least, the pragmatic coalition sought tax cuts to stimulate investment and raise stock prices.[3] In addition to advocating the policies outlined in *Recuperación económica*, the pragmatic neoliberal coalition continued to seek greater access to the policy process. Meanwhile, individual peak associations continued to press for sector-specific policies that were compatible with the items of general agreement and were designed to avoid intersectoral conflict that could unravel the coalition.

The balance of economic interests within the coalition allowed for accommodations that made the pragmatic coalition and its policy proposals possible. Internationalist economic interests both among and within the peak associations clearly dominated the pragmatic neoliberal coalition. They were not radical neoliberal interests because they had a heavier concentration in *fixed assets* (extractive industries in logging, fishing, and mining) rather than liquid assets. The coalition also included in a subordinate position landowners and industrialists who produced for domestic markets. Because it was dominated by fixed-asset rather than liquid-asset internationalists, the coalition was not opposed to sectoral policies in principle, especially in credit and taxation. But because it favored an open economy, it frowned upon tariffs as a means to protect domestic markets.

The pragmatic coalition was not without its tensions, as CPC debates over the tariff question between 1983 and 1984 revealed. The debates also offered evidence that fixed-asset internationalists, not producers for domestic markets, dominated the new capitalist policy coalition, a marked reversal of the situation in the gradual policy period discussed in Chapters 4 and 5. Commensurate with guidelines set by the General Agreement on Trade and Tariffs, the Sociedad de Fomento Fabril (SFF) had demanded a differentiated tariff schedule ranging from zero to 35 percent depending on the national content of a product. But, in a replay of events during the period of gradual economic adjustment, the SFF was once again outvoted in the CPC. The Sociedad Nacional de Agricultura (SNA), the Cámara Nacional de Comercio (CNC), the Sociedad Nacional de Minería (SONAMI), and the Cámara Chilena de la Construcción (CChC) opposed the SFF's proposals. They preferred a low across-the-board tariff in the 15 to 20 percent range. As a result of these alignments in the CPC, tariff structure was not on *Recuperación económica's* agenda.[4] In response to unrelenting pressure from the SFF, the CPC held yet another survey on the issue of differentiated tariffs in 1984, and the situation remained unchanged. The other member associations of the CPC again rejected the SFF's proposals.[5] They preferred protection via a high real exchange rate and barriers to unfair international competition—dumping.[6] As a result, these mechanisms became part of the official policy position of the pragmatic neoliberal coalition.

Tariff policy remained a divisive issue that threatened the cohesiveness of the coalition. Yet, for a number of reasons, the split over the tariff question was not sufficiently acute to drive the SFF from the coalition. First, the SFF agreed with the other member associations on many policy initiatives, especially with respect to reflation. Second, the pragmatic coalition did recommend somewhat higher levels of protection than those that existed, though they were not the SFF's preferred policy instruments. Equally

TABLE 7.1 Composition of Industrial Exports, 1983 (Millions of US$)

| Sector | Amount | %Total Exports | %Industrial Exports |
|---|---|---|---|
| Total Exports | 3,835.5 | | |
| Mining | 2,296.6 | 59.9 | |
| Farm & Sea | 327.5 | 8.5 | |
| Total Industrial Exports | 1,211.4 | 31.6 | |
| Semi-Traditional Industrial Exports | 518.8 | 13.5 | 42.8 |
| Fish Meal | 307.1 | | |
| Paper & Cellulose | 208.0 | | |
| Printed Matter | 3.7 | | |
| Non-Traditional Industrial Exports | 692.6 | 18.0 | 57.2 |
| Foods | 116.8 | 3.0 | 9.6 |
| Beverages | 10.8 | 0.3 | 0.9 |
| Wood[a] | 116.4 | 3.0 | 9.6 |
| Chemicals[b] | 109.8 | 2.9 | 9.1 |
| Basic Metals[c] | 284.5 | 7.4 | 23.4 |
| Metal & electric manufactures | 20.3 | 0.5 | 1.7 |
| Transport Materials | 29.0 | 0.8 | 2.4 |
| Miscellaneous | 8.7 | 0.2 | 0.7 |

[a]Mainly pine logs ($102.8 million).
[b]Mainly petroleum and derivatives ($66.5 million).
[c]Mainly molybdenum oxide ($122.8 million).

*Source:* Banco Central de Chile, *Memoria Anual* (Santiago: Imprenta Nacional, 1980).

important, the pragmatic coalition supported sectoral policies as long as they served to redress market distortions or promoted exports. Thus, in alliance with at least one other association (SONAMI), the SFF began in 1984 to lobby for the introduction of a drawback system (reimbursement for the import duties on components used in the manufacture of exports).[7] The CPC quickly supported those efforts.[8] Given the composition of industrial exports, shown on Table 7.1, it was clear that nontraditional manufactured exports needed some incentives if they were to expand.[9] They only constituted about 26 percent of industrial exports; the bulk was in the category of semi-elaborated industrial products.

## The Pragmatic Neoliberal Coalition and Policy Change

The pragmatic neoliberal coalition had been advocating a consistent set of policy alternatives to radical neoliberalism since the end of 1982. Yet its proposals did not bring significant policy change until the peak associations hammered out their differences and presented a united front. Their new unity was expressed in several ways, such as the policy accommodations of *Recuperación económica*, a commitment to acquire greater access to policy formulation, and the pursuit of principled sectoral policies. Between July 1983 (when the CPC released *Recuperación económica*) and the end of 1984, the nascent coalition extracted substantial concessions from the government.[10] Table 7.2 shows that the fiscal deficit for 1983 stood at just under 4 percent of GDP in 1983 and close to 5 percent in 1984. Real short term interest rates (30 to 90 days) declined from an annual average of 35.1 percent in 1982 to 15.9 percent in 1983 and 11.4 percent in 1984.[11] The government also demonstrated a commitment to higher real exchange rates.[12] Moreover, the authorities decreed a tax reform in January 1984 that approximated the one proposed by the CPC and individual peak associations. In order to stimulate investment, the reform reduced personal income taxes and gave tax credits to retained profits.[13] Inflation, however, stood closer to government goals than those of the private sector: 23 percent for 1983 and 1984, as measured by the variation in the CPI from December to December.[14]

The concessions did not end there. In May 1984, the government developed an internal debt rescheduling program more consistent with CPC demands. Small and medium debtors of the "productive" (i.e., nonfinancial) sector could renegotiate 100 percent of their liabilities, large debtors up to 76 percent. The terms of the loan were ten years with a two year grace period at 5 percent real interest at first and then 6 percent.[15] The authorities also instituted sectoral policies found in *Recuperación económica*. For example, in August 1984, the Ministry of Urban Affairs and Housing began a triennial housing and public works program developed by the CChC.

Furthermore, the government responded to many of the sectoral demands of the other peak associations, none of which incited intersectoral conflict even though some were not in *Recuperación económica*.[16] In March 1983, the SFF exulted when tariffs rose from 10 percent to 20 percent across-the-board. Then, in August 1983, officials slapped a 15 percent tariff on textiles products, shoes, aluminum products, gas meters, and matches. A few months later, the tariff was extended to wood, paper, rubber, and clay and enamel (construction) products. Industry was also promised a drawback policy, which was instituted between 1985 and 1988.

Agriculture benefitted from an array of programs. The government backed purchasing orders first for wheat (in October 1982) and then, by

TABLE 7.2 Key Domestic and International Economic Indicators, 1970-1988

| Year | GDP (%) | CPI | Fiscal Deficit %GDP | Interest Rates (30-90 days annualized) | Real Wage Index | Real Exchange Rate Index | Internat'l Reserves Millions of US$ | Copper ¢/lb | Oil $/bb (average) | World Interest Rates US Prime |
|------|------|------|------|------|------|------|------|------|------|------|
| 1970 | 2.1 | 32.5 | 2.9 | – | 100.0 | 76.6 | 393.5 | 64.2 | – | – |
| 1971 | 9.0 | 20.0 | 11.2 | – | – | – | 162.7 | 42.3 | – | – |
| 1972 | -2.9 | 77.9 | 13.5 | – | – | – | 75.8 | 48.6 | 2.8 | – |
| 1973 | -7.1 | 352.9 | 24.6 | – | – | – | 167.4 | 80.8 | 3.7 | 8.0 |
| 1974 | 1.0 | 504.7 | 10.5 | – | 68.1 | 99.9 | 94.0 | 93.3 | 12.3 | 10.8 |
| 1975 | -12.9 | 374.8 | 2.6 | 121.0 | 65.9 | 136.4 | -129.2 | 55.9 | 12.8 | 7.9 |
| 1976 | 3.5 | 211.9 | 2.3 | 51.4 | 67.8 | 110.6 | 107.9 | 63.6 | 13.7 | 6.8 |
| 1977 | 9.9 | 92.0 | 1.8 | 39.4 | 74.8 | 92.2 | 273.3 | 59.3 | 13.0 | 6.8 |
| 1978 | 8.2 | 40.1 | 0.8 | 35.1 | 79.6 | 111.4 | 1.058.0 | 61.9 | 13.0 | 9.1 |
| 1979 | 8.3 | 33.4 | -1.7 | 16.6 | 86.1 | 114.8 | 2.763,8 | 89.8 | 18.6 | 12.7 |
| 1980 | 7.8 | 31.2 | -3.1 | 12.2 | 93.5 | 100.0 | 4,073.7 | 99.2 | 31.9 | 15.3 |
| 1981 | 5.5 | 9.5 | -1.7 | 38.8 | 101.9 | 87.2 | 3,775.3 | 79.0 | 36.1 | 18.9 |
| 1982 | -14.1 | 20.7 | 2.3 | 35.1 | 102.0 | 98.7 | 2,577.5 | 67.0 | 33.6 | 14.9 |
| 1983 | -0.7 | 23.1 | 3.8 | 15.9 | 91.0 | 116.1 | 2,022.7 | 72.2 | 29.7 | 10.8 |
| 1984 | 6.3 | 23.0 | 4.8 | 11.4 | 91.2 | 122.4 | 2,055.9 | 62.5 | 28.7 | 12.0 |
| 1985 | 2.4 | 26.4 | 3.1 | 11.1 | 87.1 | 150.0 | 1,886.7 | 64.3 | 26.4 | 9.9 |
| 1986 | 5.7 | 17.4 | 2.2 | 7.7 | 90.5 | 164.6 | 1,778.3 | 62.3 | 13.8 | 8.3 |
| 1987 | 5.7 | 21.5 | 0.8 | 9.4 | 88.7 | 170.0 | 1,871.1 | 80.8 | 17.8 | 8.2 |
| 1988 | 7.4 | 12.7 | – | 7.2 | 94.5 | – | 2,133.6 | 117.9 | 14.2 | 9.3 |

*Source:* Eduardo Silva, "The Political Economy of Chile's Regime Transition: From Radical to Pragmatic Neo-Liberal Policies." Reprinted from *The Struggle for Democracy in Chile, 1982-1990*, edited by Paul Drake and Iván Jaksic, by permission of the University of Nebraska Press, Copyright © 1991 by the University of Nebraska Press.

December 1983, for corn, wine, and oils.[17] New credit lines charged substantially lower real interest, 8 percent in comparison to 14 percent at the beginning of 1983. The government also made special loans available to grain and cereal growers. Wheat growers benefitted first in 1982, but by February 1985 all traditional crops were covered.[18] Moreover, reference prices for beets appeared in 1982, followed by price bands for oil producing plants (July 1984) and wheat (November 1984).[19] (A reference price for wheat was established in 1982.) In 1983, Agriculture Minister Prado pledged to retain import surcharges on dairy products.[20] The government had established those surcharges in November 1982, after the SNA had demanded them in October.[21]

Commerce and the financial sector also obtained government assistance. In the first half of 1983, the CNC asked the administration for special loans for working capital, which were subsequently conceded by the Central Bank.[22] Meanwhile, the financial sector may have received as much as seven billion dollars in aid between 1982 and 1985, counting such items as the preferential dollar, Central Bank purchases of unrecoverable loans, debt rescheduling and emergency loans.[23]

## Power Resources and Policy Change

That the new policies reflected proposals developed by the pragmatic coalition supports the argument that a coalitional shift affected policy change after the collapse of radical neoliberalism. But this still does not explain how the pragmatic coalition managed to translate its agenda into policy. What power resources did the pragmatic coalition wield? What channels to the policymaking process did it command? The discussion begins with an examination of two important background conditions: international factors and coalition cohesion. It continues with an analysis of the crucial but unintended role of political instability in the ascent of the pragmatic coalition; the chapter concludes by showing how cabinet shuffles and the system of interaction between capital and the state in policy formulation clinched the link between coalitional change and policy shifts.

*The International Economy and Coalition Cohesion.* Since radical neoliberal policies had depended on the easy availability of foreign loans, the Latin American debt crisis strengthened the pragmatic neoliberal coalition. Lasting changes in the international financial picture made fixed-asset sectors of the economy (export and domestic-market producers), rather than financial services, the most important contributors to economic growth.[24] The absence of foreign lending made a return to radical neoliberal policies all but impossible during this period.[25]

Chile's commitment to repaying its foreign obligations gave internationally oriented fixed-asset producers the upper hand within the pragmatic neoliberal coalition. Chile, like other Latin American nations, had to export for its balance of payments and hard currency reserves to meet the targets established by the IMF and other international financial institutions. Loan conditionality strengthened export-oriented groups such as those represented by SONAMI and the CNC, as well as the export sectors of the SFF and, especially, the SNA. They were now the main source, aside from involuntary lending from international commercial banks and IMF loans, of the hard currency needed for debt service and economic recovery. By the same token, the debt crisis assured a long-term dearth of voluntary lending to Latin America, meaning that producers for domestic markets could no longer be ignored, as they had been by the radical coalition. Chile had to create local substitutes for foreign products to cut its import bill and build trade surpluses. Moreover, the export sector simply could not absorb the high levels of unemployment (20 to 30 percent) that were generating political instability. Producers for domestic markets in industry, agriculture, and construction could; this earned them a junior position in the coalition.

External factors made the pragmatic coalition a feasible alternative to the failed radical neoliberals, but they were not sufficient to produce significant policy change. Formulating integrated policy proposals and forging a cohesive coalition to advocate them were also crucial, but insufficient, factors. For example, when the coalition was in its embryonic stage and merely voiced scattered policy demands it achieved little success. Once the peak associations negotiated a common policy agenda under the auspices of the CPC, their well-developed, integrated proposals amounted to a coordinated program for economic recovery, not just isolated demands. Thus, if called upon, the pragmatic coalition now had the wherewithal to participate in policy formulation effectively.

*The Threat of a Multiclass Coalition.* In early 1983, external factors and coalition cohesion alone failed to elicit substantive policy change. Much more pressure than that which the private sector alone could generate had to be brought to bear on Pinochet. The sudden mobilization of the masses and the explosive emergence of a political opposition in the middle of 1983 provided that pressure.

Social and political unrest erupted shortly after Finance Minister Carlos Cáceres announced his "Emergency Program" in March 1983. The scale of the economic debacle and the extent of joblessness—with little hope of relief due to Cáceres' tepid commitment to reflation—ignited the protest movement. Given the effectiveness of past repression, the sudden rebirth of civil society took everybody by surprise, including the movement's own organizers. Although the opposition did not achieve its goals, the protest movement had far-reaching unintended consequences for public policy, economic growth patterns, and the nature of the relationship between business and the state in Chile. Those unintended consequences eventually turned Chile into a model of macroeconomic management for developing nations.

Beginning in May 1983, the Chilean labor movement, middle-class professional associations, opposition political parties, and shantytown dwellers staged a series of monthly national days of protest. Flourishing opposition groups demanded Pinochet's resignation and an immediate and full transition to democracy. In short, the military government's project for political and social transformation was in jeopardy, and Pinochet's rule was under challenge.[26]

Mass mobilization and party opposition strengthened the pragmatic coalition's negotiating position with the government in two ways. First, since Chile's depressed economy had sparked the opposition movement, Pinochet needed economic programs that would spur economic growth.[27] The pragmatic coalition provided such programs. Second, the main opposition alliance strove to include capitalists. The opposition inadvertently bolstered the pragmatic coalition in its negotiations with the government by raising the specter of a multiclass political movement for democratization that might involve disgruntled capitalists. As a result, the military government's economic policy concessions, including changes in the policymaking process to involve businessmen in policy formulation, were largely an effort by Pinochet to regain the unconditional loyalty of Chilean capitalists. Chapter 8 explores the issue of capitalist's loyalty to the regime in more detail. The present section draws out the implications of the coalition's greater participation in the policy process for the connection between coalition formation and policy change.

The fact that the opposition was very conciliatory towards capital lends credibility to the counterfactual claim that had the military government continued to stonewall the pragmatic coalition some capitalists might have negotiated with the opposition. There can be little doubt that in 1983 and 1984 the centrist opposition wanted to form an implicit alliance with capitalists. Its discourse explicitly linked the prospects for meaningful economic policy change to democratization. The opposition then appealed for capitalist support by proposing economic policies that closely corresponded to those advocated by the pragmatic coalition. Opposition policy statements, moreover, exploited the wedge between manufacturers for domestic markets in industry and the internationalists within the pragmatic coalition by appealing to the loyalties of the former.

These, of course, were the tactics of the dominant, centrist (or center-left) opposition coalition, which was led by the Christian Democratic party

(PDC) and included the Radical party as well as more social-democratic (reformed) leftists in the Bloque Socialista. In August of 1983, this coalition became known as Alianza Democrática (AD). They pledged to uphold private property rights, manage the foreign debt, and pursue prudent macroeconomic policies. They also supported a mixed economy, sectoral economic policies (especially industrial policy and debt relief), rapid economic reactivation, and tougher negotiations with the IMF to extract enough financing to reflate the economy without heavy inflation.[28] In other words, Alianza Democrática tried to assuage the military and entrepreneurs that an early transition to democracy, with substantial revisions to the 1980 Constitution, would not mean a reversion to "socialism." In return, Alianza Democrática hoped that capitalists and dissident military groups (soft-liners) would join their cause.

Meanwhile, the Communist party and more militant Marxist socialists had formed a separate coalition—the Movimiento Democrático Popular (MDP). They too claimed that the principle of private property would be upheld, but they advocated a much stronger state role in the economy, major economic reforms, and radical redistribution programs.[29]

At first, both Alianza Democrática and the MDP vied for control of the mass protest movement that began in May 1983. Alianza Democrática quickly managed to gain the upper hand the same year and largely dominated organized labor, professional associations, and the student movement. Beginning in 1984, the MDP began to gain ground among the unemployed in the shantytowns.[30] Since the AD was stronger than the MDP among organized groups, and represented a much broader political spectrum, it sought to establish itself as the valid interlocutor with the military government over the issue of democratization. Alianza Democrática counted on the support of significant conservative sectors in this endeavor as will be seen in the section on ministerial changes.

Beginning in January 1984, Alianza Democrática attempted to form an explicit alliance with capitalists in order to wrestle the pace and content of political liberalization away from the military government. The PDC spearheaded the effort with the publication of *Proyecto alternativo*.[31] The multivolume *Proyecto alternativo* contained official PDC economic and social policy statements that were an integral part of the party's project for a transition to democracy. It also spelled out what had been more or less implicit up to then: That the opposition was committed to the principle of gradualism and did not contest capitalists' overriding concerns regarding economic policy change. The document consistently reinforced the positions that the AD had advanced in 1983. It stressed moderate economic policy reform, macroeconomic stability, private property rights, and a mixed economy, defined as a combination of state regulation and investment.[32]

The *Proyecto alternativo* called for an explicit alliance with capitalists for democratization based on *concertación social*: a social pact between political parties, capital, and labor.[33] This idea stood at the core of the PDC's strategy to win over capital, or to at least keep it from opposing a political transition that differed from the one stipulated in the Constitution of 1980. In pursuit of such a social pact, the Christian Democrats organized a series of workshops in late 1984. The purpose of the workshops was to identify the assurances capitalists required and to establish which of those guarantees would be acceptable to labor. Property rights were the main issue for capital. They sought a commitment to private enterprise and an affirmation that expropriation and heavy state competition would remain a thing of the past. Labor wanted changes in the labor code to facilitate collective bargaining, better working conditions, and higher wages. As will be seen, capitalists essentially got what they wanted before 1988 while labor's demands had to wait until the first democratic government for attention, and even then business retained the upper hand.

While the opposition maneuvered to gain the loyalty of disgruntled capitalist groups (especially producers for domestic markets), capitalists threatened to join the multiclass opposition coalition against the dictatorship. Although they approached the subject indirectly, their insinuations added to the regime's, especially its leader's, insecurity. The pragmatic coalition issued veiled warnings that its support for the military regime was not unconditional.

The timing of such statements was significant. For example, when the CPC released *Recuperación económica* and circulated it among the highest decision-making circles of the government in July 1983, it stressed that its economic program was a negotiating platform and that it did not seek a break with the regime. However, some of the SFF's leaders diffidently cautioned that such statements did not preclude such a break entirely.[34] At the same time, and in the same tone and style, CPC president Jorge Fontaine emphasized that business sought a dialogue with the government, not a confrontation. Fontaine also stated that the authorities should recognize that the very "survival of the free enterprise system in Chile was at stake," for current economic recovery programs could only lead to "perdition."[35] The implicit threat of this statement lay in the historical memory of the rhetoric used by business groups against Salvador Allende. It was common knowledge that the CPC and the SFF mounted the assault against Allende only when they became convinced that the "survival of the free enterprise system was at risk."[36] For Pinochet, this delicate situation was compounded by the fact that breakaway capitalist groups, most notably in the SFF and the SNA, might ally with medium and small-scale industrialists and farmers who were noticeably more active in their opposition to the regime than large-scale businessmen and landowners.[37]

*Political Instability, Cabinet Changes, and Coalitional Triumph.*
Between the middle of 1983 and the beginning of 1984, Pinochet faced increasing challenges to his rule. In response, he began to replace ministers according to his assessment of the political opposition's strength. As long as opposition forces remained divided, seemingly momentous changes were little more than smokescreens, and deflationary policy continued. When they threatened to unite, significant shifts in economic cabinet positions and policy followed.

Throughout most of 1983, the situation must not have seemed hopeless to Pinochet, even though he faced a combative, cohesive private sector demanding economic recovery and a strong middle and lower-class opposition calling for a speedy transition to democracy. These opposition forces remained unconnected, which permitted Pinochet to alternately repress one while placating the other. Thus, despite severe difficulties, the opposition was manageable. Accordingly, Pinochet's appointments to high-level economic policymaking positions did not mark a great departure from radical neoliberalism, as shown in Table 7.3. He placed representatives of the pragmatic coalition in subordinate cabinet positions to appease the budding pragmatic coalition and to blunt its increasingly strident discontent with deflationary policies. Continuing the trend established in 1982, policy changes were slight.

The first set of cabinet changes occurred in February of 1983. Pinochet replaced superminister Rolf Lüders with Carlos Cáceres (moved up from the Central Bank) as minister of finance and Manuel Martín was placed subordinate to him as minister of economy. Cáceres was a nonradical internationalist who had been sympathetic to the Chicago boys. By virtue of his position he was in ultimate control of policymaking. Martín, by contrast, clearly represented the interests of domestic market producers, and he developed an economic recovery program that was remarkably close to CPC proposals.[38] He was being manipulated unwittingly, however. His real function was to deflect the growing energies of the business opposition onto a subordinate ministry. Meanwhile, the real power, Finance Minister Cáceres, unveiled his highly restrictive emergency plan in March 1983.

Pinochet's plan backfired. Cáceres made policy but the combination with Martín did not blunt the CPC's offensive. It intensified it. The CPC rejected Cáceres' plan and counterattacked with *Recuperación económica* in June and July. Cáceres, as previously shown, was forced to give in on a number of points, principally fiscal deficit levels, inflation, tax reform, and protection for domestic market producers. Not surprisingly, friction developed between Martín and Cáceres.[39]

The situation worsened for Pinochet in August of 1983. The opposition began making overtures to a highly disgruntled private sector, promising to respect the social market economy and to fulfil key aspects of the economic recovery program. Important business sectors listened carefully and considered the possibilities. Confronted with a potential alliance between the business and political oppositions, Pinochet increasingly selected cabinet members who were either direct representatives of the pragmatic coalition or men who were representative of those interests. The trickle of policy changes that began in 1982 increased and became a flood in April 1984.

In August 1983, the monthly demonstrations against the military government were getting larger, and the mainstream political opposition formally proclaimed its unity with the creation of Alianza Democrática. At the same time, the AD proceeded to make overtures to the pragmatic neoliberal coalition by linking the implementation of its economic policy proposals to speedy redemocratization. Businessmen did not reject the AD's overtures out of hand. This highly charged atmosphere brought Pinochet's first major cabinet change: He appointed Sergio O. Jarpa, a well-known political figure with close ties to traditional business sectors, as minister of interior.

Jarpa's appointment had two immediate political consequences. First, the pragmatic coalition was pleased by Jarpa's commitment to economic recovery along the lines of *Recuperación económica*, Jarpa even pressured Pinochet to dismiss Cáceres and to provide him with an economic team dedicated to rapid economic reactivation, a key goal of the CPC.[40] Second, because Jarpa believed economic reactivation should be accompanied by more accelerated political liberalization than the one contemplated in the 1980 Constitution, he offered hope to the opposition that a transition to democracy could be negotiated. Jarpa was convinced that a concurrent process of economic and political change was the only way to defuse Chile's crisis, but he did not support a transition as rapid as the opposition would have liked. Jarpa quickly established negotiations with Alianza Democrática. The key topics discussed were hastening the timetables for congressional and presidential elections, the role of the armed forces in the new government, and the form and function of future democratic political institutions. By the same token, both Jarpa and the AD pointedly excluded the MDP from the dialogue.

Ever defiant, Pinochet soon demonstrated that neither move was what it appeared to be, meaning an admission of defeat. Instead, it soon became evident that Pinochet had used Jarpa to drive a wedge between the business and political oppositions and to diffuse the force of the mass mobilization movement by drawing Alianza Democrática to the negotiating table. A few months later, all illusions about a rapid transition to democracy were dashed when the dialogue between Jarpa and Alianza Democrática broke down after it became clear that Pinochet had not given him negotiating

TABLE 7.3 Conglomerates and Key Government Economic Institutions, 1983-1987

| Institution/ Position | Name | Tenure | Conglomerate Affiliation of Official | Conglomerate Type | If not in Conglomerate Official is Executive of Firms in Sectors that are | Official Linked to Finance Sector [a] | Official Is Chicago Boy |
|---|---|---|---|---|---|---|---|
| Ministers of Finance | Cáceres | 02/83-04/84 | Ibáñez-Ojeda | Neutral | | Yes | |
| | Escobar | 04/84-02/85 | | MNC | | Yes | |
| | Büchi | 02/85- | | | | | |
| Ministers of Economy | Martín | 04/83-08/83 | Lúksic | MDM/Competitive | | Yes | |
| | Passicot | 08/83-04/84 | | | | | |
| | Collados | 04/84-07/85 | | | Construction | | |
| | Délano | 07/85-07/87 | | | Internat'l Mkt. Oriented | | |
| Central Bank Presidents | Errázuriz | 1983-1984 | BHC | Radical Internat'l | | Yes | |
| | Ibáñez | 1984-1985 | | | | Yes | |
| | Seguel | 1985- | | | | | |
| Vice Pres. | Tapia | 1982-1983 | Matte | Internationalist | | Yes | Yes |
| | Ossa | 1983-1984 | | | | | |
| | Ruiz | 1984-1985 | | | Internat'l Mkt. Oriented | | |
| | Serrano | 1985- | | | | | |

| | | | | | | |
|---|---|---|---|---|---|---|
| CORFO[b] Vice Presidents | Ramírez<br>Pérez<br>Hormazábal | 03/81-08/83<br>08/83-12/83<br>12/83- | | | | |
| Budget Office | Costabal | 1981-1984 | Matte/Lúksic Edwards | Internat'l & MDM/C Radical Internat'l | Yes | Yes |
| Directors | Fuenzalida<br>Selume | 1984-1985<br>1985- | | | | |
| Ministers of Agriculture | Prado | 12/81- | (Agro-export/import) | | | |

Neutral: Supermarket business links it to both domestic market food industry and international commerce (imports); also important in higher education (business school).
MDM/Competitive: Fixed-asset firms concentrate in internationally competitive manufactures for domestic markets.
MNC: Multinational Corporation.
[a] Official is on the board of directors of, an executive with, or consultant to a private financial institution.
[b] All CORFO Vice Presidents were army officers.

*Source:* Colegio de Periodistas, *Diccionario biográfico* (Santiago: Editorial Universitaria, selected years); Company annual reports, Superintendencia de Asociaciones Bancarias y Financieras, *Nómina del directorio de instituciones financieras* (Santiago: n.p., selected years); *Hoy* no. 346, March 7, 1984; Fernando Dahse, *El mapa de la extrema riqueza* (Santiago: Editorial Aconcagua, 1979).

authority.[41] In a similar manner, Pinochet frustrated Jarpa on economic policy. He ignored Jarpa's petitions for cabinet-level changes in the economic ministries that would have paved the way for reflationary policies. On the contrary, Pinochet replaced Economy Minister Martín with a more malleable and neutral figure—Andrés Passicot, a Chicago school sympathizer who nonetheless declared that his ministry would take on a more active role in economic management.[42] Pinochet, however, could not afford to snub the pragmatic coalition quite so callously. In an attempt to mollify the pragmatic coalition, he appointed Modesto Collados, a direct representative of the pragmatic coalition, minister of urban development and housing. President of the CChC just before his appointment, Collados immediately put into effect a public works and construction plan that the CChC had prepared under his direction for *Recuperación económica*. In fact, the plan had been a condition he placed on acceptance of the job.[43]

Meanwhile, Cáceres' commitment to austerity and the grudging tone of his concessions to the pragmatic coalition earned him increasingly acerbic criticism from businessmen and landowners. The criticism, Alianza Democrática's unrelenting attempts to draw the pragmatic neoliberal coalition into *concertación social*, the private sector's continued flirtation with the AD, and the unabated monthly days of mass protest combined to persuade Pinochet to appoint a new cabinet in April 1984. At all costs he had to avert the union of the business and political oppositions. The new ministers of economy and finance—Modesto Collados and Luis Escobar—embodied the pragmatic coalition's hopes and aspirations. Chilean entrepreneurs breathed a collective sigh of relief. With these appointments, state institutions in the economic sector became heavily biased in favor of the pragmatic coalition. More importantly, a new system of interaction between capital and the state—one in which organized business participated fully in the policy formulation process—was ushered in. These events rekindled upper class loyalty to Pinochet and dashed the opposition's hopes for a broad multiclass alliance.

Escobar incarnated the pragmatic coalition: He was an internationalist who would not neglect the interests of producers for domestic markets. Escobar had been minister of economy during Jorge Alessandri's administration in the early 1960s. Thus, he was closely identified with a relatively gradual project of capitalist modernization. Escobar also had extensive ties to both international finance and Chilean manufacturers for domestic markets (through the Banco de Fomento de Valparaíso, a regional industrial development bank). He favored an expansionary monetary policy, a differentiated tariff schedule, and greater fiscal deficit spending. It was hoped that because Escobar had once been the Chilean representative to the IMF and World Bank, he could get better terms from them, which would allow him to implement reflationary policy.

Collados had headed two public works-related ministries during the Frei administration in the mid-1960s. As president of the CChC (the office he held just prior to becoming minister) he had advocated an expansion of the money supply based on a policy of controlled emissions. Although he did not support differentiated tariffs, Collados developed a triennial plan that emphasized sectoral policies such as construction, public works, and protection for agriculture, and he also devised a solution to the crisis of the financial institutions.

In addition to these top two appointments, the retention of Prado as minister of agriculture and Lira as minister of mines reinforced the pragmatic coalition's institutional strength. Prado (a landowner) had primary interests in agricultural exports and secondary investments in production for domestic markets. Lira was a prominent member of SONAMI, the mine owners' association.

Modifications in the policy process reinforced the connection between the ministries, the pragmatic coalition, and policy outcomes. Ever since de Castro's departure in early 1982, peak associations had developed position papers and discussed them in ad hoc meetings with Pinochet and cabinet officials. However, they had little or no participation in the commissions and study groups that actually made policy, except when the new tax legislation was created under Cáceres. With Collados and Escobar, access to policymakers and participation in policymaking became more routine, which increased their direct influence on policy outcomes.

Participation by sectoral peak associations in the elaboration of Collado's triennial plan was perhaps the most dramatic example of these connections. The associations were an integral part of the plan's sectoral commissions. As a result, the sectoral planning groups that were created drew heavily from the programs that individual peak associations had elaborated for *Recuperación económica,* subsequently refined in many cases.

Collados, in May 1984, created a second avenue of participation: the Social and Economic Council (SEC). The SEC brought together representatives of the private, public, and labor sectors to discuss policy recommendations and demands. Although it was limited to an advisory role, the SEC served as an additional formal and regular meeting place between business and government.[44] Moreover, the SEC's economic commissions gave private sector representatives added organizational support for refining positions and a powerful public forum. The SEC was, after all, part of the authoritarian regime's "new institutionality," which provided more effective channels of participation and representation to the private sector than good old political democracy.

The importance of these developments is that during this period a new system of interaction between capital and the state emerged: Businessmen and landowners associated with the pragmatic coalition, or who supported its economic program, were installed in the most important economic policymaking institutions of the state, from the finance ministry on down to the line ministries for economy, agriculture, mining, and others. Business peak associations, working within the parameters of the policy consensus of *Recuperación económica*, directly participated in the formulation of sectoral policies, debt relief, and other policies. The fluid, partially institutionalized, system of communication contributed to a much more flexible policy style.

Nevertheless, the direct representation of capitalists and landowners in the state also led to conflicts. The tensions within the pragmatic coalition over the issue of protection were embodied in the Collados-Escobar economic team, which led to conflicts that affected policy coordination and efficacy. These divisions came close to unravelling the pragmatic coalition and proved to be Minister of Finance Escobar's unmaking. Part of the problem was that Pinochet had shifted the locus of power within the hierarchy of ministries from finance to economy. Escobar supported the SFF's position on a differentiated tariff schedule and pushed hard to implement it, reopening intersectoral conflict and placing him in a direct confrontation with Collados—his superior in the new cabinet hierarchy—and the pragmatic coalition. A differentiated tariff policy violated the accepted parameters for sectoral policy that the coalition had agreed to in 1983. Pinochet sided with Collados. Escobar, in turn, resorted to arbitrary measures to raise selected tariffs and generate more income for fiscal coffers. He slapped up to a 15 percent tax surcharge on the existing 20 percent customs tariff on approximately 200 items. The SFF applauded his move, but it angered other groups (SONAMI and the CNC in particular). Later Escobar raised the flat tariff from 20 percent to 35 percent, angering even the SFF, because prices for essential imports increased too much. Sharp criticism of Escobar's actions led to his dismissal in February 1985. As the next section shows, his replacement ushered in a period in which the evolving system of interaction between the state and capital was refined with profound consequences for the consolidation of the pragmatic neoliberal coalition and for Chile's future.

### Consolidation of Pragmatic Neoliberalism, 1985-1988

In 1983 and 1984, the pragmatic coalition won many policy changes in direct and indirect negotiations with the military government. Tables 7.2 and 7.5 show results of the changes. They set Chile on a solid course of economic recovery, albeit with even higher levels of social inequality. Low real exchange rates, declining interest rates, and a fiscal stimulus that left a deficit of 4.8 percent of GDP in 1984 produced a 6.3 percent rise in overall GDP with inflation steady at 23 percent, and a 9.4 point increase in the industrial production index.

Pleased with its accomplishments, the pragmatic coalition, through the CPC and the sectoral peak associations, busied itself after 1984 with the preservation of those policies. Table 7.2 shows that the coalition was successful on many counts. For example, real wages remained low, interest rates continued to decline, and high real exchange rates prevailed. Sectoral policies, such as limited protection for domestic market producers (especially in agriculture) and public works projects for the construction sector, were also maintained. Differentiated tariffs were permanently removed from the policy agenda. These successes meant that between 1985 and 1988 there were essentially only two major issues pending for the pragmatic coalition. Industry (the SFF) wanted laws to promote nontraditional exports, and capitalists in general supported a renewal of the sale of state-owned or controlled assets to the private sector. The outcome, predictably, did not disappoint them.

But the period between 1985 and 1988 has a significance that goes beyond the coalition's continued success in policy advocacy. Both the economic policies and the modifications in the way the state interacted with capital enlarged and stabilized the pragmatic neoliberal coalition itself. These developments, in turn, contributed to sustained economic growth. Validated by renewed economic growth and rising investment rates, the pragmatic coalition was consolidated, providing stability to Pinochet's regime during the transition to democracy in 1988 and establishing a system of state-capital relations that persists until today. This system of interaction also laid the foundation for a flexible approach to market reforms; and the ultimate success of those policies made Chile a model of macroeconomic stability and sustained economic growth.

## Industrial Export Promotion, Privatization, and Coalition Consolidation

The promotion of nontraditional exports and more privatization were the two new substantive policy demands that the pragmatic coalition raised between 1985 and 1988. An enduring political consequence of the implementation of these two policies was that they contributed to the consolidation of the pragmatic neoliberal coalition. One eased tension within the coalition; the other enlarged its material base. Together, they established the basis for renewed investment in production as opposed to financial speculation.

*Nontraditional Export Promotion.* In advocating nontraditional exports, industrialists presented well thought out, technically supported arguments for their case. Although the government responded slowly, it steadily promulgated export promotion laws. The SFF's main demand was the devolution of a hefty value-added tax and customs tariff on the imported inputs for industrial products destined for export. The first decree came in December 1985. It was not wholly to the SFF's liking because it was geared to small and medium producers. A second decree, more in line with the SFF's position, appeared in May 1988. A host of additional measures related to storage and financing materialized between those dates.[45] These decrees promoted exports of nontraditional industrial products, basically manufactures as opposed to semi-elaborated primary products.

The drawbacks strengthened the internationalist component of the SFF, which enhanced the SFF's ties to the pragmatic coalition, especially after its defeat in the long, divisive battle over differential tariffs. The new decrees also facilitated an expansion of exports, which added to foreign exchange earnings.  The SFF had been aware of these potentially beneficial consequences for business unity from the outset and framed demands and proposals along those lines.  The promotion of nontraditional exports fueled economic growth and reinforced cohesive business support for pragmatic neoliberalism, which indirectly led to greater political stability.[46]

Taken together, drawbacks, high exchange rates, and slightly higher tariffs during this period worked so well as substitutes that the differentiated tariff was dropped from the SFF's list of demands. With that, a major source of intersectoral conflict within the pragmatic coalition was resolved. Marginal increases in protection worked because industrial firms that were not globally competitive had been wiped out in an earlier period.[47] Although the industrial sector's share of GDP fell from 29 percent to 21 percent between 1974 and 1980, the industrial production index in Table 7.4 shows that by 1979 most industrial subsectors with economies of scale had managed to adjust by borrowing, modernizing, consolidating, and merging.[48] Moreover, Table 7.5 reveals that between 1983 and 1987 most of them also managed to recover and surpass 1979 levels of production.

Finally, the SFF tended to be satisfied with the minimal protectionist measures advocated by the pragmatic coalition because most of the members of its elected council were linked to firms in industrial subsectors that had managed to adjust by 1979; and their companies, moreover, often dominated the subsectors in which they participated, which virtually assured their business prospects.[49] A juxtaposition of Tables 7.4 and 7.6 shows that with the exception of nine members exclusively tied to subsectors that had not adjusted well by 1979, the rest operated in subsectors that could compete with the relatively low tariff protection that existed through 1978, although not with levels as low as those of the radical neoliberal period that followed.[50] Reinforcing the point, Table 7.6 shows a heavy concentration of SFF elected members in the chemical (351-2), metal products (381), machinery (382), and electrical goods (383) subsectors, which had all managed to adjust prior to 1979.  Consequently, for most of the SFF's elected board, high real exchange rates and tax surcharges on selected imports could well take the place of differentiated tariffs.

*Privatization.* Privatization proceeded on two distinct tracks. One involved the delicate matter of the transfer of companies once controlled by defunct core internationalist conglomerates, firms that were now in receivership. When the government took over some of Chile's main financial institutions, it also acquired control over companies that had high levels of unrecoverable debt with banks placed in receivership or liquidated.[51] For the privatization process to proceed companies had to be separated from the control of banks in which the government had intervened. It was a slow process because the government needed to address the firms' debt problems before their rationalizing commissions could sell them, whether by public auction or directly to interested buyers.[52] For the most part, the situation had not been resolved in mid-1985. Business leaders wanted the government to move more quickly,[53] and the SFF and the CNC met with the minister of economy in August to discuss the issue.[54] In the end, although it was not the solution preferred by business leaders, the problem was dealt with on a company-by-company basis.[55]

Privatization of public enterprises proceeded differently. The firms themselves were not in financial straits. There was no need for difficult negotiations between government, rationalizing commissions, and potential buyers. The main debate concerned which firms to privatize and to what extent. Between 1985 and 1988, as the plebiscite over Pinochet's rule neared, the list of firms to be privatized and the amount of assets to be transferred grew. The commission responsible for ruling on privatization consisted of the ministers of finance, economy, ODEPLAN, CORFO and a representative of Pinochet. The only civilians involved were the ministers of finance and economy. The private sector, of course, favored extensive privatization.[56]

The wave of privatization that ensued after 1985 led to a reapportionment of wealth in national and foreign conglomerates. The shifting of assets reinforced the dominance of *fixed-asset* producers for international markets over producers for domestic markets and consolidated the economic base of the pragmatic neoliberal coalition. The pattern of acquisitions shows that the largest surviving conglomerates chose to seize firms that complemented their present activities.[57] Fixed-asset internationalists such as the Angelini and Matte groups had managed their affairs more conservatively during the boom years and emerged as the most important economic groups after the economic collapse of 1983. They expanded their industrial export capability in the fish, wood pulp, and paper industries through the acquisition of two huge holding companies, COPEC (Angelini) and Inforsa (Matte).[58] Another economic group, Lúksic, bought the Compañía Cervecerías Unidas thereby exponentially increasing its share of the food and beverage markets,

TABLE 7.4 Industrial Production Index, 1976-1980 (1979 = 100)

| | 1976 | 1977 | 1978 | 1979 | 1980 | % Change 1978/79 | % Change 1979/80 |
|---|---|---|---|---|---|---|---|
| General Index | 85.2 | 93.8 | 100.8 | 108.6 | 114.9 | 7.7 | 5.8 |
| **UIIC** | | | | | | | |
| Consumer Goods | 87.8 | 90.8 | 94.0 | 96.5 | 99.9 | 2.7 | 3.5 |
| 311-2 Food | 106.1 | 102.3 | 103.9 | 105.8 | 115.8 | 1.8 | 9.5 |
| 313 Beverages | 100.5 | 120.6 | 133.5 | 147.6 | 150.1 | 10.6 | 1.7 |
| 314 Tobacco | 131.3 | 140.9 | 146.2 | 148.1 | 155.8 | 1.3 | 5.2 |
| 321 Textiles | 61.5 | 67.9 | 73.3 | 72.4 | 60.6 | 1.2 | -16.3 |
| 322-4 Footwear & Clothing | 74.4 | 87.9 | 85.2 | 85.8 | 85.2 | 0.7 | -0.7 |
| 332 Furniture & Wood Accessories | 72.2 | 59.8 | 58.5 | 83.4 | 127.7 | 42.6 | 53.1 |
| 342 Printing & Publishing | 57.8 | 54.6 | 56.8 | 64.1 | 65.9 | 12.9 | 2.8 |
| 390 Miscellaneous Manufac. | 88.5 | 79.4 | 85.3 | 66.8 | 73.7 | 21.7 | 10.3 |

| Intermediate Products | 90.4 | 101.9 | 109.1 | 121.0 | 127.1 | 10.9 | 5.0 |
|---|---|---|---|---|---|---|---|
| 331 Wood exc. Furniture | 79.5 | 86.6 | 74.6 | 89.3 | 99.7 | 19.7 | 11.6 |
| 341 Cellulose and Paper | 109.2 | 124.8 | 120.2 | 129.8 | 141.7 | 8.0 | 9.2 |
| 323 Leather exc. Footwear | 65.8 | 57.5 | 64.1 | 49.0 | 45.8 | -23.6 | -6.5 |
| 355 Rubber | 77.2 | 99.3 | 78.2 | 89.1 | 86.1 | 13.9 | -3.4 |
| 351-2 Chemical Products | 87.9 | 110.7 | 109.6 | 124.8 | 141.8 | 13.9 | 13.6 |
| 354 Peroleum, Coal & By-prod. | 115.1 | 119.5 | 136.2 | 142.6 | 136.7 | 4.7 | -4.7 |
| 369 Nonmetallic Minerals | 79.1 | 87.3 | 96.3 | 114.3 | 122.2 | 18.7 | 6.9 |
| 371-2 Basic Metals | 118.2 | 122.0 | 144.5 | 161.9 | 160.5 | 12.4 | -0.9 |
| 381 Metal manuf. exc. Machinery | 63.1 | 67.7 | 97.6 | 97.3 | 99.6 | -0.3 | 2.4 |
| Machinery & Transport Equipment | 59.8 | 78.7 | 94.9 | 113.9 | 130.6 | 41.1 | 14.7 |
| 382 Machinery exc. elec. mach. | 104.3 | 145.2 | 97.1 | 127.8 | 110.1 | 31.6 | -13.9 |
| 383 Electric Mach. & Appliances | 65.3 | 72.7 | 98.0 | 115.2 | 131.6 | 17.6 | 14.2 |
| 384 Transport Equipment | 36.8 | 59.2 | 99.4 | 107.2 | 138.3 | 7.8 | 29.0 |

*Source:* Banco Central de Chile, *Memoria Anual* (Santiago: Imprenta Nacional, 1980).

TABLE 7.5 Industrial Production Index, 1980-1987 (1968 = 100)

| | 1980 | 1981 | 1982 | 1983 | 1984 | 1985 | 1986 | 1987 | %Change 1983/84 | %Change 1983/87 |
|---|---|---|---|---|---|---|---|---|---|---|
| General Index | 106.5 | 107.4 | 90.1 | 94.5 | 103.9 | 104.0 | 112.8 | 117.3 | 9.9 | 24.1 |
| UIIC | | | | | | | | | | |
| Consumer Goods | | | | | | | | | | |
| 311-2 Food | 103.7 | 110.2 | 111.6 | 112.8 | 130.8 | 127.1 | 138.9 | 132.7 | 16.0 | 17.6 |
| 313 Beverages | 96.8 | 105.0 | 89.8 | 93.3 | 94.0 | 96.5 | 97.4 | 96.2 | 0.7 | 3.1 |
| 314 Tobacco | 105.3 | 92.1 | 76.8 | 76.9 | 81.2 | 80.7 | 83.1 | 82.0 | 5.6 | 6.6 |
| 321 Textiles | 97.1 | 91.3 | 67.0 | 76.0 | 95.1 | 101.6 | 120.1 | 126.1 | 25.1 | 65.9 |
| 322 Clothing | 123.1 | 145.3 | 79.3 | 81.5 | 95.9 | 104.0 | 115.0 | 124.6 | 17.7 | 52.9 |
| 324 Footwear | 69.3 | 71.9 | 59.9 | 71.2 | 69.7 | 66.4 | 67.2 | 66.5 | -2.1 | -6.6 |
| 332 Furniture exc. Metallic | 114.4 | 108.3 | 67.0 | 56.3 | 77.2 | 87.6 | 133.5 | 222.7 | 37.1 | 295.5 |
| 342 Printing & Publishing | 185.0 | 185.5 | 168.1 | 163.5 | 166.5 | 147.3 | 175.6 | 187.6 | 1.8 | 14.7 |
| 390 Miscellaneous Manufac. | 110.6 | 167.3 | 77.0 | 79.2 | 81.3 | 63.4 | 66.2 | 70.1 | 2.7 | -11.5 |

**Intermediate Products**

| | | | | | | | | | | |
|---|---|---|---|---|---|---|---|---|---|---|
| 331 Wood exc. Furniture | 80.0 | 75.4 | 59.8 | 70.3 | 79.0 | 75.6 | 77.5 | 92.9 | 12.4 | 32.1 |
| 341 Cellulose and Paper | 90.7 | 98.8 | 82.5 | 94.8 | 98.7 | 104.0 | 110.6 | 111.9 | 4.1 | 19.0 |
| 323 Leather exc. Footwear | 108.7 | 120.7 | 90.6 | 89.8 | 88.8 | 76.2 | 70.3 | 64.0 | -1.1 | -28.7 |
| 355 Rubber | 123.9 | 112.9 | 76.4 | 110.3 | 127.9 | 122.3 | 112.7 | 121.0 | 16.0 | 9.7 |
| 351 Industrial Chemical Prod. | 100.1 | 88.9 | 69.8 | 84.2 | 88.9 | 90.8 | 91.0 | 103.1 | 5.6 | 22.4 |
| 352 Other Chemical Products | 103.6 | 114.5 | 104.8 | 95.3 | 101.3 | 100.8 | 108.3 | 123.6 | 6.3 | 29.7 |
| 353 Petroleum Refining | 95.2 | 90.5 | 70.0 | 80.4 | 80.3 | 80.5 | 84.6 | 90.9 | -0.1 | 13.1 |
| 354 Petroleum & Coal By-prod. | 35.1 | 67.4 | 84.1 | 78.1 | 76.8 | 69.2 | 68.3 | 68.6 | -1.7 | -12.2 |
| 356 Plastics | 100.5 | 117.9 | 108.0 | 115.6 | 135.9 | 157.2 | 178.1 | 199.4 | 17.6 | 72.5 |
| 361 Clay, Ceramics & Crockery | 254.7 | 164.7 | 31.2 | 152.3 | 292.2 | 334.0 | 351.8 | 368.6 | 91.9 | 142.0 |
| 362 Glass & By-products | 94.5 | 88.1 | 47.1 | 78.8 | 74.8 | 86.8 | 102.9 | 96.0 | -5.1 | 21.8 |
| 369 Nonmetallic Minerals | 116.9 | 134.2 | 74.2 | 96.6 | 104.5 | 108.0 | 127.2 | 113.6 | 8.2 | 17.6 |
| 371 Basic Metals/Iron & Steel | 115.5 | 103.5 | 68.4 | 87.4 | 104.7 | 103.2 | 105.7 | 110.3 | 19.8 | 26.2 |
| 372 Basic Metals/Non-ferrous | 97.5 | 96.2 | 105.5 | 106.2 | 110.9 | 107.6 | 112.3 | 114.2 | 4.4 | 7.5 |
| 381 Metal Manuf. exc. Machinery | 101.0 | 107.4 | 83.8 | 82.8 | 83.5 | 90.5 | 97.7 | 109.9 | 0.8 | 32.7 |

**Machinery & Transport Equipment**

| | | | | | | | | | | |
|---|---|---|---|---|---|---|---|---|---|---|
| 382 Machinery exc. elec. mach. | 134.1 | 130.8 | 58.6 | 50.2 | 64.8 | 56.3 | 73.1 | 84.5 | 29.1 | 45.6 |
| 383 Electric Mach. & Appliances | 113.8 | 108.8 | 59.5 | 70.4 | 84.8 | 86.5 | 109.5 | 125.0 | 20.5 | 77.6 |
| 384 Transport Equipment | 117.1 | 107.7 | 63.2 | 42.9 | 44.7 | 55.9 | 50.3 | 57.2 | 4.2 | 33.3 |

*Source:* Banco Central de Chile, *Boletín Mensual* (Santiago: Imprenta Nacional, selected years).

TABLE 7.6 SFF Council: Industrial Economic Interests, 1982-1985 (by CIIU Classification)

| Member Name | Domestic Market Internationally Noncompetitive Sectors | | | | | | | | | | | | | | | MDM/C | | Export | |
|---|---|---|---|---|---|---|---|---|---|---|---|---|---|---|---|---|---|---|---|
| | 321 | 324 | 331 | 342 | 351 | 352 | 355 | 356 | 361 | 362 | 371 | 381 | 382 | 383 | 384 | 390 | 311-2 | 341 | 372 |
| Abumohor | x | | | | | | | | | | | | | | | | | | |
| Agüero | | | | x | | | | | | | | x | x | | | | | | |
| Arteaga | | | | | x | x | | | | | | x | x | | | | | | |
| Ayala | | | x | | | | | | | | | | | | | | | x | |
| Behrmann | | | | | | | | | | | x | x | x | | | | | | |
| Briones | | | | | | | | | | | | | | | | x | | | |
| Casanova | | | | | | | x | | | | | | | | | | | | |
| Ceruti | | | | | | | | | | | | x | x | | | | | | |
| Claro | | | | | | | | | | x | | x | x | x | | | | | |
| Daroch | | | | | x | x | | | x | | | x | x | | | | | | |
| Eguiguren | | | | x | | x | | | | | | | | | | x | | | |
| Friedman | | | | | | | | | | | | | | | | x | | | |
| Garib | x | | | | | | | | | | | | | | | | | | |
| Ipinza | | x | | | | | | | | | | | | | | | | | |
| Izquierdo | | | | | | | | | | | | | | | | | x | | |
| Krumm | | | | | x | | | | | | | | | | | | | | |
| Kunstmann | | | | | x | x | | | | | | | | | | | | | |

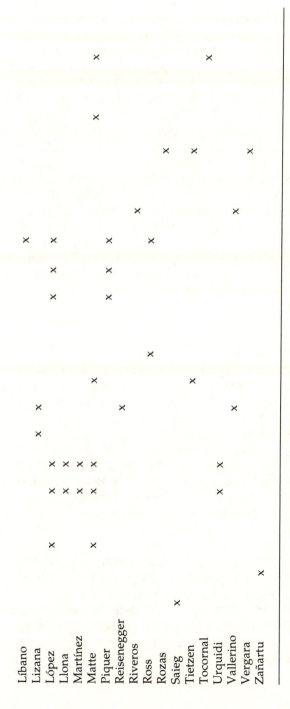

MDM/C: Manufactures for domestic markets in internationally competitive sectors.

*Sources:* SFF, *Memoria Anual,* selected years; Colegio de Priodistas, *Diccionario biográfico* (Santiago: Editorial Universitaria, selected years); SFF, *Informativo SFF,* selected numbers; Superintendencia de Asociaciones Bancarias y Financieras, *Nómina del directorio de instituciones financieras* (Santiago, n.p., selected years); conglomerate company annual reports.

a sector that exported very little but that did not need high levels of protection. A minority of the large firms for sale, like the consumer durable firm Compañía Tecno Industrial (bought by Sidgo Koppers) required only the slightly higher levels of protection advocated by the pragmatic coalition.

Privatization, however, also allowed for an influx of transnational corporations, which would become allies of the pragmatic neoliberal coalition. Complementing the influence of the pragmatic coalition's internationally oriented sector, the foreign economic actors gained entry in one of three ways. First, Chilean conglomerates such as Angelini, Matte, and Lúksic went into partnership with foreign concerns because they could not absorb the heavy debts acquired along with their new companies. Second, some foreign economic groups bought Chilean firms that had good export potential or could compete with international products, such as in the food and beverage industries. This was the case of BANESTO, a Spanish group.[59] Others expanded their presence in local financial markets. Third, the privatization of public enterprises proper also led to an influx of foreign buyers, especially through debt-equity swaps. International concerns bought heavily into public utilities (telephones and electricity), pharmaceuticals, nitrate-based chemicals, steel, and coal mines.[60]

## External and Institutional Factors
## in Coalition Consolidation

The strengthening of the economic base of the pragmatic coalition and the easing of tensions within it were crucial to its consolidation. The basis for an enduring policy coalition was set and the foundation for economic growth based on production rather than financial speculation was laid. The lasting impact of pragmatic neoliberalism on Chilean politics can only be explained if two additional factors are taken into account. International conditions and institutional factors—mainly cabinet appointments and the institutionalization of access to the policymaking process—further consolidated the new capitalist coalition, reequilibrating both the pragmatic neoliberal economic model and the relationship between capitalists and the military government.

*International Economic Change.* International conditions worked to the pragmatic neoliberal coalition's advantage. The lingering debt crisis and the long-term unavailability of foreign loans continued to make fixed-asset producers for international and domestic markets the best generators of foreign exchange and employment. Other developments in the world economy also strengthened the pragmatic coalition, such as declining oil prices, falling international interest rates, and rising copper prices. Once the economy began to grow again in 1985, these external factors reinforced the pragmatic coalition by obviating the need to lobby for higher fiscal deficits (one of the key countercyclical policies of the previous period). Lower oil bills and higher copper receipts let Chile sustain economic growth without exceeding IMF-set deficit levels. In other words, businessmen and landowners could now afford to support orthodox stabilization and be more "neoliberal." Of course, savings squeezed out of the middle and lower classes through low wages and salaries contributed mightily to the upper classes' recovery.

*The System of Interaction Between Capitalists and the State.* Pinochet's response to the new system of interaction between capitalists and the state established the key condition for the consolidation of the pragmatic neoliberal coalition and ensured the coalition's lasting impact on Chilean politics. Pinochet reduced the direct influence of businessmen in the cabinet and, therefore, in the policymaking process; but he did not eliminate their role in policy formulation and implementation. This change eased tension in the pragmatic coalition and made economic policy measures more coherent.

Pinochet placed the Ministry of Finance, the Central Bank, and the Office of Budget under the command of neutral career bureaucrats. Now that financial agencies were once again at the apex of the hierarchy of ministries, no final decisions were under the direct control of business interests. Hernán Büchi, the new minister of finance, emerged as the central actor. Büchi was a neutral figure with no direct private economic interests and a long career in the Chilean bureaucracy under Pinochet. In keeping with the regime's commitment to honoring international obligations, and befitting the balance of forces in the pragmatic coalition, Büchi favored the internationalist groups; but he did not ignore the needs of domestic market producers.

Büchi was not a businessman, and he represented a return to a more technocratic policymaking style. Nevertheless, he did not isolate himself or remain aloof from private sector representatives. The new minister was someone who would consult, accommodate, and negotiate. At the same time, his independence enabled him to arbitrate conflicts among business groups. That quality, more than anything else, helped soothe tensions within the pragmatic coalition.

However, businessmen and landowners retained control over the line ministries that regulated their sectors, such as the ministries of economy, agriculture, and mining. Again, as befitting the balance of forces within the pragmatic coalition, the men who headed those ministries largely represented the internationalists within the coalition, although they also had a stake in domestic market production. This was particularly true for the Ministry of

Agriculture, where Jorge Prado remained in office. Economy Minister Juan Délano, the successor of Collados, also reflected the interests of the dominant coalition. He was vice president of the CNC at the time of his appointment and shared the CNC's commitment to low tariffs with protection against unfair competition (dumping). Samuel Lira, closely linked to SONAMI, continued as minister of mines. This pattern of appointments gave sectoral peak associations easy informal access to the policymaking process. Of course, these ministers were ultimately beholden to the decisions of the minister of finance and the head of the Central Bank who gave cues on how to respond to the petitions of businessmen and landowners.

In addition to these informal channels, more institutionalized ones also gave sectoral peak associations access to the policymaking process. To begin with, when Délano became minister of economy in early 1986, he organized standing national commissions for internal and external commerce and industry. These commissions gave the CPC and its member associations a place on the working groups that made policies, such as the drawbacks that emerged in 1985 and 1988.[61] The private sector's inclusion on the national commissions complemented its increasing participation on planning boards and legislative committees. Délano had been a high-ranking member of the Social and Economic Council that also had commissions bringing together business leaders and undersecretaries of state. The new commissions in the economy ministry took that concept one step further.

The Social and Economic Council itself underscored the ties between members of the pragmatic coalition and the government. Pinochet recognized the SEC's value as an added instance of collaboration between the private sector and the executive. He ordered his economic ministers to make sure that one of their ranking members were always present at the working sessions of the SEC's various economic commissions.[62]

Peak association leaders also gained entrance into another important policymaking arena: the junta's legislative commissions, in which each branch of the armed forces had its own well-staffed commission. The Constitution of 1980 required the creation of these commissions as part of its effort to establish a "legislative process" in the transition to protected democracy. "Legislative bills" circulated among peak associations, allowing them to make observations, recommendations, and to lobby against certain provisions if desired. In addition to these factors, business leaders, as well as the junta, could introduce legislation.[63]

A review of the system of interaction between capital and the state suggests several conclusions. In contrast to previous periods, technocrats stood at the apex of the policymaking hierarchy; below them, businessmen and landowners who were part of the pragmatic neoliberal coalition, or whose economic interests were similar to those of the coalition, headed the line ministries. Organized business had ample access to these policymakers and participated fully in policy formulation. This arrangement permitted the formulation of sectoral policy that was in line with a more pragmatic approach to economic reform: aid to exports and defense of national production with as little distortion of market signals as possible. These conditions were established when the pragmatic neoliberal coalition formed in 1983. The extent to which they were not violated reflects the persistence of the coalition. Moreover, the CPC continued to intervene as the business interlocutor of choice on all issues of general interest to the private sector— again based on agreements worked out during the formation of the pragmatic neoliberal coalition.

One of the positive consequences of this system of interaction for organized business has been its professionalization. In the 1970s, only the SFF had a technical department capable of analyzing and developing policy proposals. Ten to fifteen years later, each of the other five sectoral associations and the CPC established sophisticated technical departments of their own. Meanwhile, the SFF's department of studies expanded even further. Professionalization enabled the business associations to speak the language of the bureaucrats in the economic ministries and agencies: the technical report informed by economic theory and supported by data. Professionalization also gave them the capacity to develop policy proposals independent of the state, to advance a policy agenda more effectively, and to defend themselves from unwanted policy initiatives.

Moreover, this system of collaboration between businessmen, landowners, and government officials facilitated a flow of information that gave policymakers clear signals that increased the likelihood of the creation of optimum investment conditions. It gave businessmen and landowners confidence that government policymakers took their interests to heart, which probably enhanced investment decisions. This factor was important to Chile's economic recovery in the mid-1980s. Table 7.2 shows that between 1984 and 1988 the economy grew at a healthy rate of 5.5 percent, interest rates declined steadily (even when the international prime rate went up in 1988), and the exchange rate kept Chilean products cheap. Equally important, total investment as a percentage of GDP climbed from about 19 percent to 23.5 percent, and the share of nontraditional exports as a percentage of total exports rose from about 29 percent in 1980 to 37 percent in 1988.[64] The economy's performance, in turn, helped stabilize Pinochet's regime and made Chile a showcase for market reforms, albeit one that ignored issues of social equity. That democratic governments subsequently have addressed the issue of extreme poverty without reducing economic growth has led many observers to hold up Chile as a model for the rest of region and beyond.

## Conclusion: Capitalist Coalitions and
## Economic Policymaking in Authoritarian Chile

The discussion of Chile's political economy to this point has shown that during the period of military rule, free market economic reforms were not solely the creation of technocrats isolated from society by a strong state. This interpretation suggests the value of redirecting analysis away from an exclusive focus on the problems of economic policy design, sequencing, and timing toward an examination of the system of interaction between the state and capital.

As for economic policy outcomes during each of the main policy periods, shifting coalitions of businessmen and landowners participated in setting policy agendas, formulated policies, and implemented them. Economic and political crises roused capitalist and landowning groups out of complacency and impelled them, project in hand, to jostle for position. For their part, rulers have their agendas too, and tend to favor one set of capitalists over another.  Which capitalist coalitions participated in policymaking depended on a complicated conjuncture of factors. On the whole, international factors, although strongly conditioning at times, were not decisive by themselves. Domestic structure—political regimes, state institutions, and organizational factors—also intervened.

In the first policy period, a core of business interests essentially set an agenda for economic change. They selected and controlled a team of young like-minded economists, many of whom had links to the major firms of the core business groups of the Monday Club, to flesh out an economic reform plan for Chile. Fixed-asset interests that were oriented toward domestic markets but that were internationally competitive dominated the core of that coalition; groups oriented toward international markets and producers for domestic markets who were internationally uncompetitive occupied a subordinate position. This balance of forces favored gradual economic restructuring. The sources of foreign savings gradually shifted toward private international finance and direct investment, bolstering this alignment of forces and its policy orientation. Domestic factors, however, proved more significant for the outcome during this period. Regime change—the breakdown of democracy—isolated uncompetitive industrial producers for domestic markets (previously the main obstacles to gradual change) from the rest of Chilean elites who preferred less protection. A "porous" military government had set up institutional channels that accommodated all of those interests, initially in correspondence with the balance of forces among them.  In part, that wider accommodation of interests took place because the newly arrived military junta worked closely with the broader social coalition that had backed the coup. Those institutional arrangements also offered space for a narrow set of competing interests based on liquid assets that backed more radical restructuring.

Changes in international and domestic factors also explained the shift in dominance from a gradualist to a radical neoliberal coalition of capitalists. In that process, a narrow core coalition of capitalists allied with a group of technocrats, many of whom shared business ties, and took advantage of their institutional toeholds within the state to generate conditions favorable to their interests. In contrast to most of the Chilean private sector, this group wanted radical neoliberal economic restructuring. A sharp increase in international liquidity boosted the radical coalition and Chicago boy technocrats, but regime change—a shift from military rule by junta to personalist rule by Pinochet—clinched its initial rise. Pinochet backed the coalition and the technocrats unconditionally and protected them from opposition by more traditional business and landowning interests. Continued high levels of international liquidity eventually brought dissident upper-class elites around as allied fractions of the core radical internationalists. The collapse of international liquidity in the early eighties led to the radical coalition's demise.

Out of the rubble, fixed-asset groups, with internationalists in the dominant position and domestic market producers subordinate to them, forged a new, broadly inclusive capitalist coalition. The lack of international liquidity bolstered fixed-asset producers; but, because Pinochet remained in power, they continued to be shut out of policymaking institutions. Pinochet responded tepidly to the pragmatic coalition's demands. It took a menace to his rule to "win." Only when capitalists threatened to join the political opposition did Pinochet ally himself with the pragmatic neoliberal coalition and open state institutions to its members, allowing them to participate fully in economic policy formulation.

This interpretation of the political economy of Chile's neoliberal economic restructuring offers some insights that may be valid for democratic governments presently engaged in the process. The principal "lesson" seems to be that, among other significant factors, the structure of the system of interaction between capitalists and the state affects policymaking styles, policy outcomes, and patterns of investment. The period of radical neoliberalism shows that rigidly ideological technocrats in an exclusionary relationship with a narrow set of liquid-asset centered conglomerates can increase the likelihood of policy inflexibility, investment in short-term financial instruments, and real estate speculation. The main features of this relationship suggest that democratic regimes are not immune to such alliances, which merely require hierarchical lines of authority among ministries with financial agencies at the apex.[65] Policymakers then establish direct links to conglomerate heads. Wider business interests, to say nothing of organized business, largely are kept out of the policymaking process. As long as the overall economy does well, other capitalists might not insist on participation, thus avoiding political problems for the democratic government. This system seems to require heavy flows of private foreign capital, a condition which largely has been restored in the world economy. Moreover, because this system of interaction responds poorly to changing conditions, it may contribute to wrenching see-saws in the economy's performance. Aside from the heavy toll on citizens, economic crises tend to have serious repercussions for political stability.

The more "successful" system of interaction presents a different structure. An authoritative hierarchy among ministries, with financial agencies at the apex, remains a key factor because it offers policy coherence. But the characteristics of the policymakers and their relationship to capitalists differs. Technocratic officials, whether career bureaucrats or not, control the heart of the system, but they remain open to interaction with capitalists as long as their demands are compatible with the general interests of the private sector. By contrast, line ministries are headed by businessmen and landowners and establish a working relationship with sectoral economic interests. They are held in check from any propensity to distort overall economic policy coherence by the financial agencies. In this arrangement, the relationship with the private sector is more institutional in that state officials deal with *organized* business groups capable of forging broad agreements on a policy agenda and able to effectively represent the general and sectoral interests for which they claim to speak. These arrangements do not necessarily have to be institutionalized, however; meaning that they do not require the creation of routinized, codified, and officially sanctioned interactions between the private and public sectors. When the organized business sector is dominated by fixed-asset interests, this structure may contribute to policies that emphasize longer term investment in production. These structures may also generate more flexible policymaking styles that can ease social tensions during crises and help find policy alternatives to face the crisis more quickly.

Nevertheless, as the concluding chapter argues, Chile's "successful" system of interaction has limitations. It proved functional for the establishment of a good business climate; a condition that in some circles had amounted to the quest for the golden fleece since the 1960s. But it remains an exclusionary relationship. Incorporating the interests of other social groups in the policy mix in ways not wholly sanctioned by business, but still commensurate with a mixed market economy, has proven difficult.

## Notes

1. For the positions of the SFF, SONAMI, ABIF, SNA, CNC on these issues, see *La Tercera de la Hora*, July 22, August 1, December 6, 1982; *Ercilla* no. 2453, 2470, August 4 and December 1, 1982, respectively; *Estrategia*, August 2-8, 1982; *El Mercurio*, August 15, 1982. Sectoral policy demands were drawn from the following sources. For the SFF, see *Informativo SFF* no. 137, August 1982; *El Mercurio* and *La Tercera de la Hora*, August 1, 1982; *Estrategia*, August 16-22, September 6-12, October 25-31, 1982; *La Tercera de la Hora*, August 27, 1982; *Ercilla*, no. 2475, January 5, 1983. For the SNA's positions, see *El Campesino* 8 and 11, August and November 1982; *Estrategia*, August 16-22, 1982. For the CNC's positions, see *Estrategia*, August 16-22, 1982; letter no. 248/82 to Minister of Finance and Economy Lüders dated October 12, 1982 following the CNC general assembly of October 7-8. For SONAMI policy positions, see *El Mercurio*, June 20, 1982; letter to Pinochet dated August 3, 1982; *Estrategia*, August 16-22, 1982. For the CChC's policy positions, see *La Tercera de la Hora*, June 20 and 27, 1982; *El Mercurio*, June 20 and December 23, 1982. For the ABIF's policy position, see *Estrategia*, August 16-22, 1982.

2. Guillermo Campero, *Los gremios empresariales en el período 1970-1983* (Santiago: ILET, 1984), pp. 277-280. The *Unidad de Fomento* (UF) was essentially a constant measure of value periodically adjusted for inflation.

3. For more details, see Confederación de la Producción y Comercio, *Recuperación económica: Análisis y proposiciones*," Santiago, July 4, 1983.

4. In terms of business association alignments on the tariff issue, the SFF issued a recommendation in favor of a differentiated tariff structure in October 1982; see SFF "Informe final de la comisión SFF para estudiar una alternativa al sistema arancelario," October 20, 1982. The SNA was opposed to differentiated tariffs so strongly that it went on record forcefully arguing against them in a position paper it presented to the CPC during the preparations for *Recuperación económica: Análisis y proposiciones*. This document was part of the CPC's files on *Recuperación económica* and carried no title or date. Moreover, in a March 1982 memorandum that gave business' definition of the ideal market economy, the CPC explicitly supported low, across-the-board tariffs. In November 1982, the SNA flatly declared itself against differentiated tariffs; see CPC minutes of the executive committee meetings no. 577, November 25, 1982. SONAMI had gone on record against such tariffs in August; see *Estrategia*, August 16-22, 1982. The finance and construction sectors were at best ambivalent.

5. CPC, minutes of executive committee meeting no. 635, December 17, 1984.

6. As early as 1982, the export sector sought selective protection against what it deemed to be unfair import competition. It supported tax surcharges on designated items for both industrialists and landowners and price bands based on the average international price historically for some traditional agricultural crops.

7. For SFF views, see SFF, "Memorandum económico: Plan alternativo de emergencia y medidas complementarias," June 1983 (document prepared for the CPC meetings of June and July 1983), "Proyecto de ley de reintegros a las exportaciones," June 26, 1984. The SFF sent a copy of the proposed bill to CPC president Jorge Fontaine. In the cover letter attached to it, dated June 27, the SFF said that it would discuss the matter with SONAMI. For SONAMI views, see SONAMI,

internal memo dated June 13, 1983. Concerning the CPC's economic recovery plan, it stressed that the plan should include export incentives for producers for domestic markets; see letter to Finance Minister Luis Escobar, no. 630, December 19, 1984. For CPC support of the drawback bill, see executive committee meeting minutes nos. 619 and 633 of July 16, 1984 and November 19, 1984.

8. CPC, minutes of executive committee meeting no. 619, July 16, 1984. They stated that the CPC met with the minister of economy to discuss the adoption of drawbacks.

9. Manufactured nontraditional exports include: foods, beverages, manufactured wood products, chemicals, iron and steel, metal and electric manufactures, and transport materials.

10. Actually, the government and the general public learned of the outline and many of the details of *Recuperación económica* at least as early as June 1983. The sectoral peak associations met in a much publicized conclave on June 4 to discuss their alternative plan at the country estate of the CPC's president.

11. Sociedad de Fomento Fabril, "Endeudamiento interno," Santiago, July 1985.

12. José Pablo Arellano, "Crisis y recuperación económica en Chile en los años 80," *Colección Estudios Cieplan* no. 24, June 1988, p. 71.

13. For a detailed account of the tax reform and its likely effects, see Manuel Marfán, "Una evaluación de la nueva reforma tributaria," *Colección Estudios Cieplan* no. 13, June 1984, pp. 27-52. For a brief summary, see José Pablo Arellano and Manuel Marfán, "25 años de política fiscal en Chile," *Colección Estudios Cieplan* no. 21, June 1987, pp. 152-158.

14. José Pablo Arellano, "Crisis y recuperación económica en Chile en los años 80," *Colección Estudios Cieplan* no. 24, June 1988, p. 76.

15. José Pablo Arellano and Manuel Marfán, "Ahorro, inversión y relaciones financieras en la actual crisis económica chilena," *Colección Estudios Cieplan* no. 20, December 1986, p. 86; and José Pablo Arellano, "La difícil salida al problema del endeudamiento interno," *Colección Estudios Cieplan* no. 13, June 1984, pp. 10-12.

16. Individual peak associations had made many of their specific demands in the position papers they had written for a June 4, 1983 meeting of the group that set the basis the final CPC document a month later. Throughout 1983 and 1984, the individual peak associations asserted and refined those demands. The SFF, the SNA, and SONAMI later developed their own detailed programs which always reaffirmed the general diagnostic and goals of the CPC document.

17. *El Campesino* 10, October 1982.

18. *El Campesino* 1-2, January-February 1985.

19. *El Campesino* 8 and 12 August and December 1984, respectively.

20. *El Campesino* 1-2, January-February 1983.

21. *El Campesino* 10 and 11, October and November 1982.

22. CNC *Memoria Anual*, 1982-1983.

23. Patricio Rozas and Gustavo Marín: *El "mapa de la extrema riqueza": 10 años después* (Santiago: Ediciones Chile-América, 1989); and José Pablo Arellano, "La difícil salida al problema del endeudamiento interno," *Estudios Cieplan* no. 13, June 1984.

24. On the Latin American debt crisis, see Miles Kahler, ed., *The Politics of International Debt* (Ithaca: Cornell University Press, 1986); Barbara Stallings and

Robert Kaufman, eds., *Debt and Democracy in Latin America* (Boulder: Westview, 1989); William L. Canak, ed., *Lost Promises: Debt, Austerity, and Development in Latin America* (Boulder: Westview, 1989); Robert Wesson, ed., *Coping with the Latin American Debt* (New York: Praeger, 1988).

25. The resumption of international liquidity is a factor that has made the recent and more drastic economic reform processes of Argentina and Mexico possible.

26. For the composition and evolution of mass mobilization and its impact on the regime, see Manuel Antonio Garretón, *Reconstruir la política: Transición y consolidación democrática en Chile* (Santiago: Editorial Andante, 1987) and "The Political Opposition and the Party System under the Military Regime," in Paul Drake and Iván Jaksic, eds., *The Struggle for Democracy in Chile, 1982-1990* (Lincoln: University of Nebraska Press, 1991).

27. Interviews with Jorge Fontaine (CPC) and Manuel Valdés (CPC and SNA), April and March 1989, respectively.

28. Alejandro Foxley, "Algunas condiciones para una democratización estable: El caso de Chile," *Colección Estudios Cieplan* no. 9, December 1982; Cieplan, *Reconstrucción económica para la democracia* (Santiago: Editorial Aconcagua, 1983).

29. *Revista Hoy* no. 343, February 15, 1984.

30. Garretón, *Reconstruir la política*.

31. *Proyecto alternativo* (Santiago: Editorial Aconcagua, 1984).

32. See "Bases de una estrategia de desarrollo económico social en democracia," *Proyecto alternativo*, vol. 2, pp. 173-265.

33. *Proyecto alternativo*, vol. 2, pp. 214-219.

34. *Qué Pasa* no. 639, July 7, 1983.

35. *Revista Hoy* no. 311, July 6, 1983.

36. For Jorge Fontaine statements to that effect, see *Revista Hoy* no. 330, November 16, 1983.

37. For the small and medium-scale entrepreneurial movement, see Guillermo Campero, *Los gremios empresariales*. Wheat producer leader Carlos Podlech offered to join the protest movement, *Revista Hoy*, no. 307, June 8, 1983. Angel Fantuzzi (ASIMET), although a supporter of Pinochet, urged an alliance between producers for domestic markets in agriculture and industry. Individual capitalists and landowners, such as Germán Riesco (SNA) and Efraín Friedman (SFF), also joined the opposition. By the same token, a noted businessman, Pablo Piñera, said that a consensus could develop between the right and labor—both understood that the regime might lash out at them, *Revista Hoy* no. 295, March 15, 1983.

38. *Revista Hoy* no. 314, July 27, 1983.

39. One may follow the debates in Guillermo Campero, *Los gremios empresariales*, and *Qué Pasa* nos. 636 and 641, of July 16 and 21, 1983.

40. For conflict between Jarpa and Cáceres, see *Revista Hoy* nos. 318, 321, 322, 326 and 335, August 24, September 14, September 21, October 19, and December 21, 1983, respectively.

41. These negotiations were the subject of numerous press accounts between the months of August and October 1983.

42. *Qué Pasa* no. 655, October 7, 1983.

43. Personal interview with Pablo Araya, director of studies of the CChC, May 1989.

44. For complaints about the insignificance of labor's views in the SEC economic commissions, see República de Chile, Consejo Económico y Social, XII reunión ordinaria, June 1985; and Augusto Lecaros Z., "Representación de los intereses de la sociedad en el Estado y Consejos Económicos y Sociales," Thesis, Instituto de Ciencia Política, Pontificia Universidad Católica, 1987.

45. Ministerio de Economía, Fomento y Reconstrucción and ASEXMA, *Medidas de fomento a las exportaciones chilenas ponen el mundo en sus manos* (Santiago: Ediciones OPLANE, 1988).

46. One may follow these debates in SFF, *Revista Industria* 87, 6, December 1984.

47. For detailed studies of deindustrialization, see Jaime Gatica Barros, *Deindustrialization in Chile* (Boulder: Westview, 1989); PREALC, "Monetarismo global y respuesta industrial: El caso de Chile," *Documento de Trabajo* no. 232, March 1984.

48. Author interviews with Gustavo Ramdohr (ASIMET), August 1988; Jaime Alé (SFF), September 1988; Jorge Fontaine (CPC), April 1989; Manuel Valdés (CPC and SNA), March 1989; available annual reports of the firms in which SFF members participated; Alejandra Mizala, "Liberalización financiera y quiebra de empresas industriales: Chile, 1977-82," *Notas Técnicas Cieplan* no. 67, January 1985.

49. The main criteria was that most SFF members were associated with companies that either produced the leading brand names or were widely recognized as one the principal firms in their industry; annual reports also occasionally give data on market shares.

50. Those nine members were executives, or owners, of firms in textiles (321), rubber and plastics (355-6), footwear and clothing (322-4), leather (323), printing and publishing (342).

51. *Qué Pasa* no. 619, February 17, 1983; also no. 647, September 1, 1983.

52. *Qué Pasa* no. 753, September 12, 1985.

53. *Qué Pasa* no. 742, June 27, 1985.

54. *Qué Pasa* no. 750, August 22, 1985; and *Revista Industria* 88, 4, August-September 1985, p. 175.

55. *Qué Pasa* no. 762, November 14, 1985.

56. See the debates on the *Estado Empresario* in SFF *Revista Industria* 87, 4 and 5, August and October 1984; and *Revista Industria* 88, 2, April-May 1985.

57. *Qué Pasa* no. 637, June 23, 1983; and no. 750, August 22, 1985.

58. COPEC, which had been controlled by Cruzat-Larraín, is one of Chile's largest holding companies. It controls some of Chile's most important fishing and timber companies and has a significant presence in petroleum product distribution, data processing, financial services (investment companies), and electrical utilities. The acquisition of COPEC strengthened Angelini's already large presence in the fishing and timber industries. Inforsa, previously controlled by the BHC group, controlled important companies in the timber industry and other industrial firms. The acquisition of Inforsa increased the Matte conglomerate's already formidable presence in the pulp and paper industry via the Papelera. For the complete picture on the size of the holding companies, see their company annual reports and financial statements to the banking superintendency of Chile.

59. Patricio Rozas and Gustavo Marín, El *"mapa de la extrema riqueza": 10 años después.*

60. For greater details, see Particio Rozas and Gustavo Marín, *El mapa de la extrema riqueza: 10 años después*.

61. Author interviews with Gustavo Ramdohr, president of ASEXMA, August 1988; Jorge Fontaine, former president of CPC, April 1989; Jaime Alé, director of planning of the SFF, September 1988; Lee Ward, director of the government's National Commission for External Commerce, December 1988; minutes of the meetings of the Subcommission for Drawback Legislation of the National Commission for External Commerce.

62. República de Chile, Consejo Económico Social, XIII reunión ordinaria, July 1985.

63. Author interview with Jaime Alé, SFF director of planning, September 1988.

64. Investment data from *La Epoca*, August 18, 1993. Export data from Table 3.2 in Eduardo Silva, "The Political Economy of Chile's Regime Transition: From Radical to Pragmatic Neo-liberal Policies," in Paul W. Drake and Iván Jaksic, eds., *The Struggle for Democracy in Chile*, pp. 104-105.

65. Guillermo O'Donnell, *Delegative Democracy* (South Bend: University of Notre Dame Press, 1992).

# 8

# Pragmatic Neoliberalism and the Politics of Chile's Transition from Authoritarianism

Chile is often portrayed as an exceptional case in recent transitions to political democracy in South America. Having had a history of deeply rooted democratic traditions it was the last of the "bureaucratic-authoritarian" regimes to redemocratize. The transition was dictated by the timetable and conditions set by the military much more than in Argentina and Uruguay; and political change took place under conditions of economic growth rather than crisis. A number of factors explain these differences. The military institution retained its cohesion and Pinochet never lost his grip over his system of one-man rule. After the economic crisis of 1983-1984, economic prosperity blunted the opposition's arguments for rapid change. Finally, business and landowning elites never suffered internal splits over the issue of regime change, and they supported the military government through the 1988 plebiscite on whether Pinochet should rule for an additional eight years. The focus of this chapter is on the factors that influenced this behavior by capitalists.

As outlined in Chapter 2, studies have argued that elite cohesion is vital for regime stability. In many of the "new authoritarian" regimes, three main conditions led to cleavages among socio-economic elites that turned into destabilizing conflicts. First, barring a severe threat from below, capitalists were less likely to support authoritarianism when they were shut out of the economic policy coalition and the policymaking process. Second, their support was eroded further when they were buffeted by economic restructuring because losers sought to protect themselves. Third, wide-spread discontent tended to erupt in the wake of the severe economic crises that accompanied efforts at profound economic change.

Most studies of Chile's political transition note that the Chilean bourgeoisie chafed under all three of these conditions, yet no major fraction of the bourgeoisie turned against Pinochet. Consequently, analysts have concluded that the cohesion of Chilean elites must have been due to another factor: Their fear of resurgent socialism.[1] Capital was frightened by mass mobilization and the character of the opposition political parties that dominated it. The specter of Unidad Popular was being revived at a time when capitalists were economically weak and had an insecure grip on their property, especially that which the government indirectly controlled as a result of the 1982-1983 banking crisis. In short, the bourgeoisie feared the threat from below more than Pinochet's imposition of economic change.

This chapter argues that the evidence suggests otherwise. Variation in the same factors that affected capitalists in other countries adequately explains the Chilean bourgeoisie's behavior. Bonapartist arguments are unnecessary and obscure some of the key dynamics of Chile's redemocratization process and the underpinnings of the current democratic regime. Memories of Allende's government were, of course, a matter of concern for Chilean businessmen and landowners; but analyses that fixate on this concern take their rhetoric too much at face value. The threat from below was considerably weaker than touted, especially after the left renovated itself in a more mildly reformist vein. More important to cohesive capitalist support for the dictatorship was the fact that capitalists and landowners forged the pragmatic neoliberal coalition; that Pinochet responded favorably to the demands of that broad alliance of businessmen and landowners; and that he included them in the policymaking process. These factors comprise the crucial difference from cases where such alliances either did not form or were consistently excluded from policymaking.

This chapter shows that the pragmatic neoliberal coalition's successes between 1983 and 1988 had several important consequences for the process of democratization in Chile. First, the *inclusion* of all major capitalist groups in the economic policy coalition, their exclusive access to the policymaking process, and the military government's policy concessions cemented the relationship between capitalists and Pinochet for the plebiscite of 1988. As a result, no major capitalist or landowning group was available to enter into an alliance for extensive political liberalization with the main opposition group, Alianza Democrática (AD), later known as the Concertación de Partidos por la Democracia, or simply Concertación.

Second, the absence of a broad multiclass movement for political democratization that included property owners had major consequences for Chile's shift from an authoritarian to a democratic form of government. For example, the military government could scrupulously adhere to the timetable and conditions for political liberalization set forth in the 1980 Constitution. There was no change in the October 1988 date for the plebiscite on Pinochet's rule. Moreover, institutional conditions that ensured a "protected" democracy in which the military retained veto power over civilian authorities, and which built in a conservative bias to economic policymaking, also remained intact.

The pragmatic coalition's success—and, conversely, Alianza Democrática's failure to build a coalition for political change that included economic elites—had a third major consequence. Between 1985 and 1988, in its efforts to ally capitalist fears of democratization, Alianza Democrática moderated its economic policy platform. Thus, as the plebiscite drew near it was clear that capitalists' rejection of Alianza Democrática had more to do with its aversion to mild reformism than fear of socialism. When Alianza Democrática failed to draw capitalists into a coalition for regime change it joined them in a tacit conservative compact to assure democratization. In a continuation of this implicit compact, the Concertación committed itself to the pragmatic neoliberal coalition's economic model in exchange for acquiescence to political change on the part of capitalists and landowners.

There were further consequences for Chile's new democracy. The main features of the system of interaction between capital and the state developed during the final years of the military dictatorship were retained. Today, technocratic policymakers set agendas for moderate policy shifts from pragmatic neoliberalism, but they continue to formulate new policy with the participation of organized business. As a result, social equity questions have been addressed only within a framework that is compatible with neoliberalism. In effect, Chile is constructing a variant of the liberal welfare state that is fully consonant with the main tenets of pragmatic neoliberalism.

## Capitalists, Pragmatic Neoliberalism, and Mass Mobilization, 1983-1985

The military government was at its weakest between 1983 and 1985. It was battered by severe economic crisis, entrepreneurial revolt, and a mass mobilization movement of middle and lower-class groups spearheaded by resurgent opposition political parties. During this period the opposition tried to wrestle control of the pace and content of the political transition—as outlined in the Constitution of 1980—away from Pinochet and his supporters. Success hinged on Alianza Democrática's ability to broaden the class base of the opposition movement by gaining the implicit or explicit support of one or more capitalist groups. To that end, Alianza Democrática attempted to convert the conflict between capitalists and the military government over economic policy into capitalist support for regime change. This strategy failed and, with it, Alianza Democrática's bid for rapid redemocratization.

Two arguments sustain the assertion that the successes of the pragmatic coalition rather than fear of radical socialism largely influenced the regime loyalties of capitalists. The first one draws attention to the actions of the main opposition group, Alianza Democrática, and its pivotal position in both the opposition movement and *vis-à-vis* regime soft-liners. Alianza Democrática persistently tried to form implicit and explicit alliances with capitalists on moderate economic policy platforms. Moreover, within the context of the emerging party system, Alianza Democrática had to negotiate the terms of political liberalization with conservative political parties, which effectively isolated the Marxist Movimiento Democrático Popular (MDP).

The second argument focuses on the relationship between the timing of mass mobilization and the fact that capital only relaxed its pressure on the government over deflationary policies after policy concessions were extracted. Capital's revolt over orthodox deflation fed Alianza Democrática's hopes that a broad multiclass alliance against the military government could be constructed. If it was the dread of socialism that motivated capitalists, they should have closed ranks with the military government shortly after the masses began to mobilize. After all, business and landowner opposition to government economic policy legitimized and fueled the political opposition movement. Nevertheless, mass mobilization erupted in May 1983 and the Confederación de la Producción y Comercio (CPC) did not soften its confrontation with the government until after the fifth monthly mass protest at the end of the year. At that time, the administration had begun to make policy concessions with the promise of more to come. The sequence of these events suggest that the pragmatic neoliberal coalition's success, as measured by economic policy change and access to economic policymaking to the exclusion of other social groups, largely explained capitalists' regime loyalties.

### Alianza Democrática's Coalition Strategy

As previously seen, the main opposition political bloc, Alianza Democrática, was a broad coalition of political parties from the center and center-left of the party spectrum, dominated by the Christian Democratic party (PDC). The Christian Democrats had surreptitiously helped the miners union to stage the first big protest in May 1983, and Alianza Democrática quickly took control of the monthly protest movement. Its goal was to turn the limited political liberalization of the Constitution of 1980 into full scale democratization. Alianza Democrática demanded free, competitive elections with full civilian participation and civil guarantees by 1985. To achieve these goals, the AD called for the political ouster of Pinochet, abrogation of the perpetual state of emergency, lifting restrictions on political party activity, the return of exiles, and restoring rights to Marxist political parties. Alianza Democrática made every effort to distance itself from the smaller and weaker leftist MDP, steadfastly rejecting all offers to work together.

Alianza Democrática understood that a smooth, rapid transition to full political democracy could not be accomplished without negotiations with conservatives and the military (minus Pinochet).[2] Alianza Democrática realized it would have to enlist the support of capitalists to accomplish its goal. To that end, Alianza Democrática sought to exploit the tension between capitalists and Pinochet over economic policy. Throughout 1983, both the PDC and Alianza Democrática attempted to form an implicit alliance with capitalists and some conservative political parties based on a moderate economic program tailored to the demands of the emerging pragmatic neoliberal capitalist and landowning coalition. The attempt was not explicit because Alianza Democrática sought the pragmatic coalition's support on the basis of shared economic policy demands, not through direct negotiation with business peak associations.

To diminish any anxiety about political change the business and landowning classes might harbor, Alianza Democrática quickly established its commitment to capitalist development. The pragmatic neoliberal coalition had asked Pinochet for reflationary economic policies and better debt repayment conditions from the IMF, without which reflation would be impossible. It also insisted on a commitment to the principle of private property—especially after the bank interventions of early 1983 and Pinochet's brief flirtation with hard-line nationalist elements that wanted the state to capitalize over 50 percent of the banks in receivership. Alianza Democrática responded by pledging respect for private property and prudent macroeconomic policies and foreign debt management. It supported sectoral economic policies, especially industrial policy and debt relief, rapid economic reactivation, and efforts to extract from the IMF the resources necessary to reflate the economy without heavy inflation.[3] In other words, Alianza Democrática tried to assuage both the military and entrepreneurs that an early transition to democracy via revisions to the 1980 Constitution did not signify a return to Unidad Popular-style socialism. To reinforce the point, the AD also pointedly excluded the MDP from the mainstream opposition coalition.

Despite the assurances of the PDC and Alianza Democrática, however, capitalists did not support the transition to democracy proposed by the opposition. To the dismay of Alianza Democrática, beginning in late September 1983 the capitalist critique of government economic policy began to abate. When the clash between capitalists and the military government diminished so did the AD's prospects for early democratization.

## Capitalists and Landowners: Between Pinochet and Mass Mobilization

Events between the eruption of mass mobilization (May 1983) and the abatement of the capitalist critique of government economic policy

(September-October 1983) reinforce the argument that the threat from below was not sufficient to explain the return of dissident business and landowning groups to the authoritarian fold. After all, it was capital's critique of Pinochet's economic policy that had fed the AD's hopes of constructing a broad multiclass alliance against the dictatorship. Moreover, the rift between Pinochet and the bourgeoisie had initially fueled and legitimized the opposition movement. Thus, if it were dread of the threat from below—which included the "socialist" AD—that largely motivated capitalists to close ranks with the military government, they would have done so shortly after the eruption of mass mobilization. Significantly, the CPC did not soften its confrontation with the military government until after the fifth national day of protest, almost half a year later. Not only that, but when mass mobilization began, instead of retreating capitalists escalated their confrontation with the regime. In July, they presented their economic recovery plan to the government and lobbied hard for it both in private and in public. Out of frustration with the government's lack of response to their proposals, the pragmatic coalition issued veiled threats that it might join the opposition.[4] And in September 1983—just before and after the fifth protest— capitalists pressed Pinochet to replace the ministers of finance and economy with men who favored reflationary policies.

In short, although Chilean capitalists worried over the potential political consequences of mass mobilization, instead of retreating from their dispute with the military government over economic policy they escalated it. The pragmatic coalition must have had some confidence that if the regime fell a complete reversal of the neoliberal experiment would not follow. Otherwise, the strategy that they did pursue—hedging bets to extract concessions from both government and opposition—would have been too risky. In other words, at the very least, capitalists felt that the threat from below was not severe enough to preclude their use of political unrest to gain negotiating leverage against Pinochet and the Chicago boys.

What induced capitalists to soften their critique of government economic policy at the end of September 1983? In the face of both massive monthly demonstrations and the mobilization of medium and small entrepreneurs, the government needed the solid support of Chilean large-scale capitalists. The defection of a significant capitalist group to either of those protesting groups would have increased the opposition's momentum significantly. As a result, the military government began to negotiate economic policy reforms along the lines suggested in *Recuperación económica* in return for a less militant business critique.[5] The threat of a multiclass opposition alliance that included capitalists enabled the pragmatic neoliberal coalition to translate its economic policy preferences into policy.

Government concessions to the pragmatic coalition began in August 1983. There were cabinet changes (Sergio O. Jarpa to the Ministry of Interior and Modesto Collados to Public Works) that held out the promise of organized business' inclusion in the policy formulation process. And the authorities began to implement some of the economic policy changes suggested in *Recuperación económica* in spite of the fact that the pragmatic coalition did not yet participate in policy formulation.

Increased access to the policymaking process, another one of the pragmatic coalition's long-standing demands, amplified the promise of economic policy change. For example, although Pinochet did not remove Finance Minister Cáceres he agreed to more frequent meetings with the CPC leadership.[6] Moreover, Cáceres' incumbency as minister of finance was uncertain, which raised the pragmatic coalition's hopes for change. Pinochet ordered a "shadow cabinet," composed of men whose views were much closer to the CPC than Cáceres'—Luis Escobar and former Minister of Economy Manuel Martín—to accompany Cáceres to the United States on a debt renegotiation mission.[7] Escobar favored reflationary policies, and Martín was closely connected to the groups that drafted *Recuperación económica*. It was commonly believed that one of them was being groomed for Cáceres' position. Business leaders also had easy access to Jarpa. Moreover, in the middle of September 1983, the military government also agreed to establish the Economic and Social Council, a CPC demand since mid-July 1983.[8]

Real concessions to the pragmatic neoliberal coalition gave credibility to the promise of policy change. In September 1983, the CPC concentrated its lobbying efforts on the issue of deficit spending.[9] It reiterated the demand, set forth in *Recuperación económica*, that such outlays reach 4 percent of GDP. A month later Cáceres complied. Deficit spending for 1984 would be around 5 percent of GDP.[10] The CPC also praised Cáceres for lowering real interest rates.[11] Overall, they fell from 35 percent in 1982 to 16 percent in 1983. In addition to these measures, the government quickly expanded housing and public works programs, as expected given Collados' appointment to the Ministry of Public Works.[12] Lastly, the CPC had advocated cutting business taxes as a means to stimulate the economy since 1982. Finance Minister Cáceres committed himself to such reform and brought the business peak associations into the process of drafting a revised tax code.[13]

Although the CPC softened its critique of government economic policy once the authorities began to negotiate over economic policy change, it did not lift all pressure. The CPC stopped demanding the resignations of Finance Minister Cáceres and Economy Minister Passicot, but it continued to press for a purge of Chicago boys who held mid-level positions in ministries and government agencies.[14] It was generally feared that they would try to impede the moderation of reforms to radical neoliberalism.[15] Furthermore, the CPC persistently lobbied for economic policy changes outlined in *Recuperación económica* not yet addressed by the government, such as a broader internal debt renegotiation bill at lower-than-market interest rates (5 percent over the Unidad de Fomento).[16] Moreover, business consistently used the document as its lobbying base in meetings with government officials. Thus, if after September 1983 business seemed less strident in the public presentation of its demands, its actual commitment and pursuit of them did not abate. And, as will be seen, the military government continued to make concessions on the basis of that document's recommendations in order to shore up capitalist support and defuse political opposition.

For capitalists, negotiation proved to be a fruitful alternative to confrontation since Pinochet was striving to keep political liberalization within the narrow bounds of the 1980 Constitution. Capitalists renewed their unconditional support for the regime once the pragmatic coalition triumphed. Its elevation to dominant coalition status occurred when the military government began to adopt its policy recommendations and placed its representatives in key state ministries. Access to the economic policymaking process and the exclusion of all other social groups cemented its dominant position.

The construction of a counterfactual highlights the risk that Pinochet would have run had he refused to bargain with the pragmatic neoliberal coalition. What might have happened if Pinochet had insisted on radical neoliberal prescriptions for the economic crisis? What if Pinochet believed that the military could rule Chile without capitalist support and that capitalists would never turn against him because of their fear of a threat from below? He could have pushed the pragmatic coalition to negotiate with the Christian Democrats. The pragmatic coalition, or significant breakaway groups, would have had an incentive to offer their tacit support for a quicker ouster of Pinochet in return for an even more moderate definition of a mixed economy. There is a possibility that a broad multiclass opposition alliance that included significant sectors of capital could have induced a split in support for Pinochet within the military junta. For example, the commanders of the air force and *Carabineros* might have concluded that Pinochet's presence was more politically destabilizing than a political opposition endorsed by important fractions of capital and prominent conservative political parties.[17]

To be sure, only desperate conditions could have driven Chilean capitalists to take such a risk. But Pinochet's continued application of orthodox deflation could have constituted such circumstances. Given Chile's severely depressed economy in 1982 and early 1983, the absence of reflationary policies were as grim a menace to the property and integrity of the surviving conglomerates as anything the PDC could have orchestrated. Capitalists understood their plight in those terms, which gave some of CPC president Jorge Fontaine's statements regarding the regime loyalties of the private sector the quality of a veiled threat. When it seemed that Pinochet would not budge, Fontaine declared that Chilean capitalists only moved against regimes when they endangered the viability of the private enterprise system.[18] Had the military government continued with orthodox deflation and the deep economic depression it produced, capitalists might have interpreted it as a "system-wide" hazard.

Another consequence of capitalists' decision to participate in an alliance against Pinochet would have been to shift the balance of power within the PDC to the right, especially since negotiation for political change would likely have included the armed forces and conservative political parties. Under those circumstances, Chilean capitalists would have had little to fear from radicals on the left, such as the MDP. The MDP would have been effectively isolated as a political force, which was the case anyway given that the AD pointedly refused to include the MDP in its mobilizations and negotiating strategies. Moreover, the MDP lost much of its capacity to mobilize in the wake of the destruction of the Communist party and the "domestication" of most of the Marxist left in Chile after 1986. Nevertheless, from the perspective of capital, negotiation with Pinochet was far preferable to striking a bargain with the PDC. With Pinochet, they would not face even relatively minor adjustments in economic policy in the interests of social equity.[19] Thus, when he showed an interest in compromising, the pragmatic coalition quickly softened its critiques to diminish the atmosphere of political crisis that gripped Chile.

## The Social Pact Option, 1984

By October of 1983 Alianza Democrática had lost its chance to promote rapid and substantial political liberalization.[20] Pinochet had broken off the "dialogue" with Alianza Democrática and capitalists had returned to the fold. In 1984, after the failure of the "implicit" alliance strategy, Alianza Democrática attempted to form an explicit social pact (*concertación social*) between capital and labor in order to win capital over, or at least to keep it from opposing a transition.[21] *Concertación social* was designed to allay capitalists' fears of democracy. To this end, the PDC sponsored a series of workshops in late 1984.[22] Capitalists voiced their concern that private property rights remain inviolable and requested ironclad commitments against expropriation and competition by state enterprises. They also worried that a new labor code might strengthen the labor movement.[23] Workers essentially wanted changes in the labor code to facilitate collective bargaining, better working conditions, and higher wages.[24]

Chilean capitalists, however, had a strong incentive to reject the *concertación social* project. Throughout 1984, cumulative economic policy concessions to the pragmatic neoliberal coalition were a testament to its increasing strength. Evidence for an expansionary economic policy came in the form of deficit spending, reduction in unemployment, and lower interest rates. A more satisfactory debt rescheduling scheme had been introduced. Moreover, the pragmatic coalition's access to, and participation in, the economic policymaking process had increased significantly. The economic ministries as of April 1984 were headed by "their" ministers (they had been part of Jorge Alessandri's conservative presidency in the late fifties and early sixties); meanwhile, purges of Chicago boys from administrative positions continued. In addition, businessmen and landowners participated in the formulation of the government's triennial plan, a three-year sectoral development program that had been sponsored by Collados when he was the chairman of the construction sector's peak association in 1983.[25] Finally, the Economic and Social Council, a government organization with advisory capacity to the state in economic and social matters, had begun to function. It was dominated by members of the business peak associations and provided additional access to government officials.[26] These were significant gains over the pre-1983 period, and they gave the pragmatic coalition's leaders the strength and security to reject participation in a social pact with labor.[27]

By 1985, capitalists had weathered the now receding economic crisis and had a relatively stable relationship with the military government. The pragmatic neoliberal coalition's next maneuver was to extract concessions from Alianza Democrática. The new dominant capitalist coalition sought to make the pragmatic neoliberal economic model an "untouchable" item in the future regime.

### Triumph of Pragmatic Neoliberalism and Opposition Response, 1986-1988

During this period, the pragmatic coalition sought to consolidate its gains. The military government had adopted the pragmatic economic model and given the coalition exclusive access to policy formulation. The creation of the national commissions for commerce and industry in the Ministry of Economy in 1986 further enhanced the role of capitalists in economic policymaking. These commissions were working groups in which the CPC and its member associations had formal participation, both in terms of proposing policy (drawbacks, for example) and in revising decree drafts.[28] Moreover, economic recovery and sustained growth solidified the terms of the bargain that held the pragmatic neoliberal coalition together. All capitalist and landowning partners prospered.

As a result of these successes, in 1986 capitalists began a campaign to perpetuate pragmatic neoliberalism. They opposed not only socialism but most government regulation or action that might vitiate pragmatic neoliberalism. Growth with austerity was their slogan. They sought to defend a model in which sectoral interests could lobby for protection and subsidies within a framework of macroeconomic stability. The latter, of course, required fiscal austerity in order to maintain the privileges of the former.

The Sociedad de Fomento Fabril (SFF) spearheaded the public debate. Throughout 1986, it proclaimed that the pragmatic neoliberal model represented the best interests of industry and the nation. Major alterations could only lead to disaster. The SFF demanded absolute respect for private property. Capitalists opposed renewed state participation in production, even joint ventures between state and private entrepreneurs. They rejected the AD's version of a mixed economy and ardently supported privatization to reduce public sector competition. They argued that Chile should maintain an open and free economy both internationally and internally via low across-the-board tariffs with high real exchange rates, protection against unfair competition when needed, and no controls on prices or foreign exchange. Tax structures, state welfare provision, and labor market arrangements should remain basically unaltered.[29]

Between 1987 and October 1988, the date of the plebiscite, the CPC, the Sociedad Nacional de Agricultura (SNA), and the Cámara Nacional de Comercio (CNC) echoed the SFF's pronouncements and declared their allegiance to Pinochet in the transition process.[30] With the formation of so-called civic committees (*comités cívicos*) in 1987 capitalists began to campaign for the regime in the coming plebiscite. The CPC publicly declared its support for Pinochet in the beginning of 1988.[31]

In response to capitalists' unwavering position and the success and international prestige of the pragmatic model, Alianza Democrática adopted an ever more conservative economic policy position. Alianza Democrática sought to assure capitalists and right-wing political parties that it was not a threat to the established order, but that it was a legitimate participant in a negotiated transition to democracy. Backing these assurances meant bargaining over the terms of the 1988 plebiscite and various anti-democratic clauses of the 1980 Constitution. Alianza Democrática gambled that its moderate economic posture would induce a negotiated transition from Pinochet's authoritarian regime to a more democratic regime than that contemplated by the 1980 Constitution. The opposition concentrated on political democratization rather than economic change.

Although Alianza Democrática had consistently supported a moderate economic program, as late as September 1985 it still favored more state participation in production than capitalists desired.[32] But with the relative economic success of the pragmatic economic model, as well as the solidification of the pragmatic capitalist coalition, the AD softened its position on state enterprise. By 1988, the opposition continued to praise a mixed economy, however, now redefined as industrial policy (targeting growth industries, supplying tax incentives for investments, and allocating special credits). It no longer mentioned state enterprise.[33] Thus, as will be seen below, the opposition limited the issue of state involvement in the economy to a discussion of distributional issues within the limits of the neoliberal model.[34]

A consequence of these concessions by the opposition was that by early 1987 capitalists admitted they no longer feared for their property rights. Instead, they recognized that not much was likely to change regardless of who won the plebiscite.[35] Their only real concern was that government intervention in markets might lead to economic instability.[36] Yet the CPC opposed even moderate economic reformism in the interests of social justice, and capitalists clung to Pinochet during the plebiscite because he shielded them from even the mildest economic change.[37]

## Capitalist Regime Allegiances
## and Chile's Transition to Democracy

Dominated by CPC members that produced for international markets and supported by domestic market producers, the rise of the pragmatic neoliberal coalition and the relative success of its economic model had several important consequences for Chile's political transition. First, the formation of the pragmatic neoliberal coalition robbed the opposition movement led by Alianza Democrática of acquiring a major capitalist ally against the military government. It gave the regime the fortitude to resist opposition demands for a more rapid transition to full political democracy. Pinochet and his supporters could bide their time and insist on a political transition within the institutional confines of the 1980 Constitution: plebiscite in 1989 with Pinochet virtually assured of his candidacy, full elections in 1990 or 1997 depending on the outcome of the plebiscite, electoral laws designed without opposition participation (with all of the consequent opportunity for gerrymandering), and full application of the pragmatic neoliberal economic model with minimal concern for social equity.

The Pinochet campaign for the October 1988 plebiscite (the *Sí* option) reflected officialdom's resurgent triumphalism. Its political advertisement stridently extolled economic gains since 1984 and compared Chile's relatively stable and growing economy to the economic disarray of fledgling democracies in neighboring Argentina, Peru, and Bolivia. Their ads also revealed a heavy-handed effort to equate the anti-Pinochet position (the *No* option) with the violence and chaos of the Allende years.

Second, the opposition was induced to further moderate its economic program. The Concertación de Partidos por el No (later Concertación de Partidos por la Democracia) emphatically stated its acceptance of the pragmatic neoliberal economic model and promised that distributional issues would be addressed within its confines. The Concertación also demonstrated its moderation by stressing social and political reconciliation in a deeply divided and traumatized polity rather than revenge for the abuses of 16 years of arbitrary rule.[38]

These concessions helped to assure a smooth political transition as stipulated by the 1980 Constitution. Since the projection of pragmatic neoliberalism was no longer at issue, the opposition minimized the risk that the transition process might be reversed.[39] In 1988, this allowed the opposition to press for a clean election, assure recognition for its victory, and to set the stage for negotiated constitutional change with conservative political parties after the plebiscite.

Events bore out the Concertación's hopes. Although it had little impact on political party, electoral districting, and congressional representation rules (majoritarian v. proportional), it did establish the right to monitor counting procedures at voting booths.[40] Moreover, during the ballot count on the night of October 5, when many worried that Pinochet might attempt to invalidate what appeared to be an opposition victory, conservative political party leaders from Renovación Nacional (RN)—the largest conservative party—and junta members Fernando Matthei (air force) and Rodolfo Stange (*Carabineros*) conceded that the Concertación seemed to be winning. Thus, they undercut any intention Pinochet might have had to annul the plebiscite's results.[41] The *No* campaign won by a comfortable margin: 54.7 percent of the vote to 43 percent for the *Sí*. Presidential and congressional elections were scheduled for December 14, 1989 and the transfer of office was set for March 11, 1990.

The stage was set for Chile's first presidential election since 1970. Christian Democratic party president Patricio Aylwin ran for the Concertación; former Pinochet minister of finance Hernán Büchi for the conservatives (Democracia y Progreso, a coalition of conservative political parties that included Renovación Nacional and Unión Democrática Independiente, the UDI); and banker-businessman-populist Francisco Javier Errázuriz campaigned on an independent ticket. Aylwin received 55.2 percent of the vote to Büchi's 29.4 percent, and Errázuriz's 15.4 percent. Of the Senate's 38 elected seats Concertación parties won 22 and Democracia y Progreso got 16.[42] In the chamber of deputies Aylwin's coalition garnered 69 seats to the conservative alliance's 48. The leftist Lista Partido Amplio de Izquierda Socialista (PAIS) obtained two seats and independents received one.[43]  The Concertación essentially conducted the presidential campaign on the same platform as the *No* crusade,[44]  while Democracia y Progreso emphasized a neoliberal/libertarian platform.[45]

## Pragmatic Neoliberalism
## and the Aylwin Administration, 1990-1994

The Concertación's concessions to the pragmatic neoliberal coalition (broad socio-economic reform for political democratization) had a third important consequence, one that is likely to affect the character of democratic politics and the range of acceptable policy options for years to come. Chile's new political institutions tend to favor the economic interests of conservative forces and places reformers at a disadvantage. The pact explicitly committed reformist political parties representing the middle class and some labor sectors to pragmatic neoliberalism. In return, businessmen, landowners, and conservative political parties accepted limited political change.

Reformers are constrained by this political bargain. Patricio Aylwin administration's social reforms have been mild and well within the confines of the pragmatic neoliberal model. One may conclude that the administration's policies were consolidating a liberal development path for Chile. Contrary to what some analysts maintain, the Aylwin government's policymakers were not building either a social-democratic or some other deeply reformist alternative.[46] In addition to this argument, this concluding section shows how Chile's tutelary democracy provides political and institutional conditions that protect capitalists and landowners from social democrats in particular, and from non-liberal social reformism in general.[47]

What differentiates a liberal from a social-democratic developmental path? Every modern state—and Chileans think of themselves as modern—has a welfare function. The question is, what type of welfare state? Gosta Esping-Andersen offers criteria for distinguishing between liberal and social-democratic welfare states. The key distinguishing feature is the degree to which social policy ties individuals to markets or protects people from them. Closely related to this question is the degree to which people can survive with a measure of dignity when they cannot work. Liberal welfare states tie individuals to markets as much as possible because they provide individuals few alternatives to survival besides working for virtually any wage as determined by relatively unregulated labor markets. They offer minimal, difficult to obtain, means-tested protection; they stigmatize public welfare recipients; and, most importantly, they encourage private insurance for the provision of the bulk of a society's welfare needs. Social-democratic welfare states buffer individuals from the vicissitudes of the market. They provide generous, easy to access universal benefits (pension, health, unemployment, child care) that people are entitled to by virtue of citizenship.[48]

The two developmental paths also differ in their assumptions about the role of the state in the economy. Liberals prefer minimal, arms-length government intervention in self-clearing markets. Social democrats favor mixed economies, meaning a strong state role in the economy (although not necessarily public ownership), and full employment. Social democracy also relies on strong labor parties and unions.

Esping-Andersen constructed his model on the basis of the experience of advanced industrial nations. Developing nations tend to lack the resources to implement a "pure" social-democratic agenda. But certain strategies crucial for the development of a social-democratic agenda are not precluded. One task consists of embedding in new labor and social laws principles that facilitate the future design of social-democratic policies as resources permit.[49] The same approach should be applied to a revision of electoral rules that shackle the development of social-democratic parties. A second feasible policy line would focus on fortifying the labor movement, as well as strengthening the role of the state in industrial policy and labor relations. The Aylwin administration accomplished little in either area.

Aylwin's government campaigned on the slogan "economic growth with equity." Undeniably, the Aylwin administration was mildly reformist and did its best to deliver on its promise. It raised and spent more funds for social programs than the dictatorship did, modestly expanding programs established during the social modernizations period of the dictatorship. Although the social safety net for the most needy was extended, for everyone else the emphasis remained on the provision of private insurance (especially in pensions and health). Monies were channeled into a new social investment fund (Fosis), which provided resources for community projects in small business development, infrastructure improvement for poor municipalities, and small-scale rural projects.[50]

These programs fit a liberal rather than a social-democratic conception of equity and contribute to the consolidation of a liberal development path. Social expenditures target the most needy sectors; a policy first introduced by the neoliberal social engineers of the military government (in the latter half of the 1980s the World Bank incorporated this idea into its structural adjustment programs, which are blueprints for liberal welfare state development). In keeping with Esping-Andersen's definition, these programs are not universal. They are meager, means-tested, and carry a stigma.[51] Everyone else must rely on the market and private insurance for survival. A heavy emphasis on inflation control as social policy to raise real incomes takes a similar approach. The notion embedded in Fosis is that productive activities are the best providers of welfare. Nowhere in Aylwin's tenure does one find the articulation of norms and principles that express an intention to insulate individuals from the market.

That the Aylwin government raised some taxes in order to increase spending for the neediest of the poor does not signify a turn to a more serious reformist, or social-democratic, agenda. The funds were destined to expanding and strengthening the liberal welfare system established under military rule. The way the Aylwin government raised taxes further revealed its commitment to mild reformism rather than bold departures. It established a 10-15 percent tax on business profits (hardly an onerous burden) that was negotiated with capitalists and right-wing parties, raised the value-added tax from 16 percent to 18 percent, and transferred some of the resources generated by modest military budget cuts to social programs.[52]

Finally, mild reformism in labor legislation does not favor the construction of social democracy in Chile either. One of the fundamental principles guiding the labor reform was sound. The Aylwin administration favored a wage policy that tied wage increases to productivity gains, satisfying neoliberal demands for wage restraint to control inflation, and keeping the government's pledge to address the decline of real wages at a time of rising corporate profitability. However, achieving that goal required legislation to strengthen unions, a key demand of the labor movement itself. Although the Aylwin administration sought to move somewhat aggressively in principle, it failed to do so in practice. As will be seen below, the political strength of the private sector—a result of the process of Chile's political transition—gutted the government's proposals.

There were three factors that protected conservatives from would-be social democrats and more serious reformist attempts, and all were a consequence of the victory of the pragmatic coalition and the Concertación's bargain with it. The remainder of this chapter briefly describes these factors and analyzes how they constrained the Aylwin government. The first factor was the commitment of the Concertación to maintain economic growth by retaining the pragmatic neoliberal economic model, which emphasized market forces and fiscal restraint.[53] This economic development strategy gave businessmen a great structural advantage. They were the primary source of investment, so the Concertación could not afford to alienate that sector.

Second, Chile's transition from authoritarianism took place within the confines of the 1980 Constitution, a charter with numerous features designed to protect conservative interests from reformists. Since it is still the law of the land, Chilean political institutions are not fully democratic, and they leave reformist Christian and social democrats at a disadvantage.[54] Because the staunchly conservative military has significant autonomy from civilian control, civilian governments must continuously gauge the armed forces' reaction to public policies. Moreover, the electoral system gerrymanders districts in favor of right-wing parties that block or water down reformist legislation. The Senate is their bastion, where quorum rules give them a veto power over all legislation, including constitutional amendments.[55]

Third, the system of collaboration between government and the private sector—developed to assuage capitalist fears of arbitrary policy and to insure steady investment—benefits business elites. This system of interaction, known as "consensus" policymaking, is only a slight modification of the one established between capital and the state under military rule after 1984. Technocrats who are members of the political parties of the Concertación now occupy most of the key economic and line ministries. They keep open lines of communication with organized business and invite them to participate in the formulation of policies. Capitalists have ample opportunity to modify most of the government's policy initiatives. Although the consensus style of policymaking formally includes labor when issues directly affect that social group, for the most part the process is biased in favor of the private sector.[56]

The relationship between capitalists and the government was not always harmonious or free of tension during the Aylwin administration. Policymakers belonged to a political bloc tied to a statist past. Consequently, businessmen were on their guard, ready to challenge any deviation from pragmatic neoliberalism and defend their "hard-earned" gains of the dictatorship era. Though acrimonious exchanges between capitalists and the Aylwin administration surfaced from time to time, maintaining a close relationship with organized business was one element of the Aylwin administration's success in maintaining a good business climate.[57] Constant communication, feedback, negotiation, and concessions on the part of government assuage capitalist fears and contribute to capitalists' invest-ment decisions. One SFF leader put this way.

> We may have our differences with the government, but if we are worried about something, or want to express our point of view on policy, all we have to do is pick up the phone and arrange a meeting. We may not get everything we want, but we rarely come away empty handed. The people in the ministries of finance and economy are all very reasonable. It gives us confidence in this government.[58]

How did these factors constrain reformist attempts that might have deviated from the path of liberal state formation? First, the Concertación had promised the pragmatic neoliberal capitalist coalition that it would maintain an export-oriented market economy, macroeconomic stability, and fiscal and wage restraint in the interest of holding down inflation. One of the Aylwin administration's biggest challenges was to convince capitalists that it would honor those commitments, immediately limiting the range of social policy the new government could attempt. It would not deficit spend, and it could not raise much financing through taxation, which business considered to be confiscation. Moreover, many changes to the tax code might discourage the private sector from investing or cause it to flee Chilean borders.[59] Attempts to introduce social policies that did not fit the liberal welfare state mold might elicit the same response.

In this manner, increased spending for existing means-tested programs targeted for the extremely poor, along with a social investment fund, were an expedient and relatively uncontroversial means for delivering on the promise of economic growth with equity. Few new government agencies were required, maintaining the commitment to a minimalist state. Production not handouts, and keeping people tied to markets and at the mercy of their employers, were at the center of the effort. Nevertheless, the programs have been relatively successful at what they were designed to do. By all indications they have reduced the level of *extreme* poverty (pauperism or absolute destitution). Aggregate figures for infant mortality, literacy, and life expectancy have all improved. Meanwhile, the needs of other social groups, such as workers, peasants, and the middle classes, largely remain unaddressed.

The direction the Concertación took on social policy might have been an act of self-censorship; a recognition of the structural power of Chilean (and foreign) capitalists. The absence of any significant industrial policy might be attributed to the same cause. Too much tinkering with existing policies might have dampened the rate of investment and economic growth. After all, private insurance in pensions and health are also investment pools. Tax and labor policy, however, were not affected by self-censorship. Policy debates on taxes and labor laws illustrate how Chile's political institutions and the system of collaboration between capitalists and the government result in an unequivocal bias in favor of the supporters of continued liberal state formation.

The Aylwin administration designed a bill to increase taxes for more social spending. The government confronted all three legacies of authoritarianism: It had to convince business of the sincerity of its promise to maintain macroeconomic stability, deal with the veto power of conservative political parties in the Congress, and cope with the consensus style of policymaking (which included business groups in policy formulation). These factors assured that direct negotiation with conservative political parties and business groups was required. Any measures that those groups opposed—in social policy or tax hikes—simply would not pass.

The negotiations centered on the taxation of corporate profits. The Aylwin administration was keen to show its commitment to maintaining high economic growth rates and macroeconomic stability. As a result, it kept its corporate tax increase proposals low (15 percent to 20 percent) and repeatedly stressed that the tax hikes would be spent on social services and not wasted on other items.[60] (VAT tax increases were relatively uncontroversial, and military budget cuts were very low so as not to upset the armed forces.) The Concertación also entered directly into negotiations with the principal right-wing party, Renovación Nacional (RN), and with Manuel Feliú, president of the CPC.

For their part, conservatives felt compelled to support the tax reform as long as the spending went for proven social programs. During the 1989 presidential campaign, they realized that conservatism was unpopular with many social groups because of its unabashed support for a dictatorship that had blatantly neglected social equity concerns. In the spirit of compromise and national reconciliation, and to boost their electoral appeal, conservatives acquiesced to slightly higher levels of taxation for existing (liberal) programs or measures that extolled the virtues of "production" versus "handouts."[61]

Of course, right-wing forces did not just give in to the government's propositions. Taking advantage of the consensus-style policymaking process established by the Concertación, conservative political parties and the CPC reduced the corporate tax increase to between 10 percent and 15 percent of profits. As expected, this did not hamper investment or impede economic growth; nor did increased social spending lead to unmanageable inflationary pressures. Since the bill was to expire in 1994, the Concertación renegotiated the terms with the CPC. The taxes were retained, but at slightly lower levels.[62]

Although the Aylwin administration proceeded cautiously on social spending and tax issues from the outset, its attempts to reform labor were more aggressive. Unions had to be strengthened for the government's plan of tying wage increases to productivity to succeed. Without more effective unions, labor could not reap the benefits of increased productivity in collective bargaining. "The legacies of the dictatorship," however, enabled conservative forces to gut the government's bill.

The government proposed a bill that reformed three key aspects of the labor code. First, the administration sought to make it more difficult and expensive to fire workers, revising the old code that allowed employers to let workers go without showing cause and to hire replacements for strikers. Second, the bill permitted unions to negotiate contracts by economic sector rather than on a company-by-company basis. Unions would gain the right to negotiate health benefits and job security clauses. Third, the draft legislation mandated that non-union employees pay union fees if they benefitted from union negotiated contracts, a condition that stopped short of the key Central Unica de Trabajadores (CUT) demand of mandatory union enrollment.[63]

Chilean capitalists, represented by the CPC and conservative political parties, opposed the bill in its entirety. Appointed Senate seats gave conservatives a majority, which forced the administration to negotiate the labor reform bill point by point with the RN. The legislation soon bogged down.[64] Business leaders also took advantage of the system of collaboration with the executive branch to lobby against the bill.[65] In the end, a bill that never addressed more than the bare minimum of labor's agenda provided the following results: Labor acquired no new capacity to capture and retain wages on the basis of increased productivity.[66] The number of unionized workers, only 14.4 percent of the labor force in 1992, remained low enough to ensure that organized labor would continue on the political sidelines.[67]

In conclusion, Chile's political transition in the late 1980s created a protected, or tutelary, democracy in the 1990s. The victory of the pragmatic neoliberal capitalist coalition in the final years of the dictatorship solidified business and landowner support for the military government and robbed the Concertación of the opportunity to create a broad-based, multiclass opposition to Pinochet. The inability of the Concertación to wrestle the pace and content of the transition from authoritarians contributed to the further moderation of its socio-economic reform agenda. For the time being, the victory of pragmatic neoliberalism has locked Chile into a path of liberal state formation and socio-economic development.

Within these constraints, the Concertación paid far more attention to social equity than the dictatorship did, reducing the level of extreme poverty and inducing capitalists to contribute more to social programs. However, the reforms are mild and do not challenge neoliberalism. They build a liberal welfare state without preparing the conditions that might lead to more substantive change.

Chile is being touted as an example of an alternative way for developing nations to respond to neoliberalism. Chile is said to be leading the way (along with Spain, perhaps) to a new social-democratic development path. The arguments made here suggest otherwise. It is worth noting that liberalism and welfare statism are not antithetical terms. The modern state has a welfare function. Liberalism, neo or otherwise, has its own conception of social equity, and a history of liberal state formation logically leads to the construction of a liberal welfare state. Without strong labor parties and unions it is unlikely that social democracy will materialize as a consequence of liberal state formation.[68]

The consolidation of a liberal pattern of state formation, with institutional features that protect conservative forces, has other implications. Although the Concertación recognizes the need for industrial policies to move Chile beyond the "easy stages" of export-oriented growth, passing such legislation will prove difficult. Most capitalists and landowners in Chile show little desire to move beyond agro-extractive exports, with minimal value-added, or financial service activities. This issue ties in with capitalists' lack of desire to improve wages and income distribution. Chilean capitalists prefer to maintain low wages as a component of their international comparative advantage, which also requires a weakly organized labor force.[69]

Chile's protected democracy places constraints on anything but a mildly reformist path that reinforces liberal welfare statism. Such basic issues as redressing a highly skewed income distribution pattern, protecting individuals from the full rigors of market forces, or promoting an industrial policy will most likely be postponed. Although extreme poverty may have been alleviated, the relative shares of income of the highest and lowest quintiles remain constant as Chile's economy grows. Moreover, the distance between the extremely poor and the "merely" poor is not so great, and the latter are still at the mercy of market forces. Little buffers them from a precarious existence and the rigors of management's tight control in the work place. Despite improvement, real wages are still very low; in fact, the present economic development model requires low wages. With the prices of goods such as education, health, housing, and clothing at world prices, they remain out of reach for many Chileans.

The triumph of the pragmatic neoliberal capitalist coalition and its impact on the transition from authoritarianism contributed to some of the main constraints to more deep-seated socio-economic reforms. So did the retention of the basic features of the system of interaction between capital and the state devised during the last years of the dictatorship: technocratic policymakers and organized business working together closely to formulate policy (the subordinate inclusion of organized labor and middle class interests notwithstanding). Two years into the Aylwin administration, the leaders of top business peak associations confirmed that easy access to the executive branch bolstered their confidence in the Concertacion's assertion that it intended to adhere to the main tenets of pragmatic neoliberalism. They also acknowledged that this system allowed them to alter proposed legislation in ways that favored their interests. By the same token, Minister of Planning and Development Sergio Molina, directly blamed the government's difficulties in addressing the issue of social equity on this system of collaboration.[70]

Chile's transition to democracy not only gave verbal guarantees to businessmen and landowners, it also provided them with strong institutional means with which to defend their interests. Those interests are anchored by a very broad definition of property rights and the view that most taxation amounts to confiscation of profits. In this context, capitalists get to define what constitutes "excessive."

In conclusion, the Chilean bourgeoisie's democratic vocation may be confined to supporting only a limited, or protected, democracy combined with a pragmatic neoliberal socio-economic model. So far the Concertación's emphasis on moderation and negotiation seems to augur well for political stability. How that emphasis translates into more political democratization, developing industrial competitive advantages, and social justice remains to be seen. Deepening political democracy in Chile requires reducing military prerogatives, which the armed forces resist, and removing the 1980 Constitution's authoritarian features, which may also prove difficult.[71] Moreover, it is an open question whether Chilean business elites would remain as committed to democracy if they were faced with real—albeit nonsocialist—challenges, such as diminished institutional veto power and the resurgence of reformist policies along the lines of Scandinavian social democracies.[72] Finding the conditions under which national capitalists cease to feel threatened by a more just society is as worthy an intellectual task as uncovering the conditions for political and macroeconomic stability.

## Notes

1. For an analysis of the regime loyalties of capitalists based on the degree of threat from below (which I argue is partly mistaken), see Jeffry A. Frieden, *Debt Development, and Democracy: Modern Political Economy and Latin America, 1965-1985* (Princeton: Princeton University Press, 1991).

2. For a description of this process as discussions among intellectuals, see Jeffrey M. Puryear, *Thinking Politics: Intellectuals and Democracy in Chile, 1973-1988* (Baltimore: Johns Hopkins University Press, 1994).

3. Alejandro Foxley, "Algunas condiciones para una democratización estable: El caso de Chile," *Colección Estudios Cieplan* no. 9, December 1982; *Qué Pasa* no. 612, December 30, 1982; no. 613, January 6, 1983; no. 647, September 1, 1983; Cieplan, *Reconstrucción económica para la democracia* (Santiago: Editorial Aconcagua, 1983).

4. Recall that when the CPC distributed "Recuperación económica" to the government, the SFF and the CPC cautioned that although the private sector did not wish to break with the government it might be forced into opposition due to government inflexibility on economic policy. For the SFF's statement, see *Qué Pasa* no. 639, July 7, 1983; for the CPC, see Jorge Fontaine's declaration in *Revista Hoy* no. 311, July 6, 1983.

5. *Qué Pasa* no. 654, October 20, 1983; and no. 655, October 27, 1983.

6. Confederación de la Producción y Comercio, minutes of executive committee meeting no. 591, September 5, 1983.

7. *Revista Hoy* no. 326, October 19, 1983.

8. *Revista Hoy* no. 313, July 20, 1983; *Qué Pasa* no. 649, September 15, 1983.

9. *Revista Hoy* no. 321, September 14, 1983.

10. *Qué Pasa* no. 655, October 27, 1983; *Revista Hoy* no. 328, November 2, 1983.

11. CPC, minutes of executive committee meeting no. 591, September 5, 1983.

12. Author interviews with CPC officials reinforced the conclusion that the government was progressively implementing the CPC's economic program. Also see *Qué Pasa* no. 655, October 27, 1983.

13. *Qué Pasa* no. 649, September 15, 1983, reported that the tax reform bill was

virtually ready to clear the legislative commission in charge of economic affairs. Business associations had ample access to the policymaking process through the legislative commissions; see Cámara Nacional de Comercio, memorandum to Minister of Finance Carlos Cáceres, no. 265/83, November 4, 1983.

14. *Qué Pasa* no. 655, October 27, 1983.

15. *Revista Hoy* no. 321, September 14, 1983; *Qué Pasa* no. 650, September 22, 1983.

16. *Revista Hoy* no. 321, September 14, 1983; *Qué Pasa* no. 655, October 27, 1983.

17. There is some evidence that this position might have developed in Mary Helen Spooner, *Soldiers in a Narrow Land: The Pinochet Regime in Chile* (Berkeley: University of California Press, 1994).

18. For Jorge Fontaine's statements to that effect, see *Revista Hoy* no. 330, November 16, 1983.

19. *Proyecto alternativo* (Santiago: Editorial Aconcagua, 1984), three volumes. Volumes one and two referred to labor law and tax reform and the need for more state intervention in the economy than under Pinochet, including the need to avert extreme property concentration as had been the case with the Cruzat-Larraín and BHC conglomerates. It also paid special attention to medium and small business.

20. *Qué Pasa* no. 653, October 13, 1983; *Revista Hoy* no. 326, October 19, 1983; and no. 328, November 2, 1983.

21. Proyecto Alternativo, *Proyecto alternativo*, vol. 2 (Santiago: Editorial Aconcagua, 1984).

22. Centro de Estudios del Desarrollo, *Concertación social y democracia* (Santiago: CED, 1985).

23. In CED, *Concertación social*, see the contributions by Fernando Léniz, "El difícil consenso económico"; Víctor Manuel Ojeda, "Los problemas de la economía y la relación empresarios-trabajadores"; Andrés Feliú, "El punto de vista de los empresarios"; and commentary by Ricardo Claro.

24. In CED, *Concertación social*, see the contributions by Guillermo Pérez, "Sindicalismo y redemocratización: Posibilidades y alcances de la concertación social"; Luis Eduardo Thayer, "Relaciones del trabajo en una institucionalidad democrática: Un enfoque jurídico"; José Ruiz di Giorgio and José Ruiz dos Santos, "Concertación social: Cambio posible y necesario"; Eugenio Díaz, "La concertación desde una perspectiva sindical de izquierda."

25. Author interviews with Jorge Fontaine, president of the CPC, and Pablo Araya, director of research, Chilean Construction Chamber, both conducted in April 1989.

26. For Chile's Economic and Social Council, see Augusto Lecaros, "Representación de los intereses de la sociedad en el estado y los consejos económico sociales," M.A. Thesis, Pontificia Universidad Católica de Chile, Instituto de Ciencia Política, 1989. I also relied on information from an author interview in May 1989 with Beltrán Urenda, the Council's director.

27. In an author interview in August 1988, Gustavo Ramdohr (ASIMET and ASEXMA), who participated in the Concertación dialogues, shared this view of capital's refusal to enter into such pacts.

28. Author interviews with Gustavo Ramdohr, president of the Nontraditional Exporters' Association (ASEXMA), August 1988; Jorge Fontaine, president of the

238 *Pragmatic Neoliberalism and Chile's Transition*

CPC, April 1989; Jaime Alé, SFF director of planning, September 1988; Lee Ward, director of the National Commission for External Commerce, December 1988; minutes of the meetings of the Subcommission for Drawback Legislation of the National Commission for External Commerce.

29. Sociedad de Fomento Fabril, "Acciones prioritarias, 1986," *Revista Industria* 89, 1, 1986; "Editorial: Los programas políticos y el sector productivo," *Revista Industria* 89, 2, 1986; "Derecho de propiedad, reforzamiento de la empresa privada y economía libre," *Revista Industria* 89, 2, 1986; "Exposición del presidente de la SFF en la 102 asamblea de socios," *Revista Industria* 89, 3, 1986; SFF, "Carta del presidente," *Memoria*, 1985/86; "Carta del presidente, *Memoria*, 1986/87; *Qué Pasa* no. 785, April 24, 1986.

30. *El Campesino* 6, June 1987; and 11, November 1987; Cámara Nacional de Comercio, *Informe económico anual, 1988* (Santiago: CNC, 1988). For the SNA's position on agrarian reform, see *El Campesino* 1-2, January-February 1986; and 11, November 1986. For the CPC's support of the SNA, see *El Campesino* 8, August 1987.

31. *El Campesino* 1-2, January-February 1988; and 5, May 1988.

32. For Alianza Democrática's program, see "Acuerdo nacional para la transición a la plena democracia," *Revista Hoy* no. 424, September 2, 1985.

33. *Estrategia*, October 17, 1988; and *La Epoca*, December 26, 1988. Also see Ernesto Tironi, *Es posible reducir la pobreza en Chile* (Santiago: Editorial Zig-Zag, 1989); and Felipe Larraín "Desarrollo económico para Chile en democracia," in Felipe Larraín, ed., *Desarrollo económico en democracia* (Santiago: Ediciones Universidad Católica de Chile, 1988).

34. Ernesto Tironi, "Democracia y mejoramiento de remuneraciones," Centro de Estudios del Desarrollo, *Materiales para Discusión* no. 178, 1987; A. García, "Crecimiento equitativo: Políticas de empleo e ingresos," Centro de Estudios del Desarrollo, *Materiales para Discusión* no. 191, 1987; Sergio Molina, "El compromiso de Chile: Crear un órden social justo," Centro de Estudios del Desarrollo, *Materiales para Discusión* no. 200, 1987.

35. *Qué Pasa* no. 833, March 26, 1987.

36. Author interviews with Jaime Alé (SFF), September 1988; Humberto Prieto (CNC), January 1989; Sergio de la Cuadra (minister of finance in 1982), September 1988. Also see *El Campesino* no. 11, November 1988; Cámara Nacional de Comercio, *Informe económico anual, 1988*, pp. 8-11; and Sociedad de Fomento Fabril, "Los industriales y la política," *Revista Industria* 91, 4, 1988.

37. This was evident in a statement loaded with neoliberal code-words that appeared in *El Campesino* 1-2, January-February 1988, p.7.

38. Latin American Studies Association, "The Chilean Plebiscite: A First Step Toward Redemocratization," *LASA Forum* 19, 4, 1989.

39. The opposition's strategic choice was consistent with the prescriptions advocated by Guillermo O'Donnell and Philippe Schmitter, *Transitions form Authoritarian Rule: Tentative Conclusions* (Baltimore: Johns Hopkins University Press, 1986).

40. Latin American Studies Association, *The Chilean Plebiscite*.

41. For events during the night of October 5, see *Qué Pasa* no. 914, November 13, 1988; and Ascanio Cavallo et al., *La historia oculta del régimen militar* (Santiago: Editorial La Epoca, 1988).

42. The Senate also has nine designated seats. One is reserved for former

presidents of the republic for life, and the others are nominated by the outgoing president for one term.

43. *La Epoca*, December 16, 1989; Steven Brager, "The Chilean Elections of 1989: An Account, an Analysis, and a forecast for the Future, (mimeo) 1990; and César Caviedes, *Elections in Chile: The Road Toward Redemocratization* (Boulder: Lynne Rienner, 1991).

44. Interview with Sergio Bitar in *Qué Pasa* no. 954, July 20, 1989; and interview with Patricio Aylwin in *Revista Hoy* no. 626, July 17, 1989. Also see *Business Latin America*, July 10, 1989; and August 14, 1989.

45. Büchi stressed that his candidacy symbolized Chile's liberation from the deleterious political style of the past that had been responsible for the collapse of democracy: political freedom without economic freedom. His platform underscored four points. First, power decentralization—a weaker presidency and more autonomy for administrative regions. Second, under his presidency Chile would become an "opportunity society" with more employment, better wages, health and housing, zero inflation, and low taxation. The third point addressed "education for liberty," with subsidies for the poor. Fourth, Chile should strengthen economic ties to its neighbors. These points drawn from *Qué Pasa* no. 954, July 20, 1989; no. 959, August 24, 1989; and no. 964, September 28, 1989.

46. For a similar view on the continuities between the military government and the new democracy, see James Petras and Fernando Ignacio Leiva, with Henry Veltmeyer, *Democracy and Poverty in Chile: The Limits to Electoral Politics* (Boulder: Westview, 1994). For an argument about the requirements for the construction of social democracy somewhere between those of the Concertación and my own, see Luiz Carlos Bresser Pereira, José María Maravall, and Adam Przeworski, *Economic Reforms in New Democracies: A Social Democratic Approach* (Cambridge: Cambridge University Press, 1993).

47. For an historical treatment of tutelary democracy in Latin America, see Brian Loveman, *The Constitution of Tyranny: Regimes of Exception in Spanish America* (Pittsburgh: University of Pittsburgh Press, 1994).

48. Gosta Esping-Andersen, *The Three Worlds of Welfare Capitalism* (Princeton: Princeton University Press, 1990).

49. This borrows from the concept of regimes in the international relations literature; see Robert O. Keohane and Joseph S. Nye, *Power and Interdependence: World Politics in Transition* (Boston: Little, Brown and Company, 1977); and Stephen D. Krasner, *International Regimes* (Ithaca: Cornell University Press, 1983).

50. For these policies, see Alan Angell, "Can Social Sector Reforms Make Adjustment Sustainable and Equitable? Lessons from Chile and Venezuela," *Journal of Latin American Studies* 27, 1, 1995; David E. Hojman, *Chile: The Political Economy of Development and Democracy in the 1990s* (Pittsburgh: University of Pittsburgh Press, 1993); Carol Graham, "From Emergency Employment to Social Investment: Changing Approaches to Poverty Alleviation in Chile," in Alan Angell and Benny Pollack, eds., *The Legacy of Dictatorship: Political, Economic, and Social Change in Pinochet's Chile* (Liverpool: Institute of Latin American Studies, The University of Liverpool, Monograph Series, no. 17, 1993); and Tarsicio Castañeda, *Combating Poverty: Innovative Social Reforms in Chile during the 1980s* (San Francisco: International Center for Economic Growth, 1992).

51. For means-tested social policies in Chile, see Pilar Vergara, "Market Economy, Social Welfare, and Democratic Consolidation in Chile," in William C. Smith, Carlos H. Acuña, and Eduardo A. Gamarra, eds., *Democracy, Markets, and Structural Reform in Latin America: Argentina, Bolivia, Brazil, Chile, and Mexico* (New Brunswick: Transaction, 1994).

52. For these policies, see *Qué Pasa* no. 955, July 27, 1989; and no. 986, March 1, 1990; also *Business Latin America*, July 23, 1990; and December 3, 1990.

53. Felipe Larraín, "The Economic Challenges of Democratic Development," in Paul Drake and Iván Jaksic, eds., *The Struggle for Democracy in Chile, 1982-1990* (Lincoln: University of Nebraska Press, 1991).

54. Brian Loveman, "¿*Misión Cumplida?* Civil-Military Relations and the Chilean Political Transition," *Journal of Interamerican Studies and World Affairs* 33, 3, 1991; and Rhoda Rabkin, "The Aylwin Government and Tutelary Democracy: A Concept in Search of Case?" *Journal of Interamerican Studies and World Affairs* 34, 4, 1992-93.

55. The Senate has nine seats appointed by Pinochet, and the selection rules heavily favor conservatives. Four of nine are held by the military and Pinochet is guaranteed a lifelong Senate appointment. The remaining appointed seats also tend to favor conservatives. For further details, see Loveman, "¿*Misión Cumplida?.*"

56. For a related argument, see Carlos H. Acuña and William C. Smith, "The Political Economy of Structural Adjustment: The Logic of Support and Opposition to Neoliberal Reform," in William C. Smith, Carlos H. Acuña, and Eduardo A. Gamarra, eds., *Latin American Political Economy in the Age of Neoliberal Reform: Theoretical and Comparative Perspectives for the 1990s* (New Brunswick: Transaction, 1994).

57. For a treatment of these themes, see Oscar Muñoz, "El desarrollo de las relaciones estado-empresa en el nuevo escenario económico: Dos ensayos," *Apuntes Cieplan* no. 106, 1991.

58. Author interview with Pedro Lizana, June 1992.

59. Author interview with Manuel Marfán, Cieplan economist, consultant to the government, and chief architect of the Aylwin administration's tax reform policy, July 1992.

60. Author interview with Manual Marfán, architect of the Concertación's tax reform strategy, July 1992.

61. Author interviews with Manuel Marfán and Manuel Feliú, former president of the CPC, both in July, 1992. Also see Manuel Feliú, *La empresa de la libertad* (Santiago: Editorial Zig-Zag, 1988).

62. For the renegotiation of the tax provisions, see Kurt Weyland, "Growth with Equity in Chile's New Democracy?" *Latin American Research Review*, forthcoming. Not all business sectors accepted increased taxation with equanimity. The SFF bitterly opposed them and remained unresigned to them after legislation was passed. They felt that the RN and Feliú had betrayed their trust. Again, however, as with the differentiated tariff issue, their opposition did not mean that taxes were passed over the interests of capital and landowners, or that the representatives of upper class elites were renegades. Once again it was a case of the SFF's isolation among other capitalist and landowning fractions. Although the rest of the peak associations were far from enthusiastic, they could live with slightly higher taxes as the price to pay for having lost the plebiscite in 1988. Author interviews during June and July 1992

with José Antonio Guzmán (president, CPC), Raúl García (general secretary, SNA), Alfonso Mujica (vice president, CNC) and Manuel Feliú, who negotiated the tax agreements with the government while president of the CPC.

63. *Business Latin America*, July 23, 1990; September 3, 1990.

64. For these points, see interview with Luis Maira (president of Izquierda Cristiana), in *Qué Pasa* no. 1021, November 5, 1990; and *Business Latin America*, September 3, 1990.

65. Author interviews with Jaime Alé (SFF), Pedro Lizana (SFF), Raúl García (SNA), Alfonso Mujica (CNC), José Antonio Guzmán (CPC and Construction Chamber), all in June and July 1992.

66. Centro de Investigación y Asesoría Sindical, "Trabajadores/Empresarios: Desafío de futuro," *Documento* no. 6, 1990.

67. This was better than the 8.5 percent low under Pinochet in 1985 but far below the high of 32.3 percent under Allende. See Kenneth Roberts, "Rethinking Economic Alternatives: Left Parties and the Articulation of Popular Demands in Chile and Peru," paper presented at the conference on "Inequality and New Forms of Popular Representation in Latin America," New York, Columbia University, March 3-5, 1994.

68. For the developmental paths of liberal and social-democratic welfare states, see Gosta Esping-Andersen, *The Three Worlds of Welfare Capitalism*.

69. These observations were brought home to me by Cecilia Montero and Alan Angell in personal communications in September 1994 and May 1995 respectively.

70. Author interviews during June and July 1992 with business leaders such as José Antonio Guzmán (CPC), Manuel Feliú (CPC); Pedro Lizana (SFF), Raúl García (SNA), Alfonso Mujica (CNC). Sergio Molina speech at a Seminar on the United Nations Development Programme's *Human Development Report, 1992*, Ex Congreso Nacional, July 16, 1992.

71. Alfred Stepan, *Rethinking Military Politics: Brazil and the Southern Cone* (Princeton: Princeton University Press, 1988); Brian Loveman, *¿Misión Cumplida?*.

72. The vehement opposition of capitalists to even the mention of constitutional change in 1992 underscores the point. Conservative political parties fully share their concerns, further highlighting the difficulties that reformists encounter in Chile's new democracy.

# Acronyms

| | |
|---|---|
| ABIF | Asociación de Bancos e Instituciones Financieras |
| AD | Alianza Democrática |
| BHC | Banco Hipotecario de Chile |
| CAPA | Comité Asesor de Política Arancelaria |
| CCC | Cámara Central de Comercio |
| CCU | Compañía Cervecerías Unidas |
| CChC | Cámara Chilena de la Construcción |
| CMPC | Compañía Manufacturera de Papeles y Cartones |
| CODE | Confederación Democrática |
| COPEC | Compañía de Pertóleos de Chile |
| CORFO | Corporación de Fomento |
| CNC | Cámara Nacional de Comercio |
| CPC | Confederación de la Producción y Comercio |
| CUT | Central Unica de Trabajadores |
| FRENAP | Frente Nacional de la Propiedad Privada |
| GATT | General Agreement on Trade and Tariffs |
| GDP | Gross Domestic Product |
| IMF | International Monetary Fund |
| ISI | Import-Substitution Industrialization |
| JAP | Junta de Abastecimiento Popular |
| MDP | Movimiento Democrático Popular |
| MNC | Multinational Corporation |
| ODEPLAN | Oficina Nacional de Planificación |
| PAIS | Partido Amplio de Izquierda Socialista |
| PDC | Partido Demócrata Christiano |
| RN | Renovación Nacional |
| SEC | Social and Economic Council |
| SFF | Sociedad de Fomento Fabril |
| SNA | Sociedad Nacional de Agricultura |
| SONAMI | Sociedad Nacional de Minería |
| UDI | Unión Democrática Independiente |
| UF | Unidad de Fomento |
| UP | Unidad Popular |
| VAT | Value Added Tax |

# Selected References

## Books and Articles

Ahumada, Jorge. *En vez de la miseria*. Santiago: Editorial del Pacífico, 1958.

Almond, Gabriel and Bingham Powell. *Comparative Politics*. Boston: Little, Brown, 1966.

*American Sociological Review* 55, June 1990.

Amsden, Alice. *Asia's Next Giant: South Korea and Late Industrialization*. New York: Oxford University Press, 1989.

Anderson, Charles W. *Politics and Economic Change in Latin America: The Governing of Restless Nations*. New York: D. Van Nostrand, 1967.

Angell, Alan. "Can Social Sector Reform Make Adjustment Sustainable and Equitable? Lessons from Chile and Venezuela," *Journal of Latin American Studies* 27, 3, 1995.

Angell, Alan and Benny Pollack, eds. *The Legacy of Dictatorship: Political, Economic, and Social Change in Pinochet's Chile*. Liverpool: The University of Liverpool, Institute of Latin American Studies, Monograph Series, no. 17, 1993.

Arellano, José Pablo. "Crisis y recuperación económica en Chile en los años 80." *Colección Estudios Cieplan* no. 24, 1988.

_____. "La difícil salida al problema del endeudamiento interno." *Colección Estudios Cieplan* no. 13, 1984.

_____. "De la liberalización a la intervención: El mercado de capitales en Chile, 1974-1982." *Colección Estudios Cieplan* no. 11, 1983.

_____. "Sistemas alternativos de seguridad social: Un análisis de la experiencia chilena." *Colección Estudios Cieplan* no. 4, 1980.

Arellano, José Pablo and Manuel Marfán. "25 años de política fiscal en Chile." *Colección Estudios Cieplan* no. 21, 1987.

_____. "Ahorro, inversión y relaciones financieras en la actual crisis económica chilena." *Colección Estudios Cieplan* no. 20, 1986.

Arriagada, Genaro. *La oligarquía patronal chilena*. Santiago: Ediciones Nueva Universidad, 1970.

Aylwin, Mariana et al. *Chile en el siglo XX*. Santiago: Emisión, n.d.

Baltra, Alberto. *Gestión económica del gobierno de la Unidad Popular*. Santiago: Editorial Orbe, n.d.

Bauer, Arnold J. "Industry and the Missing Bourgeoisie: Consumption and Development in Chile, 1850-1950," *Hispanic American Research Review* 70, 2, 1990.

_____. *Chilean Rural Society from the Spanish Conquest to 1930*. New York: Cambridge University Press, 1975.

Baytelman, David. "Problems of Collective Land Exploitation in Chilean Agriculture." In Federico Gil, Ricardo Lagos, and Henry A. Landsberger, eds., *Chile at the Turning Point: Lessons of the Socialist Years, 1970-1973*. Philadelphia: Institute for the Study of Human Issues, 1979.

Berger, Suzanne, ed. *Organizing Interests in Western Europe*. New York: Cambridge University Press, 1981.

Bitar, Sergio. "The Interrelationship between Economics and Politics." In Federico Gil, Ricardo Lagos, and Henry A. Landsberger, eds., *Chile at the Turning Point: Lessons of the Socialist Years, 1970-1973*. Philadelphia: Institute for the Study of Human Issues, 1979.

Blondel, Jean. *Political Parties*. London: Wildwood House, 1978.

Bottomore, T.B. *Elites and Society*. New York: Basic Books, 1964.

Bresser Pereira, Luiz Carlos, José María Maravall, and Adam Przeworski. *Economic Reforms in New Democracies: A Social Democratic Approach*. Cambridge: Cambridge University Press, 1993.

Business Latin America. *Trading in Latin America: The Impact of Changing Policies*. New York: n.p., 1981.

Campero, Guillermo. *Los gremios empresariales en el período 1970-1983: Comportamiento sociopolítico y orientaciones ideológicas*. Santiago: Instituto Latinoamericano de Estudios Transnacionales, 1984.

Campero, Guillermo and José A. Valenzuela. *El movimiento sindical en el régimen militar chileno, 1973-1981*. Santiago: Instituto Latinoamericano de Estudios Transnacionales, 1984.

Canak, William L. *Lost Promises: Debt, Austerity, and Development in Latin America*. Boulder: Westview, 1989.

Cardoso, Fernando Henrique. "Entrepreneurs and the Transition to Democracy in Brazil." In Guillermo O'Donnell, Philippe C. Schmitter, and Laurence Whitehead, eds., *Transitions from Authoritarian Rule: Comparative Perspectives*. Baltimore: Johns Hopkins University Press, 1986.

_____. *Dependency and Development in Latin America*. Berkeley: University of California Press, 1978.

_____. *Las ideologías de la burguesía industrial en sociedades dependientes: Argentina y Brasil*. México: Siglo XXI, 1971.

Carriere, Jean. *Landowners and Politics in Chile: A Study of the Sociedad Nacional de Agricultura, 1932-1970*. Amsterdam: Centrum voor Studie en Documentatie von Latijns-Amerika, 1981.

Castañeda, Tarsicio. *Combating Poverty: Innovative Social Reforms in Chile During the 1980s*. San Francisco: International Center for Economic Growth, 1992.

Castillo Velasco, Jaime. *Las fuentes de la Democracia Cristiana*. Santiago: Editorial del Pacífico, 1963.

Cauas, Jorge and Sergio de la Cuadra. "La política económica de la apertura al exterior en Chile." *Cuadernos de Economía de la Universidad de Chile*, August-December, 1981.

Cavallo, Ascanio, Manuel Salazar, and Oscar Sepúlveda. *La historia oculta del régimen militar*. Santiago: Editorial La Epoca, 1988.

Caviedes, César N. *Elections in Chile: The Road Toward Redemocratization*. Boulder: Lynne Rienner, 1991.

Centro de Estudios del Desarrollo. *Concertación Social y Democracia*. Santiago: CED, 1985.

Centro de Estudios Públicos. *"El Ladrillo": Bases de la política económica del gobierno militar chileno*. Santiago: Centro de Estudios Públicos, 1992.

Centro para el Desarrollo Económico y Social de América Latina. *América latina y desarrollo social*. Santiago: n.p., 1965.

Chalmers, Douglas and Craig Robinson. "Why Power Contenders Choose Liberalization." *International Studies Quarterly* 26, 1, 1982.

Collier, David. *The New Authoritarianism in Latin America*. Princeton: Princeton University Press, 1979.

_____. "The Bureaucratic-Authoritarian Model: Synthesis and Priorities for Future Research." In David Collier, ed., *The New Authoritarianism in Latin America*. Princeton: Princeton University Press, 1979.

Conaghan, Catherine M. *Restructuring Domination: Industrialists and the State in Ecuador*. Pittsburgh: University of Pittsburgh Press, 1988.

Conaghan, Catherine M. and Rosario Espinal. "Unlikely Transitions to Uncertain Regimes? Democracy without Compromise in the Dominican Republic and Ecuador." *Journal of Latin American Studies* 22, 3, 1990.

Conaghan, Catherine M., James Malloy, and Luis Abugattas. "Business and the Boys: The Politics of Neoliberalism in the Central Andes." *Latin American Research Review* 25, 2, 1990.

Conniff, Michael L., ed. *Latin American Populism in Comparative Perspective*. Albuquerque: University of New Mexico Press, 1982.

Correa Prieto, Luis. *El Presidente Ibáñez: La política y los políticos*. Santiago: Editorial Orbe, 1962.

Crouch, Colin, ed. *State and Economy in Contemporary Capitalism*. New York: St. Martin's Press, 1979.

Dahl, Robert. *Polyarchy: Participation and Opposition*. New Haven: Yale University Press, 1971.

Dahse, Fernando. "El poder de los grandes grupos empresariales nacionales." *Contribuciones FLACSO*, June 1983.

_____. El mapa de la extrema riqueza. Santiago: Editorial Aconcagua, 1979.

De la Cuadra, Sergio and Salvador Valdés. "Myths and Facts about Instability in Financial Liberalization in Chile: 1974-1983." In Philip L. Brock, ed., *If Texas Were Chile: Financial Risk and Regulation in Commodity Exporting Economies*. San Francisco: Institute for Contemporary Studies, 1992.

Deyo, Fredric C. *The Political Economy of the New Asian Industrialism*. Ithaca: Cornell University Press, 1987

Di Tella, Torcuato. "Populism and Reform in Latin America." In Claudio Véliz, ed. *Obstacles to Change in Latin America*. London: Oxford University Press, 1965.

Di Palma, Giuseppe. *To Craft Democracies: An Essay on Democratic Transitions*. Berkeley: University of California Press, 1990.

Domhoff, William G. *The Power Elite and the State: How Policy Is Made in America*. New York: Aldine de Gruyter, 1990.

Dooner, Patricio. *Periodismo y política: La prensa de derecha e izquierda*. Santiago: Editorial Andante, 1989.

Dos Santos, Theodonio. "The Structure of Dependence." *American Economic Review* 60, May 1970.

Drake, Paul W. *The Money Doctor in the Andes: The Kemmerer Missions, 1923-1933*. Durham: Duke University Press, 1989.

_____. *Socialism and Populism in Chile, 1932-52*. Urbana: University of Illinois Press, 1978.

_____. "The Political Responses of the Chilean Upper Class to the Great Depression and the Threat of Socialism." In Frederic Cople Jaher, ed., *The Rich, the Well Born and the Powerful.* Urbana: University of Illinois Press, 1973.

Drake, Paul W., ed. *Money Doctors, Foreign Debts, and Economic Reforms in Latin America from the 1980s to the Present.* Wilmington: Scholarly Resources, 1994.

Drake, Paul W. and Iván Jaksic, eds. *The Struggle for Democracy in Chile, 1982-1990.* Lincoln: University of Nebraska Press, 1991.

Drake, Paul W. and Eduardo Silva, eds. *Elections and Democratization in Latin America, 1980-85.* San Diego: Center for Iberian and Latin American Studies, Center for U.S.-Mexican Studies, Institute of the Americas, 1986.

Edwards, Sebastian and Alejandra Cox-Edwards. *Monetarism and Liberalization: The Chilean Experiment.* Cambridge: Ballinger, 1987.

Ellsworth, P.T. *Chile: An Economy in Transition.* New York: Macmillan, 1945.

Epstein, Edward C. "Legitimacy, Institutionalization, and Opposition in Exclusionary Bureaucratic-Authoritarian Regimes: The Situation of the 1980s." *Comparative Politics* 17, 1, 1984.

Espinoza, Juan G. and Andrew Zimbalist. *Economic Democracy: Worker's Participation in Urban Industry, 1970-73.* New York: Academic Press, 1978.

Evans, Peter. *Dependent Development: The Alliance of Multinational, State, and Local Capital in Brazil.* Princeton: Princeton University Press, 1979.

Evans, Peter, Dietrich Rueschmeyer, and Theda Skocpol, eds. *Bringing the State Back In.* New York: Cambridge University Press, 1985.

Falcoff, Mark. *Modern Chile.* New Brunswick: Transaction, 1989.

Ffrench-Davis, Ricardo. "El problema de la deuda externa y la apertura financiera en Chile." *Colección Estudios Cieplan* no. 11, 1983.

_____. *Políticas económicas en Chile, 1952-1970.* Santiago: Ediciones Nueva Universidad, 1973.

Finer, F.E., ed. *Vilfredo Pareto: Selected Writings.* New York: Praeger, 1966.

Fleet, Michael. *The Rise and Fall of Chilean Christian Democracy.* Princeton: Princeton University Press, 1985.

Fontaine, Arturo. *Los economistas y el Presidente Pinochet.* Santiago: Editora Zig-Zag, 1988, second edition.

Foxley, Alejandro. *Latin American Experiments in Neoconservative Economics.* Berkeley: University of California Press, 1983.

_____. *Reconstrucción económica para la democracia.* Santiago: Editorial Aconcagua, 1983.

_____. "Algunas condiciones para una democratización estable: El caso de Chile." *Colección Estudios Cieplan* no. 9, 1982.

Frank, Andre Gunder. *Capitalism and Underdevelopment in Latin America.* New York: Monthly Review Press, 1967.

Frieden, Jeffry. *Debt, Development, and Democracy: Modern Political Economy and Latin America, 1965-1985.* Princeton: Princeton University Press, 1991.

_____. "Winners and Losers in the Latin American Debt Crisis: The Political Implications." In Barbara Stallings and Robert Kaufman, eds., *Debt and Democracy in Latin America.* Boulder: Westview, 1989.

_____. "Classes, Sectors, and Foreign Debt in Latin America." *Comparative Politics* 21, 1, 1988.

Furtado, Celso. *Economic Development of Latin America: Historical Background and Contemporary Problems.* New York: Cambridge University Press, 1976, second edition.

Garcés, Joan E. *Allende y la experiencia chilena.* Barcelona: Editorial Ariel, 1976.

García, Alvaro. "Crecimiento equitativo: Políticas de empleo e ingresos." *Centro de Estudios del Desarrollo,* Materiales para Discusión no. 191, 1987.

García, Pío. "The Social Property Sector: Its Political Impact." In Federico Gil, Ricardo Lagos, and Henry A. Landsberger, eds., *Chile at the Turning Point: Lessons of the Socialist Years, 1970-1973.* Philadelphia: Institute for the Study of Human Issues, 1979.

Garretón, Manuel Antonio. *The Chilean Political Process.* Boston: Unwin Hyman, 1989.

_____. *Reconstruir la política: Transición y consolidación democrática en Chile.* Santiago: Editorial Andante, 1987.

Garretón, Manuel Antonio and Tomás Moulián. "Procesos y bloques políticos en la crisis chilena." *Revista Mexicana de Sociología* 41, 1, 1979.

Garretón, Oscar Guillermo. "Concentración monopólica en Chile: Participación del estado y de los trabajadores en la gestión económica." In, n.a., *Economía política en la Unidad Popular.* Santiago: Editorial Fontanella, 1975.

Gatica Barros, Jaime. *Deindustrialization in Chile.* Boulder: Westview, 1989.

Geddes, Barbara. "The Politics of Economic Liberalization," *Latin American Research Review* 30, 2, 1995.

Gerschenkron, Alexander. *Economic Backwardness in Historical Perspective.* Cambridge: Belknap Press of Harvard University Press, 1962.

Gil, Federico. *The Political System of Chile.* Boston: Houghton-Mifflin, 1966.

Gil, Federico, Ricardo Lagos, and Henry A. Landsberger, eds. *Chile at the Turning Point: Lessons of the Socialist Years, 1970-1973.* Philadelphia: Institute for the Study of Human Issues, 1979.

Goldstein, Judith. "The Political Economy of Trade: Institutions of Protection." *American Political Science Review* 80, 1, 1986.

Gómez, Sergio. "Organizaciones rurales y políticas estatales en Chile: Coyunturas de conflictos y de consensos." *FLACSO,* Documento de Trabajo no. 392, 1988.

_____. "Polémicas recientes sobre el sector agrario." *FLACSO,* Documento de Trabajo no. 294, 1986.

_____. "Nuevos empresarios y empresas agrícolas en Chile." *FLACSO,* Documento de Trabajo no. 277, 1986.

_____. *Los empresarios agrícolas.* Santiago: Instituto de Capacitación e Investigación en Reforma Agraria, 1972.

Gourevitch, Peter A.. *Politics in Hard Times: Comparative Responses to International Crises.* Ithaca: Cornell University Press, 1986.

_____. "Breaking with Orthodoxy: The Politics of Economic Policy Responses to the Great Depression of the 1930s." *International Organization* 38, 1, 1984.

_____. "The Second Image Reversed: The International Sources of Domestic Politics." *International Organization* 32, 4, 1978.

_____. "International Trade, Domestic Coalitions, and Liberty: Comparative Responses to the Crisis of 1873-1896." *Journal of Interdisciplinary History* 8, 2, 1977.

Graham, Carol. "From Emergency Employment to Social Investment: Changing Approaches to Poverty Alleviation in Chile." In Alan Angell and Benny Pollack, eds., *The Legacy of Dictatorship: Political, Economic, and Social Change in Pinochet's Chile*. Liverpool: The University of Liverpool, Institute of Latin American Studies, Monograph Series, no. 17, 1993.

Grayson Jr., George. "Chile's Christian Democratic Party: Power, Factions, and Ideology," *Review of Politics* 31, 1, 1969.

_____. El Partido Demócrata Cristiano chileno. Buenos Aires: Editorial Francisco Aguirre, 1968.

Griffith-Jones, Stephany and Osvaldo Sunkel. *La cisis de la deuda y del desarrollo en América Latina: El fin de una ilusión*. Buenos Aires: Grupo Editor Latinoamericano, 1987.

Grunwald, Joseph, ed. *Latin America and the World Economy: A Changing International Order*. Beverly Hills: Sage Publications, 1978.

Haggard, Stephan. *Pathways from the Periphery: The Politics of Growth in Newly Industrializing Countries*. Ithaca: Cornell University Press, 1990.

Haggard, Stephan and Robert Kaufman, eds. *The Politics of Economic Adjustment: International Constraints, Distributive Conflicts, and the State*. Princeton: Princeton University Press, 1992.

Hall, Peter A., ed. *The Political Power of Economic Ideas: Keynesianism across Nations*. Princeton: Princeton University Press, 1989.

Hamilton, Nora. *The Limits of State Autonomy: Post-Revolutionary Mexico*. Princeton: Princeton University Press, 1982.

Handelman, Howard and Thomas G. Sanders. *Military Government and the Movement Toward Democracy in Latin America*. Bloomington: University of Indiana Press, 1981.

Hartlyn, Jonathan and Samuel A. Morley. *Latin American Political Economy: Financial Crisis and Political Change*. Boulder: Westview, 1986.

Hirschman, Albert. *Journeys Toward Progress*. Garden City: Doubleday, 1966.

Hojman, David E. *Chile: The Political Economy of Development and Democracy in the 1990s*. Pittsburgh: University of Pittsburgh Press, 1993.

Hurtado, Carlos. *De Balmaceda a Pinochet: Cien años de desarrollo y subdesarrollo en Chile, y una disgresión al futuro*. Santiago: Ediciones Logo, 1988.

Ianni, Octavio. *Crisis in Brazil*. New York: Columbia University Press, 1970.

Ikenberry, John G. "The Irony of State Strength: Comparative Responses to the Oil Shocks of the 1970s." *International Organization* 40, 1, 1986.

Ionescu, Ghita and Ernest Gellner. *Populism: Its Meanings and National Characteristics*. New York: Macmillan, 1969.

Jeannerette, Teresa. "El sistema de protección a la industria chilena." In Oscar Muñoz, ed., *Proceso a la industrialización chilena*. Santiago: Ediciones Nueva Universidad, 1972.

Jobet, Julio César. *Ensayo crítico del desarrollo económico-social de Chile*. Santiago: Editorial Universitaria, 1955.

Johnson, Dale L. "Dependence and the International System." In James D. Crockcroft, Andre Gunder Frank, and Dale L. Johnson, eds., *Dependence and Underdevelopment: Latin America's Political Economy*. Garden City: Anchor Books, 1972.

Kahler, Miles, ed. *The Politics of International Debt*. Ithaca: Cornell University Press, 1986.

Katzenstein, Peter J. *Small States in World Markets: Industrial Policy in Europe.* Ithaca: Cornell University Press, 1985.

_____. editor. *Between Power and Plenty: Foreign Economic Policies of Advanced Industrial States.* Madison: University of Wisconsin Press, 1978.

Kaufman, Edy. *Crisis in Allende's Chile: New Perspectives.* New York: Praeger, 1988.

Kaufman, Robert R. "Liberalization and Democratization in South America: Perspectives from the 1970s." In Guillermo O'Donnell, Philippe C. Schmitter, and Laurence Whitehead, eds., *Transitions from Authoritarian Rule: Comparative Perspectives.* Baltimore: Johns Hopkins University Press, 1986.

_____. "Industrial Change and Authoritarian Rule in Latin America: A Concrete Review of the Bureaucratic-Authoritarian Model." In David Collier, ed., *The New Authoritarianism in Latin America.* Princeton: Princeton University Press, 1979.

_____. *The Politics of Land Reform in Chile, 1950-1970.* Cambridge: Harvard University Press, 1972.

_____. *The Chilean Political Right and Agrarian Reform.* Washington D.C.: Institute for the Comparative Study of Political Systems, 1967.

Kay, Cristóbal. "Agrarian Reform and the Transition to Socialism." In Philip O'Brien, ed. *Allende's Chile.* New York: Praeger Publishers, 1976.

Kay, Cristóbal and Patricio Silva, eds. *Development and Social Change in the Chilean Countryside: From the Pre-Land Reform Period to the Democratic Transition.* Amsterdam: Centrum voor Studie en Documentatie von Latijns-Amerika, 1992.

Kirsch, Henry W. *Industrial Development in a Traditional Society: The Conflict of Entrepreneurship and Modernization in Chile.* Gainesville: University of Florida Press, 1977.

Krasner, Stephen. "Sovereignty: An Institutional Perspective." In James Caporaso, ed., *The Elusive State.* Newbury Park: Sage, 1989.

_____. *Defending the National Interest: Raw Materials Investments and U.S. Foreign Policy.* Princeton: Princeton University Press, 1978.

Landsberger, Henry and Tim McDaniel. "Hypermobilization in Chile, 1970-73." *World Politics* 28, 4, 1976.

Larraín, Felipe. "The Economic Challenges of Democratic Development." In Paul Drake and Iván Jaksic, eds., *The Struggle for Democracy in Chile, 1982-1990.* Lincoln: University of Nebraska Press, 1991.

_____. *Desarrollo económico en democracia.* Santiago: Ediciones Universidad Católica de Chile, 1988.

Latin American Studies Association. "The Chilean Plebiscite: A First Step Toward Redemocratization" *LASA Forum* 19, 4, 1989.

Lijphart, Arend. *Democracies: Patterns of Majoritarian and Consensus Government in Twenty-One Countries.* New Haven: Yale University Press, 1984.

_____. "The Comparable Cases Strategy in Comparative Research." *Comparative Political Studies* 8, 2, 1975.

_____. "Comparative Politics and the Comparative Method." *American Political Science Review* 65, 3, 1971.

Lindblom, Charles. *Politics and Markets.* New York: Basic Books, 1977.

Linz, Juan. "An Authoritarian Regime: Spain." In Erik Allardt and Yrjo Littunen, eds., *Cleavages, Ideologies, and Party Systems.* Helsinki: Academic Bookstore, 1964.

Loveman, Brian. *The Constitution of Tyranny: Regimes of Exception in Spanish America*. Pittsburgh: University of Pittsburgh Press, 1994.

_____. *Chile: The Legacy of Hispanic Capitalism*. New York: Oxford University Press, 1979.

_____. *Struggle in the Countryside: Politics and Rural Labor in Chile, 1919-1973*. Bloomington: Indiana University Press, 1976.

Maira, Luis. "The Strategy and Tactics of the Chilean Counterrevolution in the Area of Political Institutions." In Federico Gil, Ricardo Lagos, and Henry A. Landsberger, eds., *Chile at the Turning Point: Lessons of the Socialist Years, 1970-1973*. Philadelphia: Institute for the Study of Human Issues, 1979.

Malloy, James M., ed. *Authoritarianism and Corporatism in Latin America*. Pittsburgh: University of Pittsburgh Press, 1977.

Mamalakis, Markos J. *Historical Statistics of Chile*. Westport: Greenwood, 1978-1989.

_____. *Growth and Structure of the Chilean Economy: From Independence to Allende*. New Haven: Yale University Press, 1976.

_____. "La teoría de los choques entre sectores." *Universidad de Chile: Instituto de Economía*, publicación no. 83, 1966.

Mann, Michael. *The Sources of Social Power, Volume 1*. Cambridge: Cambridge University Press, 1986.

Marfán, Manuel. "Una evaluación de la nueva reforma tributaria." *Colección Estudios Cieplan* no. 13, 1984.

Maritain, Jaques. *Christianity and Democracy*. Santiago: Charles Scribner's Sons, 1947.

Martner, Gonzalo. *El gobierno del Presidente Salvador Allende, 1970-1973*. Concepción: Ediciones LAR, 1988.

Maxfield, Sylvia. *Governing Capital: International Finance and Mexican Politics*. Ithaca: Cornell University Press, 1990.

_____. "National Business, Debt-Led Growth, and Political Transition." In Barbara Stallings and Robert Kaufman, eds., *Debt and Democracy in Latin America*. Boulder: Westview, 1989.

McDaniel, Tim. "Class and Dependency in Latin America." *Berkeley Journal of Sociology* 21, 1976-77.

Menges, Constantine. "Public Policy and Organized Business in Chile: A Preliminary Analysis." *Journal of International Affairs* 20, 2, 1966.

Migdal, Joel. *Strong Societies and Weak States: State-Society Relations in the Third World*. Princeton: Princeton University Press, 1988.

Miliband, Ralph. *The State in Capitalist Society*. New York: Basic Books, 1969.

Millán, René. *Los empresarios ante el estado y la sociedad*. Mexico: Siglo XXI Editores, 1988.

Mizala, Alejandra. "Liberalización financiera y quiebra de empresas industriales: Chile, 1977-82." *Notas Técnicas Cieplan* no. 67, 1985.

Molina, Sergio. "El compromiso de Chile: Construir un orden social justo." *Centro de Estudios del Desarrollo*, Materiales para Discusión no. 200, 1987.

Monteón, Michael. *Chile in the Nitrate Era: The Evolution of Economic Dependence, 1880-1930*. Madison: University of Wisconsin Press, 1982.

Moore, Barrington, Jr. *The Social Origins of Dictatorship and Democracy: Lord and Peasant in the Making of the Modern World*. Boston: Beacon, 1966.

Moran, Theodore H. *Multinational Corporations and the Politics of Dependence: Copper in Chile*. Princeton: Princeton University Press, 1974.

Mosca, Gaetano. *The Ruling Class*. New York: McGraw Hill, 1939.

Moulián, Tomás. "Las fases del desarrollo político chileno entre 1973 y 1978. *FLACSO Chile*, Documento de Trabajo no. 155, 1982.

Moulián, Tomás and Pilar Vergara. "Ideología y política económica." *Colección Estudios Cieplan* no. 9, 1980.

Moulián, Tomás and Isabel Torres Dujisin. *Discusiones entre honorables: Las candidaturas presidenciales de la derecha, 1938-1946*. Santiago: FLACSO, n.d.

Movimiento de Acción Unitario Popular. *El libro de las 91: Las empresas monopólicas y el área social de la economía chilena*. Santiago: Ediciones Barco de Papel, 1972.

Muñoz, Oscar. "El desarrollo de las relaciones estado-empresa en el nuevo escenario económico: Dos ensayos." *Apuntes Cieplan* no. 106, 1991.

_____. editor. *Proceso a la industrialización chilena*. Santiago: Ediciones Nueva Universidad, 1972.

_____. editor. *Crecimiento industrial de Chile, 1914-1965*. Santiago: Universidad de Chile, Instituto de Economía y Planificación, segunda edición, 1971.

Muñoz, Oscar and Ana María Arriagada. "Orígenes políticos y económicos del estado empresarial en Chile." *Estudios Cieplan* no. 16, 1977.

Nordlinger, Eric A., Theodore J. Lowi, and Sergio Fabrini. "The Return to the State: Critiques." *American Political Science Review* 82, 3, 1988.

Nove, Alec. "The Political Economy of the Allende Regime." In Philip O'Brien, ed., *Allende's Chile*. New York: Praeger Publishers, 1976.

Novoa, Eduardo. "Vías legales para avanzar hacia el socialismo." *Revista Mensaje*, 1971.

O'Brien, Philip. *The Pinochet Decade*. London: Latin American Bureau, 1983.

_____. editor. *Allende's Chile*. New York: Praeger Publishers, 1976.

O'Brien, Philip and Paul Cammack, eds. *Generals in Retreat: The Crisis of Military Rule in Latin America*. Manchester: Manchester University Press, 1985.

O'Brien, Tomas F. *The Nitrate Industry and Chile's Crucial Transition: 1870-1891*. New York: New York University Press, 1982.

O'Donnell, Guillermo. *Delegative Democracy*. South Bend: University of Notre Dame Press, 1992.

_____. "Reflections on the Patterns of Change in the Bureaucratic-Authoritarian State." *Latin American Research Review* 12, 1, 1978.

_____. "Corporatism and the Question of the State." In James M. Malloy, ed., *Authoritarianism and Corporatism in Latin America*. Pittsburgh: University of Pittsburgh Press, 1977.

_____. *Modernization and Bureaucratic-Authoritarianism: Studies in South American Politics*. Berkeley: Institute of International Studies, University of California, 1973.

O'Donnell, Guillermo and Philippe C. Schmitter. *Transitions from Authoritarian Rule: Tentative Conclusions about Uncertain Processes*. Baltimore: Johns Hopkins University Press, 1986.

O'Donnell, Guillermo, Philippe C. Schmitter, and Laurence Whitehead, eds. *Transitions from Authoritarian Rule: Comparative Perspectives*. Baltimore: Johns Hopkins University Press, 1986.

Offe, Claus and H. Wiesenthal. "The Two Logics of Collective Action: Theoretical Notes on Social Class and the Political Form of Interest Representation."

*Political Power and Social Theory* 1, 1, 1980.

Oppenheim, Lois Hecht. *Politics in Chile: Democracy, Authoritarianism, and the Search for Development.* Boulder: Westview, 1993.

Petras, James F. *Latin America: Bankers, Generals, and the Struggle for Social Justice.* Totowa: Rowman and Littlefield, 1986.

_____. "Nationalization, Socioeconomic Change, and Popular Participation." In Arturo Valenzuela and Samuel Valenzuela, eds., *Chile: Politics and Society.* New Brunswick: Transaction Books, 1976.

_____. *Politics and Social Forces in Chilean Development.* Berkeley: University of California Press, 1970.

Petras, James and Fernando Ignacio Leiva, with Henry Veltmeyer. *Democracy and Poverty in Chile: The Limits to Electoral Politics.* Boulder: Westview, 1994.

Pike, Frederick B. *Chile and the United States, 1880-1962.* Notre Dame: University of Notre Dame Press, 1965.

Portes, Alejandro and Douglas Kincaid. "The Crisis of Authoritarianism." *Research in Political Sociology,* 1, n.n., 1985.

Poulantzas, Nicos. *Political Power and Social Classes.* London: New Left Books, 1973.

Prats, Carlos. *Memorias: Testamento de un soldado.* Santiago: Pehuén Editores, 1985.

Programa de Economía para América Latina y el Caribe. "Monetarismo global y respuesta industrial: El caso de Chile." *Prealc,* Documento de Trabajo no. 232, 1984.

*Proyecto alternativo.* Santiago: Editorial Aconcagua, 1984, three volumes.

Przeworski, Adam. "Some Problems in the Study of Transitions to Democracy." In Guillermo O'Donnell, Philippe C. Schmitter, and Laurence Whitehead, eds., *Transitions from Authoritarian Rule: Comparative Perspectives.* Baltimore: Johns Hopkins University Press, 1986.

Puryear, Jeffrey M. *Thinking Politics: Intellectuals and Democracy in Chile, 1973-1988.* Baltimore: Johns Hopkins University Press, 1994.

Putnam, Robert D. *The Comparative Study of Political Elites.* Englewood Cliffs: Prentice Hall, 1976.

Raczynski, Dagmar. "Reformas al sector salud: Diálogos y debates." *Colección Estudios Cieplan* no. 10, 1983.

Ramos, Joseph. *Neoconservative Economics in the Southern Cone.* Baltimore: Johns Hopkins University Press, 1986.

Remmer, Karen and Gilbert Merkx. "Bureaucratic-Authoritarianism Revisited." *Latin American Research Review* 17, 2, 1982.

Reyna, José Luis and Richard S. Weinert, eds. *Authoritarianism in Mexico.* Philadelphia: Institute for the Study of Human Issues, 1977.

Risse-Kappen, Thomas. "Public Opinion, Domestic Structure, and Foreign Policy in Liberal Democracies." *World Politics* 43, 4, 1991.

Rogowski, Ronald. *Commerce and Coalitions: How Trade Affects Domestic Political Alignments.* Princeton: Princeton University Press, 1989.

_____. "Political Cleavages and Changing Exposure to Trade." *American Political Science Review* 81, 4, 1987.

Rojas, Alejandro. *La transformación del estado: La experiencia de la Unidad Popular.* Santiago: Ediciones Documentas, 1987.

Roxborough, Ian. "The Chilean Opposition to Allende." In Philip O'Brien, ed., *Allende's Chile.* New York: Praeger, 1976.

Roxborough, Ian, Philip O'Brien, and Jackie Roddick, eds. *Chile: The State and Revolution*. London: Macmillan, 1977.

Rozas, Patrico and Gustavo Marín. *El mapa de la extrema riqueza: 10 años después*. Santiago: Ediciones Chile-América, 1989.

Ruiz-Tagle, Jaime. *El sindicalismo chileno después del plan laboral*. Santiago: Programa en Economía y Trabajo, 1985.

Rustow, Dankwart. "Transitions to Democracy: Toward a Dynamic Model." *Comparative Politics* 2, 3, 1970.

Sanfuentes, Andrés. "Los grupos económicos: Control y políticas." *Colección Estudios Cieplan* no. 15, 1984.

Santa Lucía, Patricia. "The Industrial Working Class and the Struggle for Power in Chile." In Philip O'Brien, ed., *Allende's Chile*. New York: Praeger, 1976.

Sartori, Giovanni. "European Political Parties: The Case of Polarized Pluralism." In Joseph Lapalombara and Myron Weiner, eds., *Political Parties and Development*. Princeton: Princeton University Press, 1966.

Schamis, Hector E. "Reconceptualizing Latin American Authoritarianism in the 1970s: From Bureaucratic-Authoritarianism to Neoconservatism." *Comparative Politics* 23, 2, 1991.

Schmitter, Philippe C. "Still the Century of Corporatism?" *The Review of Politics* 36, 1, 1974.

_____. *Interest Conflict and Political Change in Brazil*. Stanford: Stanford University Press, 1971.

Schneider, Ben Ross. "The Career Connection: A Comparative Analysis of Bureaucratic Preferences and Insulation." *Comparative Politics* 25, 3, 1993.

Scully, Timothy R. *Rethinking the Center: Party Politics in Nineteenth and Twentieth Century Chile*. Stanford: Stanford University Press, 1992.

Sigmund, Paul E. *Multinationals in Latin America: The Politics of Nationalization*. Madison: University of Wisconsin Press, 1980.

_____. *The Overthrow of Allende and the Politics of Chile, 1964-1976*. Pittsburgh: University of Pittsburgh Press, 1977.

Silva, Patricio. "Technocrats and Politics in Chile: From the Chicago Boys to the Cieplan Monks." *Journal of Latin American Studies* 23, 2, 1991.

Skidmore, Thomas. *The Politics of Military Rule in Brazil*. New York: Oxford University Press, 1988.

_____. *Politics in Brazil, 1930-1964: An Experiment in Democracy*. New York: Oxford University Press, 1967.

Skocpol, Theda. *States and Social Revolutions: A Comparative Analysis of France, Russia, and China*. Cambridge: Cambridge University Press, 1979.

Smith, Peter H. "Crisis and Democracy in Latin America." *World Politics* 43, 4, 1991.

Smith, William C. *Authoritarianism and the Crisis of the Argentine Political Economy*. Stanford: Stanford University Press, 1989.

Smith, William C., Carlos H. Acuña, and Eduardo Gamarra, eds. *Latin American Political Economy in the Age of Neoliberal Reform: Theoretical and Comparative Perspectives for the 1990s*. New Brunswick: Transaction, 1994.

Spalding, Rose J. *Capitalists and Revolution in Nicaragua: Opposition and Accommodation, 1979-1993*. Chapel Hill: University of North Carolina Press, 1994.

Spooner, Mary Helen. *Soldiers in a Narrow Land: The Pinochet Regime in Chile*. Berkeley: University of California Press, 1994.

Stallings, Barbara. "Political Economy of Democratic Transition: Chile in the 1980s." In Barbara Stallings and Robert Kaufman, eds., *Debt and Democracy in Latin America*. Boulder: Westview, 1989.

———. *Banker to the Third World: U.S. Portfolio Investment in Latin America, 1900-1986*. Berkeley: University of California Press, 1987.

———. *Class Conflict and Development in Chile*. Stanford: Stanford University Press, 1978.

Stallings, Barbara and Robert Kaufman, eds. *Debt and Democracy in Latin America*. Boulder: Westview, 1989.

Stepan, Alfred. "The New Professionalism of Internal Warfare and Military Role Expansion." In Alfred Stepan, ed., *Authoritarian Brazil: Origins, Policies, and Future*. New Haven: Yale University Press, 1973.

Stevenson, John Reese. *The Chilean Popular Front*. Westport: Greenwood, 1945.

Sunkel, Guillermo. *El Mercurio: Diez años de educación político-ideológica, 1969-1979*. Santiago: Instituto Latinoamericano de Estudios Transnacionales, 1983.

Tapia Videla, Jorge. "The Difficult Road to Socialism: The Chilean Case from a Historical Perspective." In Federico Gil, Ricardo Lagos, and Henry A. Landsberger, eds., *Chile at the Turning Point: Lessons of the Socialist Years, 1970-1973*. Philadelphia: Institute for the Study of Human Issues, 1979.

Threlfall, Monica. "Shantytown Dwellers and People's Power." In Philip O'Brien, ed., *Allende's Chile*. New York: Praeger Publishers, 1976.

Thorp, Rosemary. *Economic Management and Economic Development in Peru and Colombia*. Pittsburgh: University of Pittsburgh Press, 1991.

Thorp, Rosemary and Laurence Whitehead, eds. *Latin American Debt and the Adjustment Crisis*. Pittsburgh: University of Pittsburgh Press, 1987.

———. *Inflation and Stabilisation in Latin America*. New York: Holms and Meier, 1979.

Tironi, Ernesto. *Es posible reducir la pobreza en Chile*. Santiago: Editorial Zig-Zag, 1989.

———. "Democracia y mejoramiento de remuneraciones." *Centro de Estudios del Dearrollo*, Materiales para Discusión no. 178, 1987.

Tomic, Radomiro. "Christian Democracy and the Government of Unidad Popular." In Federico Gil, Ricardo Lagos, and Henry A. Landsberger, eds., *Chile at the Turning Point: Lessons of the Socialist Years, 1970-1973*. Philadelphia: Institute for the Study of Human Issues, 1979.

Tulchin, Joseph H. and Augusto Varas. *From Dictatorship to Democracy: Rebuilding Political Consensus in Chile*. Boulder: Lynne Rienner, 1991.

Valdés, Juan Gabriel. *La Escuela de los Chicago: Operación Chile*. Buenos Aires: Grupo Editorial Zeta, 1989.

Valenzuela, Arturo. "The Military in Power: The Consolidation of One Man Rule in Chile." In Paul W. Drake and Iván Jaksic, eds., *The Struggle for Democracy in Chile, 1982-1990*. Lincoln: University of Nebraska Press, 1991.

———. *The Breakdown of Democratic Regimes: Chile*. Baltimore: Johns Hopkins University Press, 1978.

Valenzuela, Arturo and Samuel Valenzuela, eds. *Military Rule in Chile: Dictatorships and Oppositions*. Baltimore: Johns Hopkins University Press, 1986.

———. *Chile: Politics and Society*. New Brunswick: Transaction, 1976.

Véliz, Claudio. "La mesa de tres patas." *Desarrollo Económico* 3, 1-2, 1963.

Vergara, Pilar. "Market Economy, Social Welfare, and Democratic Consolidation in

Chile," In William C. Smith, Carlos H. Acuña, and Eduardo Gamarra, eds., *Democracy, Markets, and Structural Reform in Latin America: Argentina, Bolivia, Brazil, Chile, and Mexico*. New Brunswick: Transaction, 1994.

_____. *Auge y caída del modelo neoliberal en Chile*. Santiago: Ediciones Ainavillo, 1985.

Vylder, Stefan de. *Allende's Chile*. Cambridge: Cambridge University Press, 1976.

Wade, Robert. *Governing the Market: Economic Theory and the Role of Government in East Asian Industrialization*. Princeton: Princeton University Press, 1990.

Wallerstein, Immanuel. *The Modern World System: Capitalist Agriculture and the Origins of the European World Economy in the Sixteenth Century*. New York: Academic, 1974.

Weir, Margaret and Theda Skocpol. "State Structures and the Possibilities for 'Keynesian' Responses to the Great Depression in Sweden, Britain, and the United States." In Peter Evans, Dietrich Rueschmeyer, and Theda Skocpol, eds., *Bringing the State Back In*. New York: Cambridge University Press, 1985.

Wesson, Robert, ed. *Coping with Latin American Debt*. New York: Praeger, 1988.

Weyland, Kurt. "Growth with Equity in Chile's New Democracy?" *Latin American Research Review*, forthcoming.

Whitehead, Laurence. "The Adjustment Process in Chile: A Comparative Perspective." In Rosemary Thorp and Laurence Whitehead, eds. *Latin American Debt and the Adjustment Crisis*. Pittsburgh: University of Pittsburgh Press, 1987.

_____. "Whatever Happened to the Southern Cone Model?" In David E. Hojman, ed., *Chile After 1973: Elements for the Analysis of Military Rule*. Liverpool: Latin American Center, Liverpool University, 1985.

Winn, Peter. *Weavers of Revolution: The Yarur Workers and Chile's Road to Socialism*. New York: Oxford University Press, 1986.

Winn, Peter and Cristóbal Kay. Agrarian Reform and Rural Revolution in Allende's Chile." *Journal of Latin American Studies* 6, 1, 1974.

Wright, Thomas C. *Landowners and Reform in Chile: The SNA, 1919-1940*. Urbana: University of Illinois Press, 1982.

_____. "Agriculture and Protectionism in Chile, 1880-1930." *Journal of Latin American Studies* 7, 1, 1975.

Wright, William E. "Comparative Party Models: Rational Efficient and Party Democracy." In William E. Wright, ed., *A Comparative Study of Party Organization*. Columbus: C.E. Merrill, 1971.

Wynia, Gary W. *Argentina in the Postwar Era: Politics and Economic Policy Making in a Divided Society*. Albuquerque: University of New Mexico Press, 1978.

Zeitlin, Maurice and Richard E. Ratcliff. *Landlords and Capitalists: The Dominant Class of Chile*. Princeton: Princeton University Press, 1988.

_____. "Class Segments: Agrarian Property and Political Leadership in the Capitalist Class of Chile." *American Sociological Review*, 41, December 1976.

## Unpublished Manuscripts

Athey, Lois E. "Government and Opposition during the Allende Years." Ph.D. Dissertation, Columbia University, 1978.

Brager, Stephen. "The Chilean Elections of 1989: An Account, an Analysis, and a Forecast for the Future." University of California, San Diego.

Cavarozzi, Marcelo. "The Government and the Industrial Bourgeoisie in Chile,

1938-1964." Ph.D. Dissertation, University of California, Berkeley, 1975.

Cusack, David F. "The Politics of Chilean Private Enterprise under Christian Democracy." Ph.D. Dissertation, University of Denver, 1972.

Lecaros, Augusto Z. "Representación de los intereses de la sociedad en el Estado y los Consejos Económicos y Sociales." M.A. Thesis, Instituto de Ciencia Política, Pontificia Universidad Católica de Chile, 1989.

Montecinos, Verónica. "Economics and Power: Chilean Economists in Government, 1958-1985." Ph.D. Dissertation, University of Pittsburgh, 1988.

Roberts, Kenneth. "Rethinking Economic Alternatives: Left Parties and the Articulation of Popular Demands in Chile and Peru," paper presented at the the conference on "Inequality and New Forms of Popular Representation in Latin America," Columbia University, March 3-5, 1994.

### Business Sources

Cámara Central de Comercio/Cámara Nacional de Comercio. *Informe económico anual, 1988*. Santiago: Cámara Nacional de Comercio, 1988.

_____. *Memoria Anual*. Annual, selected issues.

_____. *Circulares*. Selected titles.

Confederación de la Producción y Comercio, minutes of executive committee meetings, selected issues.

_____. *Recuperación económica: Análisis y proposiciones*. Santiago, July 4, 1983.

Sociedad de Fomento Fabril. *Revista Industria*. Monthly, selected issues.

_____. *Informativo SFF*. Monthly, selected issues.

_____. *Memoria*. Annual, selected issues.

_____. "Endeudamiento interno." Santiago, July 1985.

_____. "Informe final de la comsión designada por la SFF para estudiar una alternativa al sistema arancelario actualmente en vigencia." Santiago, October 20, 1982.

Sociedad Nacional de Agricultura. *El Campesino*. Monthly, selected issues.

Sociedad Nacional de Minería. *Boletín Minero*. Monthly, selected issues.

### Government Sources

Banco Central de Chile, Comité Asesor de Política Arancelaria. Minutes of November 22, 1974.

Banco Central de Chile. *Estudios monetarios III: Seminario de mercados de capitales auspiciado por la Organización de Estados Americanos*. Santiago; n.p., 1974.

_____. *Memoria Anual*. Santiago: Imprenta Nacional, selected issues.

_____. *Boletín Mensual*. Santiago: Imprenta Nacional, selected issues.

Corporación de Fomento de la Producción. *Privatización de empresas y activos, 1973-1978*. Santiago: Gerencia de Normalización de Empresas, n.d.

República de Chile, Consejo Económico Social. *Reuniones ordinarias*. Santiago: Edimpres, 1984-1989.

Ministerio de Economía, Fomento y Reconstrucción and ASEXMA. *Medidas de fomento a las exportaciones chilenas ponen el mundo en sus manos*. Santiago: Ediciones "OPLANE," 1988.

## Periodicals and Dailies

*Business Latin America*. New York, weekly.
*El Mercurio*. Santiago de Chile, daily.
*Ercilla*. Santiago de Chile, weekly.
*Estrategia*. Santiago de Chile, weekly.
*La Epoca*. Santiago de Chile, daily.
*La Tercera de la Hora*. Santiago de Chile, daily.
*Latin America Regional Reports*. New York, weekly.
*Qué Pasa*. Santiago de Chile, weekly.
*Revista Hoy*. Santiago de Chile, weekly.

## Author Interviews

All interviews were conducted in Santiago de Chile between July 1988 and June 1989, and June-July 1992.

Jaime Alé (SFF)
Pablo Araya (CChC)
Guillermo Campero (ILET sociologist)
Washington Cañas (CNC)
Sergio de la Cuadra (Central Bank and minister of finance under Pinochet)
Hernán Danús (Mining Engeneer's Institute)
Jorge Desormeaux (Universidad Católica, economist and businessman)
Guillermo Elton (CNC)
Cristián Eyzaguirre (CMPC executive)
Manlio Fantini (SONAMI)
Manuel Feliú (CPC)
Jorge Fontaine (CPC)
Juan Andrés Fontaine (Central Bank under Pinochet)
Ricardo Ffrench-Davis (Member of Frei government economic team)
Efraín Friedman (SFF)
Alejandro Foxley (Ciepan and opposition shadow cabinet)
Claudio Gaete (CChC)
Raúl García A. (SNA)
José Antonio Guzmán (CPC)
Dominique Hachette (Universidad Católica economist, consultant)
Eduardo Klein (businessman)
Christopher Lynch (U.S. Embassy, economic section)
Pedro Lizana (SFF)
Rolf Lüders (BHC director and former minister of finance)
Sergio Molina (minister of finance under Frei)
Alfonso Mujica (CNC and CPC)
Oscar Muñoz (Cieplan economist)
Víctor Oettinger (ProChile)
Jaime Palma (ministry of economy, internal commerce bureau)
Alvaro Plaza (Universidad Católica School of Business)
Humberto Prieto (CNC)

Gustavo Ramdohr (ASEXMA/ASIMET)
Carlos Recabarren (CNC)
Tássilo Reisengger (SFF)
Carlos Rodríguez (SONAMI)
Raúl Sáez (CORFO and coordinating minister for finance and economy under Pinochet)
Orlando Sáenz (SFF)
Andrés Sanfuentes (PDC economist and early economic advisor to the junta)
Eladio Susaeta (businessman)
Beltrán Urenda (CES)
Manuel Valdés (SNA)
Juan Ignacio Varas (Private sector representative to CAPA for CPC)
Juan Villarzú (Businessman, Central Bank under Frei, early economic advisor to Pinochet)
Lee Ward (ministry of economy)

## Prosopographical Data Sources

Colegio de Periodistas. *Diccionario biográfico de Chile*. Santiago: Editorial Universitaria.
*Directorio de empresas y ejecutivos*. Santiago: ITV Editores, 1978-1988.
*Directorio de instituciones de Chile*. Santiago: Silber Editores, 1986-1988.

Directorships from Company Annual Reports, 1970-1987:
(Companies in parenthesis were subsidiaries of the main firm listed)
_____. Agrícola Nacional.
_____. Banco Hipotecario de Chile.
_____. Bodega y Viñedos Sta. Emiliana.
_____. Carozzi.
_____. Cemento Cerro Blanco Polpaico.
_____. Cementos Bío-Bío.
_____. Compañía Cervecerías Unidas (Agrícola Victoria Ltda., Aguas Minerales Cachantún, Cevecería Santiago Ltda., Compañía Cevecería Nacional Ltda., Compañía de Renta La Porteña, Embotelladora del Sur Ltda., Embotelladora Modelo Ltda., Embotelladora Viña del Mar Ltda., Fábrica de Envases Plásticos Ltda., AFP Provida, Inversiones Socinver).
_____. Compañía de Petróleos de Chile—COPEC (Abastecedora de Combustibles, Sociedad Nacional de Oleoductos Ltda., Compañía Lubricantes de Chile Ltda., Apex Petroleum, Administradora de Estaciones de Servicio Ltda., Sociedad de Inversiones de Aviación Ltda., Sociedad Austral de Electricidad, Empresa Eléctrica de la Frontera, Empresa Eléctrica Pilmaiquén, Sociedad Hidroeléctrica Melocotón Ltda., Compañía de Carbones de Chile, Celulosa Arauco y Constitución, Forestal Arauco Ltda., Forestal Celco Ltda., Compañía Forestal de Chile Ltda., Forestal Pedro de Valdivia Ltda., Servicios Forestales Naheulbuta, Transportes Tranaquepe, Sociedad Pesquera Guanaye Ltda., Pesquera Marazul Ltda., Sociedad de Aeronavegación Pesquera Ltda., Sociedad Pesquera Coloso, Pesquera San José de Coquimbo, Corporación de Productores de Harina de Pescado–Corpesca, Sociedad Nacional de Procesamiento de Datos Ltda–Sonda,

Sonda Computación Ltda., Westham Trade Corporation, Sociedad de Computación Binaria, Tecnología en Información y Comunicaciones, Distribuidora y Comercial Abastible Ltda., ABC Inversiones Ltda., Puerto Lirquén, Cía. de Turismo de Chile Ltda.).

_____. Compañía Chilena de Navegación Interoceánica (Affiliates: Agencias Universales, Naviera Antofagasta, Naviera Arica, Agunsa Estibas Ltda., Modal Trade).

_____. Compañía de Consumidores de Gas de Santiago (Comercial Gasco Ltda., Importadora y Distribuidora Comercial Gasco Ltda., Cemento Polpaico, Sociedad Elctro-Industrial Popaico).

_____. Compañía Industria Azúcar (COIA).

_____. Compañía Industrial (Indus).

_____. Compañía Industrial de Tubos de Acero (CINTAC).

_____. Compañía Industrial El Volcán.

_____. Compañía Manufacturera de Papeles y Cartones, CMPC (Forestal Mininco, Forstación Nacional, Sociedad Recuperadora de Papel Ltda., Empresa Distribuidora de Papeles y Cartones Ltda., Envases Impresos Ltda., Productos de Papel Ltda., Productos Sanitarios Ltda., Muellaje San Vicnete Ltda., Chilena de Moldeados, AFP Summa, Aserradero San Pedro, Exportadera de Papel Sociedad Comercial Ltda., Sociedad Administradora Carena Ltda., Viviendas Económicas San Pedro Ltda., Comercial Río Laja Ltda., Servicios Forestales Escuadrón Ltda., Sociedad Forestal Crecex Ltda., Sociedad Agrícola y Ganadera Monteverde Ltda., Promociones Forestales Crecex Ltda., Inversiones Candelaria Ltda., Exportadora e Importadora CMPC Internacional Ltda.).

_____. Compañía Minera de Tocopilla.

_____. Compañía Minera de Valparaíso (Hidroeléctrica Guardia Vieja, Muelles y Bosques Ltda., Cominco, Forestal Cominco, Puerto de Lirquén, Forestal y Pesquera Callaqui, Forestal y Pesquera Copahue Ltda., CMPC, Productos Industriales y Forestales, Coindustria, Forestal Coindustria, Viecal, Sardelli Investment).

_____. Compañía Naviera Arauco.

_____. Compañía Tecno Industrial (Sociedad Manufacturera de Electroartefactos, Coresa, Vitroquímica, Industria Procesadora de Acero, Proyectos-Tecnología y Matrices Ltda., Cía. Elaboradora de Metales, Central de Servicios Técnicos Ltda, Fundición Industrial Cruz).

_____. Consorcio Nieto Hermanos.

_____. Cristalerías de Chile (Cristal Plásticos Ltda, Cristaleías Videcor Chile Ltda, Empresa Nacional de Explosivos, Marítima de Inversiones, Reicolite, Sociedad Turística Península Pucón, Sodex, Sociedad Anónima de Navegacón Petrolera).

_____. Famela-Somela.

_____. FENSA.

_____. Industria Forestal, Inforsa.

_____. La Rosa Sofruco.

_____. Lucchetti (Consorcio Nieto Hnos., Agromaule Ltda, Productos Alimenticios Italpasta Ltda., Comercial Lucchetti Ltda., Madeco.

_____. Mademsa.

_____. Pesquera Indo.

_____. Pesquera Eperva.

_____. Química Metalúrgica Tocopilla.

_____. Sociedad Industrial Pizarreño.

_____. Sud Americana de Vapores.

_____. Viña Santa Carolina (Viña Ochagavía, Watts Alimentos, Sociedad Distribuidora Santa Carolina Ltda., Consorcio Vitivinícola Miraflores. Ltda., Sociedad Agrícola Santa Carolina Ltda., Línea Aérea del Cobre.

_____. Viña Undurraga.

Banks and Financieras, 1973-1988: *Superintendencia de Bancos e Instituciones Financieras'* "Nómina de los bancos y sociedades financieras," provided the directorships of all financial institutions, both Chilean and foreign for the years 1979-1988. The Superintendencia also kindly furnished all available company annual reports for Chilean financial institutions for the years 1973-1978.

Insurance Companies, 1970-1988: Directorships for all insurance companies.

# Index

Agriculture, 5, 7, 19-20, 30, 32-36, 41, 67, 77, 81, 83, 86, 108, 112, 116, 126-127, 153, 160, 179, 182, 191, 193
Aguirre Cerda, Pedro, 32
Air force, 88, 109, 119, 222, 227
Alessandri, Arturo, 30, 32-33
Alessandri, Jorge, 39, 47, 78, 116, 156, 158, 162, 190, 224
Alianza Democrática (AD), 187, 216-220, 223-226.
*See also* Opposition alliance
and capitalists, 184, 190, 216-219, 223- 225
and economic policy, 184, 217-220
Allende, Salvador, 1, 11, 29, 33, 39-40, 44-45, 48-49, 53-55, 57, 65-66, 69-70, 74-75, 79-81, 85, 89-90, 103-105, 109, 185, 216, 227
Allied capitalist fractions.
*See* Power bloc
Andean Common Market, 66, 79
Andean Pact, 111
Argentina, 4-5, 10-11, 24, 65, 97, 103, 137-138, 215, 226
Armed forces, 88, 109, 119, 129, 187, 204, 223, 230, 233, 236
Army, 109, 119, 141, 163
Arteaga, Domingo, 157
Article 14 loans.
*See* Capital accounts
Asociación de Bancos e Instituciones Financieras (ABIF).
*See* Peak associations
Automatic adjustment, 137, 139, 141, 150, 152-154, 156, 164.
*See also* Exchange rate, fixed
Ayala, Ernesto, 158
Aylwin, Patricio, 227, 230
Aylwin administration, 228-233, 235

Balance of payments, 38, 79, 101, 141, 155, 182
Baraona, Pablo, 118, 123, 126
Bardón, Alvaro, 140
Bilateral loans, 38, 79
Bolocco, Enzo, 82
Bonapartism, 12, 216
Bourgeoisie, 4-6, 8-10, 19, 21, 30, 32-33, 39, 42, 44, 80, 84-85, 88, 103, 215-216, 220, 235
comprador, 6
industrial, 5-6
Brazil, 11, 24, 65, 97
Brick, the, 69, 73-77, 86-87, 89-90, 99-100, 107, 130, 167.
*See also* El Ladrillo
Büchi, Hernán, 203, 227
Bureaucratic-authoritarianism (BA), 7, 215
Bureaucrats, 11, 21-22, 129, 203, 205, 208
Business climate, 208, 231
Business opposition, 45, 186

Cáceres, Carlos, 163, 182, 186-187, 190-191, 221
Cámara Central de Comercio.
*See* Peak associations
Cámara Chilena de la Construcción.
*See* Peak associations
Cámara Nacional de Comercio.
*See* Peak associations
Capital accounts, 137, 140, 144
Article 14, 140, 144
Capital markets, 68, 74, 80-81, 87, 103, 105, 107-108
Capitalist coalitions
dominant, 5, 8-11, 20-23, 29-30, 32, 36, 55, 66-67, 77, 80, 90, 97, 128-129, 152, 163, 204, 207, 222, 224

gradualist, 45, 65-69, 71, 76, 78, 83,
    85-89, 97-99, 101, 106, 109-110,
    123, 129-130, 207
pragmatic, 23, 39, 138-139 155-168,
    173-179, 181-183, 185-188, 190-195,
    202-205, 207, 216-226, 230-231,
    234-235
    and cohesion, 161-162, 165, 174-
        175, 177, 182, 192-195, 202-203
    and formation, 138, 156-168
    and opposition, 174, 183, 185,
        187, 207, 217, 219-220, 222,
        224-228, 231, 234-235
radical internationalist, 110-112, 123-
    124, 128-130, 138-141, 148-150,
    166, 167
    and consolidation, 119, 123-124,
        129-130, 138, 140, 144, 148
    and formation, 99-108, 11-112,
        116, 129
    and Pinochet, 99, 109-113, 117,
        119, 123, 129-130, 138, 154
Capitalists, 1-6, 10-12, 17-25, 29, 31, 34,
    36, 40, 42-43
domestic market producers, 22, 30-
    32, 38, 71, 73, 80-81, 98, 102, 116,
    138-139, 145, 150, 152, 156-160,
    162-163, 173, 176-177, 181-183,
    185-186, 190, 195, 202, 206-207,
    226
fixed-asset domestic market
    internationally competitive, 19-20,
    66, 71, 73, 83, 85, 88, 98-100, 113,
    129, 155-156, 183, 206-207, 226
fixed-asset internationally
    noncompetitive, 19-20, 67, 76, 79,
    83, 89, 98, 127, 129, 144, 163, 206
fixed-asset internationally oriented,
    20, 83, 150, 152, 155-159, 163, 173,
    176-177, 181-182, 191, 195, 202-
    203, 206-207
fixed-asset producers, 19, 150, 156-
    159, 166, 181, 202, 207-208
liquid asset, 19-20, 67, 71, 73, 78, 80,
    83, 97, 100, 128, 140, 151,
    166, 173, 177, 107
Carabineros, 109, 222, 227
Casanova, Bruno, 158

Cauas, Jorge, 82, 108-109
Central Bank, 36, 74, 82, 86, 102, 105,
    107-108, 123-124, 126, 140-141,
    152, 161, 163-165, 181, 186, 203-204
Central Unica de Trabajadores (CUT),
    223.
    *See also* Labor, organized
Chicago boys, 5, 40, 74-75, 107-112,
    124-125, 130, 139-141, 149, 151-
    156, 165, 173, 186, 220-221.
    *See also* Technocrats
    and conglomerates, 47, 74, 85, 88,
        98-99, 107, 140-141, 151-152, 155-
        156, 165
    and Pinochet, 109-111, 124, 151, 154,
        220
Christian Democratic party (PDC), 39-
    44, 47-49, 52-53, 55-57, 73-75, 85-
    86, 88, 107-110, 148, 183-185, 218-
    219, 222-223, 227
Civic Committees, 225
Civil society, 84, 182
Class conflict.
    *See* Conflict
Collados, Modesto, 190-192, 204,
    221, 224
Collective bargaining, 185, 223, 233
Comité Asesor de Política Arancelaria
    (CAPA), 82, 124
Communist party, 33-34, 36, 223
Concertación de Partidos por la
    Democracia, 216-217, 227-228,
    230-235.
    *See also* Opposition alliance
    and capitalists, 216-217, 228, 230-
        231, 233-235
    and economic policy, 217, 227, 230,
        232-234
Concertación social, 185-223
Confederación de la Producción y
    Comercio.
    *See* Peak associations
Confederación Democrática (CODE),
    53
Conflict
    class, 40, 54
    intersectoral, 19, 29, 31-33, 56, 81,
        103, 124, 127-129, 150, 152, 159-160,

177, 179, 192, 194
intraclass, 3, 6, 19, 23, 33, 38
intrasectoral, 38, 68, 87
Conglomerates
Angelini, 49, 113, 195
Banco Concepción, 140-141
Banco Hipotecario de Chile (BHC),
47, 49, 70, 73-74, 83, 100-101, 105,
112-113, 130, 140-141, 147, 151, 165
core, 89, 107, 138-141, 151-152, 162,
165-167
Cruzat-Larraín, 73, 100-101, 105,
108-109, 112-113, 118, 130, 140,
144, 151
Edwards, 47, 49, 70-71, 73-74, 77, 85-
87, 100-101, 108, 113, 130, 140-141,
163
foreign, 77-78, 140, 195
formerly traditional, 113
internationalist, 71, 73, 85, 88, 98-
103, 105-112, 116, 118-119, 123,
127-130, 140-141, 144, 148, 150-
152, 155, 162-166, 195
internationally competitive, 71, 74,
77, 85, 88, 98-100, 102, 130, 141
Lúksic, 49, 71, 77, 101, 195, 202
Matte, 47, 49, 55, 71, 77, 85, 101, 113,
116, 156, 158, 195, 202
radical international, 98-103,
105-108, 110-112, 116, 118-119,
123, 128-130, 140, 144, 152, 163,
166
traditional, 71, 73, 102, 105-106, 109-
111, 113, 127-128, 163, 207
Constitution of 1980, 23, 25, 149, 184-
185, 187, 204, 216-219, 222, 225-
227, 230, 326
Construction, 7, 44-45, 148, 150, 179,
182, 190-191, 193, 224
Corporación de Fomento (CORFO),
34-36, 38, 56, 85, 108-109, 140-141,
195
Corporatism, 56-57
Counterfactual, 183, 222
Coup coalition, 56-57, 68, 73-75, 129-
130
Crisis, 18, 23, 77, 79-80, 187, 191, 208,
215-217, 222-224

economic, 10-11, 57, 68-69, 97, 138,
155-157, 160, 166-167, 176, 215,
222, 224
international, 98, 103, 138, 166, 174,
181-182, 202
political, 11, 25, 53, 68-69, 79, 97, 167,
223

Danús, Luis, 141, 163
de Castro, Sergio, 82, 108-109, 123, 140-
141, 154, 161-162, 191
de la Cuadra, Sergio, 141, 163-165
Debt crisis, 138, 166, 174, 181-182, 202
Debt relief, 156, 165, 176, 184, 192, 219
Debt rescheduling, 157, 162-163, 179,
181, 224
Deflation, 68, 88, 97-98, 101-102, 110-
112, 125, 167, 173, 186, 218, 222-
223
Délano, Juan, 204
Democracia y Progreso, 227-228
Democratic breakdown, 29, 167, 206
Democratization, 1-4, 6, 9-12, 17, 22-25,
29, 109-110, 183-187, 215-219
and capitalists, 24-25, 57, 109,
185, 207, 216-217, 223, 228, 235-236
political transition, 9, 11-12, 23-24,
57, 174-175, 184, 186-187, 193, 204,
215, 219, 225-226
redemocratization, 4, 12, 187, 215-
216
Devaluation, 66, 87, 139, 150-151, 154,
156-157, 159, 161-163
Domestic structure, 18, 138, 206
and factors, 3, 80, 98, 129, 206-207
Dominant fraction of capital, 5, 9, 11,
30, 32, 66, 80, 85, 97-98, 128-129,
152, 163, 207
Dumping, 125-126, 152, 157-159, 161,
177, 204
Drawbacks, 162, 176, 178-179, 194, 204,
224

Economic crisis
*See* Crisis, economic
growth, 1,4, 10, 12, 25, 23-24, 30, 36,
68, 73, 79, 113, 129, 145, 149, 154,
160, 162, 173-175, 181, 183, 193-

194, 202-203, 205, 215, 229-230,
     232-233
power, 22, 81, 89, 98, 100, 102-103,
     113, 129, 154
reactivation, 112, 157, 184, 187, 219
recovery, 1, 10, 21, 47, 129-130,
     159, 164-165, 173-176, 182, 185-
     187, 192, 205, 220, 224
shocks, 30, 32, 128
Eguiguren, Gonzalo, 158
El Ladrillo, 69, 73.
     *See also* Brick
El Mercurio, 47, 70, 77, 101, 113, 127
Elections, 39-41, 48, 218, 226-227
congressional, 41, 52-53
municipal, 41
presidential, 33-34, 39, 53, 227
timetables, 187
Elite cohesion, 161, 181-182, 215
Emergency economic program, 176,
     181-182, 186
Employment, 33, 42, 54, 81-182, 98,
     107, 138, 162, 173, 182, 202, 224
Encuentro del Area Privado, 48
Escobar, Luis, 190-192, 221
Exchange rate, 36, 66, 105, 163, 205
fixed, 137, 141, 148, 150-154, 156
     *See also* Automatic adjustment
high, 126, 156, 158, 176-177, 192-194,
     225
policy, 152
Export sector, 4, 21, 31-32, 38, 42, 67-
     68, 73, 79-80, 86, 100, 102-103, 110,
     112-113, 116-117, 127, 129, 139,
     145, 148, 150-158, 162, 176, 178,
     181-182, 191, 193-195, 202, 205, 234
Expropriation, 42, 44-45, 52, 185, 223.
     *See also* Nationalization
External credit, 138.
     *See also* Foreign savings
External factors, 18, 21-22, 79, 98, 102,
     128-129, 138, 182, 203
External shocks, 17, 31, 102, 151

Fatherland and Freedom, 55
Feliú, Manuel, 223
Financial intermediation, 110, 138, 140
Financial liberalization, 68, 98-99, 107,

112, 144, 148
deregulation, 98, 144, 148
sector reform, 68, 99, 107, 112
Financial speculation, 1, 9, 101, 193,
     202
Financial system, 41, 103-104, 137-138,
     152
Financieras, 105, 106-164
Financiers, 31-32, 80, 103, 153
Fiscal deficit, 149, 173, 176, 179, 186,
     190, 203
Fontaine, Jorge, 55, 73, 78, 157, 159,
     185, 223
Foreign capital, 41-42, 79, 103, 208.
     *See also* Multinational and
     transnational corporations
Foreign exchange, 4, 32, 36, 38, 79, 97,
     101-103, 126, 140, 144, 149, 154,
     162, 173, 176, 194, 202, 225.
     *See also*  Hard currency
Foreign savings, 38, 98, 107-108, 129,
     138, 150, 155, 206.
     *See also* External credit
Frei, Eduardo, 39, 56-57, 66, 74, 78-79,
     81, 191
administration, 74, 78-79, 81, 191
Frente Nacional del Area Privado
     (FRENAP), 48-49
Friedman, Milton, 5, 101

General Agreement on Trade and
     Tariffs (GATT), 177
Great Depression, 1, 6, 30-32, 35-36,
     138
Gremialismo, 54-55
Gremios, 54-55

Harberger, Arnold, 5, 101
Hard currency, 32, 79-80, 102, 105-106,
     157, 182.
     *See also* Foreign exchange

Ideology, 3, 7, 10, 25, 74-75, 88,
     107, 125, 154
free market, 154
Import duties, 111, 148, 178.
     *See also* Tariffs
Import-substitution industrialization

(ISI), 4-5, 29-30, 32-33, 35, 38, 65-66, 79, 129

coalition, 11, 29-30, 33, 36, 39, 67, 79, 80

and industrialists, 85, 103, 112

Industrial policy, 34-35, 153, 184, 291, 226, 229, 232, 235

Industry, 5, 7, 20, 30-35, 38, 41, 45, 67, 77, 79, 81-82, 108, 127, 153, 157-158, 167, 179, 182-183, 193, 204, 224-225.

*See also* Manufacturers

Inflation, 4, 38, 42, 48, 68, 74, 77, 88, 97, 101-102, 107, 138, 149, 151, 157, 164, 173, 176, 179, 184, 186, 192, 219, 229-231, 233

Institutional power, 18, 88, 108, 123, 155

Interaction between state and capital, 2, 4-5, 9, 21-22, 25, 65, 67, 84, 86, 89, 98-99, 106, 112, 123, 129-130, 138, 161, 174, 181, 190-193, 203-208, 217, 231, 235

*See also* System of interaction

Interest rates, 36, 105, 107-108, 111, 125, 139, 150-157, 162, 164-165, 176, 179, 192-193, 202, 205, 221-222, 224

International financial institutions, 182.

*See also* International Monetary Fund and Multilateral lending institutions

International liquidity, 22, 129, 138, 144, 153, 161, 166, 207

International Monetary Fund (IMF), 79, 173, 182, 184, 190, 203, 219.

*See also* International financial institutions and Multilateral lending institutions

International reserves, 137, 141, 150, 155

Intersectoral conflict.

*See* Conflict, intersectoral

Interventions, 42-43, 45, 49, 52, 105, 195, 219

Intraclass conflict.

*See* Conflict, intraclass

Intrasectoral conflict.

*See* Conflict, intrasectoral

Investment, 2, 5, 8-11, 21-23, 30, 35, 66-68, 73, 77, 81, 97-99, 101, 103, 107-108, 110, 112-113, 129-130, 141, 153, 157, 173, 175-176, 179, 184, 191, 193, 205-208, 226, 229-232, 233

Ipinza, Eugenio, 158

Jarpa, Sergio, 187, 190, 220-221

Joint ventures, 34, 41, 85, 225

Junta, military, 5, 47, 65, 81, 85, 87, 107-109, 119, 126, 129-130, 204.

*See also* Military government and Regime, military

Junta de Abastecimiento Popular (JAP), 47-48, 52-54

Kast, Miguel, 144

Kelly, Roberto, 73, 85-86

Krumm, Fernando, 158

Labor, 2, 4-5, 18, 22, 33-36, 38-41, 45, 47-48, 56-57, 74, 77, 79, 88, 119, 148-149, 166, 168, 173, 191, 223-225, 228-235

code, 144, 185, 223, 233

legislation, 33, 38, 164, 229-230, 232, 234

markets, 4, 225, 228

movement, 4, 225, 228

organized, 4, 30, 35-36, 39, 68, 81, 123, 184, 234-235

*See also* Confederación Unica de Trabajadores

parties, 5, 229, 234

strikes, 30, 36, 149

Land reform, 44, 56, 117

Landowners, 2-6, 8-11, 17-19, 23-35, 29-36, 39-40, 42-44, 52-56, 66-69, 77, 84, 88-89, 97, 103, 111, 113, 117-118, 123-128, 130, 139, 150-155, 175-177, 190-192, 203-206, 208, 216-217, 219, 224, 228, 234-235

Left, renovation, 1, 4, 24, 184, 216, 223

Legislative commissions, 119, 204

Léniz, Fernando, 85-86, 108-109

Lira, Samuel, 191, 204

Lizana, Pedro, 158
Llona, Alberto, 158
Lüders, Rolf, 165-166, 186

Macroeconomic policy, 183-184, 219
    stability, 184, 193, 225, 231-232, 236
Manufacturers, 30-32, 34, 36, 44, 47, 56,
    66.
    *See also* Industry
    for domestic markets, 30-31, 76, 80-
        81, 83, 127, 159, 183, 190
    uncompetitive internationally, 127
    *See also* Capitalists, fixed-assets
Marquez de la Plata, Alfonso, 118, 141
Martín, Manuel, 186, 190, 221
Matte, Benjamín, 55
Matthei, Fernando, 222
Mexico, 11, 24
Middle classes, 2, 18, 30, 33-34, 40-41,
    47-48, 52, 54, 56, 68, 74, 123, 137-
    138, 148, 150, 168, 183, 186, 203,
    217, 228, 232, 235
Military government, 3-5, 10-12, 22, 25,
    56-58, 65-66, 69-70, 85, 87, 98-100,
    109-111, 165, 183-184, 187, 192,
    202, 206, 215-224, 226, 229, 234.
    *See also* Junta, military and Regime,
        military
Mine owners, 31, 34, 36, 56, 76, 191.
    *See also* Peak associations; SONAMI
Ministry of Agriculture, 36, 86,
    108, 118, 163, 192, 203, 204
Ministry of Economy, 36, 82, 85-87,
    108, 110, 118, 123, 126, 140, 162-
    165, 186, 190, 192, 195, 203-204,
    220-221, 224, 231
Ministry of Finance, 36, 81-82, 86, 107-
    108, 110, 123, 140-141, 161-165,
    182, 186, 190, 192, 195, 203-204
Ministry of Interior, 187, 220
Ministry of Mines, 191, 204
Ministry of Urban Development and
    Housing, 179, 190
Mixed economy, 30, 184, 222, 225-226
Mobilization, 9, 29-30, 216-220
    of business, 30, 42, 44, 49, 53-55, 69-
        70
    of center-left, 29, 39-40, 139, 182-183,

187, 217-220.
*See also* Protest movement
    timing of, 218
Monday Club, 45, 47-49, 57, 69-71, 73-
    77, 86, 99-100, 107, 109, 111-112,
    130, 206
Monetarism, 4
Movimiento de Acción Gremial, 55
Movimiento Democrático Popular
    (MDP), 184, 187, 218-219, 223
Multiclass alliance, 10, 29, 33-34,
    41, 56, 139, 168, 174, 182-183, 185,
    190, 216, 218, 220, 222, 234
Multilateral lending institutions, 38,
    39.
    *See also* Multilateral financial
        institutions and IMF
Multinational corporations (MNCs),
    83, 128, 163.
    *See also* Foreign capital and
        Transnational corporations

National Commissions, 204, 224
National Party (PN), 42-44, 74
Nationalization, 29-30, 39-45, 47-49, 56,
    70, 77, 80-81, 103, 104.
    *See also* Expropriation
Navy, 73, 86, 109, 111, 119
Neoliberalism
    gradual, 2, 11, 20, 25, 65-67, 76, 87,
        89, 105, 130, 156, 167
    radical, 10, 45, 57, 66, 73-74, 97-99,
        101, 108, 110-113, 117-119, 128,
        130, 137-140, 148, 150-153, 156,
        161, 166-167, 173-174, 179, 181,
        186, 207, 221-222
    pragmatic, 1-2, 11, 25, 65, 67, 139,
        156, 173, 205, 215, 217, 225, 227-
        228, 230, 235
Nontraditional exports, 33, 35, 42, 80,
    178, 193-194, 205

Oil prices, 79-80, 98, 101-102, 128,
    202-203
Opposition alliance, 183, 220, 222.
    *See also* Alianza Democrática
        and Concertación de Partidos
Organizational factor, 174, 206

Organized business, 8, 19, 21, 54, 67, 69, 78, 87, 89, 99, 102, 108, 124, 149, 151, 155, 160-161, 166, 174-176, 190, 205, 208, 217, 221, 231, 235.
*See also* Peak associations

Papelera (CMPC), 47, 53, 156, 158
Partido Amplio de Izquierda (PAIS), 227
Passicot, Andrés, 190, 221
Peak associations, 6-7, 9, 20-22, 31, 35, 42-45, 48, 52-54, 56-57, 67, 69, 76-78, 81-84, 86-90, 124-125, 128, 130, 144, 148-158, 160, 167, 175-177, 179, 182, 191-193, 204, 219, 221, 224, 235.
*See also* Organized business
Asociación de Bancos e Instituciones Financieras, (ABIF)148, 159
Cámara Central de Comercio (CCC), 31, 36, 55, 76-77, 86
Cámara Chilena de la Construcción (CChC), 45, 76, 148, 159, 177, 179, 190-191
Cámara Nacional de Comercio (CNC), 148, 152-153, 159, 161, 177, 181-182, 192, 195, 204, 225
Confederación de la Producción y Comercio (CPC), 47-59, 52, 54-55, 67, 69, 73, 75-77, 81-82, 86-90, 124-125, 139, 150-153, 156-165, 167, 173-179, 185-187, 193, 204-205, 218, 220-222, 224-226, 233-234
Sociedad de Fomento Fabril (SFF), 33-36, 38, 43, 45, 47-49, 52, 54-55, 70, 73-83, 85-86, 90, 104, 108, 124-128, 144-145, 148, 152-154, 157-161, 163, 177-179, 182, 185, 192, 194-195, 205, 225, 231
Sociedad Nacional de Agricultura (SNA), 31, 33-34, 36, 43-44, 52-55, 74, 76-78, 86, 103, 118-119, 124-128, 144-145, 148, 152-154, 159-161, 163, 177, 181-182, 185, 225
Sociedad Nacional de Minería (SONAMI), 31, 36, 76-77, 148, 152-

153, 159, 161, 177-178, 182, 191-192, 204
*See also* Mine owners
Petrodollars, 103, 129
Pinochet, 18, 22-24, 54, 69, 99, 109-113, 123-126, 157, 160-168, 182, 185-187, 190-191, 203-25, 215-223, 225-227
and capitalist support, 4, 9, 24-25, 113, 129, 139, 166, 168, 174, 185-186, 190, 215-217, 219-220, 222-223, 225-226, 234
and Chicago boys, 5, 57, 69, 99, 109-112, 119, 123-124, 138, 151, 155, 164, 167, 207
and conglomerates, 99, 112, 117, 119, 123, 129-130, 162-163, 165, 174, 203
and one-man rule, 5, 22, 57, 65, 109-112, 138, 151, 155, 164, 167, 207
and organized business, 54, 124, 126, 157, 160-161, 163-164, 167, 174, 185, 187, 191, 203, 207, 216, 221-222, 225
and policy inflexibility, 112, 161, 174, 223
and political opposition, 24, 139, 148, 183, 217-218, 220, 222-223, 225
Piñera, José, 144
Plebiscites, 24, 119, 148, 195, 215-217, 225-227
No option, 227
results of 1988, 227
Sí option, 226
Pliego de Chile, 53
Policy agenda setting, 3, 69, 89
Policy debates, 8, 20, 70, 75-76, 78, 99, 101, 110, 118, 124, 127, 150, 153
Policy formulation, 4-5, 8, 11, 21-23, 25, 35, 66-67, 69, 83, 85-86, 88-90, 98-99, 106-108, 111, 125, 128-130, 160-161, 164, 166, 174-175, 179, 181-183, 190, 203, 205, 207, 221, 224, 232
Policy networks, 25, 100, 106, 139, 151
Policy style, 2, 9, 99, 123, 130, 192, 203, 207
flexible, 192, 208

inflexible, 9, 99, 123, 130, 207
Policymaking process, 2-3, 5-7, 21-25,
    29, 65, 89, 123-124, 175-176, 181,
    202-204, 221-124, 233
    access to, 3, 5, 9-10, 22-25, 36, 54, 57,
        84, 102, 140, 148, 161, 165, 176,
        202, 204, 208, 215-216, 221-222
    consensus style, 231-233
    participation, 6, 17, 23, 36, 43, 99,
        123, 148, 167, 175, 183, 203, 224
Political instability, 168, 181-182, 186
Political liberalization, 23-24, 184, 187,
    216, 218, 22-223
Political opposition, 12, 139, 148, 174,
    182, 186-187, 190, 207, 218, 222
Popular Front, 33-36
Power bloc, 20, 71, 138, 140, 150
    allied capitalist fractions, 20, 99, 112,
        139, 144, 149-152, 155, 166, 207
Prado, Jorge, 163, 166, 181, 191, 204
Preferential dollar, 157-158, 165, 181
Price bands, 153, 181
Price floors, 67, 77, 126, 159, 165
Price supports, 32, 86, 126-127, 159
Privatization, 74, 86-87, 97-98, 101-105,
    109, 111-112, 193, 195, 202
Property rights, 53, 184-185, 223, 226,
    235
Protected democracy.
    *See* Tutelary democracy
Protection, 5, 19-20, 24, 29-32, 33-36,
    66-68, 70, 76-79, 81-83, 97, 125-127,
    139, 150, 152-154, 156, 159, 164-
    165, 177, 186, 191-194, 202, 204,
    206, 225, 228
Protest movement, 182-184, 190, 218,
    220.
    *See also* Mobilization, center-left
Proyecto alternativo, 184-185
Public investment, 110, 153

Radical internationalists, 75, 98-104,
    106, 108, 123-124, 128-129, 138,
    150, 154, 166, 207
Radical neoliberals, 69-70, 83, 99, 108-
    109, 117, 119, 123, 167, 175, 182
Radical party, 34-35, 184
Receivership, 166, 195, 219

Recuperación económica, 176-177, 179,
    185-187, 190-192, 220-222
Reflationary policy, 32, 161, 164, 173-
    174, 176-177, 182, 184, 190, 219-222
Reformist policy, 33-34, 36, 39, 43, 56-
    57, 216, 228-231, 235-236
Regime, 4-5, 7-11, 17-25, 55-56, 75, 90,
    98-100, 112-113, 149-150, 183, 215-
    218, 222-226
    authoritarian, 4, 7, 9-10, 22-25, 55,
        81, 83-85, 113, 123, 128-130, 155,
        185, 191, 215, 225
    change, 10, 17-18, 81, 139, 150, 193,
        205-207, 215, 217
    democratic, 18, 22, 24, 40, 123, 207,
        216, 225
    loyalties, 4, 9-11, 17, 21, 23-24, 29, 36,
        40, 49, 56, 162, 183, 185, 217-218,
        222-223, 226
    military, 5, 8
    *See also* Military government and
        Junta, military
    structure, 18, 22, 67, 78, 83, 88, 98-99,
        102, 106, 112, 119, 123, 129-130,
        138-140, 144, 149, 160, 166-167, 206
    *See also* State institutions and State
        structure
Renovación Nacional (RN), 227, 233-234
Requisitions, 42, 43, 52
Rodríguez, Pablo, 55

Sáenz, Orlando, 45, 48, 55, 70, 73, 79,
    85-86, 101, 104, 108, 112, 125
Sáez, Raúl, 85, 108
Sahli, Raúl, 125
Second Convention of the CPC, 87
Sectoral policy, 5, 19-20, 150-151,173-
    174, 176-179, 191-193, 205
Sequencing and timing
    economic policy, 1, 69, 87, 160,185,
        206
    mass mobilization, 218
Shock treatment, 69, 101, 108-109,112,
    123
Social and Economic Council (SEC),
    191, 204
Social democratic, 4, 24, 184, 228-230,
    234

Social democrats, 228-230
Social equity, 1-2, 4, 12, 23, 88, 205,
    217, 223-235
  extreme poverty, 205, 232, 234-235
  justice, 226, 236
Social groups, 3, 18-19, 21-22, 35, 54,
    65, 83-85, 123, 138, 155, 208, 218,
    222, 231-233
  class-based, 8, 9, 17, 19, 22, 30
Social market economy, 77, 104, 187
Social modernizations, 144, 229
Social policy, 2, 112, 175, 184, 228-229,
    231-232
Socialism, 4, 7, 39-41, 68, 80, 97, 187,
    219, 225, 227, 236
  fear of, 4, 216-220
  *See also* Threat from below
Socialist party, 24, 33-34, 36, 184, 227
Sociedad de Fomento Fabril .
  *See* Peak associations
Sociedad Nacional de Minería
  *See* Peak associations
Soza, Francisco, 109
Stabilization, economic, 1, 38-39, 66-67,
    70
Stange, Rodolfo, 227
State competition, 185, 223
State enterprise, 4, 10, 34, 85, 97, 105,
    112, 193, 223, 226
State formation, 4, 231-232, 234
State institutions, 2, 18, 22, 25, 66-67,
    99, 106, 119, 165, 167, 190, 206-207.
  *See also* Regime structure and
    State structure
State purchases, 153, 181
State structure, 3, 7, 10-11, 17-18, 22,
    25, 65.
  *See also* Regime structure and
    State institutions
Subsectoral organizations, 124
System of interaction between state
    and capital, 2, 21-22, 25, 76, 89, 98-
    99, 106, 112, 123, 129-130, 138, 174,
    181, 190-193, 203-208, 217, 231, 235
  *See also* Interaction between state
    and capital

Tariffs, 30-31, 34-36, 66-68, 88, 137-138,

    158-160, 163, 204, 225.
  *See also* Import duties
  differentiated, 33, 35-36, 153, 156,
    159, 177, 190-195
  increases, 33, 179, 192, 194
  reductions, 66, 76-82, 98-99, 101, 110-
    111, 117-118, 123, 125-127, 137
Tax policy, 32, 42, 157, 176-177, 191-
    192, 194-195, 225
  cut, 153, 176, 221
  incentive, 179, 226
  increase, 192, 194, 230, 232-233
  reform, 86, 179, 186, 191, 232
  relief, 161, 176
  and social spending, 230
Technocrats, 1-5, 7, 10-11, 22, 65, 67,
    69, 88-89, 98, 106, 111-112, 123,
    129-130, 138, 141, 152, 174, 203-
    204, 206-208, 217, 231, 235.
  *See also* Chicago boys
Threat from below, 9-11, 24-25, 215-
    216, 220, 222.
  *See also* Socialism, fear of
Timing.
  *See* Sequencing and timing
Trade surplus, 182
Transnational corporations, 158, 202.
  *See also* Foreign capital and
    Multinational corporations
Triennial Plan, 179, 191, 224
Tutelary democracy, 228
  *Also* Protected democracy, 57, 204,
    235

Undurraga, Sergio, 86
Unemployment, 33, 82, 138, 162,
    173, 182, 224, 229
Unidad de Fomento (UF), 176, 222
Unidad Popular (UP), 9, 29-30, 40-45,
    47-49, 52-54, 56, 68, 74, 80, 86, 97,
    103, 105, 216, 219
Unión Democrática Independiente
    (UDI), 227
Universidad Católica de Chile/
    Catholic University, 98, 124-125
University of Chicago, 5, 74, 98, 101
Upper classes, 5-7, 9-12, 17, 21, 23-24,
    29-31, 34-36, 39-40, 42-43, 68, 76,

84, 138, 148, 166, 174-175, 190, 203, 207
Uruguay, 4-5, 11, 65, 97, 103, 137-138, 215

Valdés, Manuel, 86
Value added tax, 223
Venezuela, 24
Villarzú, Juan, 109

Wages, 42, 203, 234-235

raises, 185
real, 173, 193, 223, 232, 235
reduction, 66, 74, 110, 156, 164, 173, 176, 230
Welfare state, 4, 29, 35, 217, 228-229
liberal, 217, 228-229, 232, 234
social-democratic, 228-230, 234
World Bank, 38, 190, 229

Zabala, José, 108

# About the Book and Author

Chile emerged from military rule in the 1990s as a leader of free market economic reform and democratic stability, and other countries now look to it for lessons in policy design, sequencing, and timing. Explanations for economic change in Chile generally focus on strong authoritarianism under General Augusto Pinochet and the insulation of policymakers from the influence of social groups, especially business and landowners. In this book Eduardo Silva argues that such a view underplays the role of entrepreneurs and landowners in Chile's neoliberal transformation and, hence, their potential effect on economic reform elsewhere. He shows how shifting coalitions of businesspeople and landowners with varying power resources influenced policy formulation and affected policy outcomes. He then examines the consequences of coalitional shifts for Chile's transition to democracy, arguing that the absence of a multiclass opposition that included captialists facilitated a political transition based on the authoritarian constitution of 1980 and inhibited its alternative. This situation helped to define the current style of consensual politics that, with respect to the question of social equity, has deepened a neoliberal model of welfare statism, rather than advanced a social democratic one.

Eduardo Silva is assistant professor of political science and a fellow of the Center for International Studies at the University of Missouri–St. Louis. He is co-editor of *Elections and Democratization in Latin America, 1980–85*, and his articles on Chilean political economy have appeared in *World Politics* and the *Journal of Interamerican Studies and World Affairs*. Silva's recent research has concentrated on the politics of conservation and sustainable development in Chile, Costa Rica, Mexico, and Venezuela.